ONE WEEK
LOAN

12 MAR 1997

1 8 FEB 2000

2 3 MAR 1998 – 5 MAY 2000

2 8 NOV 1998

2 2 MAY 2000

The Determinants of Small Firm Growth

Regional Policy and Development Series

Throughout the industrialised world, widespread economic restructuring, rapid technological change, the reconfiguration of State intervention, and increasing globalisation are giving greater prominence to the nature and performance of individual regional and local economies within nations. The old patterns and processes of regional development that characterised the post-war period are being fundamentally redrawn, creating new problems of uneven development and new theoretical and policy challenges. Whatever interpretation of this contemporary transformation is adopted, regions and localities are back on the academic and political agenda. *Regional Policy and Development* is an international series which aims to provide authoritative analyses of this new regional political economy. It seeks to combine fresh theoretical insights with detailed empirical enquiry and constructive policy debate to produce a comprehensive set of conceptual, practical and topical studies in this field. The series is not intended as a collection of synthetic reviews, but rather as original contributions to understanding the processes, problems and policies of regional and local economic development in today's changing world.

Ron Martin,
Department of Geography,
University of Cambridge

The Determinants of Small Firm Growth

An Inter-Regional Study in the United Kingdom 1986–90

Richard Barkham, Graham Gudgin,
Mark Hart and Eric Hanvey

with the assistance of John Fagg and Ian Stone

Regional Policy and Development Series 12

Jessica Kingsley Publishers
London and Bristol, Pennsylvania

Regional Studies Association
London

The right of the Richard Barkham, Graham Gudgin, Mark Hart and Eric Hanvey to be identified as authors of this work has been asserted by them in accordance with the Copyright, Designs and Patents Act 1988.

First published in the United Kingdom in 1996 by
Jessica Kingsley Publishers Ltd
116 Pentonville Road
London N1 9JB, England
and
1900 Frost Road, Suite 101
Bristol, PA 19007, U S A

and Regional Studies Association (Registered Charity 252269)

Library of Congress Cataloging in Publication Data
A CIP catalogue record for this book is available from the Library of Congress

British Library Cataloguing in Publication Data
A CIP catalogue record for this book is available from the British Library

ISBN 1-85302-331-0

Printed and Bound in Great Britain by
Athenaeum Press, Gateshead, Tyne and Wear

Contents

List of Tables

Acknowledgements

There were a number of individuals and organisations who were an integral part of the research project upon which this book is based. Most of all, we would like to acknowledge our gratitude to Ian Stone (University of Northumbria at Newcastle) and John Fagg (Worcester College) who played an active and critical role in the design and implementation of the survey methodology.

In the creation and maintenance of the three regional industrial databases held at the Northern Ireland Economic Research Centre (NIERC) we were particularly grateful to the provision of data by the Local Enterprise Development Unit (LEDU) in Northern Ireland, the Leicestershire County Council and Market Location for Leicestershire, and the HERTIS Information for Industry held at the former Hatfield Polytechnic in Hertfordshire. Access to the Wearside industrial database was generously provided by Ian Stone.

To the owner-managers of the 174 small firms surveyed in the study we proffer a special thank you for allowing and tolerating our intrusions to an already hectic work schedule. The time spent with these firms has certainly added to our understanding of the small business sector in general and the process of growth in particular. We hope that in some small way there was a return benefit to these firms and their owners.

In the preparation of this manuscript we are indebted to the professional and patient support of Jane Shaw at NIERC who managed, without complaint, to work miracles with the many drafts that arrived on her desk.

Finally, we would like formally to thank the two referees who commented extensively on an earlier draft of the book. Their comments have enabled us to clarify many of the arguments we develop, but of course the usual disclaimer applies.

Richard Barkham, *University of Reading*
Graham Gudgin, *Northern Ireland Economic Research Centre, Belfast*
Mark Hart, *University of Ulster*
Eric Hanvey, *Northern Ireland Economic Research Centre, Belfast*
September 1995

CHAPTER 1

Introduction

Intro:
- link to SME +
UK.

Background

For those who have observed changes in economic development over the last 25 years, one of the most striking, if least expected, trends has been the rising importance of the small firm. The first 25 years after the last war were characterised by stable economic growth and an absence of recession, under conditions of limited competition with barriers to trade still relatively high. In this situation large bureaucratic organisations were able to thrive. They could plan ahead with reasonable certainty and were not under competitive pressures as strong as those of succeeding years.

Since then, and approximately since 1970, economic conditions have been more difficult and much more volatile. Economic growth has been slower, certainly in the United Kingdom but also in the industrial world as a whole. Competition has removed whole industries and reduced once mighty firms to shadows of their former selves. Deep recessions have made it difficult to plan and to commit large-scale capital investment.

It is in these less promising circumstances that small firms have thrived. Their flexibility and their ability to occupy and develop niche markets have better fitted them to survive in conditions of fluctuating demand. Difficult economic circumstances may wipe out thousands of existing small businesses, but many thousands more are always ready to replace them, bringing new products, new ideas, new people and new energy to fill the gaps left by closures. The sheer commitment of owners rather than managers has given small businesses an edge in many sectors. Of course there remain many things which small firms cannot do as well as large companies. For many products the economies of scale still dictate large-scale production and huge amounts of capital. But over a wide range of activities, high-tech as well as traditional, small firms have become an increasing force.

Small firms are of particular importance in countries or regions which cannot attract or do not want to attract multi-nationals. In a more slowly growing world with endemic unemployment there has been too little multi-national investment to go around, and policy makers have been driven to seek jobs and growth in often small and family-owned businesses.

This has been particularly the case in Northern Ireland, one of four areas in the UK which form the test-beds for the ideas in this book. Northern Ireland's violent image has made it difficult to attract inward investment, and much money and attention have instead been directed towards indigenous and other existing industry. Partly as a result, firms employing less than 50 people have grown in importance from 10 per cent of manufacturing output twenty years ago to 30 per cent now. This leaves a much more diverse economy than before, less vulnerable to shocks and to decisions made outside the local area.

In the United Kingdom as a whole, the 1980s were a highly favourable decade for enterprise and the small firm sector in particular. The renaissance of the small business sector over this period has been widely documented, with a great deal of attention being paid to the rapid rise in the numbers of self-employed and in the numbers of firms. Whilst this is an important dimension to economic growth, of greater significance in the longer term is the growth and survival of small firms. Over the last decade it has been clearly established that small firms account for a substantial, and growing, proportion of total employment in the United Kingdom. The most recent evidence, relating to 1987–89, shows that the smallest firms (i.e. those employing less than 10 persons) have accounted for a disproportionately large share of total job creation in relation to their overall share of employment (Daly *et al.* 1992).

The formation of new businesses has been intensively studied and is now well understood. The same cannot be said about the subsequent growth of new businesses. This is an important issue for national economies and the evidence to date is well summarised in Storey (1994). It is also an important issue for regional economies. The most recent regional evidence on the growth performance of small manufacturing firms (Gudgin *et al.* 1989; Hart *et al.* 1993a), taken together with geographical variations in the formation rates of new enterprise (Hart, Harrison and Gallagher 1993b), indicates that over a number of time-periods there have been considerable differences in the ability of certain regions to generate sufficient numbers of *successful* small firms.

For example, a Northern Ireland Economic Research Centre (NIERC) study, using specially created industrial databases which include information on virtually all manufacturing establishments, examined the process of job generation in Northern Ireland, the Republic of Ireland and Leicestershire (Gudgin *et al.* 1989). Dramatic differences were observed in the employment growth of surviving small manufacturing firms in these three areas. In particular, the growth of surviving small firms from 1973 through to 1986 in Leicestershire was twice as rapid as in Northern Ireland and almost six times as fast as in the Republic of Ireland. Market conditions and industrial structure could not on their own provide an explanation for these large differences. Instead, a heavy reliance upon local markets, combined with problems related to their relative competitive position (Hitchens and O'Farrell 1987; 1988a; 1988b), were thought to be more plausible explanations of the inferior performance of small firms in Northern Ireland and the Republic of Ireland.

However, a later comparative study undertaken by the same research team at NIERC revealed a sharp reversal in the fortunes of surviving small manufacturing firms in Northern Ireland over the period 1986–90 (Hart *et al.* 1993a). Despite relatively slow growth in local demand, surviving Northern Ireland firms grew much faster than their counterparts in Leicestershire and the Republic of Ireland in this later period. It was suggested that this could, in part, be associated with the impact of government financial assistance provided by the Local Enterprise Development Unit (LEDU), the small business agency in Northern Ireland. As a result of these trends, the small firm sector in Northern Ireland employed 30,418 persons, representing 27.6 per cent of total manufacturing employment. The comparable figure for 1986 was 25.3 per cent (27,233 employees). This example clearly illustrates the growing importance of the small indigenously-owned firm to a regional economy such as Northern Ireland.

While both of these studies have added greatly to our knowledge of how cohorts of surviving firms have performed in different regions over time, they have been less than helpful in actually explaining why spatial and temporal differences have emerged. Accordingly, this book presents the results of a detailed study which, prompted by the conclusions of the 1973–86 NIERC study, set out to investigate the determinants of growth in small manufacturing firms in four UK regions: Northern Ireland, Leicestershire, Wearside and Hertfordshire. The study was based on a detailed face-to-face interview survey of 174 small firms and the owner-managers who run them, and looked at the growth performance of established small firms over the period 1986–90. The focus on the manufacturing sector was predicated on the belief that it is this sector which is of crucial importance to the achievement of long-term sustainable economic growth in local and regional economies.

The main objective of the study was to conduct an in-depth analysis of the determinants of growth in established small firms. One of the key questions addressed was the extent to which the characteristics of the owner-manager or the main decision-maker could influence growth. The characteristics in question were broadly defined as the educational background, work experience, and motivations of the main decision-maker within the firm. Furthermore, we were interested in the manner in which these characteristics were linked to the business development activities undertaken by the firms – for example, process, product and/or market development. The main hypothesis to be tested was that the characteristics of the owner-manager have a significant effect on the growth performance of the firm, through the management strategies and business practices they choose to adopt. In other words, the emphasis was upon influences *internal* to the company in the explanation of small firm growth whilst controlling for the influence of *external* or environmental variables. Thus, the survey concentrated on gathering information under the following three broad headings:

- the nature of the firm (i.e. size, product markets and location)
- the characteristics of the owner-manager
- business development strategies

The ultimate objective of the project is to contribute to the policy debate on how government agencies can help companies to achieve faster growth.

Measures of Growth

There is no general agreement on how firm size should be measured and therefore there is a wide variation in the growth variables used by researchers (O'Farrell and Hitchens 1988). A firm's size may be measured according to its revenues or profits or by the amount of human and physical capital it employs. Researchers in the fields of geography and economics have tended to use employment to indicate firm size because aggregate employment is a key variable with which policy makers are concerned, and because the measurement of this variable is relatively simple. Researchers in finance tend to make use of variables drawn from company accounts to measure size since this is consistent with the aspects of the business with which they are chiefly concerned.

There is an important difference between company growth and its financial performance. Firms may perform well without growing, and similarly (from a financial perspective) a growing firm may be performing badly. Performance is generally taken to relate to the efficiency with which management utilises a company's assets in the quest for profits. Generally speaking, measures of perform-ance seek to relate resources employed to profits made. There are a wide variety of measures available to assess a company's performance – most of which are of a financial nature.

The study of growth in small firms says relatively little about the performance of these firms. Growth may imply that a satisfactory level of performance is being achieved but it does not guarantee it. The 1980s saw many firms show spectacular growth only to be followed by precipitate decline. Subsequent analysis showed these firms to have grown quickly on the basis of debt finance, the interest payments on which could not be met in the economic downturn. It is entirely possible that growth in any group of small firms may be based on rapid increase in debt. This might be expected to have occurred in the South East region during the 1980s due to the high levels of business confidence engendered by low interest rates and rapid economic growth. Some confirmation of this hypothesis is found in the very high rates of small business failure experienced in the South East in the late 1980s. Furthermore, it is high performance rather than high growth that will tend to attract capital to a region. It is recognised that company growth may be correlated with financial performance but this should not always be taken for granted and is clearly conditional upon the length of the time period studied.

Growth is often of more interest to economists and public policy makers than financial performance, although it is understood that at least adequate profitability is always necessary and high profitability is important. Growth is important for generating wealth and jobs. If growth also entails a rising market share, then it also indicates underlying competitiveness as long as some form of subsidy is not involved. The interest of this study primarily in growth rather than profitability stems from the need for economic expansion and jobs in areas of high unemployment. Our interest is in the extent to which small firms can contribute to economic expansion and an understanding of how policy makers might intervene to encourage or at least facilitate more rapid growth.

In this research little emphasis is placed on performance measures or profitability. In part, this is because profits are very difficult to measure precisely in small firms (BDO Stoy Hayward 1995). Also, it reflects the fact that profits and growth may for periods of time be inversely correlated. For instance, companies which spend more on product development, marketing or training may have a lower return on capital than firms which minimise such expenditures. The former companies may, however, experience much faster growth. Similarly, highly profitable firms may choose to distribute their profits or to invest in assets which do not contribute to growth in a local economy.

Growth may be measured in terms of the resources employed by the firm, in which case employment or some measure of assets could be used. Alternatively, growth may be measured in terms of the output produced by the firm, in which case turnover is the appropriate variable. Although in the long run movements in these size variables are correlated, in the short and medium term it may be possible for any one of them to advance significantly without any movement in any of the others. For example, sales and assets can increase substantially without there being any corresponding impact on employment. Clearly, increased sales will ultimately lead to an increase in the level of resources utilised by the firm, but increased productivity may lead to there being a considerable lag between sales growth and the growth of assets and employment. Certainly, over a period as short as four years the correlations between these variables may be low.

Measurement of each of these variables poses difficulties. The least problematic of the various possible measures of growth is turnover; it is easy to measure and is always recorded. From an economic perspective, sales are a relatively good indicator of size and therefore growth. Sales may be considered a precise indicator of how a firm is competing within a market, and indeed firms themselves tend to use it as a measure of their own performance. Any analysis of company growth should at least in part be based on changes in turnover. If for reasons of policy or other research factors a measure of resource utilisation is required, employment is to be preferred to assets because accounting conventions prevent the accurate measurement of the latter. In this study turnover is taken as the principal measure of company size, and hence of company growth. Employment is a subsidiary measure mainly reflecting our interest in regional economic development.

Structure of the Book

Chapter 2 outlines the conceptual background to the project based on a wide-ranging literature review. Chapter 3 discusses in some detail the methodology adopted for the owner-manager survey and presents brief profiles of the four regions in which the survey work took place. Chapter 4 presents the results of a multivariate regression analysis and a series of models are presented in an attempt to identify the strongest influences on small firm growth. Chapters 5 and 6 look at each of the variables in the preferred model and discuss the interrelationships between these and other important variables not in the model. Although the survey was not designed to investigate or to measure differences between regions in the growth of small firms it did include a range of locational conditions covering parts of England together with Northern Ireland. Chapter 7, therefore, describes the differences in the growth performance of small firms between the four study areas and attempts to account for these differences within the framework of the model presented in Chapter 4.

In order to fully understand the factors affecting the growth performance of the surveyed firms in the period 1986–90, Chapter 8 examines the relative importance of a range of constraints to growth. The final chapter summarises the main conclusions of the analysis and discusses their implications for small firm policy. Of particular interest will be to consider the results of this analysis for the operation of LEDU's growth-oriented corporate strategy.

CHAPTER 2

Small Firm Growth
Towards a Synthesis

The Pivotal Role of the Entrepreneur

The aim of this chapter is to outline the work of economists and others on the growth of small firms and to provide a conceptual framework for the empirical analysis that follows. Despite the increasing importance of the growth of surviving cohorts of small firms to the economy the development of a theoretical under-standing of the process of small firm growth is a matter of much contention. It is argued that it is the very nature of the change from a small to a large firm that makes the development of theory difficult. The internal organisation of large and small firms is so fundamentally different that to develop a theory of firm growth that operates along a size continuum is somewhat spurious (Storey 1994).

One aspect of this internal organisation was described by Penrose (1959) who argued that as firms expand, new managers are drawn in who require training and who need to be integrated into the existing organisational framework of the firm. The abilities and experience of new management personnel added to those already in the firm will lead to further potential for expansion, including the diversification into new product areas. However, Penrose hypothesised that there may be managerial costs to higher growth which can eventually erode profitability. The existence of this 'Penrose effect' will depend upon the speed and ease with which new managers can be successfully integrated into the firm without its overall efficiency becoming impaired.

For the purposes of understanding the process of small firm growth, however, Penrose (1959) concluded that the differences in the administrative structure (for example, the size and sophistication of the management team) of the very small and the very large firms are so great that they cannot be regarded as part of the same growth process. Furthermore, the possibility of the operation of a 'Penrose effect' within growing small firms should caution against the acceptance of theoretical developments which see small firm growth as simply the initial or early stages of an overall 'stage model' of firm growth.

More generally, O'Farrell and Hitchens (1988) demonstrate that the schools of thought which might be expected to shed light on the issue of small firm growth (industrial economics, stochastic theory, neo-classical economics and business strategy) in fact do nothing of the sort. They state: 'at present an adequate explanatory framework within which to analyse the growth of small owner-managed manufacturing enterprise has not been developed. We are still seeking a theory which will simultaneously explain the infrequency of the phenomenon and account for the major processes underlying growth' (p.1380).

Much of the recent economic literature on the determinants of small firm growth and development has tended to focus on a combination of a life cycle effect (i.e. younger small firms grow faster than older small firms) and economic variables, especially financial variables, for an explanation of growth (see, for example, Acs and Audretsch 1990; Reid 1993). However, as Barreto (1989) has argued the 'removal' of the 'human elements' from modern micro-economic theory was an inevitable consequence of the development of a model of the firm which would appeal in terms of consistency and robustness. Thus, within economics, as the work of Reid and others illustrate, there persists an allegiance to a model of small firm growth which essentially denies a role to the owner-manager or entrepreneur. Consequently, they engage in empirical enquiry into the growth of small firms which fails to address the key questions of entrepreneurial characteristics and motivations and how they may be translated into business strategy.

We would argue for a broader conceptual framework which introduces these missing 'human elements'. As with Penrose (1959), we see firms as collections of individuals with abilities which influence the form and direction of growth. In this respect we also align ourselves to two important schools of thought on the economics of entrepreneurship. First, the Austrian and neo-Austrian schools of economic thought which, although adopting a neo-classical approach, assign a crucial role to the entrepreneur in directing and re-directing resources within a constant state of disequilibrium in the market place. Most notable is the work of Kirzner (1973) who argued that it is the alertness and superior perception of entrepreneurs which cause the factors of production to be reallocated towards equilibrium. Therefore, the entrepreneur assumed a necessary, or pivotal, role in the adjustment process as markets moved towards equilibria.

Second, the work of Schumpeter (1934) develops a more specific and restrictive role for the entrepreneur in his or her influence upon the economic cycle. In essence, Schumpeter's 'great' entrepreneur is one who *only* provides a new product or new production process through the mechanism of different or untried combinations of inputs. Thus, the entrepreneurial action, defined in this way, is solely confined to a discrete change in product or process rather than a gradual evolution of design and, as a result, shifts the economy on to a higher production function.

Both Schumpeter and Kirzner were defining the concept of entrepreneurship and not obviously seeking to explain the determinants of small firm growth. Nevertheless, their work clearly provides an important conceptual framework within which an understanding of the performance of small firms and their contribution to economic change can be developed. As Barreto (1989) states:

'entrepreneurship in any or all of its different roles is essential if we are to understand how the market system generates change and growth' (p.143).

Despite the obvious tensions with micro-economic theory, research into the firm, and in particular the small firm, must continue to embrace methodologies which can assess the contribution of the individual owner-manager(s) to firm growth and hence economic development. For Barreto (1989) the resolution of this tension is beyond doubt: 'as economics moves towards relaxing the core assumptions, towards incorporating "human elements" and towards explaining technological change, the entrepreneur will re-appear in micro-economic theory' (p.143–4).

The literature on entrepreneurship and business strategy offers many promising insights into the nature of the growth process. This said, there are still many problems in attempting to utilise this body of theory and evidence to formulate a general model of firm growth. One of these is that much of the modern literature on entrepreneurship stemming from economics, such as the work of Casson (1982), has not been tested. On the other hand the literature on entrepreneurial psychology, education, motivation and strategy has produced a mass of contradictory findings which have resulted in a wide range of theoretical interpretations of the data supplied. Variety.

However, one useful typology to consider when relating entrepreneurial or owner-manager characteristics to firm growth is the distinction between *craftsmen* and *opportunist* entrepreneurs. First put forward by Smith (1967), this categorisation has been supported in a number of subsequent studies (Boswell 1973; Smith and Miner 1983; Cooper and Dunkleberg 1986). The craftsman entrepreneur is characterised by low levels of formal education, high technical ability, lack of managerial orientation, limited business goals and a disinclination to plan ahead. The opportunist entrepreneur has a degree-level education, a long-held ambition to start a firm and make it grow large, diverse business experience and a high level of managerial capability.

Craftsmen entrepreneurs tend to start firms characterised by relatively low growth, small-batch subcontracting type production and paternalistic management, and seek a competitive advantage based on price, quality and company reputation. The opportunist entrepreneur will form a company based on a new product or process, in which professional management techniques are employed, growth is the explicit objective and competition is on the basis of innovation and marketing effort. Despite criticism from researchers such as Stanworth and Curran (1976) numerous studies have indicated that the craftsman/opportunistic differentiation is a meaningful one. It is an objective of this project to examine the validity of incorporating this typology in any framework which seeks to understand the determinants of small firm growth.

Use to Support Storey.

The Determinants of Small Firm Growth

The empirical evidence

Company growth is clearly influenced by a wide range of factors. Some of these are external to the firm and outside the control of the owner-manager. Others are internal, and within the competence of owner-managers to control or at least influence. Many of the external factors concern the wider economic environment. They include the growth of demand for the company's product, the prices of competitors, costs of supplies and/or labour. Other costs include interest rates, while the availability of finance may also fluctuate from time to time. The regulatory framework within which companies operate may also change over time and differ between places.

Many of these external factors are influenced by national governments. Although they vary between countries, they can be relatively constant within a single country at a particular point in time. Some factors may, however, vary between regions. These include the costs of labour and especially of property. Government financial assistance is also often available only in designated areas. Although this study is concerned in part with differences between regions, it does not consider differences between countries. For this reason, it is factors internal to the company which are of more concern than those which are external. This is not to deny the great importance of external factors. Rather, our approach is to focus mainly on factors which cause growth differences between companies operating within a single country over the same period in time. The variation in growth between companies under these conditions is still huge, and thus shows that internal factors are of great importance.

A common way of abstracting from the influence of external factors is to use one or more company control variables which include a range of external influences. One of these is location. This captures some of the influence of local variations in product demand, production costs, government assistance and other geographically specific factors. Another is the product group or industry. This captures influences which vary systematically between industries such as demand, costs and regulations.

In a recent and comprehensive review of the small firm growth literature, Storey has extended this broad view of the influences on company growth (see Storey 1994). Storey concludes that the growth process in small firms is driven by a combination of three basic components. These are:

1. The characteristics of the entrepreneur(s)/owner-manager(s).

2. The characteristics of the small firm.

3. The range of business development strategies.

These three components are *not* mutually exclusive and may combine in a number of ways to influence growth in small firms.

Within each of these three sets of factors, Storey summarises the individual elements which other researchers have shown through various surveys to have had an impact upon growth. In the discussion that follows we draw heavily upon Storey's comprehensive summary of the literature to outline the conceptual framework adopted in this project. It should be noted that Storey's criterion for including a study in his review was that they must have used quantitative (preferably multivariate) analysis. The studies considered were largely those from the United Kingdom and the United States of America.

Storey identified 15 entrepreneurial characteristics which empirical studies had related to the set-up and growth of small firms (Table 2.1). The overall conclusion was that the direct relationship between the background of the entrepreneur and growth would appear to be relatively limited. However, some consistent evidence across the various empirical studies was apparent. The most important characteristics to emerge were that individuals founding and managing rapidly growing small firms tend to have been:

- motivated by market opportunities
- relatively well educated
- in previous managerial positions
- in their middle years.

Finally, there was some evidence to suggest that more rapidly growing small firms were more likely to be formed by groups or teams of entrepreneurs.

Turning to the second component – the firm itself – six separate company characteristics have been consistently investigated with respect to their impact on small firm growth (Table 2.2). The overall conclusion from the results of the various studies is that all these 'control' variables are important in understanding the process of small firm growth. Some of these, such as location and industrial sector, fall within what was identified earlier as external factors in the process of small firm growth.

The impact of the final component influencing growth, that of business strategy, is examined in Table 2.3. The studies reviewed by Storey assessed 14 distinct elements of business strategy for their impact on small firm growth. The key points to emerge are that growth can be associated with strategies to:

- share equity with external individuals/organisations
- create and operate effectively a strong management team
- occupy and exploit market niches where competition is less severe and where quality advantages can be maximised.

Storey's review confirms the need to include in any investigation of small firm growth variables which reflect the internal characteristics of the firm. The following section outlines in detail the conceptual basis to the approach adopted in this project.

Table 2.1. The Entrepreneur

	Barkham (1992)	Hakim (1989)	Woo et al. (1989)	Kinsell et al. (1993)	Johnson (1991)	Storey, Watson and Wynarczyk (1989)	Jones (1991)	Macrae (1991)	Wynarczyk et al. (1993)	Storey (1982a)	Storey (1994)	Dunkelbert et al. (1987)	Dunkelberg and Cooper (1982)	Kalleberg and Leicht (1991)	Solem and Steiner (1989)	Reynolds and Miller (1988)	Westhead and Birley (1993a)	Reynolds (1993)
1 Motivation	+			+	+	+			x			x					x	
2 Unemployment push				x	x				−	−	−						x	−
3 Education	x		x	+	+	+	+	+	x	x	(+)	x	+	x	x	x	x	+
4 Management experience	+		x	x		+		+			x	−	+		x	x	x	
5 Number of founders	+		+	+		(+)						+			x		x	+
6 Prior self-employment				x		x					x	−		x		x	x	
7 Family history											+						x	
8 Social marginality (ethnic)							+		+			x					x	
9 Functional skills							x		x									
10 Training			−															
11 Age			x	(+)		x		x	x		(+)	−	−	−	x	x	x	+
(Age)²				(−)							−							
12 Prior business failure						x		x	x						x	x	x	−
13 Prior sector experience			x			x	−				+	x		x	x	x	x	
14 Prior firm size experience			x	x		x						x	−	x			+	−
15 Gender		x	x	x	x	x	−	x	x	x	x	x		x	x	x	x	+

Key:

+ Positive relationship between the element and growth of the firm

− Negative relationship between the element and growth of the firm

( ) Relationship present in a univariate context, but weak in a multivariate context

x Element not shown to be significant in influencing growth

Source: Storey (1994)

Table 2.2. The Firm

	Cambridge Small Business Research Centre (1992)	Dunne and Hughes (1992)[a]	Westhead and Birley (1993a)	Barkham (1992)	Varyham and Kraybill (1992)	Storey (1994)	Hakim (1989)	Kalleberg and Leicht (1991)[b]	Jones (1991)	Dunne, Roberts and Samuelson (1989)	Johnson (1989)	Reynolds and Miller (1988)	Macrae (1991)	Storey et al. (1987)
1 Age	–	–			–	+	–	x	–	(–)				–
2 Sector/markets	+	+	+	x	+	+	x	+	+			+	x	x
3 Legal form						+	+	+			+	+		
4 Location	+						+	+	+		+			
5 Size	–	–			–		+	+	–		+	+		–
6 Ownership	x				+					+				

Notes: [a] Dunne and Hughes measure growth in terms of net assets
[b] Kalleberg and Leicht measure growth in terms of business earnings

Key:
+ Positive relationship between the element and growth of the firm
– Negative relationship between the element and growth of the firm
0 Relationship present in a univariate context, but weak in a multivariate context
x Element not shown to be significant in influencing growth

Source: Storey (1994)

Table 2.3. Strategy

	Woo et al. (1989)	Dunkelberg et al. (1987)	Macrae (1991)	Cambridge Small Business Research Centre (1992)	Kinsella et al. (1993)	Solem and Steiner (1989)	Wynarczyk et al. (1993)	Storey et al. (1989)	Kalleberg and Leicht (1991)	Westhead and Birley (1993a)	Birley and Westhead (1990)	Siegel et al. (1993)
1 Workforce training				x	x		x	(+)				
2 Management training			+		(+)		x				+	
3 External equity				+	(+)	+		(+)				
4 Technological sophistication				+		+		x	x			+
5 Market positioning			+			+		(+)	x	x	+	+
6 Market adjustments												
7 Planning	+				(+)							
8 New product introduction	+	+			x	+	+	(+)	x	x	x	
9 Management recruitment			+				+	(+)				+
10 State support				(+)	(+)			(+)		x	x	
11 Customer concentration			x		x			x		−		
12 Competition									x	x	x	
13 Information advice		+		+	x			(+)		x		
14 Exporting				x	(+)			(+)		x		

Key: + Positive relationship between the element and growth of the firm
− Negative relationship between the element and growth of the firm
( ) Relationship present in a univariate context, but weak in a multivariate context
x Element not shown to be significant in influencing growth

Source: Storey (1994)

The Key Variables

The intention in this study was to develop an approach which would bring together research in economics, organisational studies and business strategy to examine the link between entrepreneurial characteristics, business strategy and small firm growth across a variety of small firm types. Such a comprehensive approach requires the collection of information in a wide range of areas. The broad categories of variables to be included in the survey are organised under the three interrelated components of growth discussed above and are presented in Table 2.4. The precise questions asked are explained in greater detail in the following chapter.

Table 2.4. The determinants of growth in small firms

Owner-manager	*The firm*	*Business strategy*
Age	Firm age	Planning
Gender	Size	External finance
Education	Industrial sector	Product development
Founder of business	Region	Process development
Career history	Legal structure	Marketing
Management experience (function, sector, size)	Ownership	Management recruitment
Other business interests		
Other business owners		

Source: After Storey (1994)

With this comprehensive set of variables included in a *single* study of the determinants of small firm growth we can move with some confidence towards an overall assessment of their relative impact. For example, to what extent is it true that, after controlling for the nature of the firm itself in terms of age, size, industrial sector and location, small firm owner-managers who are highly motivated, well educated, have a range of managerial experience and who have created well balanced top management teams are those who will achieve the greatest growth? More important, perhaps, for the debate on the effectiveness of small firm policy, is the extent to which growth is a function of the adoption of particular business strategies – which may in turn be linked to the characteristics of the owner-manager. Such strategies would include product and process development, the search for external equity/finance, aggressive and systematic marketing, recruitment of key management personnel and the development of clear business objectives. These important questions can be readily examined within the framework adopted in this study.

Although we have included motivation as one of the key characteristics of the owner-manager (see Table 2.4) it should be stressed that its measurement will *not* involve the adoption of one of a number of psychological models which are currently available. These models include:

- psychodynamic models, which emphasise the impact of early life experiences (e.g. Kets De Vries 1977)
- social development models, which argue that 'entrepreneurship' can be wholly understood in terms of the type of situation encountered and the social groups to which the individual relates (e.g. Gibb and Ritchie 1981)
- personality trait models, which attempt to discover a set of traits which differentiate the entrepreneur from other groups (e.g. McClelland 1961).

The reason for rejecting this resource-intensive approach in our investigation of the determinants of small firm growth is based quite simply on the lack of consistent supporting evidence in studies of this type (Chell 1986). We prefer, instead, to focus on the measurement of motivation by concentrating on the qualities of the person and how they might influence or react to the impact of particular stimuli (environments or situations). These qualities, or 'person variables', according to Chell, include:

- the skills of the entrepreneur
- how the entrepreneur perceives the environment
- the awareness of the entrepreneur and the expectations of growth
- what outcomes (growth/expansion) are valued by the entrepreneur
- what the objectives of the entrepreneur are and how they will be achieved.

Thus, this research aims to examine the influence of such 'objective' person variables on performance rather than the more imprecise and difficult to measure psychological variables.

Conclusion

An important area of literature which underpins this study is that which deals with the relationship between the characteristics of the owner-manager/entrepreneur and the growth performance of the small firm. Many different aspects of the owner-manager's background and personality have been related to the performance of the firm they run and the strategies they adopt. Based on this comprehensive review of the literature, the framework adopted for the quantitative analysis of small firm growth in this study has identified three main components which will be examined to assess their *relative* impact on growth. These components are the background of the owner-manager(s), the nature of the firm itself and the business development activities undertaken by the owner-managers in the firm.

CHAPTER 3

Methodology

[handwritten: objective of work.]

Introduction

The main objective of this study was to conduct an in-depth analysis of the determinants of small firm growth, and in particular to explore the relationship between the growth of established small firms and the characteristics of their owner-managers. The main hypothesis, as discussed in the previous chapter, was that the characteristics of the owner-manager have a significant effect on the performance of the firm, both through their abilities and experience and through the management strategies and business practices they choose to adopt. In other words, the emphasis in the study was placed upon the extent to which *internal* as opposed to *external* variables account for growth in the small firm. Furthermore, given the geographical variations in the growth performance of surviving small firms referred to in Chapter 1, we were interested in the extent to which there were regional differences in the explanation of small firm growth. To properly test these hypotheses a detailed interview survey of established small firms was undertaken. This provides data on the range of variables required to construct a comprehensive multivariate model of small firm growth. As Storey (1994) correctly argues, it is only with the construction of such models that the process of small firm growth can be properly investigated.

Sample Selection

Although the study was not designed specifically to explain regional variations in small firm growth the survey was, nevertheless, carried out in four regions within the United Kingdom in order to evaluate the extent to which the determinants of small firm growth varied geographically and to control for unspecified regional effects on small firm growth. The selection of the areas was dictated by several factors. First, there were interesting contrasts in their geographical position ranging from Hertfordshire in the south east, through Leicestershire in the East Midlands to the peripheral regions of Northern Ireland and Wearside. This range of locations permits both the comparison of the importance of owner-manager characteristics between regions and an assessment of the importance of external factors, within the various regional economies, on firm growth. Second, the availability of establishment/firm-level data (name, address, ownership details, industrial sector, employment data and date of formation) for the manufacturing sectors in these areas facilitated the identification of an appropriate sample. NIERC already maintains such industrial databases for Northern Ireland and Leicestershire, and, as part of this study, a similar database was created for Hertfordshire.[1] One of the major strengths of this research project which cannot be understated is the availability of industrial databases for each of the four regions included in the survey. These databases contain information on virtually all manufacturing establishments in the regions and enabled the identification of an appropriate sample. As a result the performance of the *full population* of small firms can be examined and some measure of the representative nature of the final sample thus determined.

The time period selected for this study – 1986 to 1990 – was conditioned first by the availability of firm-level data on the total population of small firms in each of the study areas and second, by the fact that it coincided with a period of rapid growth in the UK economy and therefore provided an excellent context within which to investigate the determinants of growth in small firms.

The survey examined the performance of established small firms, defined as firms employing less than 50 full-time employees at the beginning of the time period and established prior to 1981, i.e. in existence at least five years before the start of the study period. Thus, firms included in the study had been trading for at least 10 years at the time of the survey which was undertaken during 1991. The focus on firms of this age was designed to remove some of the growth volatility which is normally associated with the start-up phase, especially in the first four years of trading (Storey and Johnson 1986; Storey 1989). The study was designed to focus on the characteristics and motivations of the individual who owns and manages his (there were no women in the study) own firm, and therefore only single plant, indigenously-owned firms were included in the survey sample.

The survey was conducted entirely within the manufacturing sector in each of the four study areas. Firms included in the sample were drawn from five distinct industrial sectors within manufacturing in an attempt to gain a representation of growing and declining sectors at a national level. This was deemed important in order to examine the hypothesis that growth in the small firm sector is not just a function of external factors – in this case factors such as demand or technological change which impact differently on individual sectors. If growth is chiefly related to the characteristics and motivations of the owner-manager then we might expect these factors to be the dominant influences on growth, irrespective of sector. In order to examine further these conflicting viewpoints it was, therefore, necessary to have a range of sectors in the survey sample representing differences in growth and technological sophistication. Thus, we included in the sample some of the

---

1   Access to the Wearside database, which is held at the University of Northumbria at
     Newcastle, was made possible by the co-operation of Dr Ian Stone.

older established sectors such as clothing (SIC 453) and mechanical engineering (SIC 32) which are dominated by mature processes, as well as electrical engineering (SIC 344 and 345) and chemicals (SIC 26), sectors that are seen as more technologically sophisticated and dynamic. The final sector was other manufacturing (SIC 48 and 49) which included some new and innovative industries (primarily plastics) which tend to evade accurate SIC coding under the 1980 classification.

As already stated, the objective of this study was to investigate the determinants of growth, and in particular fast-growth, in the small firm sector. Therefore, a final and most important element of the sample selection was to ensure that fast-growth firms were adequately represented in the survey. Using employment change over the period 1986–90 as a measure of growth, the sample was divided into three growth categories:

1. Fast-growth (100% employment growth or more)

2. Medium/slow-growth (1–99% employment growth)

3. Static/declining (zero or negative employment change)

The distinction between the fast- and slower-growth categories was an arbitrary one, but it was felt that a small firm that had at least doubled its employment size over a four-year period would genuinely constitute a fast-growth firm.

The original intention was to construct a survey sample equally divided between the three growth categories in each of the four study areas and the five industrial sectors indicated above. Firms were randomly sampled within these stratifications. Therefore, the intention was to interview 50 owner-managers in each region across the specified sectors while attempting to stratify in terms of growth category.

There were, however, some difficulties experienced in the implementation of the sampling framework. First, there were some problems in identifying fast-growth companies from the Hertfordshire and Leicestershire databases due to the inconsistent recording of company employment change by the organisations who compiled the original registers upon which the NIERC databases were based. Second, it was difficult to identify sufficient fast-growth companies in Wearside to meet our one-third target in each study area. This was a function of its smaller geographical size which meant that the population of small firms was considerably smaller than in the other three study areas. A further complication was that the clothing sector was under-represented in Wearside. Third, the inclusion of the required proportion of fast-growth companies in *each* of the study areas was hampered by the fact that the owner-managers of these companies were very difficult to contact and arrange a lengthy interview. Some were simply too busy to participate in the survey. A detailed discussion of the characteristics of the 174 small manufacturing firms who finally participated in the survey is presented later in this chapter (see Characteristics of the Survey Respondents, p.22).

The Questionnaire

A formal questionnaire was seen as the best method of collecting data, but at the same time there was no wish to interrupt the flow of conversation during the interview and therefore a semi-structured questionnaire was used. This provided the degree of consistency needed across the various categories of firm (region, sector and growth rate) and permitted the possibility of obtaining an in-depth, yet personal profile from each of the surveyed firms. In all instances the aim was to interview the individual who could be described as the dominant decision-maker within the firm. In the few cases where this was not possible, the interviewee was either a shareholder or senior manager who was actively involved in the strategic decision-making process within the firm. The questionnaire took between 45 minutes and 2 hours to complete, depending on the size and sophistication of the firm and it's management team as well as the willingness of the owner-manager to engage in detailed discussion of the various aspects of the firms activities and performance. The questionnaire was divided into six main sections (see Appendix p.145 for the full version):

1. Background company characteristics
2. Measures of growth
3. Owner-manager qualifications and work experience
4. Motivations of owner-manager
5. Business development activities
6. Constraints on growth

1. Background company characteristics

This section sought data on the background characteristics of the firm in terms of its age, ownership and legal structure, the number of owners/partners and their role in the management of the firm, other business interests of the owner(s), and the precise industrial activity/ product range.

2. Measures of growth

This section of the questionnaire sought information on the growth of employment, turnover, total assets and profits in each firm. Although the questionnaire asked for annual data on these variables it was often only possible to obtain data for 1986 and 1990. Financial data, particularly that relating to profits, was not obtained from all the survey firms as a result of some owner-managers deciding not to release what they saw as sensitive information about their firm.

3. Owner-manager qualifications and work experience

Questions in this section concentrated on collecting detailed data on the personal characteristics of the owner-manager, and where possible the whole strategic management team. In particular, attention was focused on information relating to educational achievement and the detailed work histories of the prime decision-maker(s) in the firm.

4. Motivations of owner-manager

This section was designed to measure the motivation of the owner-manager in pursuing growth in the firm over the study period. This has traditionally been a difficult aspect of individual behaviour to measure and for the purposes of this study it was decided that the *specific* objectives the individual had set for the business for the precise 1986–90 period would be examined. In each case the respondents were required to record their motivations four years previously. The main interest was in establishing to what extent growth was a major objective for the owner of the firm. There were several very similar questions on this issue included in the questionnaire, which attempted to test the consistency of the interviewee's responses. A motivation or desire for growth is not in itself a sufficient condition for business growth over a specific period. Rather, it needs to be translated into a strategic plan which is designed to achieve the overall goal. Therefore, questions were included to ascertain whether the owner-manager had a coherent business strategy capable of fulfilling the objective that had been set. However, it could again be argued that the existence of a coherent business strategy is not sufficient evidence of a motivation to grow. Thus, the survey went one step further by seeking to establish what aspects of the strategy had actually been implemented by the owner-manager.

5. Business development activities

This section of the questionnaire contained a number of questions designed to probe in detail the nature of the business development activities undertaken by the owner-manager. For example, the owner-manager was asked to outline the activities the firm had undertaken in terms of product, process and market development.

It should be stressed that all the questions in sections 4 and 5 focused on the specific time period 1986–90, and each interviewee was constantly reminded to answer only with respect to this period and not to talk about the objectives of the business in general since its establishment or, indeed, possible future intentions. In this way the analysis can be seen to link the motivations, objectives and strategies of the owner-manager to the *actual* growth performance of the firm in a particular time period.

6. Constraints on growth

The last section examined some of the most common constraints on small firm growth, both internal and external, and the extent to which the owner-manager felt that they had hindered the performance of the firm *in the period 1986–90*. The range of issues investigated included the level of overall demand, competition, labour market conditions, finance, relationships with other firms, business information and premises.

The data file on each of the surveyed firms contains 240 variables which cover these six broad areas in the questionnaire.

Characteristics of the Survey Respondents

One of the strengths of this research project was the ability to utilise full population information upon which to base detailed survey work. This section examines the characteristics of the survey respondents in order to establish the rigour of the sampling methodology, and to present some broad assessment of the representative nature of the final sample.

The initial intention to obtain 50 respondents from each of the study areas, while controlling for growth performance and broad industrial sector, proved more difficult than at first envisaged for the reasons already discussed (see Sample Selection, p.17). The major problem occurred in Wearside where it was only possible to obtain 25 respondents which conformed to the sampling frame. Overall, therefore, 174 small firm owner-managers participated in the survey and the distribution of the businesses in terms of growth category, region, industrial sector, employment size, and age are presented in Tables 3.1–3.6. Two of the respondents did not provide any employment information for the period 1986–90, and turnover data was only provided by 148 of the surveyed firms.

The objective to obtain equal numbers of small firms in the three employment growth categories (i.e. one-third in each) was not achieved with only 42 of the respondents (24.4%) being categorised as 'fast-growth' (Table 3.1). Whilst the

Table 3.1. Survey respondents by growth category average growth rate

Growth category	No of firms	%	Average growth rate (1986–90) %		
			Emp	Turnover	(No)
Fast-growth	41	24.4	212.3	156.4	(34)
Slower growing	63	37.8	36.4	46.2	(59)
Static/declining	68	37.8	-15.4	5.0	(54)
Total	**172***	**100.0**	**59.8**	**56.6**	**(147)**

Source: NIERC Small Firm Growth Survey
Note: * Two firms failed to provide employment data

Table 3.2. Survey respondents:
growth category by region and industrial sector

Region	Fast-growth	Slower growing	Static/ declining	All firms
Northern Ireland	18 (36.0)	15 (30.0)	17 (34.0)	50
of which:				
chemicals	2	0	0	2
mech eng	11	6	12	29
elect eng	3	2	1	6
clothing	–	2	4	6
other mfg	2	5	–	7
Leicestershire	10 (20.4)	22 (44.9)	17 (34.7)	49
of which:				
chemicals	–	4	1	5
mech eng	3	6	8	17
elect eng	1	3	2	6
clothing	2	4	3	9
other mfg	4	5	3	12
Hertfordshire	9 (18.7)	15 (31.2)	24 (50.0)	48
of which:				
chemicals	–	–	2	2
mech eng	2	6	12	20
elect eng	5	6	7	18
clothing	–	–	1	
other mfg	2	3	2	7
Wearside	5 (20.0)	13 (52.0)	7 (28.0)	25
of which:				
chemicals	–	–	–	–
mech eng	3	6	3	12
elect eng	1	3	3	7
clothing	1	4	1	6
other mfg	–	–	–	–
Total	**42**	**65**	**65**	**172**

Source: NIERC Small Firm Growth Survey

quota was achieved for the Northern Ireland sample the other three study areas only contained 20 per cent of 'fast-growth' firms (Table 3.2). The problem in achieving the required number of 'fast-growth' firms in the mainland study areas was a function of an under-representation of firms in the chemicals sector, especially pharmaceuticals, combined with the greater difficulties experienced by the research team in obtaining interviews with the owner-managers of these better performing firms.

Table 3.1 also presents data on the average growth rates in each of the three pre-determined growth categories. One of the interesting points to emerge is that for 'fast-growth' small firms average employment growth is higher than growth in turnover, thus implying negative productivity growth. Confining the calculation of average employment growth to only those 34 firms who provided turnover data, a growth rate of 224.6 per cent is recorded, which confirms this conclusion. For the other two categories of growth, the average rate of turnover growth in the 1986–90 period was slightly higher than the average rate of employment growth, thus implying modest productivity growth.

The issue of productivity is important for small firms as they seek to remain competitive in the market place, and, therefore, the occurrence of negative productivity growth suggests that the response to falling sales in the market place is sluggish with respect to employment levels. This may reflect the fact that smaller firms have less flexibility in adjusting employment levels to changes in demand. Marginal changes in turnover may not easily translate into a discrete unit of employment either because the change in turnover is too small to justify laying off or recruiting an extra worker, or because the balance and variety of skills required may be disturbed.

The regional distribution of the surveyed firms is presented in Table 3.3 along with a comparison of average growth rates measured in terms of percentage employment and turnover change over the period 1986–90. Average growth rates are very variable between small firms in the four study areas with the highest rates of employment and turnover growth recorded in Northern Ireland, and, perhaps surprisingly given its south-east England location, the lowest growth rates were found in Hertfordshire respondents. There is also a contrast between the areas in terms of productivity with small firms in Northern Ireland and Wearside experiencing a small increase compared to a decline in the other two areas. Restricting the analysis to only those firms providing employment and turnover data confirms this observation for all the regions except Northern Ireland where an average employment growth of 86.6 per cent was slightly higher than average turnover growth.

With respect to industrial sector, Table 3.4 reveals that just under half the survey respondents were trading within the mechanical engineering sector, with a further 21.5 per cent in electrical engineering. Average growth rates vary quite markedly between the five sectors with the highest employment growth rates being recorded by firms in the electrical engineering and other manufacturing (i.e. plastics) sectors.

Table 3.3. Survey respondents by region and average growth rate

Region	No	%	Average growth rate (1986–1990) %		
			Emp	Turnover	(No)
Northern Ireland	50	29.1	77.9	84.1	(41)
Leicestershire	49	28.5	53.6	48.4	(40)
Hertfordshire	48	27.9	46.5	29.3	(42)
Wearside	25	14.5	61.4	70.9	(24)
Total	**172**	**100.0**	**59.8**	**56.6**	**(147)**

Source: NIERC Small Firm Growth Survey

Average growth rates in turnover also vary greatly between the five sectors with the highest rates being recorded in arguably the more growth-oriented sectors of chemicals, electrical engineering and other manufacturing. Only in the nine firms in the chemicals sector does average turnover growth exceed that of average employment growth.

Table 3.4. Survey respondents by industrial sector and average growth rate

Sector	No	%	Average growth rate (1986–90) %		
			Emp	Turnover	(No)
Chemicals	9	5.2	42.6	96.6	(8)
Mechanical eng	78	45.3	59.7	53.9	(63)
Electrical eng	37	21.5	70.0	62.2	(33)
Clothing	22	12.8	40.4	33.6	(20)
Other manfg	26	15.1	67.0	61.8	(23)
Total	**172**	**100.0**	**59.8**	**56.6**	**(147)**

Source: NIERC Small Firm Growth Survey

Table 3.5 shows the employment size distribution of the small firms included in the survey. There was no attempt made to control for size at the time of sample selection but the final sample reflected the full range of firm size within the small firm sector. As one would expect, average growth rates in employment were correlated by size with the smallest firms (in 1986) experiencing the fastest growth over the period. The same was true for average growth in turnover, but in terms of productivity it was the larger firms in the sample which recorded small gains over the 1986–90 period.

Table 3.5. Survey respondents
by employment size (1986) and average growth rate

No of Employees	No	%	Average growth rate (1986–90) %		
			Emp	Turnover	(No)
1–5	33	19.2	131.2	66.9	(29)
6–10	39	22.7	68.8	66.9	(32)
11–25	60	34.9	34.5	49.6	(48)
26–50	40	23.2	30.2	48.7	(38)
Total	**172***	**100.0**	**59.8**	**56.6**	**(147)**

Source: NIERC Small Firm Growth Survey
Note: * Two firms failed to provide employment data

As indicated above, a firm had to be operating for at least 10 years before it could be included in the sample. Table 3.6 reveals the decade in which the survey respondents were established. Nearly one-fifth (18.6%) were established at the very start of the 1980s, with the majority of the remainder indicating a formation date in the 1970s. Again, not surprisingly, average growth rates in employment and turnover were highly correlated with age. The younger the firm, especially those formed in 1980–81, the faster the rate of growth. Turning again to the issue of productivity, it is generally the older firms in the sample, that is, those set up in the 1960s or earlier, which had experienced productivity growth in the 1986–90 period.

Table 3.6. Survey respondents by date of formation and average growth rate

Date of formation	No	%	Average growth rate (%)		
			Emp	Turnover	(No)
Pre-1960s	26	15.1	14.0	38.2	(23)
1960s	35	20.3	27.1	38.9	(31)
1970s	79	45.9	69.6	51.1	(67)
1980–81	32	18.6	108.5	108.0	(26)
Total	**172***	**100.0**	**59.8**	**56.6**	**(147)**

Source: NIERC Small Firm Growth Survey
Note: *Two firms failed to provide a date of formation

How Representative is the Sample?

It is important to establish to what extent the sample reflects the population of small firms in each of the four study areas. As discussed above, the samples of firms for the survey were drawn randomly within three strata of fast-, medium- and slow-growing firms. Attempts were made to draw firms equally from the three strata. However, this was more successful for Northern Ireland than for other areas, partly reflecting the better quality of background data and a high degree of co-operation from businesses. In the other areas it was sometimes difficult to persuade faster growing firms to take part in the survey, and firms initially identified as fast-growing proved to be slower growing, once data was forthcoming directly from the firm. These problems led to a particular under-representation of fast-growth firms in the Wearside sample.

In the case of the two southern areas – Leicestershire and Hertfordshire – there were also fewer fast-growth companies among the population of small firms (Table 3.7). This contributed to a difficulty of including fast-growing firms within the sample for these areas. The outcome for Leicestershire and Hertfordshire was that fast-growing firms were over-represented in the sample due to the attempt to obtain an equal distribution across the three growth categories. The proportion of fast-growing firms in the sample was higher than for the population of small firms in Northern Ireland, Leicestershire and Hertfordshire. Slower growing firms were

Table 3.7. Small firms classified by rate of employment growth (1986–90) (%)

	Fast growing	Slower growing	Declining	%	Total no of firms
Northern Ireland					
Population	21.9	32.5	45.5	100	(818)
Survey	36.0	30.0	34.0	100	(50)
Leicestershire					
Population	12.6	36.4	51.0	100	(884)
Survey	20.4	44.9	34.7	100	(49)
Hertfordshire					
Population	7.7	28.8	63.6	100	(365)
Survey	18.7	31.2	50.0	100	(48)
Wearside					
Population	22.4	41.5	36.0	100	(147)
Survey	20.0	52.0	28.0	100	(25)

Sources: NIERC Industrial databases
NIERC Small Firm Growth Survey

broadly represented in proportion to their presence in the population with the exception of Wearside. Declining firms were under-represented in each of the four areas.

The net result was that average employment growth was higher in the sample firms than in the population in all of the four areas (Table 3.8). The 144 firms for which full information was available, increased their employment by 61 per cent over the four-year period. This compares with 29 per cent for the population of small firms within the targeted sectors in the four survey areas. Differences in growth between the populations of firms in Northern Ireland, Leicestershire and Hertfordshire were reflected, and to some extent exaggerated, in the sample. The main exception was Wearside, the area with the fastest growing *population* of firms. Among the *sample* firms in Wearside, average employment growth was above average but second to Northern Ireland. In both the populations and the sample there was a clear difference in employment growth between the two more northerly areas of Northern Ireland and Wearside and the two southerly areas of Leicestershire and Hertfordshire. This difference also emerges in the growth of turnover among the sample companies. The relative position of the areas is, however, similar whether growth is measured in terms of employment or turnover. In particular, Northern Ireland was the fastest growing area on both measures among the survey firms. As indicated above however, it is likely that growth in Wearside is underestimated.

Table 3.8. Average regional employment growth rates by growth category: population versus survey respondents

Growth category	*Average growth rates (%)* *1986–90 (Employment)*							
	NI		*Leics*		*Herts*		*Wearside*	
	Pop	*Survey*	*Pop*	*Survey*	*Pop*	*Survey*	*Pop*	*Survey*
Fast-growth	195.5	197.4	257.9	205.4	228.5	224.9	284.8	257.2
Medium-growth	37.4	45.2	33.4	35.5	30.7	34.9	38.5	29.6
Static/declining	-21.8	-19.9	-12.3	-12.4	-15.4	-13.2	-17.5	-19.4
Total	**31.9**	**77.8**	**26.4**	**53.6**	**19.1**	**46.5**	**50.1**	**61.4**

Sources: NIERC Industrial databases
          NIERC Small Firm Growth Survey

Looking at each of the growth categories in turn, it is clear that there is a remarkable consistency between the rate of employment growth recorded by the survey respondents and that of *all* small firms in each of the four regions (Table 3.8). Overall, these *sample* and *population* comparisons would tend to support the conclusion that the 174 surveyed firms are broadly representative of the small firm sector within the targeted sectors in each of the four regions.

Approach to Data Analysis

From the outset the aim was to develop a model of small firm growth capable of being estimated and quantified within the framework of Ordinary Least Squares (OLS) regression. However, the nature of the data and the diversity of influences on small firm growth prevented the adoption of the approach apparently used by most researchers in economics – namely the derivation of precise hypotheses from economic theory and their formal testing by econometric techniques. In fact, in attempting to understand the issue of small firm growth there are a variety of problems which necessitate an approach to data analysis which is perhaps more familiar in sociology than economics. These problems or issues are explained briefly below.

First, as discussed in Chapter 2, there is insufficient theory or, rather, there are too many poorly developed theoretical approaches, to provide a useful *a priori* guide to the factors which affect small firm growth (Casson 1982; O'Farrell and Hitchens 1988). Related to this, and perhaps because of it, empirical analysis has tended to be partial in the sense of focusing on the influence of single variables such as education and motivation rather than a multivariate approach, and has, as a result, yielded inconsistent results (Storey 1994). However, at the outset of the research there was uncertainty as to which of the variables identified by the literature search – and by the researchers' intuition – would be most important, although, *a priori*, the expectation was that it would be some combination of entrepreneur, firm and business strategy variables.

A second issue relates to the way in which data on small firms has been gathered. Although in the eyes of many researchers questionnaire surveys are an objective means of obtaining data it is not clear that this is always the case. Respondents to questionnaire surveys differ in intelligence, ideology, class and experience – even within a specific group such as owner-managers. In a similar way, any group of researchers contains important differences. Because of these differences, a relatively short and direct interview may not be the most appropriate way of establishing the truth of a situation despite the expertise of the interviewers and the relatively objective nature of the questions. To minimise the possibility of data loss through partial recollection, misinterpretation, inadvertent lack of truthfulness and biased recording, several different questions were included at different points in the questionnaire on the same issue. The result of this, in short, was that there were several variables measuring the same characteristic. At the start of the analysis there was no way of knowing which was the most accurate.

A third difficulty in analysing the data relates to what can best be described as indirect effects. It is possible that some variables, say for instance education, have direct and indirect effects on firm growth. The direct effect, for example, is that education simply improves all decision making so education is highly correlated with growth. The indirect effect may be that education also improves product innovation which is itself correlated with firm growth. If this is the case the coefficient on the education variable will understate the influence of education on firm performance.

There is a technique, used largely in sociology, designed to measure indirect effects, known as 'path analysis'. The approach consists of a series of recursive regression equations in which the independent variables, through which the indirect effects are supposed to work, themselves become dependent variables to be explained in terms of a reduced set of independent variables. This approach was not adopted for two reasons. First, where the number of potential independent variables is large the computational difficulties are immense. Second, the meaning of the path coefficients is unclear where dependent variables are binary in nature (i.e. the use of dummy variables). Nevertheless, the need to examine indirect effects was recognised and was addressed through a series of cross-tabulations of the dependent variables. An indication of where indirect effects are occurring is given by showing where the significant variables in the model cross-correlate with other survey variables.

A fourth minor problem with the analysis relates to the fact that many of the variables are simple categorisations. For example, education is measured by the presence or absence of a qualification. A fifth and final small problem is that of collinearity. Certainly there is collinearity of those variables ostensibly measuring the same characteristic. However, there is also the danger of collinearity in dummy variables created to represent categories, and indeed between certain variables measuring apparently unrelated characteristics.

The theoretical and practical problems described above led to an approach to statistical analysis which is best described as 'guided model building'. This approach consists of formulating a variety of models in which the overall hypothesis that firm growth is the product of entrepreneurial, firm and strategy variables remains constant but the individual variables within each category change. Changing the variables within each category was necessary because there was more than one variable measuring the same characteristic and because the significance of some characteristics, in a multivariate framework, was not certain. As Storey (1994) points out, many of the factors commonly supposed to influence small firm growth have never been tested within a multivariate framework. The models were assessed according to three criteria: a priori reasoning and evidence, overall explanatory power and individual variable significance.

With this approach to data analysis it would be true to say that the study is concerned as much with model building as model testing. The model presents that combination of variables which has the greatest ability to explain variance in the data – subject to the broad hypothesis outlined above. One corollary of taking this approach is that many of the variables for which data was collected are omitted from the model on the grounds that they are not significantly related to the dependent variable. These omitted variables are of interest in themselves and some of them are discussed in the next chapter.

A final issue relates to the precision of the estimates produced by the regression analysis. One dependent variable is based on change in turnover over the period 1986–90. In most cases survey respondents needed to consult their company's accounts to be able to provide the financial information they were asked for, namely total assets, profits and turnover. Very few were able to recollect these items of data but some were. In general, where data was provided by recollection, it was rounded to the nearest £1000. There is a possibility, albeit remote, that the data provided in such a way was inaccurate. However, it is the view of the interviewers that such inaccuracies as exist are slight, random and rare.

CHAPTER 4

Entrepreneurial Attributes and Business Strategy Influences on Company Growth
Quantitative Results

Introduction

The 240 variables obtained from the survey were tested for their influence on growth in company output over the period 1986–90. A number of variables were individually correlated with growth in turnover. Of greatest interest, however, is the multiple correlation of all of those variables which were collectively and simultaneously correlated with growth in a statistically significant manner.

A number of regression equations are reported in this chapter which include all of the statistically significant variables or subsets of them. The value of this approach is that the coefficients attached to each variable in the equation are partial, i.e. they measure the impact of each variable *independently* of all others in the equation. This is important. Undertaking market research, for instance, is associated with a large boost to growth.[1] Some of this boost reflects the advantages gained from the market research itself. Another part, however, reflects the attributes of those types of owner-manager likely to undertake market research. A multiple regression equation goes a long way in disentangling these various influences. In addition, some variables which are not individually correlated with growth can be seen to be important when other factors are controlled for. Conversely, other variables cease to be significantly associated with growth when included in combinations with other variables. One example is years of education. This increases growth, but appears to work mainly through an increased likelihood of adopting growth strategies including market research and product development. When these strategies are included the 'underlying' education variable drops out. A more detailed discussion of the interrelationship between the dependent variables is developed in Chapters 5 and 6.

The preferred equation is shown in Table 4.1. The equation shows the maximum number of variables which had a simultaneous and statistically signifi-

---

1   See Table 4.1, p.33.

Table 4.1. Preferred equation for real change in company turnover 1986–90

		Variable	Multiple regression equation	Single regression equations
Company	1	Size	-0.14*	(-0.01)
characteristics	2	NI	0.26*	0.23
	3	Leics	(0.00)	(-0.13)
	4	Wear	(0.16)	(0.10)
	5	Mech	(-0.23)	(-0.04)
	6	Chem	(-0.20)	(0.24)
	7	Other	(-0.02)	(0.18)
	8	Elec	(-0.14)	(-0.02)
Owner-manager	9	Age	-0.01	-0.11
characteristics	10	Proforg	0.35*	(0.17)
	11	Founder	(0.12)	(0.11)
	12	Othbus+	0.26*	0.31*
	13	Othbus	0.43*	(0.20)
	14	Otherown	0.19*	(0.09)
Business strategies:				
Aims	15	Growprof	0.19*	0.25*
	16	Market	0.24*	0.22
	17	Margins	0.40	(0.32)
	18	Prodproc	0.19	(0.07)
Methods	19	Markres	0.27*	0.49*
	20	Agent	-0.36*	(-0.07)
	21	Newprod	0.03	0.04*
	22	Capsuc	0.21*	(0.12)
	23	Capfal	0.34	(0.21)
	24	Newmach	0.15	0.24
	25	Diverse	-0.19*	(0.04)
Constraints on growth	26	Demand	-0.29*	-0.42*
		Constant	1.83*	
		No of cases	138	138
		Adj r squared	0.51	
		F	6.48	
		Standard error	0.38	

Note: The figures are regression coefficients. These are statistically significantly different from zero at the 5% probability level (t test) unless otherwise stated. Starred coefficients are significant at the 1% level. Coefficients in parentheses are not significant at the 5% level. The multiple regression equation 1 excludes 6 cases from Leics with extreme values for the variable NEWPROD. The coefficients in the second column are derived from single regression equations including one variable at a time together with a constant term.

Source: NIERC Small Firm Growth Survey

cant influence on growth in output. In line with the framework developed in Chapter 2 they are grouped into four categories:[2]

1. Company characteristics
2. Owner-manager characteristics
3. Business strategies
   (a) Aims
   (b) Methods
4. Constraints on growth.

The inclusion of any individual variable indicates a significant association but cannot in itself say anything conclusive about causation. With many of the variables there is the possibility of reverse causation, simple association and, in the case of certain variables, *ex post* rationalisation. For instance, it seems most plausible that market research leads to faster growth. It is possible, however, that the reverse is true and that firms which grew faster for other reasons were more likely to undertake market research. Similarly, faster growing firms were found to be owned by those more oriented towards marketing as a strategy for growth. Again a straightforward causal interpretation seems most appropriate, but it could be that successful owners rationalised their success after the event by stressing their attention to marketing.

All of the variables included in the equation in Table 4.1 are those where we believe that causation is direct from that variable to growth. Nevertheless, the possibility of *ex post* rationalisation remains and cannot be excluded given the nature of this study. In one group of variables, constraints to growth, this problem is of particular concern. These are the constraints to growth. For instance, several companies stated that shortage of demand had constrained their growth. In some cases this view could obscure the fact that other factors including the quality of the product or the price might have caused the problem of lack of demand. It is also not obvious *a priori* at what rate of growth the constraints become operative. A lack of demand might in principle prevent a rapidly growing firm from doing even better. In practice, however, most firms which cited demand as a constraint on growth grew slowly and not rapidly, and it is reasonably clear that this constraint is at least associated with slow growth (see Chapter 8). Interpretation remains somewhat problematic but the inclusion of a wide range of alternative variables in a single equation increases the probability that any independent impact of the **demand** variable is likely to measure a true demand constraint. However, results are reported with and without the inclusion of this factor (see Table A4.2 – Equation 5, p.53). Certain other variables are potentially *ex post* rationalisations of events and this is dealt with in the text as appropriate.

---

2   A definition of each of the variables contained in the subsequent analysis is provided in Table A4.1.

The results in the previous chapter are based on growth calculated as simple percentage change $(X_1-X_0/X_0)*100$ where X_0 is turnover in 1986 and X_1 turnover in 1990. For statistical purposes this variable has the drawback that it is highly skewed. To eliminate the problem of heteroscedasticity therefore, a transformation of the simple percentage change was made using natural logarithms. The dependent variable in all of the equations is $Ln(X_1/X_0)$. Using $Ln(X_1/X_0)$ also has the advantage that coefficients in the regression equation represent, approximately, the percentage change in the dependent variable for a given absolute change in the independent variable.[3] For clarity of exposition, where regression coefficients are

---

3 Technical Note

When growth takes place on a continuously compounded basis X_1 can be calculated from X_0 by the formula

(1) $X_1 = X_0 e^{rt}$ where e is the base for natural logarithms
  r is the growth rate
  t is the number of times period

from (1) it can be seen that

$$\frac{X_1}{X_0} = e^{rt}$$

and therefore

$r = Ln((X_1/X_0)^{1/t})$

since in this case t = 1

$r = Ln(X_1/X_0)$

with r being the continuously compounded growth rate. The coefficients in the equations are left in log form because logs have the useful property that:

change in Ln X relative change in X itself.

For example: if $X_0 = 50$ and $X_1 = 60$

change in Ln X = 4.1 - 3.9 = 0.2

change in X itself = 60 - 50

$$\frac{}{50} = 0.2$$

note $(Ln X_1 - Ln X_0 = Ln(X_1/X_0))$

One slight problem with using $Ln(X_1/X_0)$ as the dependent variable is that the equivalence between the actual change in X and $Ln(X_1/X_0)$ is less precise as $(X_1 - X_0)$ grows large. However, for the sake of simplicity, the coefficients in the equations remain in log form and are referred to as percentage changes. To differentiate the percentage growth rates derived from the equation from simple percentage change those from the equations are italicised.

referred to as percentages (i.e. market research is associated with a 27% increase in growth), they are italicised. Other percentages are left as normal text.

The R^2 value shows the proportion of the total variation in growth between companies which is accounted for by the equation. The R^2 value of 0.51 for the multiple regression equation presented in Table 4.1 (p.33) indicates that this equation accounts for 51 per cent of all the variation in turnover growth between companies. The remaining 49 per cent is unaccounted for and will be due to other factors not investigated in the study, as well as some which might be viewed as random or chance influences and also measurement error. As indicated in Table A4.1 (p.52) many of the independent variables are 'dummy variables' indicating the presence or absence of an attribute. The sample size for each equation was the 144 firms for which full data was available, less six Leicestershire companies with extreme values for the number of improved products **(newprod)**. However, there were difficulties in obtaining accurate data on product development from six companies in the Leicestershire sample. As a result, these companies with very high reported numbers of product improvements were, as noted above, excluded from the main equation in Table 4.1 (p.33) which is thus based on a sample of 138 companies.[4]

The full model contains 26 variables and is complex in its interpretation. In order to focus on some of the major influences on firm growth two 'reduced form' models containing the strongest variables have been developed. The overall explanatory power of the 'reduced form' models is lower but they have the merit of providing some guidance as to the most important determinants of growth in small firms.

The Preferred Model Equation

The multiple regression equation in Table 4.1 (p.33) contains all of the variables found to be simultaneously and significantly associated with growth as well as some which are, in classical statistical terms, insignificant. The variables in the latter category are mainly in the group labelled 'company characteristics'. In the literature much emphasis is placed on size, sector and region as being important influences on firm growth (O'Farrell and Hitchens 1988; Storey 1994). In this preferred equation most, although not all, of this type of factor were found *not* to be significant. Other variables in the equation were better able to account for growth differences between regions or industries. The insignificant sector and region dummy variables were, however, retained in the model to demonstrate this fact.[5] The information in the multiple regression equation in Table 4.1 (p.33) represents a plausible picture of small firm growth. Two characteristics of the firm signifi-

---

4   An equation including these 6 companies is reported in equation 2 in appendix A4.2 (p.53).
5   An equivalent equation including only statistically significant variables is included as equation 3 in Appendix Table A4.2 (p.53).

cantly affected growth. The smaller the firm was at the start of the period **(size)** the faster it grew. A location in Northern Ireland **(NI)** enhanced growth during this period, relative to a location in Hertfordshire (which is used as a base for locational comparisons). Other locations were not significantly different from Hertfordshire. There was no significant difference in growth between industrial sectors.[6]

The type of entrepreneur associated with the faster growing firms was relatively young **(age)**, a member of a professional organisation **(proforg)**, worked as part of a larger entrepreneurial team **(otherown)**, and had a network of other business interests which are mainly legally independent and separate small firms. In some cases the existence of these other businesses is an advantage **(othbus+)**. In other cases the businesses are unconnected **(othbus)**. Most of these characteristics were highly significant influences on growth. There was also some evidence that firms still run by their founders **(founder)** grew faster, but in this equation the variable was not statistically significant.[7] Attempts were made to include a range of variables measuring the owners' qualifications and work experience. None of these were significantly associated with growth in the full equation.

Four business 'aims' were significantly associated with company growth. Sixty two per cent of owner-managers said that expansion of profits **(growprof)** was a highly important goal. In these firms growth was significantly faster than in the others. Similarly the 37 per cent of firms in which marketing was viewed as a very important strategy **(market)** grew faster. The aim of improving margins through price increases or cost reductions **(margins)** was confined to only 4 per cent of companies, but was again associated with faster growth. Finally, the aim of improving the production process **(prodproc)** held by 28 per cent of firms was found to be positively associated with growth in the full equation. With each of these four variables the association was highly significant and increased growth over four years by around twenty percentage points except for the variable **'margins'** where the boost to growth was twice as large. As will be seen in Chapter 5, these strategy aims tend to be associated with different types of owner-manager.

The remaining business strategy variables in this equation are classed as business 'methods' rather than business 'aims'. Several of these are highly significant in their association with growth, some in positive directions, others negatively. Undertaking formal market research **(markres)** was strongly associated with growth. Twenty three per cent of firms were in this category and most of these were among the fastest growing companies. Selling methods also affected growth. In particular firms which used agents to sell their products **(agent)** tended to grow slowly. Undertaking market research was associated with a 27 percentage point increase in growth. This was more than offset, however, in firms which used selling

---

6   A more detailed discussion of these 'company characteristics' can be found in Chapter 5 (The influence of company characteristics, p.54).

7   The equation omitting this variable is reported as equation 1 in Appendix Table A4.2 (p.53).

agents. These had an average effect of lowering growth by 36 percentage points (Table 4.1, p.33).

Product development was significantly associated with company growth. The larger the number of improvements made to products (newprod) the faster the growth of the company. Firms which attempted to raise external capital were also faster growing. This was true of the 57 per cent of firms which successfully raised external capital (capsuc), but also of the small number (6%) which tried but failed in their attempt (capfal). Firms which used investment in new machines to improve the production process (newmach) grew faster. Finally, those firms with a diverse range of products (diverse) were associated with slow growth to a significant degree. The growth rate of firms with more diversified products was reduced by 19 percentage points.

One variable representing constraints to growth was included in the equation. This was demand as a constraint on growth (demand). Those respondents who said that lack of demand had constrained their growth were revealed in the equation of Table 4.1 (p.33) to have a growth rate which was 30 percentage points slower than in unconstrained companies. Other potential constraints, for example labour shortages, lack of finance, etc. were found not to be significantly associated with growth. The only other significant constraint on growth was lack of management time (mantime). This was highly statistically significant and positively associated with growth, which indicates that faster growing companies were more likely to be constrained by internal organisational factors. This would tend to lend support to the argument of Penrose (1959) who stated that there may be managerial costs to fast growth which in turn impairs efficiency. However, in this case, the only realistic interpretation was that the direction of causation was from growth to constraint and the variable was consequently omitted from the equation.

The equation in Table 4.1 (p.33) accounts for half of the very large variation in growth between companies. The high explanatory power (R-square) achieved in this equation confirms the value of the approach to small firm growth adopted in this study. It is the characteristics of the entrepreneur and the strategies he or she adopts[8] which largely determine the growth of the small enterprise. Company characteristics including size, location and sector appear to be influential but in a relatively minor way. To a large part, growth in small firms derives, as envisaged in Chapter 2, from the skills, values and motivations of the entrepreneur and the strategy he or she adopts with regard to, *inter alia*, innovation, marketing and market research.

The results contained in the multiple regression equation in Table 4.1 (p.33) confirm the conceptualisation of small firm growth presented in Chapter 3 in another important way. Although in a large minority of the survey firms there was more than one 'entrepreneur', we chose to identify the lead entrepreneur and focus the analysis on this individual. Since growth appears to be a function of the

---

8   'He' generally. All owner-managers in this study are male.

characteristics of the lead entrepreneur, this appears to be a justified approach. This is not to say that there are no advantages in 'team' entrepreneurship. The equation, which includes a dummy variable **otherown** (indicating the influence of other owners), shows that team-run firms grow faster than single-entrepreneur firms. However, where teams exist there appears always to be a pre-eminent decision maker and it seems justifiable, given the current state of knowledge, to focus on this individual.

The equation also provides insight into the complex interaction of entrepreneurial characteristics, strategy and constraints. The very complexity of the processes involved in growth perhaps explains why there have been few previous attempts to investigate these in a multivariate approach. However, this omission has hindered the development of a theory of growth in small firms which clearly requires a multivariate approach. The equation in Table 4.1 (p.33) cannot be regarded as in any way definitive. It clearly requires replication and further elaboration and development. It is, however, indicative and suggests a number of interrelated hypotheses which will be explored further in Chapters 5 and 6.

The Multiple and Single Impact of Factors

The importance of a multiple regression equation, as has been said, is that it identifies the impact of each influence on growth independently of other influences. This helps to identify a 'true' effect. In particular a number of significant influences can be identified which otherwise might be missed. The partial regression coefficients from the preferred equation can be compared with the individual impact of each variable to demonstrate the importance of controlling for other factors. The results are presented in Table 4.1 (p.33) which also includes the coefficient for each factor obtained from single regressions including only one explanatory variable at a time. Since single regressions have typically been used in previous research on the growth of small firms, it is instructive to compare the two approaches.

As can be seen, several of the variables which are significantly associated with growth in the multiple regression equation (column one of Table 4.1, p.33) are not significant in simple regressions. This indicates that their impact is only revealed once other factors are controlled for. Company size **(size)** is one such factor, membership of professional organisations **(proforg)** is another, and the presence of multiple owners of a single business **(otherown)** is a third.

Several factors are clearly identified as highly significant even in simple regressions. These are market research **(markres)**, product development **(newprod)** profit oriented aims **(growprof)**, ownership of related businesses **(othbus)** and, finally, a lack of demand constraint **(demand)**. A comparison of columns 1 and 2 in Table 4.1 (p.33) shows that the coefficients in each case are smaller in the multiple regression equation. This indicates that the independent impact of each variable is smaller when other factors are controlled for. In other words, the multiple regression eliminates indirect impacts associated with each variable.

The relative importance of each variable is indicated both by the statistical significance and the size of the coefficients in Table 4.1 (p.33). Another instructive way of examining the relative importance of each variable is to examine what each contributes to the explanatory power of the equation when introduced in turn. This is achieved by starting with the variable with the highest R^2 value and adding variables in turn, in a stepwise fashion, in order of their contribution to explanatory power.

The results of such a stepwise regression are shown in Table 4.2 (p.41). This shows that the market research variable **(markres)** can alone account for 14 per cent of the variation in growth between companies. The addition of the demand constraint variable **(demand)** adds a further 10 per cent. Together these account for a quarter of the variation in growth, and hence contribute half of the explanatory power of the full preferred equation. As before, we should note that although the exercise of undertaking market research may account for much of the importance of the **markres** variable, its impact on growth is also likely to reflect the characteristics and other abilities of those most likely to undertake market research. Even so, it is interesting that only two variables can contribute so much to the equation. They indicate that the growth of a company's market is important and that market research is a key factor in expanding the company's market share.

Almost all of the remaining 24 variables in the equation individually raise the explanatory power by under two percentage points. The lesson here seems to be that growth is influenced by a large number of individually small factors. This helps to explain why the causes of growth are so difficult to identify and to comprehend. It also explains why the growth of small firms is not adequately captured in economic theory which, typically, includes only a small set of mathematically tractable variables. It also seems likely that much of the remaining 'unexplained' half of the inter-company variation in growth is accounted for by a plethora of even smaller influences. These are not likely to be statistically significant in studies with relatively small samples and will be particularly difficult to identify.

Having said this, the possibility remains that major influences may have been overlooked. The regional analysis in Chapter 7 suggests that some cost factors come into this category, although regional cost differences should be captured by the locational variables included in the equation. Another set of omitted variables may be those concerned with individual drive and motivation. However, as discussed in Chapter 2, we took the view that the range of contradictory evidence from psychological studies on this issue rendered the inclusion of these variables problematical. Furthermore, we would contend that several aspects of individual motivation are also likely to be incorporated in the business aims variables which are included in the full equation.

Table 4.2. Contribution of variables to the explanatory power of the preferred equation

	Cumulative R^2	Addition to R^2	Single equation R^2
Markres	0.144	0.144	0.144
Demand	0.247	0.103	0.113
Growprof	0.270	0.023	0.046
Margin	0.287	0.017	0.008
Founder	0.302	0.015	0.003
Proforg	0.317	0.015	0.007
Market	0.339	0.022	0.031
Age	0.358	0.019	0.033
Prodproc	0.373	0.015	-0.004
Othbus	0.385	0.012	0.004
Size	0.403	0.018	-0.007
Othbus+	0.421	0.018	0.050
Diverse	0.435	0.014	-0.006
Capsuc	0.445	0.010	0.006
Newprod	0.458	0.013	0.060
Other	0.466	0.008	0.007
Capfal	0.474	0.008	0.000
Newmach	0.479	0.005	0.035
NI	0.483	0.004	0.032
Agents	0.492	0.009	-0.006
Otherown	0.501	0.009	-0.001
Wear	0.511	0.010	-0.003
Mech	0.516	0.005	-0.006
Elec	0.514	-0.002	-0.007
Chem	0.514	0.000	0.002
Leics	0.510	-0.004	0.003

No of cases 138

Note: The multiple correlation coefficient (R^2) values in column 1 and 2 are obtained from a stepwise regression in which variables are introduced in the order indicated above.

Source: NIERC Small Firm Growth Survey

The Reduced Form Model

As is obvious from the foregoing sections, it is not easy to summarise the message of the full preferred equation. A large number of factors acting independently affect company growth. This is especially true in the case of business strategy where, in addition to one or two obvious and crucial strategies, there are a number of minor variables which have an impact on growth. The previous section showed how the variables can be ranked to indicate their contribution to the explanatory power of the full equation. In one attempt to produce a simpler equation from this exercise we have arbitrarily included only the first eight of the marked variables of Table 4.2 into a single regression equation. The results of this process are shown in Table 4.3 which we term the 'reduced form' model. By its nature the reduced form model simplifies what appears to be a very complex process. Nevertheless, the fact that the regression explains 36 per cent of the variance with eight variables instead of the original 26, and that these variables are plausible in terms of our original conceptualisation of firm growth, we can be confident in making some comments as to the most important factors influencing firm growth.

Table 4.3. A reduced form equation for growth in company sales

		Coefficient
Markres		0.41*
Demand		-0.37*
Growprof		0.16
Margins		0.43
Founder		0.23*
Proforg		0.27*
Market		0.20*
Age		-0.01
Constant		(0.34)
No of cases	138	
adjusted R^2	0.36	
F	10.54	
Standard error	0.43	

Note: Coefficients are statistically significant at the 5% level unless starred which indicates a 1% level of significance. Values in parentheses are not significant at the 5 per cent level.

Source: NIERC Small Firm Growth Survey

Even when the number of variables in the model is constrained, it is still quite clear that it is a combination of the characteristics of the entrepreneur and the strategies that he or she pursues that influences growth. In essence, the fast-growing firm can be located in any sector and any part of the country and have any initial size. The important thing is that the key decision maker be young, technically competent, the founder of the firm and profit oriented. In terms of strategy two factors stand out: a reliance on formal market research for information and recognition of the importance of marketing. Also influential in terms of strategy for a small subset of firms is a strong emphasis on use of cost and price as a means of competing.

One important variable omitted from Table 4.3 is product development **(newprod)**. This may reflect the measurement difficulties – especially in the Leicestershire sample. If the six omitted extreme values are reintroduced into the analysis then product development emerges as one of the key influences on growth. This is shown in Table 4.4 which is presented even though we have reservations about the accuracy of measurement.

Table 4.4. Reduced form equation including product development outliers

Variable	Coefficient	Cumulative R^2
Markres	0.45*	0.15
Newprod	0.01	0.19
Founder	0.30*	0.22
Age	-0.01*	0.23
Margin	0.56*	0.26
Market	0.22*	0.28
Otherown	0.18	0.30
Proforg	0.21	0.31
Constant	(0.29)	

No of cases	144
adjusted R^2	0.31
F	9.13
Standard error	0.45

Note: Coefficients are statistically significant at the 5% level unless starred which indicates a 1% level of significance. Values in parentheses are not significant at the 5 per cent level.

Source: NIERC Small Firm Growth Survey

Several points emerge from the analysis of the reduced form equation in Table 4.4. The regression equation shows the two most important variables to be: reliance on market research **(markres)** and the capability of the firm to introduce new products and modify old ones **(newprod)**. Alone, these two variables explain 19 per cent of the variance in the data. This tells us that ultimately the characteristics of the entrepreneur are less important that the strategies he or she pursues. This is useful from the perspective of small firm policy formation. Certain characteristics of the entrepreneur, such as age and whether he or she is the founder, are impossible to change. However, it is perfectly possible to devise policies which will help entrepreneurs, whatever their background, to make their firms more flexible in terms of product development and more systematic, proactive and objective in their acquisition and use of market intelligence.

Another point is that, in terms of business strategy, the reduced form model in Table 4.4 (p.43) indicates that the best firms stay close to their customers and innovate to stay ahead of the game. The marketing half of this description is a major message of our research. The innovation part must be advanced more tentatively due to potential measurement problems. Even so, it is fully plausible that to grow, the small firm needs to pay close attention to the market and to change its products so that they are always different and better than those of their competitors. This type of strategy, as Douglas (1993) points out, amounts to nothing more, in Porter's terminology, than product differentiation (see Porter 1980).

Irrespective of the value of the reduced form models, it must be emphasised that moving from the reduced form model to the full model by adding variables does have a significant effect on the explanatory power of the equation. Furthermore, most of the additional variables are significant at high levels. Although it is useful to distil the process of small firm growth to its essential components, in reality the process is extremely complex. As stated earlier, there is more than one type of entrepreneur that may achieve growth and more than one group of strategies.

Company Characteristics, Owner Characteristics and Strategy

As a final examination of the individual factors we can separately analyse them in their three broad groups. Regressing individually each of the three groups of variables in the model yields some useful insights into the nature of the interrelationships between the variables in the model. This is done in Table 4.5. Taking first equation 4.5.1 in which the company characteristics alone are regressed on growth, the first thing to note is that the overall explanatory power of the model is low. Although some of the variables are individually significant, size sector and region are, in aggregate, unimportant influences on growth even in an equation of their own. That initial size **(size)** is not significant in equation 4.5.1, or on its own, indicates, as already discussed, that it is cross-correlated with one or more of the

Table 4.5. Partial equations for real change in company turnover, 1986–90

Variable type	Variable name	4.5.1 Company characteristics	4.5.2 Entrepreneurial characteristics	4.5.3 Strategy aims	4.5.4 Strategy methods	4.5.5 Strategy aims and methods
Company characteristics	Size	(-0.04)				
	NI	0.32*				
	Leics	(0.02)				
	Wear	0.28				
	Mech	(0.12)				
	Chem	0.47				
	Other	0.39*				
	Elec	(0.20)				
Owner-manager characteristics	Age		-0.01*			
	Othbus		0.34			
	Proforg		0.24			
	Founder		0.25*			
	Othbus+		0.34*			
	Otherown		(0.11)			
Business strategies: Aims	Growprof			0.22		0.18
	Margins			(0.34)		0.53*
	Market			0.20		0.17
	Prodproc			(0.07)		(0.11)

Table 4.5. Partial equations for real change in company turnover, 1986–90 (continued)

Variable type	Variable name	4.5.1 Company characteristics	4.5.2 Entrepreneurial characteristics	4.5.3 Strategy aims	4.5.4 Strategy methods	4.5.5 Strategy aims and methods
Business strategies: Methods	Markres				0.39*	0.36*
	Agent				(-0.21)	(-0.27)
	Newprod				0.03	0.04*
	Capsuc				(0.17)	0.20
	Capfal				(0.33)	(0.34)
	Newmach				0.18	0.18
	Windex				(-0.07)	(-0.11)
	Constant	(0.48)	0.59	(0.03)	(-0.02)	(-0.20)
	No of cases	138	138	138	138	138
	Adj R-square	0.05	0.14	0.07	0.19	0.28
	F	1.98	4.85	3.70	5.70	5.75
	Standard error	0.52	0.49	0.52	0.48	0.46

Note:　Coefficients are statistically significant at the 5% level unless starred which indicates a 1% level of significance. Values in parentheses are not significant.

Source:　NIERC Small Firm Growth Survey

entrepreneur or strategy variables. Only when the latter variables are introduced in the full equation does **size** become significant. A company's presence in Northern Ireland **(NI)** has, at least in the period of the study, a strongly beneficial influence on company growth. The coefficient on this variable is positive and significant in all of the equations which contain the company variables. The precise interpretation of this variable is left to the next chapter.

The Wearside **(Wear)** variable also has a positive and significant coefficient in equation 4.5.1 but this disappears in the full model. This means that the growth performance of firms in the Wearside region can at least partly be explained in terms of entrepreneur and strategy variables. The benign regional influence we expected, given the aggregate growth data (NIERC 1992), is apparently too weak to be statistically significant in the full model.

The broad sector in which a company operates seems to have little influence on growth even when personal characteristics and strategy variables are omitted. The significance of the 'other manufacturing' sector variable **(other)** disappears in the full model indicating that it is entrepreneur and business strategy variables that are more important. Since the 'other manufacturing' sector tends to contain firms whose products are too new to be classified it is quite plausible for there to be a link between this sector and some vector of firm and strategy variables where the latter indicate motivation and innovative capability. Companies in the Chemicals sector **(chem)** grew faster than those in most other sectors. Again this influence proves insignificant in the full model. The likelihood is that owners in this sector are more likely to have growth-promoting characteristics and strategies. Once these are explicitly included in the full equation there is no further advantage from the sector itself.

Taken as a group the entrepreneur variables in equation 4.5.2 have considerably more explanatory value than the company characteristic variables although not as much as the group of strategy variables (equation 4.5.5). As before, it is clear that young, technically competent founders with multiple business interests are likely to have faster growing firms. What this reduced form equation adds to our knowledge is the fact that alone, this set of variables explains only a relatively small proportion of the variations in growth between companies.

One entrepreneur variable, 'multiple owners of a single firm' **(otherown)**, is not significant in this equation. This is somewhat surprising given the *a priori* expectation that this would be a strong and independent variable. It is worth noting that **otherown** is also not significant when regressed alone on growth. Analysis shows that **otherown** becomes significant when the strategy variables are introduced into the equation. This indicates a degree of cross-correlation between the influence of other owners and the business strategy variables. In other words, there is some tendency for the firms which utilise growth, inducing business strategies to be the multi-owner firms. Nevertheless, when the direct impact of business strategy is controlled there is an additional independent benefit that flows from the firm being run by a team of owners.

The single most important group of factors are the strategy variables. Strategy *aims* are of some distinct importance but less so than strategy *methods*. An equation containing only variables describing strategy *aims* has low explanatory power (equation 4.5.3) and only two variables which are statistically significant. It is noteworthy, however, that the two are profit motivation **(growprof)** and market orientation **(market)**.

An equation containing only variables describing strategy *methods* (equation 4.5.4) performs much better with an explanatory power of (R^2) 19 per cent. In such an equation the most significant variable is market research **(markres)**. Also significant are product development **(newprod)** and the introduction of new machinery to improve the production process **(newmach)**.

What is evident from this exercise is that an equation which contains a range of *both* entrepreneurial characteristics and business strategy indicators together with a few relevant company characteristics and external constraints, performs much better than any model which focuses on just one group of factors. This is partly because a wide range of factors influence growth, but also because there is evidence of subtle interactions. Some strategies are most appropriate for certain types of owner but not all. At this point it is sufficient to note that several strategy variables only become statistically significant when included in a full equation containing controls for company and, especially, entrepreneurial characteristics. Among these are raising external capital **(capsuc, capfal)**, use of selling agent **(agent)** and product diversification **(diverse)**. Conversely, the importance of a firm having multiple owners **(otherown)** only emerges fully in an equation in which the strategy variables are included.

Omitted Variables

The survey generated a large number of variables of which under 10 per cent were subsequently found to be significantly related to company growth in the preferred equation. Some of the variables which were excluded were clearly duplicates or alternative measures of variables which were included. However, a considerable number of variables were not in this category. They represented hypotheses which were not supported by the survey data.

As indicated above, a wide range of variables measuring the qualifications and experience of the entrepreneurs were rejected. Only membership of professional organisations **(proforg)** was included. The exclusion of other variables (e.g. those indicating university graduate status or years in education) is likely to be because the impact was indirect, and more direct management strategy variables dominated the qualification variables, leading to their exclusion.

Surprisingly, however, other aspects of entrepreneurs' experience were simply not associated with growth. For instance, 'a wide spread of previous experience' was not found to be significantly associated with faster growth. The full list of excluded variables measuring the attributes of entrepreneurs is given in Table 4.6.

Table 4.6. Owner-manager variables not found to be significantly related to growth

O levels or equivalent only

A levels or equivalent only

degree or equivalent only

vocational qualification

science qualification

business qualification

engineering qualification

jobs prior to joining or starting a firm

a wide spread of previous job experience

previous experience is relevant to current job

managerial experience

higher managerial experience

worked or studied abroad

production background

marketing experience

research and development experience

administrative or finance experience

Source: NIERC Small Firm Growth Survey

A number of common management strategies were found not to be associated with growth in any of the equations generated. Improving financial management, seeking new markets and, most surprisingly, 'producing a high quality product' were all strategies in this category. It may be that these strategies are common features of the small firm and hence they are not able to discriminate between companies when we examine the causes of growth.

Several marketing strategy variables were also found to be insignificant in the equations. Spending on advertising was one of these, and attendance at trade fairs was another. Other excluded strategies included the use of marketing consultants, increasing the number of sales staff and entering into joint agreements with other companies. One omission from the list of management strategies associated with growth was the 'introduction of new staff or staff training' as a means of improving the production process. This fits a picture of small firms giving a low priority to raising skills levels among their production employees.

It is also possible, and indeed likely, that some important variables were omitted from the survey altogether. The omission of these may help to account for the fact that the preferred equation explained only half of the inter-company variation in growth. As suggested above, one class of variables omitted from the survey were those measuring psychological or personality traits which may be associated with company growth. These are difficult and laborious to measure. Our conclusions from the extensive literature on this topic were that the research results are not impressive (see The key variables, p.15). Our preference was to investigate objective characteristics (such as age), aims and strategy methods. These are likely to be correlated with personality traits. Future research could test the degree of association between these sets of factors. Given our reservations about using psychological variables we decided it was more important to focus on factors which can be easily measured by those involved in small firms policy. Variations between companies in the price and quality of their products and the costs of their inputs were not measured in this study. Price and quality are difficult to compare between companies, and it is not obvious to us that studies which have attempted to do so have necessarily been successful. For instance the studies of Hitchens and O'Farrell (1987, 1988a, 1988b) compared these factors between firms in Northern Ireland, south-east England, South Wales and west central Ireland. Their conclusions of major deficiencies in the competitiveness of Northern Ireland's small firms appear to be contradicted by subsequent evidence that Northern Ireland's small firms were growing much faster than in the Republic of Ireland and Hertfordshire (south-east England) during the period which coincided with the Hitchens and O'Farrell studies (Hart *et al.* 1993).

Our preference has been to focus on aims and strategies and to investigate whether these were in fact correlated with growth. More intensive future research might, however, investigate whether stated strategies in fact correlate with objective pricing behaviour or the requirement of product quality. It would be important to know, for instance, whether firms recognise when their prices relative to product quality are out of line with competitors, and whether they respond rapidly to the problem. If such a problem were to persist, as suggested by Hitchens and O'Farrell for Northern Ireland, our interest would focus again on the entrepreneurial characteristics and strategies which permit this to happen.

In this study problems of slow growth in small firms were, however, not associated with peripheral regions, including Northern Ireland, but in central and southern England. Chapter 7 examines in detail the differences in growth between the four study areas and attempts to account for these differences using the equations discussed above. There is the possibility that the growth differences may be a product of regional differences in costs. In the survey, questions about costs were omitted. A view was taken that a study of costs requires more detailed investigation than was possible here. Our research strategy was one which used regional 'dummy' variables **(NI, Leics, Wear, Herts)** to act as proxies for any significant regional contrast in costs. In fact, as discussed above, statistically significant growth contrasts were observed between Northern Ireland and Hertfordshire. We cannot be sure, however, that this contrast was exclusively a reflection of cost advantages in Northern Ireland.

Conclusions

The process of guided model building identified 25 factors which have a statistically significant and largely independent influence on small firm growth. It is clear that growth in small firms is a complex process. However, it has been possible to identify a range of influences on growth which together form a plausible explanation of why some firms grow much faster than others. The conclusion of this chapter is that a mix of particular personal characteristics and qualifications together with appropriate strategy aims and methods are conducive to faster growth.

Those who succeeded in this study were younger owners with professional qualifications who own a number of businesses (indicating a degree of entrepreneurial drive), working with others to run their businesses. The strategy aims were often profit-oriented recognising the key importance of marketing. Another successful strategy was based on attention to improvements in the production process and, in a few cases, attention to cost or price cutting.

Among the strategy methods employed, the use of formal market research was clearly important as was direct contact with customers and the avoidance of selling through agents. It was also advantageous to have a narrow rather than diverse range of products. Not surprisingly, those firms which sought to raise external capital grew faster, although during this period of national credit expansion, few firms experienced a financial constraint on growth. One important business strategy was product development. There was evidence from the study that a strategy of incremental product improvement ranked alongside market research as a key means of accelerating growth. Concerns about the reliability of the responses to this part of the survey have, however, led us to be cautious about the true extent of the importance of this variable and further research is needed.

It is also clear that small firms can achieve growth in a variety of different ways. Policy makers will therefore need to avoid an approach to small business support that is dogmatic. A range of policies should be developed as well as a flexibility of approach. The importance of this research is that it can be used by policy makers to understand how individual small firms might improve their growth prospects. The policy implications of the research are dealt with more fully in the concluding chapter. The next two chapters explore the meaning of the individual variables in much greater depth.

Appendix

Table A4.1 Variables included in multivariate equations

Dependent variables

lturnrat: Log of the ratio of company turnover in 1990 to turnover in 1986

Independent variables
Company characteristics

size: Turnover of firm in 1986

NI: Location in Northern Ireland
Leics: Location in Leicestershire
Wear: Location in Wearside
Herts: Location in Hertfordshire

mech: Company products mainly in mechanical engineering
elec: Company products mainly in electrical engineering
chem: Company products mainly in chemicals
cloth: Company products mainly in clothing
other: Company products mainly in other manufacturing

Entrepreneurial characteristics

age: Age of principal owner/manager
proforg: Principal owner/manager is a member of a professional organisation
founder: Principal owner/manager was a founder of the business
othbus: Principal owner/manager owns other unrelated businesses
othbus+: Principal owner/manager owns other related businesses
otherown: The company has several active owner/managers

Business strategy aims

growprof: Growth in profits was viewed as highly important
market: Marketing was viewed as a highly important part of company strategy
margin: Company strategy was to compete on price
prodproc: Improving the production process was an important company strategy during the survey period

Business strategy methods

markres: The company undertakes formal market research
agent: Selling agents were used by the company
newprod: Number of improvements made to company products
capsuc: Successful efforts were made to raise external capital
capfal: Unsuccessful efforts were made to raise external capital
newmach: Investment in new plant and machinery was used as a means of improving the production
diverse: (Utton's) Index of product diversity

External constraints on growth

demand: Lack of demand was cited as a constraint on growth in output
mantime Shortage of management time was cited as a constraint on growth in output

Source: NIERC Small Firm Growth Survey

Table A4.2 Variations on the preferred equation for real change in company turnover, 1986–90

		Equation 1	Equation 2	Equation 3	Equation 4	Equation 5
Company	Size	-0.15*	-0.14*	-0.14*	-0.13*	-0.13*
Characteristics	NI	0.27*	0.19	(0.19)		0.32*
	Leics	(0.00)	(0.03)		(0.05)	(-0.03)
	Wear	(0.19)	(0.14)		(0.14)	(0.19)
	Mech	(-0.20)	(-0.25)		(-0.19)	(-0.25)
	Chem	(-0.17)	(0.22)		(-0.21)	(-0.27)
	Other	(-0.00)	(0.05)		(-0.04)	(-0.02)
	Elec	(-0.10)	(-0.18)		(-0.15)	(-0.19)
Owner-manager	Age	(-0.01)	-0.01	(-0.01)	-0.01	-0.01
characteristics	Proforg	0.33*	0.38*	0.32*	0.36*	0.34*
	Othbus+	0.25*	0.25*	0.23*	0.22	0.28*
	Othbus	0.42	0.40	0.45*	0.40*	0.42*
	Otherown	0.18	0.18	(0.13)	0.20	0.25*
	Founder				(0.15)	(0.15)
Business strategies:						
Aims	Growprof	0.20*	0.17*	0.22*	0.18	0.16
	Margins	0.41	0.41	0.44	(0.33)	0.46
	Market	0.24*	0.23*	0.21*	0.25*	0.23*
	Prodproc	0.17	0.19*	0.16	0.22*	0.19
Methods	Markres	0.24	0.32*	0.25*	0.33*	0.25
	Newprod	0.04*	0.02*	0.03*	(0.03)	0.04*
	Capsuc	0.23*	0.20	0.18		0.21
	Capfal	0.34	0.24	(0.30)		0.39
	Newmach	0.15	(0.15)	0.16	0.16	0.20
	Agent	-0.40*	-0.31*	-0.32	-0.30	-0.40*
	Diverse	-0.21*	0.20*	-0.21*	-0.21*	-0.16
Constraints	Demand	-0.30*	-0.30*	-0.34*	-0.30*	
	Constant	2.05*	1.72*	1.90*	1.96*	1.62*
	No of cases	138	144	138	138	138
	adjusted R^2	0.51	0.53	0.49	0.48	0.46
	F	6.60	7.24	8.0	06.24	5.66
	Standard error	0.38	0.37	0.38	0.39	0.39

Note: Coefficients are significant at the 5% level, unless starred which indicates a 1% level of significance. Coefficients in parentheses are not significant.

Equation one reproduces the equation of Table 4.1 but without the variable **'founder'**. Equation 2 includes six Leicestershire firms omitted from the preferred equation. Equation 3 includes only the statistically significant variables from Table 4.1. Equation 4 reproduces the equation of Table 4.1 without the variables **capsuc** and **capful**, while equation 5 reproduces the same without the variable **demand**.

Source: NIERC Small Firm Growth Survey

CHAPTER 5

Explanations of Variations in Growth
The Owner-manager

Introduction

Having examined the full equations explaining differences between companies in growth of sales, the following two chapters are concerned with a more detailed discussion of the individual variables shown to be significant. The overall aim is to compare and interpret the result of our analysis against the wider literature on small firm growth. Of particular interest is the way in which some variables act as 'proxies' for a wider set of factors which are not in themselves significant or specified in the model. In other words, certain owner-manager, strategy and firm variables have an indirect influence on firm growth through their association with other variables that appear in the preferred model presented in Chapter 4.

This chapter is solely concerned with those variables reflecting the characteristics of the owner-manager while Chapter 6 concentrates on the wide range of business strategy variables. Before dealing with these two large sets of variables the discussion briefly addresses the importance of the characteristics of the firm itself in the overall explanation of growth.

The Influence of Company Characteristics

Theory and research point to three potentially important influences on firm growth: firm size, geographical location and industrial sector (acting as a proxy for demand). Variables have been created to control for the effects of these influences and we have retained them in the model even though some of them are statistically insignificant. Despite emphasis in the literature on factors such as region (O'Farrell and Hitchens 1988; Storey 1994), sector (Storey 1994) and size (Evans 1987a; 1987b; Jovanovic 1982) the equations in Chapter 4 showed that there is very little explanatory power in a model of firm growth containing only these variables (see Table 4.5, pp.45–46). Nevertheless, we discuss below some of the reasons for this outcome within a general review of the major theoretical debates on firm growth.

Firm Size

The law of proportionate effect, or 'Gibrat's Law', states that a firm's growth is independent of its size. A corollary of this proposition is that growth is random with respect to size and the size distribution of industrial firms will be highly skewed with many small firms and few large ones. The economic effect of this is that industry will become progressively more concentrated until a steady state distribution is achieved. Many studies of company size distributions of firms have shown them to be skewed in the predicted manner, that is to be log-normal, and this has generally been taken as confirmation of the law of proportionate effect (Hart and Prais 1956; Hymer and Pashigian 1962; Simon and Bonini 1958; Singh and Whittington 1975).

Despite the general confirmation that the size distribution of firms is log-normal, studies have also pointed to the fact that small firms grow faster than large firms. For example, recent analysis of United States data by Evans (1987a; 1987b) and Hall (1987) and United Kingdom data by Dunne and Hughes (1990) has shown quite clearly that size and growth are negatively correlated. In other words, small firms appear to have grown faster than larger firms over recent decades. The advantage of small firms has not, however, been great enough to do more than weaken the general rule that size and growth rate are unrelated.

There are a number of possible reasons why smaller firms achieve higher growth rates than larger firms. First, small firms may be more flexible than large firms. It may be easier for an organisation with few workers and one chief decision-maker to react to changes in the market or pursue new areas of business than larger firms. Larger firms have an advantage in terms of access to capital, and possibly, information, but their ability to be entrepreneurial may be impeded by the competing interests of workers, managers and shareholders and also the tendency of systems, designed to increase efficiency, to decay into unresponsive bureaucracy (the so-called Penrose effect discussed in Chapter 2). Certainly over the last 20 years or so small firms have performed well in the sectors of the economy collectively known as high-technology industry (Oakey, Rothwell and Cooper 1988). The increasing instability of the world economy since the early 1970s and the emergence of information technology may have led to a change in the balance of competitive advantage in favour of small firms and against large firms.

Alternatively, it is possible that the generally observed faster growth of small firms is due to a form of survivor bias. In any cohort of firms some will do well and grow, others will do badly and fail. Since failed firms disappear, they will not be recorded in the data set and so mean growth rate is inflated. It is possible to regard large firms conceptually as being a collection of small firms (establishments, branches and subsidiaries), some of which do well and some of which do badly. In the case of the larger firm, however, the poor performance of the failed 'small firm' element is retained in the overall performance figures for the company and as a result the mean growth is reduced.

Another explanation for an inverse relationship between size and growth relates to the markets in which small firms operate. Many small firms operate in niche markets in which they have no cost disadvantage relative to large firms. They may supply a specialised product or be protected by geographical isolation. It is easy for these firms to grow rapidly to fill these niche markets but expansion into wider markets will eventually lead them into direct competition with larger firms who possess superior cost advantages. To expand without competition these firms need to find other niche markets and this may be difficult. Even if small firms do not operate in niche markets, high profitability and rapid expansion will soon attract the attention of other, generally larger, firms and the resultant competition will reduce the growth of sales.

A further consideration in this general discussion of firm size and growth is that firms cannot increase in size at the same rate for ever. Compound growth is exponential and a firm which doubled in size annually would quickly grow beyond the organisational ability of even the most capable management team. Jovanovic (1982) articulates this point well when he argues that the speed at which the mean and variance of growth rates decline with age and increasing size depends on the distribution of managerial ability across the population.

Since there are strong empirical and theoretical grounds for believing size and growth are related, we included a size variable in the model. Turnover in the base year, 1986, is our basic measure of size. To eliminate non-linearity the natural log of the size variable is entered in the model. It should also be noted that the effect of inflation has been removed so the turnover data is in 1990 prices. Thus, the variable **size** is expressed as the log of turnover in 1986.

The coefficient on the size variable is negative and significant, in line with prior expectations (see Table 4.1, p.33). The smaller the firm, the higher the growth rate in any period. Since both the size variable and the dependent variable are in the form of natural logs we interpret the coefficient on the size variable as an elasticity. A 100 per cent increase in the size of the firm period reduced the growth rate by 14 per cent. Put another way, a firm with £50,000 of sales in 1986 grew on average 14 per cent faster than a firm with £100,000 of sales.

With respect to the influence of size on growth, this research confirms the results of other studies, namely that smaller firms grow faster than larger ones. It is not possible to say precisely which of the above explanations are primarily responsible for this effect. However, since our sample consists entirely of firms that survived throughout the period it is possible to reject the survivor bias hypothesis. The higher growth of smaller firms is more likely to be due to a combination of factors such as their sub-optimal size, greater flexibility, less risk averse and their position in niche markets.

Sector and Region

As explained in Chapter 3, our sample of firms was drawn from five manufacturing sub-sectors. The sample was stratified in this way to control for the effect of industrial sector on differences in growth rates between companies. The prior expectation was that sector would not have an important influence on firm growth on the grounds that we do not envisage growth as a simple mechanistic response to the particular product market within which firms operate. Rather, we see companies as being essentially similar in their response to (sectorally) different external circumstances (McKenna and Orrit 1984). While it may seem obvious that growth in the markets for individual products will affect the growth of companies supplying those products, this influence is neither as automatic nor as strong as might be imagined. There are a number of reasons for this. First, increases in production can be achieved by an expansion in the number of firms as well as an expansion in size of existing firms. Second, factors influencing the market share of companies within any given market appear to be more variable than differences in market growth *per se*. Third, individual small companies can switch between markets. The view taken here is that differences in the aims and abilities of the owner-manager are more important than variations in demand for products in explaining differences in company growth rates (Boswell 1973). Nevertheless, there is some evidence that there are significant differences in growth between sectors (Storey 1994), so the effects of this variable were examined in our analysis.

Sector-specific influences on firm growth are represented in the model by dummy variables acting as proxies for sectoral growth rates. The coefficients on the sector dummies represent differences in sectoral growth relative to the base category, Clothing. The regression equation with only the company characteristic variables (see Table 4.5, pp.45–46), showed that two of the sector dummies are significant. However, when included in the preferred equation with the owner-manager and strategy variables all of the sector variables are insignificant, confirming, to an extent, our prior expectation (see Table 4.1, p.33). It might be argued that controlling for the influence of sector at two digit SIC level is too imprecise and that sub-sectoral dummies are required. Such an approach was rejected because of the large number of additional variables it would have required and consequent effect on the degrees of freedom. In any case sub-sectoral variations in market growth are usefully 'mopped up' by the dummy variable indicating demand is a constant, namely, **demand.**

Recent research has pointed to the impact of location on small firm growth (O'Farrell and Hitchens 1988; Storey 1994). Although the causal mechanism is poorly specified, transport costs, labour skill and availability, the quality of local infrastructure and services and the availability of private and public sector finance are among the many supply side factors which may vary between regions and, therefore, systematically affect the ability of small firms to grow. In addition, regional variations in demand are often cited as important factors. Consequ[...] we have attempted to control for regional effects by drawing our sample of [...]

firms from four contrasting regions: Hertfordshire, Leicestershire, Northern Ireland and Wearside. Three regional dummy variables were included in the model of small firm growth for Leicestershire, Wearside and Northern Ireland. Hertfordshire was used as the base category and hence not explicitly included in the equation. The regional dummy variables, therefore, indicate contrasts relative to Hertfordshire.

In the full equation (see Table 4.1, p. 33) the coefficient on Leicestershire **(Leics)** is negligible and insignificant, on Wearside **(Wear)** it is positive but insignificant but on Northern Ireland **(NI)** the coefficient is strongly positive and significant. Having controlled for factors internal to the firm there is clearly an additional benefit to the small firm of being located in Northern Ireland. This benefit can be seen to have increased the growth rate by 26 per cent and is therefore of some importance. In an equation containing only company characteristic variables the Wearside variable **(Wear)** is significant (see Table 4.5, pp.45–46). However, this significance disappears in the full equation, indicating that the positive growth effects of Wearside can be explained in terms of the other 'internal' factors. This is not true of the Northern Ireland effect which remains significant in both equations.

That Northern Ireland bestows some benefits on small companies should not be entirely surprising. As we have already seen in Chapter 3, small firms in Northern Ireland (and Wearside) over the period 1986 to 1990 grew much faster than those located in Leicestershire and Hertfordshire. One possible explanation for this is that small firms benefit from public sector assistance in Northern Ireland and Wearside. A more detailed analysis of the effects of public sector assistance to the small firm sector in Northern Ireland can be found in Hart *et al.* (1993) which reviews the activities of the Local Enterprise Development Unit (LEDU), the small business agency. The overall conclusion of that study was that public sector support had given a boost to growth in surviving small indigenously-owned firms in the late 1980s. Another potential cause of the location effect is a regional disparity in costs, particularly wage costs, which favoured the peripheral areas in the period of the study. The issue of regional effects is complex and important and is dealt with more fully in Chapter 7.

The Influence of Owner-Manager Characteristics

The remainder of the chapter concentrates on a more detailed discussion of the manner in which the characteristics of the owner-manager can influence the rate of growth within the small firm. However, the emphasis will not be confined to only those variables found to be significant in the regression equations reported in Chapter 4, but will include other owner-manager variables in an attempt to unravel the indirect influences on growth. The discussion will be organised around the following six groups of variables:

- founder or non-founder

- education and career history

- age
- number of other owners
- ownership of other firms
- objectives.

Founders and Non-Founders

An important division among small business owner-managers is between those who have founded their firms and those who took control through some other route such as purchase or inheritance. For a number of reasons, our expectation was that the presence of the founder would enhance growth. First, starting a firm requires a high level of personal drive, tenacity and problem solving ability. Once the firm is started this entrepreneurial drive might be expected to carry through into business development activities. Second, Cross (1981) has shown that individuals who start manufacturing firms tend, in their previous employment, to start on the shop floor but have a career history which includes a rapid rise to a managerial position. Thus, we would expect the firm founder to have both managerial skills and a strong knowledge of the technology of production. Acting against the likely benefits of having a founder in the firm is the tendency for entrepreneurs to make poor managers in that they tend to focus too much on future business opportunities and too little on the management of existing projects. Nevertheless, since we are dealing with firms of at least ten years of age we expected the impact of having a founder in the company to be beneficial on the grounds that management procedures for existing products would be well established. Finally, other studies have also found a positive relationship between founders and growth (see for example, Boswell 1973).

Our prior expectation about the impact on growth of the presence of the founder is only partially confirmed by the regression results of Chapter 4. The preferred equation presented in Table 4.1 (p.33) indicated a positive but statistically insignificant impact for founders. Controlling for other effects which might be expected to be related to founder (i.e. objects of business strategy), the presence of such an individual raises the growth rate of the firm by 12 per cent. However, in the 'reduced form' model (see Table 4.3, p.42) the variable becomes significant and its estimated impact on the growth rate nearly doubles to 23 per cent. It was also the case that no statistically significant relationship between **founder** and growth was found in the univariate equation (see Table 4.1, p.33). The implication, therefore, is that in this later equation the variable 'founder' is acting as a composite for a range of other variables. A comparison of the two equations would suggest that the presence of other owners and the involvement in other business interests are in some way represented by the 'founder' variable.

Dividing the sample into founder and non-founder firms and ex average growth in turnover indicate that founder firms grow at an avera per cent whilst non-founder firms grow at an average of 20 per cent. Cl variability of growth in founder-run firms prevents it being significant in the univariate analysis. To help us understand more precisely the reasons why the presence of a founder in the firm influences growth, the variable 'founder' was cross-tabulated with the other entrepreneurial and business strategy variables in the survey. This shows that founders (110 cases) differ in many respects from their non-founding (63 cases) counterparts.[1] In terms of the business strategies adopted they were less likely to:

- have engaged in a sales and marketing strategy: 24 per cent compared to 41 per cent of non-founders

- indicate that they had aimed to grow over the period 1986–90: 63 per cent compared to 81 per cent of non-founders

- have introduced any new products: 56 per cent compared to 78 per cent of non-founders

- have employed more sales personnel: 13 per cent compared to 29 per cent of non-founders.

Founders also differed from non-founders on a range of personal characteristics. Founders tend to:

- have had no formal qualifications: 42 per cent had no qualifications while only 15 per cent had degrees. However, 30 per cent of founders possessed a vocational qualification

- be slightly older: 49 per cent were over 50 years of age compared to 30 per cent of non-founders

- have had a career history which was very relevant to their current business activity:[2] 76 per cent compared to 41 per cent of non-founders

- have been involved in a production capacity in their previous job: 83 per cent compared to 52 per cent of non-founders

- have had a wider spread of experience:[3] 13 per cent compared to 9 per cent. Further, 25 per cent of non-founders did not have a previous job which indicates that they had inherited the current business

- be involved in sub-contracting activities in their current business: 57 per cent compared to 35 per cent of non-founders

1 The relationships are only included in the list of bullet points if they are shown to be significant in a Chi-square test at the level of 5 per cent or lower. This is true for all subsequent lists of bullet points.
2 Defined as having primarily worked in the same industrial sector.
3 Defined as having worked in a range of industrial sectors and occupied a number of managerial positions.

be advanced to explain this finding. First, few previous studies have examined all possible influences on small firm growth in one model. Second, studies have tended to focus only on strategy or entrepreneurial characteristics. The inclusion of strategy and company characteristic variables in our model seems to have the effect of reducing the importance of entrepreneurial variables. This does not mean that the entrepreneurial characteristics mentioned above are necessarily unimportant but rather that their effects may be indirect. For instance, vocational education may be important because it influences the strategy of the entrepreneur. In examining the influence of strategy on growth performance in Chapter 6 we attempt to examine further the ways in which entrepreneurial characteristics operate indirectly on the process of growth.

The one career variable which is significantly associated with growth, **proforg**, has a strong impact on growth as shown in Table 4.1 (p.33). The coefficient on this variable indicates that the presence of an entrepreneur who is a member of a professional organisation raises the growth rate by 35 per cent. Although the regression coefficient is theoretically the most meaningful, in that other influences on growth are controlled for, it is also useful to divide the population of firms into two groups based on the **proforg** variable and to examine the difference between the mean growth of each group. Table 5.1 shows that firms run by owner-managers who are members of a professional organisation grew by 47 per cent over the period whilst others grew at the mean rate of only 25 per cent.

Table 5.1. Membership of a professional organisation and growth

	No of cases	Mean growth %	Std deviation
Without membership	117	25	52
With membership	27	47	61
Whole sample	**144**	**29**	**54**

Source: NIERC Small Firms Growth Survey.

Twenty-seven owner-managers indicated that they were members of a professional organisation. Unfortunately, information about the particular professional organisation to which the owner-manager belonged was not sought and so the interpretation of this variable is somewhat speculative. However, analysis of the 16 questionnaires in which we do have relevant data reveals that in 14 cases the professional association is a technical or scientific organisation with the most frequently mentioned being the Institute of Engineers. This suggests that membership of a professional organisation is associated with a high degree of practical scientific or engineering competence although this interpretation must be treated with caution for the reasons mentioned above. There are a number of reasons why this may be conducive to growth.

Practical or technical competence gives an owner-manager the ability to respond to changes in the market by developing new products or improving or adapting existing ones or, alternatively, by improving the production process. A theoretical understanding of technology, and how it may be applied, allows creative solutions to be made to new market situations. Less well trained owner-managers may not be so flexible with respect to the changing competitive environment. In short, technical competence allows owner-managers to do what they do better in ways which could give competitive advantage in terms of cost leadership and also product differentiation, whichever is the chosen strategy. Membership of a professional organisation indicates that a very high standard of vocational education has been achieved and that the professional network offers access to information on recent technological developments.

The main characteristics of the 27 owner-managers who indicated that they were members of professional organisations can be summarised as follows:

- 37 per cent have a degree, compared with 16 per cent for non-members of professional organisations
- most (74%) have had previous managerial experience especially in larger firms (59%)
- 50 per cent held managerial positions in areas other than production including sales and marketing and Research and Development in particular, compared to only 14 per cent in the rest of the sample
- one-third (33%) had a wide spread of experience compared to 9 per cent in the rest of the sample.

On this basis it is possible to hypothesize that gaining professional status, say in engineering, gives an individual certified transferable skills which allows the individual to easily move between companies. In so doing the individual has the opportunity to gain a wide range of experience and attain a high level of responsibility. All of these factors we would expect to be positively associated with entrepreneurial performance. Furthermore, it should be remembered that membership and career progression are themselves a function of ability and motivation. However, the fact that only **proforg** of the educational or experience variables is significant in the model suggests that it is technical competence augmented by a range of relevant experience that is the crucial factor.

Perhaps it should not seem surprising that high-level vocational qualifications are associated with growth in small manufacturing firms. A generalisation of this finding that might tentatively be advanced is that it is the level and appropriateness of qualifications in relation to the business which influences success in running a small firm. However, it is not suggested that in all industries membership of professional bodies would be the key entrepreneurial variable. Rather, growth is likely to be higher where the owner-manager has achieved a high level of technical competence and experience in the field in which he or she is operating.

To what extent does membership of a professional organisation influence business strategy? An examination of the range of business development activities undertaken by those owner-managers who were members of a professional organisation revealed that, compared to non-members, they were:

- more likely to have introduced six or more new products: 22 per cent compared to 10 per cent of the rest of the sample

- more likely to have spent a proportion of turnover on process development: 33 per cent compared to 11 per cent

- more likely to have recruited sales staff: 33 per cent compared to 16 per cent.

There is a strong relationship between the number of new products, orientation towards growth, use of advertising and propensity to export. High technical competence as indicated by membership of a professional organisation is associated with product innovation and the ability to produce a standardised product range rather than customised products. We have already used the terms 'opportunist' and 'craftsman' entrepreneur derived from Smith's study of small firms in Michigan. Membership of professional organisation **'proforg'** is clearly in the category of 'opportunist entrepreneurs'.

Two other factors are worth noting with respect to membership of professional organisations. First, owner-managers with this characteristic tend to be broadly associated with the larger small firms in the survey, thus underlining the importance of this factor to growth performance. Second, the peripheral regions in our study, Wearside and Northern Ireland, were almost devoid of this type of entrepreneur (Table 5.2). If there is a link between this variable and the growth of the firm, as this work would tend to suggest, the development of innovative small manufacturing may be retarded in the regions lacking the entrepreneurial, technically qualified individuals. This point is explained further in Chapter 7 which investigates in detail the regional dimension to our model of small firm growth.

Table 5.2. Membership of a professional organisation by region

	No	% of Sample	Sample Size
NI	1	3.7	50
Herts	12	24.5	49
Wearside	2	8.0	23
Leicestershire	12	24.0	50
Total	**27**	**100**	**172**

Source: NIERC Small Firm Growth Survey

Age of the Entrepreneur

We can hypothesise that age of the owner-manager can proxy four factors which affect small firm growth performance. The first factor, skill and experience is positively related to age. The older the owner-manager the greater the practical problem-solving ability of the individual. The second factor, flexibility, is negatively related to age. The older the owner-manager, the ability and willingness to make a fundamental strategic change of direction for the business diminishes. The third factor, motivation to work hard, is also negatively related to age. As the owner-manager accumulates wealth, this wealth provides an income and this reduces the need for income generated from work. In other words, the older the owner-manager the greater the incentive to live off earlier investment rather than invest additional time and resources in the hope of a future pay-off. The fourth factor is physical energy, which generally reduces with age. These four processes will interact differently in every individual, but given that three of the factors are negatively associated with age, we would expect growth rates to decline in the older age groups.

Table 5.3 shows the age distribution of owner-managers in the survey as well as the mean growth rate for each group. In general, the pattern is as suggested by our hypotheses. The highest growth is achieved by owner-managers in the 31 to 40 years of age group with growth declining thereafter until the age group '61 and over' where it increases slightly. The high growth associated with 'elderly owner-managers' shows that it is difficult to generalise about the affect of age on small firm growth. In the survey there were a number of firms run by highly enthusiastic and capable owner-managers over the age of 65. One of these was the inventor of the ubiquitous Corby Trouser Press.

Table 5.3. Age distribution of owner-managers

	Frequency	*Per cent*	*Mean Growth Rate (%)*
20–30	7	4.0	26
31–40	30	17.2	55
41–50	64	36.8	30
51–60	54	31.0	14
61+	19	11.0	21
Total	**174**	**100.0**	

Source: NIERC Small Firm Growth Survey

On the basis of *a priori* reasoning, and the fact that there were relatively few owner-managers in the under-thirty age group, we decided that the most appropriate functional form for the age variable would be linear (and a non-linear variable does not improve the equation). The expectation was that the coefficient on the variable **age** would be negative and significant, and it can be seen from Table 4.1 (p.33) that this was in fact the case. Thus, the older the owner-manager the slower the growth of the firm. Furthermore, the age of the owner-manager has a relatively strong impact on the growth of the firm. Each year that is added to the age of the lead owner-manager reduces the four-year growth rate by approximately *one* per cent. Thus, the firm of a 50-year-old owner-manager grew 10 per cent less over the four-year period than a 40-year-old owner-manager.

To examine the reasons why age influences firm growth, owner-managers were divided into three age groups which were cross-tabulated with other survey variables. The three age groups were younger (up to 40), middle aged (41 to 50), and older (51 plus). The major findings were as follows:

- older owner-managers are more likely to have the aim 'restrain business growth': 47 per cent in the older category as opposed to 31 per cent in the middle-aged group and 22 per cent among younger owners

- a higher proportion of younger and middle-aged owner-managers had a formal business plan: 32 per cent of the younger group, 42 per cent of the middle-aged group and only 22 per cent of the older group

- older owner-managers are less likely to introduce or improve new products: 52 per cent of the older group introduced one or more improvements or products compared with 70 per cent of the 41–50 middle-aged group and 78 per cent of the younger group.

These results indicate that there is some link between age and motivation to grow. Younger owner-managers are more interested in growth and are more likely to engage in business development activities designed to foster this growth. On the other hand, the cross-tabulation analysis also indicated that age and experience were related:

- older owner-managers were more likely to possess a career history very relevant to their current job: 77 per cent of the older group compared with 61 per cent of the middle group and 38 per cent of the younger group

- older owner-managers were more likely to have had more jobs: 45 per cent of the older group have had four or more jobs as compared to 25 per cent of the middle-aged group and 14 per cent of the younger group

- older owner-managers were less likely to own other businesses: 25 per cent of the older group do as opposed to 27 per cent of the middle group and 46 per cent of the younger group

- older owner-managers were more likely to be the founders of their firms: 74 per cent of the older group were founders compared with 56 per cent of the middle and younger age groups.

The younger owner-managers appear to be less well experienced in career terms. Such a profile is not surprising since the younger owner-managers have had less time to gain experience and, furthermore, many of them had inherited their firm. It would seem, therefore, that the more intensive business development activities of the younger owner-managers are related to motivation and ambition. The younger owner-managers do seem more flexible and less 'set in their ways' than the older owner-managers. They appear more likely to seek improvements in the way their firms are run.[6]

Number of Owners

Although strenuous efforts were made to speak to the main decision-maker in each of the survey firms, in some cases it was clear that decisions were jointly made by several owners. Table 5.4 shows the distribution of firms by the number of owners. Just over one quarter of the managed firms had only one owner while nearly half had two owners. Clearly, there were a small number of firms owned by teams of individuals. Although the survey includes data on owners, other than the one interviewed, it was decided to represent their influence by means of a dummy variable indicating simply the presence of other owners.

Table 5.4. Number of owners in the firm

Number of Owners	Number of Firms	Per cent
1	47	27.0
2	84	48.3
3	23	13.2
4	9	5.2
5	4	2.3
6	1	0.6
7	1	0.6
10	1	0.6
11	1	0.6
Total	**171**	**100**

Source: NIERC Small Firm Growth Survey

6   **Age** was not the only age variable tried in the model. Since data was available on the personal details of the other owner-managers, we investigated the impact of a variable indicating average age of entrepreneurs. This has no affect on the r-square and was itself not significant. This gives support to the approach adopted which was to concentrate the analysis on the lead or dominant owner-manager. Furthermore, we experimented with other functional forms of **age**. In particular we examined whether a series of dummy variables could successfully differentiate the high-growth younger owner-managers from the slower growing, older owner-managers. These variables had no more explanatory power than the simple continuous variable.

An alternative way of handling the data, where two or more owners took decisions, would be to include in the model variables giving average values appropriately weighted for characteristics such as age or years in education. These types of variables were tried but they generally proved insignificant and failed to increase r-squared over models based on the single owner-manager variables. The main reason for this is that in most cases the interviewee is the main decision maker and accordingly, his or her characteristics most influenced the firm. However, it might also be that a simple averaging of values is too unsophisticated a means of modelling a firm with more than one owner. To take a simple example of a firm run by a 60-year-old owner-manager with, say, a degree, and a 20-year-old with no qualifications. The older owner-manager provides the decisions and the young owner-manager the hard work. Simply averaging values would totally distort the capabilities of this management team.

Another way of representing the presence of other owners is by creating a variable that differentiates between the number of other owners. Dummy variables were created for the categories 'one other owner', 'two other owners', 'three other owners' and 'four plus other owners'. The pattern of significance is interesting. The 'one', 'two' and 'four plus' dummies were significant but the 'three' dummy was not. However, in the interests of parsimony, only one dummy variable is used in the model indicating the presence of other owners. This variable is designated **otherown** and indicates the presence of more than one active owner in the firm. It can be seen that the presence of other active owners improves the growth rate of the firm over the five year period by 19 per cent. Why do multi-owner firms show better growth? Although the questionnaire provides some insight into this issue it was not primarily designed to look at the dynamics of the management team and, therefore, further research is required on this issue. However, based on the results obtained, a number of hypotheses may be put forward.

The first hypothesis relates to the possible existence of 'independence only' owner-managers. Well-documented in the literature, this type of owner-manager is concerned mainly with personal autonomy subject to making a reasonable living. Growth is not identified as an important objective (see Collins, Moore and Unwalla 1964; Stanworth and Curran 1976). This type of individual may be more likely to become an independent owner-manager rather than work as part of a team because he or she does not wish to be subject to the competing demands of close colleagues. As can be seen from Table 5.5, firms with one or two owners tend to show less desire to grow but this is not very pronounced and is not statistically significant. It would appear, therefore, that the 'number of owners' affects growth in other ways.

A second hypothesis is that even if one owner is responsible for decision-making, multi-owner firms have a greater range of skills available to them. A single owner-manager has to be competent in the whole range of business skills including production, personnel, buying, selling and finance. Having other owners in the firm allows different members of the team to specialise, which will improve

strategic decision making and strategy implementation in the small firm. This could
be a source of competitive advantage for the multi-owner firm over the single-
owner firm. Of course, the danger for multi-owner firms is that the owners will
fall into dispute with one another. Little conflict was observed among owners in
this study but this may simply be the result of survivor bias.

Table 5.5. Aim to grow by number of owners in the firm

	Number of owners							
	One		Two		Three		Four or more	
	No.	%	No.	%	No.	%	No.	%
Aim to grow	31	(66)	57	(68)	18	(78)	15	(75)
Not aim to grow	16	(34)	27	(32)	5	(22)	5	(25)

Source: NIERC Small Firm Growth Survey

It has been suggested, by Gibb and Dyson (1984), that some owner-managers
simply do not have time to sit back and think about new ideas for the growth or
survival of their business. It is possible that team-run firms form a better context
for the generation of new business ideas. Questions on the constraints to growth
provide an opportunity to test this proposition. Single-owner firms were more
likely to record lack of management time as a constraint on growth compared to
multi-owner firms.

In conclusion, this analysis has revealed that multi-owner firms show better
growth than single-owner firms. The most plausible explanation for the effect of
multi-owner teams relates to skill complementarity and specialisation in decision-
making. An owner-manager team, even if the majority are subordinate to the leader,
releases a greater range of skills to the business than the individual owner-manager
has at his or her disposal. This means that decisions are potentially better made
and implemented.

Ownership of Other Firms

At the outset of this project it was our view that existing research on small firms
had paid too little attention to networks of firms which, though legally independent, are owned by a single owner-manager. This view stemmed from an earlier
study of regional variations in owner-managership which collected data on over
100 new firms in each of the regions of the South East, the North East and the
West Midlands (Barkham 1989). During fieldwork aimed at establishing the
validity of certain other propositions (see Barkham 1989) it was found that many
of the most dynamic owner-managers would own more than one firm. Sometimes
these additional firms would be related with one perhaps marketing the goods of
another, at other times the businesses would not be related in activity but would

share common services. Often the idea for a new business would arise from the experience of running another.

For this reason, owner-managers in our survey were asked whether they, or any of the other owners, had any business interests outside the firm and whether these provided any advantages to the firm in question. Our prior expectation for the relationship between ownership of other businesses and growth was that they would be positively related. Ownership of more than one business is perhaps symptomatic of a certain restless search for profitable opportunities, characteristic of the more dynamic entrepreneur (Chell and Haworth 1992), but more than this, networks of small firms can provide support for one another in tangible and intangible ways.

The variables which indicate the ownership of other businesses are **othbus+** and **othbus**. **Othbus+** indicates that the interviewee or his co-owners had other businesses which they saw as offering advantages to the firm, whereas **othbus** indicates other firms were owned but they were not seen as providing an advantage. Interestingly, the coefficient on both variables is positive and significant, and, strangely, is stronger for **othbus**. This suggests that it is the owner-managers that are qualitatively different rather than that there exists helpful linkages between the firms. The fact that the coefficient on **othbus+** is the lower of the two might suggest that linked businesses depress growth. However, the difference between the two coefficients is not itself significant and may be due to random variation. More detailed investigation into the nature of the links between businesses and how they might affect growth is clearly warranted. Outlined below are some observations from the survey.

Within the sample just over one quarter of the interviewees (52 cases) indicated that they, or the other owners, had other business interests. Of these, 16 were described as being not advantageous to the firm. No additional information was available on 20 of the 52 businesses mentioned. Of the 32 on which data was obtained, 11 represented new unrelated firms started in response to a perceived market opportunity. One other case was an unrelated business owned by the same family. In the remaining 22 cases the firms were interrelated in some way. In four cases the related company formed the marketing arm of the manufacturing firm. A further four firms had been set up to sell the same product into a different market. This is an important finding. Most small firms research, including this study, confines itself to single independent legal entities. However, the legal entity may not in all cases be conterminous with the economic entity. It may in some cases be necessary to consolidate data from a number of firms, the nexus of which is a single owner-manager, in order to get closer to economic reality, in the same way that large firms consolidate the accounts of their subsidiaries for financial reporting purposes.

Of the remaining firms, it is possible to classify two as producing related products which provide market opportunities for the main firm, four as selling related products and sharing resources, and six as having sprung up as the result of the owner-manager seeing an opportunity in a market related to that of the current firm.

It is one of the shortcomings of this study that the links between these networks of firms were not investigated more extensively. The limited information available suggests that only four linked firms are actually sharing resources. Nevertheless, the degree of interrelationship between the firms in the 'group' may be greater than this. Being part of a network may bestow growth enhancing advantages on the small firm that were not identified in the interview. These externalities could range from shared market information to advantages in the capital markets and greater ability to spread the cost of expensive consultancy services such as those provided by the large accountancy and law firms. Moreover, operating within a 'group' might offer indirect advertising benefits. Successful transactions by one firm may lead to sales in another either by accident or by design.

Examination of the link between multiple business ownership and the other survey variables revealed that owners of more than one business are:

- less likely to be sub-contractors: 35 per cent compared to 55 per cent

- younger: 33 per cent are under 40, compared to 17 per cent in other cases

- better educated: 31 per cent have degrees as compared with 13 per cent of single-owners

- less likely to have vocational qualifications: 14 per cent compared to 30 per cent for single-owners

- more likely to engage in market research than single-owners: 39 per cent as compared to 13 per cent of single-owners

- more likely to have entered into agreements with other firms: 33 per cent have agreements compared with 17.5 per cent of single-owners

- more likely to export: 60 per cent export as compared with 41 per cent of single-owners

- more likely to place more emphasis on turnover growth: 58 per cent consider it very important compared to 41 per cent of single-owners.

The picture is quite clear. Ownership of other businesses is associated with a group of well-educated young owner-managers who are growth and export orientated and aware of the need for good market information. As has been said, the likelihood is that this variable picks out the 'restless', dynamic, owner-managers (see Chell and Haworth 1992) who are continually on the search for new market opportunities. This type of owner-manager will start a business and expand it as fast as possible, but if it fails to fully occupy him new opportunities will be sought and new firms created to 'house' them.

Objectives of the Owner-Manager

It is important to examine the stated objectives of the owner-manager because of the light these may shed on overall motivation. It is our contention that the motivation of the owner-manager is a key factor in determining the growth of the business, and both theoretical and empirical studies of firm growth have shown this to be the case. In the life of the small firm there are numerous stages at which the owner-manager can opt to maintain the firm at its current size or to grow further (Churchill and Lewis 1983). This is not to suggest that growth is easily available to all small firms and that all the owner-manager has to do is choose it. Far from it. Some small firm owner-managers face an almost insatiable demand for their product whilst others operate in situations of stable or falling demand. The point is that growth is not an automatic response to market conditions. For growth to occur the owner-manager has to pursue it as an objective. Entrepreneurial motivation is a necessary, but not sufficient, condition for growth. To paraphrase Boswell (1973): no matter how favourable market conditions it is the choices of the owner-managers which ultimately decide the growth outcome in a small firm.

Although in this section we consider the objectives of the owner-manager, we do not believe that this is the only, or even the most important, way in which motivation can be assessed. First, as we have already seen, motivation is linked with other key owner-managerial characteristics such as age. Age is essentially a description not an analytical variable but, nevertheless, it may capture a host of motivational factors better than other variables. Second, motivation to grow should have a tangible outcome in terms of business development activities. The next chapter examines the impact of business development activities on growth and these provide a useful alternative way in which motivation to grow can be assessed. Another approach is to conduct psychological or psychometric testing of owner-managers in order to measure the inherent predisposition of the owner-manager to commit effort to the goal of firm growth. Much research in the field of owner-managership has been conducted along these lines. Whilst interesting and relevant, this research has yielded contradictory results (Leff 1979; Chell 1986). As explained in Chapter 2, in this research we have confined ourselves to the study of owner-managerial objectives, and the strategies through which the objectives are realised.

Data on objectives was obtained in three ways. First, interviewees were asked to state the main objectives of the management, as contained in the business plan or as determined by informal decisions. The responses to these questions were very diverse but were capable of being grouped into six categories (Table 5.6, section A). Many firms had more than one objective. Second, interviewees were asked to rank on a scale of one to three the importance of growth in turnover, assets, employment and profits. The frequency with which these were ranked with a three (considered very important) is contained in Table 5.6, section B.

Table 5.6. Owner-manager motivation

	Frequency	*%*
Section A: Main aims		
Obj 1 Expand firm	139	50
Obj 2 Restrain growth	62	36
Obj 3 Improve products/product range	47	27
Obj 4 Improve production	29	17
Obj 5 Other business developments	14	8
Obj 6 Other personal	19	11
Section B: Focus of growth		
Asset growth very important	32	18
Turnover growth very important	81	47
Profit growth very important	107	62
Employment growth very important	23	13
Section C:		
Aim to grow	121	70
	n = 174	

Source: NIERC Small Firm Growth Survey.

Third, interviewees were asked if they had aimed to grow over the period 1986–90 and the responses to this question are shown in Table 5.6, section C.

The reason for making several attempts to get data on objectives is that the subject is value-laden and it is sometimes difficult to get owner-managers to discuss it in a detached and objective fashion. An attempt was made, therefore, to corroborate the answers to one question with the results of others. One weakness with all of the indicators of objectives is that, by definition, they rely on interviews conducted *ex post*. It is possible that the same answers would have been obtained *a priori* but it is not possible to be certain of this. Each variable was measured as a dummy taking a value of one if the aim was present (or important) and zero if it was absent.

Table 5.6 indicates, contrary to the assertions of some researchers (see, for example, Stanworth and Curran 1976) that growth appears to be a common objective amongst small firm owner-managers. Between 70 and 80 per cent of owner-mangers said that they were interested in expanding their firms in some way. This finding does not correspond with the common view that the majority of owner managers are mainly interested in independence. Just under half of owner-managers indicated that they were mainly building up their firms through product and process development and only 11 per cent described themselves as running their firms with purely personal objectives in mind.

None of the objectives in section A of Table 5.6 represented by a dummy variable was significant in the model as a factor contributing to the growth of turnover. Although this may seem surprising, the high frequency with which firms expressed an aim of expansion means that this aim is unlikely to discriminate between the successful and unsuccessful firm. It is perhaps more surprising that the other objectives are not negatively related to growth. However, the lack of relationship between aims and achieved growth does perhaps indicate that the stated aims are more than *ex post* rationalisation of what was subsequently achieved.

Asking owner-managers if they aimed to achieve growth is a rather general question. More precise questions about whether the growth motive was focused on profits, turnover, assets or employment proved to be more revealing. One variable created from the data in section B of Table 5.6 was significant in the growth equation. The dummy variable **growprof** indicates that the owner-manager considered growth in profits to be very important. This variable is positively associated with growth and is statistically significant. Table 4.1 (p.33) indicates that owner-managers rating growth in profits as highly important increased their growth rate by *19* per cent. This coefficient is low compared with others in the equation but it nevertheless offers some insight into the orientation of owner-managers who achieve growth. Most small firms are under-capitalised and at a relative disadvantage in the capital markets. In this situation, asset-growth and employment-growth are irrelevant. Of more importance is turnover-growth and profit-growth is seen as of greatest importance. Profits benefit cash-flow, justify investment decisions and, importantly, may be used for further expansion. Few objectives are worthwhile if they are at the expense of profits. In the long term all objectives should be orientated towards increased profitability.

Although the equations of Chapter 4 show that there is a link between growth and the importance attached to profit by owner-managers, it cannot be said on the basis of this evidence that profit leads to growth in small firms, though this is probably true. The interpretation of the variable, therefore, focuses on what it reveals about the owner-manager. It is more likely that this variable indicates a degree of rational, clear thinking which might be expected to be associated with the more highly performing owner-managers. Alternatively, it may be that a lack of importance attached to profits is symptomatic of a general lack of motivation, or lack of care about the business, which feeds through into slow growth in turnover.

Why firms which are not strongly profit orientated are able to survive in the market for so long is one question that might be asked. The answer may lie in the fact that in small firms the owners are the major, or the only, providers of equity capital – in the form of their own savings or retained profit. The point is that a competitive return is not required on this equity. Furthermore, it is perfectly possible for small business owner-managers to accept less than their opportunity wage. This allows them a certain amount of latitude to enjoy the satisfaction of being in business whilst not having the competitive pressure to keep profits commensurate with the risk profile of the business.

Since there is no necessary financial advantage in employment growth *per se* for the owner-manager it is strange to see even some importance attached to these factors. We observed during our interviews that some owner-managers appeared to run their firms in a paternalistic manner and to see themselves as having a socially important role in the community. The creation of jobs is seen as an important aspect of that role. No doubt this is the reason for the importance attached to employment growth.

It may seem especially surprising that the **growturn** variable, indicating a strong desire to expand turnover, was not significant, given that growth in turnover is the chosen growth measure in the study. Clearly some benefit is to be gained from turnover growth since it may establish market share, which is the basis of profit growth in subsequent periods. Furthermore, the higher the turnover the greater the chance of sales of complementary goods and repeat business. However, the message of this analysis is that for long term growth, the owner-manager has to aim for maximum profitability. An orientation towards sales growth seems to be of limited value probably because it does not necessarily bring about profit growth and may actually denude the firm's cash resources.

CHAPTER 6

Explanations of Variations in Growth
Business Strategy

Introduction

The purpose of this chapter is to examine the way in which the choice of business strategy can influence the rate of growth within the small firm. Certain business strategies will impact on growth regardless of the type of owner-manager that is running the firm and, in the same way, certain owner-managers will do better than others irrespective of the business strategy they pursue. It is also quite likely that some strategies are more suited to some types of owner-manager than to others. A complicating factor in this analysis, as discussed in Chapter 5, is that there are several inter-relationships between the owner-manager variables and the business strategy variables. The inclusion of owner-manager and strategy variables in the same model was meant to isolate the impact of business strategies *per se*. Nevertheless, the interpretation of the model is complex and the aim in this chapter is to explore in more detail the impact of business strategy on growth and the inter-relationships with the characteristics of the owner-manager.

Porter (1980) defines three generic business strategies: cost leadership, product differentiation and, for the small firm, focus on a niche market. Whilst recognising the importance of this conceptual framework, the approach of our survey was that these strategies could be disaggregated into a series of more precise business development activities. As well as knowing whether a firm is pursuing cost leadership or product differentiation strategies, it is helpful to know how each of these strategies is being achieved. Accordingly, data on a wide range of business development variables was collected in the survey (see Table A6.1, pp.96–98).

Our main findings, presented in Chapter 5, are that marketing strategies were most strongly associated with company growth. The important variables in this respect are: the importance attached to marketing by the owner-manager, a desire to improve sales and marketing, the undertaking of market research and an emphasis on pricing as a strategy. Although the results are less strong, the model indicates that growth is associated with product development as indicated by the number of new products, although it is negatively associated with a diverse product range. Furthermore, an emphasis on improving process and using new plant and machinery to achieve this end appears important. Finally, growth is unsurprisingly found to be strongly associated with a desire to use external capital to finance expansion irrespective of whether this desire was actually realised. In the rest of the chapter we explore more fully the implications of these findings.

Business Development Variables

Marketing and Market Research

The prior expectation in conducting this research was that there would be a strong relationship between marketing activity and growth. There are many aspects to marketing strategies and marketing activities and there is no single means of measuring them. As a result, attempts were made to measure a variety of aspects of marketing and several of the resulting variables proved to be strongly associated with growth within the full equation in Table 4.1 (p.33). These variables are all binary in nature and indicate whether the firm has undertaken market research **(markres)**, had a strong emphasis on marketing **(market)**, or had used price changes to influence sales **(margins)**.

Market Research

Twenty per cent of firms (36 firms) in our survey undertook systematic market research during the period. Those that did so are identified in the model by the dummy variable **markres**. Market research is defined as formal research conducted to obtain data on the location, requirements and spending power of potential customers. The coefficient on the variable is large, positive, and significant; doing market research raised a company's growth rate by 27 per cent. Thus, if the direction of causality is as we suggest, undertaking market research is a highly important influence on the growth of the firm. This is not surprising as Peters and Waterman (1982) argue that 'excellent' companies will attempt to stay close to their customers by being aware, through formal and informal research, of even subtle changes in the requirements of their customers. At a more theoretical level, Casson (1982) and Barkham (1989) place strong emphasis on the formal acquisition of information for the conduct of successful owner-managerial activity. While it remains possible that willingness to undertake market research acts as a general discriminator between more able and less able owner-managers, the inclusion within the model of variables measuring owner-manager characteristics and motivation reduce this possibility. In our view the act of undertaking market research is, in itself, a direct stimulator of growth.

Analysis of the interrelationships between market research and other survey variables reveal that it is related to other factors that are associated with growth. In particular it was found that:

- 39 per cent of owner-managers who own other businesses did market research as opposed to only 13 per cent of single business owner-managers

- 49 per cent of graduate owner-managers undertook market research as opposed to 14 per cent of non-degree holders

- 27 per cent of owner-managers who aimed to grow over the period did market research as compared with only 6 per cent of non-growth orientated owner-managers

- 26 per cent of owner-managers who stated that profits were highly important did market research as compared with 12 per cent of non-profit orientated owner-managers

- 27 per cent of owner-managers who stated that they actively sought customers did market research as compared with 9 per cent who did not actively seek customers

- 30 per cent of firms that advertise did market research as opposed to 12 per cent of firms that did not advertise

- 29 per cent of firms that export do market research as compared with 13 per cent of non-exporters.

The conclusion to be drawn from these findings is that market research tends to be undertaken by the better educated, growth orientated owner-managers. Because education variables do not appear explicitly in the full equation, coefficient on the **markres** variable may represent, in part, an indirect indicator of levels of education. Graduate owner-managers emerge as an important group in this research. They are identified in the model through what they do (e.g. market research) rather than what they are. It may well be that high levels of education are very helpful in undertaking market research or in utilising it successfully but, nevertheless, the results of market research are in themselves likely to be an additional important factor in understanding growth. For these reasons, we conclude that market research itself is a significant variable since education alone is not significant in the model. Of course, it is also the case that 'seeking customers', 'advertising' and 'exporting' are components of a successful marketing strategy. Since these activities tend to go together with one another they do not appear independently in the full model. In this sense **markres** acts as a proxy for a whole group of marketing activities.

An interesting finding from our research is that firms in Northern Ireland undertake market research to a much greater extent than firms in other regions: 34 per cent of Northern Ireland firms as compared with 22 per cent of Hertford-shire firms, 20 per cent of Wearside firms and 6 per cent of Leicestershire firms. Another way of looking at this is that 47 per cent of the survey firms which undertook market research are located in Northern Ireland. Also, 31 per cent of Northern Ireland firms doing market research have been assisted by the small firms agency Local Enterprise Development Unit (LEDU) as opposed to only 15 per cent of firms not doing market research. Since government grants for market research are available in Northern Ireland through LEDU, it seems likely that government policy has, in this respect, had an impact on the number of firms undertaking market research and, because of the importance of this variable to growth, can be judged to have had some measure of success.

This interpretation is to some extent confirmed by the results of the full equation minus the market research dummy variable. Dropping **markres** makes the Northern Ireland dummy more significant, indicating some degree of interrelationship between Northern Ireland and market research. However certain other variables are affected by the removal of **markres** although these effects do not affect the overall interpretation of the model since they tend to be significant variables becoming more significant and non-significant variables becoming less so. There is one exception to this. Dropping **markres** reduces the statistical significance of **prodproc** below the 5 per cent level. **Diverse** reduces in significance but remains significant at the 5 per cent level in the new model. Variables that improve their significance are **capsuc**, **growprof**, and **othbus+**. From this it would seem that market research is associated with a number of business development variables and without its inclusion in the model the true effects of these variables are not discernible.

Marketing Orientation

An effective marketing strategy is an important component of small business success yet many small businessmen who are excellent in production are poor at marketing. Marketing is different from market research because the latter consists only of gathering information whereas the former implies a conscious attempt to promote products within a market and perhaps also to feed back information from customers into the production process. Sixty-two owner-managers in our survey indicated that they attached importance to marketing as a strategy and this is represented in the equation as the dummy variable **market**. This variable appears within the full model alongside, but distinct from, the variable indicating that the firm undertook market research. The coefficient attached to the variable **market** is positive and significant firms placing importance on marketing grew *24* per cent more than firms that do not. It is also worth noting that a focus on marketing leads to faster growth irrespective of whether market research is undertaken.

What is the significance of this result? At a theoretical level we might observe, as does Casson (1982), that firm formation is not the costless and trivial activity it appears in neo-classical economics. Running a successful small firm may often, or even usually, involve creating a market for the products of that firm. This may be done with enthusiasm and skill by some, but not by all, owner-managers. Within certain limits, choice or awareness will cause the effort put into marketing to vary between owner-managers. Our research shows that those firms that do place an importance on marketing will generate greater growth.

It could be argued that we are confusing direct and indirect effects in that firms producing their own products will, as a matter of course, put more emphasis on marketing than those involved in subcontracting. Since firms producing their own products have more scope to expand than subcontractors, growth is the result of market opportunity not marketing *per se*. However, no significant difference is observed in this study between subcontractors and non-subcontractors with respect to marketing activity.

The data indicate that work-history has a slight impact on the likelihood that an owner-manager will adopt a marketing strategy. Only 30 per cent of owner-managers with a production background indicate that it is important, as compared with 49 per cent of 'white collar' owner-managers. In addition, the goals of the owner-manager seem to be related to marketing. Forty-one per cent of owner-managers who stated that they aimed to grow over the period attached importance to marketing, as opposed to 23 per cent of the others. That the emphasis attached to marketing is carried through to action is indicated by the fact that 60 per cent of firms placing emphasis on marketing actually engage in advertising, as opposed to 45 per cent who do not, and 29 per cent of those who emphasise marketing use marketing consultants as opposed to 15 per cent of the non-marketing orientated firms.

There appears to be a marked regional effect on the adoption of marketing as a strategy (Table 6.1). Firms in Northern Ireland are more likely than those in other regions to attach importance to marketing. Wearside firms are the poorest in this respect with Hertfordshire and Leicestershire firms giving almost equal importance to this strategy. This tends to reinforce the earlier point that the high importance attached to marketing by small firms in Northern Ireland is due to the widespread availability of grants, in particular those specifically intended to improve marketing. Of the 29 Northern Ireland firms that attach importance to marketing, 18 (62%) have been assisted by LEDU and 4 (13%) have been assisted by the Industrial

Table 6.1. Regional variations in marketing as a strategy

Region	Firms indicating marketing as important	
	No	%
NI	29	58
Herts	16	33
Wearside	4	16
Leics	13	26
	x^2 significant at 0.05%	

Source: NIERC Small Firm Growth Survey

Development Board. Although we lack the data to prove that the assistance has been in the form of direct help with marketing, it seems likely that it has. A link between public sector involvement with small firms in Northern Ireland and the high level of importance attached to marketing is likely since LEDU believe in the importance of marketing as a means of helping small firms sell outside the local Northern Ireland market in order to enhance their growth prospects.

Other Marketing Variables

A comprehensive marketing strategy consists not only of promotional activity but also of astute price manipulation. Our questions on strategy revealed that only six survey companies identified price as a strategic variable. **Margins** is a dummy variable which indicates those firms that were actively using price to achieve their strategic objectives. The coefficient on the variable is strong, positive, and significant in the full model. There are two ways of examining the impact of this variable on growth. First, Table 4.1 (p.33) shows that firms using price as a strategic variable grow *40* per cent faster than firms that do not. Alternatively, the sample of firms can be split into those that use this strategy and those that do not. The former show a mean growth of *59* per cent over the period and the latter only 28 per cent.

We do not know from our interviews whether the price adjustments referred to by owner-managers were up or down. It is possible that some companies are 'buying' short-term growth at the expense of margins and long run viability. However, the fact that the survey firms have survived for at least 10 years suggests that such price adjustment as is being practised is not of this nature but a considered strategic response to market conditions. A broader interpretation of the data is that the better managed, more efficient firms have more price flexibility than less well managed firms and are able to capitalise upon this as circumstances demand. Whatever the precise nature of the pricing strategy, it remains true that firms using this approach grew substantially faster when all other variables in the model are taken into account.

Owner-managers in the survey were asked whether they were actively engaged in seeking customers. A number of owner-managers admitted that they were not, preferring to allow their reputation to attract customers. A variable **seekcust** was created to indicate which firms were actively engaged in seeking customers. This variable was not significant in our full model. However, it was possible to refine the analysis. If a firm indicated that it was actively seeking customers they were asked what method was used. Table 6.2 shows the means by which small firms actively engage in customer search. Advertising, sales personnel and contacts are, not surprisingly, the most frequent responses. We created dummy variables to represent each of these methods and included them in the model. The only variable significantly associated with growth is **agents** which indicates the firm uses agents to seek customers. However, this method of achieving sales is negatively associated with growth.

Table 6.2. How small firms actively seek customers

	No	%
Agents	18	10
Sales personnel	36	21
Contacts	44	25
Consultants	0	0
Tender	5	3
Tradefairs	15	9
Advertising	38	22
Other	16	9

Source: NIERC Small Firm Growth Survey

A number of interpretations of this finding are possible. The more ambitious growth-orientated entrepreneurs may view the use of agents as inferior to other sales methods as a means of long-term growth in market share. More direct methods are likely to improve the flow of information between customer and company. There may also be a problem of monitoring and control in the use of agents. Small firms that rely on agents to sell their products may have their progress impeded because they have not the resources to monitor the activities of agents. It takes a great deal of time and effort to set up a network of agents and frequent contacts to ensure that agents are actively marketing the product. Small firms may not have the resources to adequately monitor their contracts with agents and so may not be getting the best out of them.

The use of agents may indicate that the managers of a firm are unwilling to take the responsibility for marketing their product. They choose a strategy of delegation which, in fact, they do not have the resources to ensure operates in their interests. Agents can very easily 'forget' products or put little effort into selling them. The lesson for the small firm may be that the use of agents is a risky strategy which, to be successful, requires a considerable investment of management time. An alternative explanation for using agents is that some managers do not have the resources, capability or confidence to sell the product overseas, but the end result is the same: poorer growth.

Product Innovation

At an intuitive level it is easy to believe that product innovation is associated with growth in small firms or indeed firms of any size. Hall (1985) states that economic success belongs to the firm or the region which can innovate and thereby stay one step ahead of the game. There are many examples of spectacular success in small firms based on innovation, especially in the field of high-technology development

(Larsen and Rogers 1984). Nevertheless, the evidence of a strong, consistent relationship between product development and growth in small firms is mixed (Storey 1994). Product development may commit the firm to long periods of research and development which ultimately do not result in exploitable technology.

In our survey we asked a number of questions about the product development activities of the firm which we have used to create three variables. **Innovation** is a variable which indicates the number of totally new products introduced by firms, that is the number of pure innovations. **Newprod2** is a variable which gives the number of products introduced which were totally new to the firm including products developed elsewhere. **Newprod** is a variable which classifies improvements to existing products as well as new products introduced by the firm. The latter most adequately represents the way in which small firms engage in product development. Small firms introduce very few new products but can be good at adopting new products and incrementally improving those that they already have in production. The data in Table 6.3 supports this interpretation. Only 12 per cent of firms in our survey have introduced totally new products. However, if we include the introduction of products new to the company and improvements to products, then 64 per cent of our firms have been active in this respect.

Table 6.3. Frequency of product development by category of product development

Products introduced	Product development (newprod)		New and bought in products (newprod2)		Completely new products (innovation)	
0	62	(36%)	95	(55%)	153	(88%)
1 to 5	84	(48%)	73	(42%)	21	(12%)
6 to 10	12	(7%)	3	(2%)		
11 to 15	9	(5%)	2	(1%)		
16 plus	7	(4%)	1	(1%)		

Source: NIERC Small Firm Growth Survey

The full equation (see Table 4.1, p.33) includes the **newprod** variable. **Newprod** is the strongest variable of the three and, unlike the other two, is highly significant if all 144 firms are included. However, its significance is lower if, as explained in Chapter 4, six firms with extreme values are excluded. Because this is a composite variable, its interpretation is slightly difficult. Furthermore, there is the possibility that one company's definition of improvement was different to another's. Nevertheless, the results show, at the very least, that growth in small firms is associated with product development. It is the firms that can react to the market by introducing new products or adapting old ones that have the strongest growth.

The explanatory power of our two other product development variables was tested by substituting them in the equation for **newprod**. The inclusion of **newprod2** in the model slightly reduces the explanatory power (adjusted r-square) of the model and the variable is itself not significant. However, the **innovation** variable has three extreme values which, if removed, make the variable insignificant. If **innovation** is included in the model the explanatory power falls still further and the variable, though positive, is again not significant.

Twenty-one firms only conduct 'pure' innovation in the sense of introducing their own, totally new, products. The growth rate of the pure innovators is much higher than other innovators, 59 per cent and 24 per cent respectively, when mean growth of the two groups is the measure. However, the standard deviation of growth in the innovators is also higher: 63 per cent compared to 51 per cent. Clearly, developing new products can be highly rewarding in business terms but it is also risky. Product development consumes cash which might be used to develop the business in less spectacular ways, and does not always produce the anticipated profits. Research into the development of high-tech firms shows that the high rates of growth achieved by some firms is usually accompanied by a high rate of failure by others in the sector (Larsen and Rogers 1984). A more cost-effective and perhaps a generally more reliable, if less rewarding, approach to business development for the small firm may be incremental product development. In so doing the small firm owner-manager needs to have a keen eye for the changing requirements of the market and the skill to adapt his or her product range accordingly.

One clear factor which emerges from the study is the negative importance of subcontracting. There is a strong negative relationship between whether a firm is classified as a sub-contractor and its tendency to generate new products as measured by the **newprod** variable. Being a sub-contractor inhibits the emergence of new products of whatever type. Ninety per cent of non-sub-contractors have new products, whereas the corresponding percentage for sub-contractors is 36 per cent. Clearly, therefore, there is less pressure on sub-contractors to innovate and, perhaps, the types of owner-managers who run them are less able to do this anyway. There also appears to be, in terms of the **newprod** variable, some regional variation in the rate of product innovation. Sixty-eight per cent of Wearside firms have no new products compared to 37 per cent in Hertfordshire, 30 per cent in Northern Ireland and only 24 per cent in Leicestershire. There are also sectoral variations in the rate of new product generation. In mechanical engineering, 59 per cent of firms registered no new product and in clothing, 32 per cent. By contrast, chemicals, albeit on the basis of fewer firms, show no firms without a product innovation, electrical engineering, 19 per cent and other manufacturing 8 per cent.

A second clear influence on product innovation is the possession of a degree. Of the 33 owner-managers who have a degree, 97 per cent indicated that they had introduced one or more new products **(newprod)** as opposed to 57 per cent of those without degrees (significant at 1% level). It is thus clear that although the possession of a degree is not a necessary condition for product innovation, on the evidence of this survey it comes close to being a sufficient condition.

Furthermore, the following relationships confirm the role of qualifications in the whole area of product development:

- the development of new or improved products was more likely to be chosen as a business development strategy by those with a degree (58%) compared to 32 per cent with no qualifications
- those with a degree were more likely to spend a proportion of their turnover on product development: 79 per cent compared to 48 per cent of those with no qualifications.

That the possession of a degree does not enter the full model as a significant independent influence on growth is partly due to the inclusion of the **newprod** variable. It might be proposed, therefore, that formal education does influence company growth, partially through the indirect impact on product innovation. We have also seen a similar point in respect of market research. Graduates appear to be beneficial to small firms. This is because they are innovative and scientific where these terms are used in their broadest sense.

Further analysis indicates some interesting links between other business objectives and innovation:

- 74 per cent of the owner-managers who said that they had aimed to grow over the period introduced new products as opposed to 43 per cent of those who had not.
- Of those that actively seek new customers, 71 per cent indicate some new products as compared with 52 per cent of those who are not active in seeking new customers.
- 86 per cent of firms that export have one or more new products as compared with only 47 per cent of those that do not export.

What can we conclude from these additional points? The introduction and improvement of products are clearly related to the qualifications and ambition of the owner-manager. This is not surprising since product development is one of the most obvious strategies for the ambitious owner-manager. There also appears to be a negative relationship between sub-contracting and innovation. This may be because the nature of sub-contracting, in which the firm operates to a brief provided by a customer, prevents the development of new products or it may be that sub-contracting as a mode of activity does not attract the ambitious and well qualified owner-manager. The significance of the relationship between exporting and product improvement should not be overlooked. Firms that wish to gain access to international markets need to be highly competitive. One of the means of achieving a competitive advantage is through product innovation. The evidence of the study is that most firms which export have been involved in product development activity. Other factors will also influence exporting, including relative cost, but without a decisive cost advantage it may be that innovative products may come close to forming a necessary condition for small firms to export.

Product Diversification

Firms in the survey frequently produced additional products which differed from the main product. Often firms received a considerable proportion of their revenue from these other products. Sometimes these are closely related to the main product and at other times less so. One of the aims of the study was to systematically collect data on the degree to which small firms were industrially diversified.

The *a priori* expectation was that diversification would reduce the likelihood of fluctuations in turnover growth but might possibly slow overall growth. The reason for this expectation is twofold. First, there is a commonly held idea that things tend to go wrong when owner-managers move out of areas that they are most familiar with. It can be the case, with large as well as small firms, that diversification is associated with a fall in profits and a slow-down in growth because the firm does not have adequate skills in the area of diversification. A related but slightly different point is that diversification and slow growth may be correlated because difficulties in one market may force a firm to move to another. Thus, overall, there was an expectation that diversification would be associated with relatively slow growth. The counter arguments are that diversification is associated with greater owner-managerial flair in the same way as multiple ownership of several small firms. The better owner-managers are more aware of market opportunities and so develop a greater range of products.

In this study the degree of diversification is represented by Utton's (1979) diversification index. This is an average of the number of products weighted by their contribution to revenue. The higher the index the greater the diversification. The coefficient on the index variable **diverse** is negative and significant, indicating that diversification is indeed associated with slower growth.

There is some evidence that diversification is associated with ownership of other firms. However, there is no evidence that declining markets influence diversification since there is no strong correlation between **diverse** and firms indicating demand as an important constraint. **Diverse** is strongly associated with those owner-managers who attached importance to diversification, but more interestingly, it is also associated with those focusing on turnover growth. It may be this emphasis on turnover growth that is the key to understanding this variable. Some firms may attempt to increase their growth through product diversification. However, if this involves less familiar technologies and markets it may place a strain on limited managerial resources and capabilities. Equally, the strategy may be pursued at the expense of profits, which in turn will impede the very growth which is being sought.

Process Innovation

Process improvement refers to the enhancement of the manufacturing process. The usual aims of process improvement would be to increase productivity and/or product quality. Our prior expectation was that improvements in the production process would be strongly associated with growth through cost reduction and improvement in product quality. Two process improvement variables are positively and significantly related to growth: **prodproc** and **newmach**. The former variable, which is the stronger, indicates that the firm had consciously chosen process improvement as a strategy to achieve its objectives. Of course, just because a firm says it has process improvement as a strategy does not mean that it has been successful in this respect. Given the difficulty in measuring process improvement, we were forced to rely on this variable. Nevertheless, as the results are in line with our prior expectations, it is possible to have some confidence in the variable. The other process variable that is significant is **newmach**, which indicates that the firm had installed new machinery in its quest for an improved process over the study period.

Fifty-two owner-managers indicated that process improvement was a business development strategy for their firms. Assuming some relationship between strategy and action, we can say that improvements in productivity and production technique enhance the growth of the firm. This is especially the case if the firm invests in new machinery, as 122 survey firms indicated that they had. From our experience of interviewing owner-managers, we believe that the **prodproc** variable indicates that the owner-manager is active and alert to all the myriad ways in which things can be improved. The biggest single improvement occurs when new machinery arrives, but, in between the periodic arrival of new capital equipment, a variety of small incremental improvements to production can be made.

An examination of the relationship between process improvement as a strategy and other owner-manager and business strategy variables revealed the following significant relationships:

- only 15 per cent of members of a professional organisation indicated process improvement as an important strategy as opposed to 32 per cent of non-members
- 20 per cent of those with management experience indicated that process improvement was an important strategy as opposed to 43 per cent without management experience

There appears to be some relationship between process improvement and sub-contractors, with 38 per cent indicating that process improvement was an important strategy as opposed to 22 per cent of non-subcontractors, as was suggested in the section on product improvement (p.83). However, this is not statistically significant. Furthermore, there is also some indication that process improvement is associated with the less experienced and less well educated owner-managers but again the relationship is not statistically significant, with 32 per cent of non-graduates indicating process improvement as a strategy compared to 21 per cent of graduates. Improving a product or introducing a new one is a risky act requiring skill and confidence. By its nature, process improvement, especially by small incremental changes, is less risky. It is possible that the **prodproc** variable picks out the more ambitious of the less skilled owner-managers, who will regard it as important since they have fewer options by which growth can be achieved. The better educated owner-managers will pursue process improvement but for them it will be a less important strategy. We may also note that process improvement as a strategy is negatively related to use of advertising and marketing as a strategy, which tends to reinforce the profile of the owner-manager associated with this strategy option.

The **newmach** variable is not associated strongly with any of the other variables except, of course, those indicating a desire to improve the production process. The usefulness of this variable lies in the fact that it has the very practical implication that, of all the methods available to improve process, investment in plant and machinery is the most effective. We investigated the hypothesis that new machinery was a proxy for the receipt of grants since over one-quarter of our survey firms come from Northern Ireland, but found no evidence of this.

The Use of External Finance

In order to expand, firms will normally have to invest. The funds for investment may come from the owners of the firm (equity, retained profit), lenders (debt) or, in some regions, public sector agencies (equity, debt, grants). Leaving aside for a moment the issue of public sector assistance, for most small firms the supply of equity will be limited to the personal savings of the owners. External equity is generally available to only a small minority of small firms who provide the prospect of outstanding capital growth. Small firms which do not fall into this category represent too great a risk for too little return and cannot attract equity funds from the general public. In addition, small firms may be internally constrained by a reluctance on the part of the owners to dilute their control over their companies. Profits are a good source of funds for investment but take time to accumulate. They may not be available in sufficient quantity at the right time for the owner-manager to take advantage of a market opportunity. Debt is a source of funds which in theory, if the project offers the prospect of normal or economic profits, is always available. Normally, debt is the most easily accessible source of long term funds for the growing small firm. As with equity, however, there is some evidence in the literature that certain owner-managers are unwilling to use debt to finance growth. The reasons for this relate to a disinclination by owner-managers to subject their firms to outside influence.

In some regions public sector agencies provide finance to small firms in the form of grants, loans and equity. In this study the region with the most public sector assistance is Northern Ireland, but Wearside also benefits from this type of support. Leicestershire and Hertfordshire firms' public sector assistance is largely restricted to national schemes such as The Business Expansion Scheme (BES). Although public sector agencies have, to a certain extent, invaded the territory of commercial finance providers, it seems likely that there is a net addition to the amount of finance flowing to the small firm sector through the activity of public sector bodies. One reason for this is that public sector agencies provide capital at below the rate deemed acceptable by the market. Since the price of capital is lower it can be presumed that the level of demand is higher. It follows from this that in an area such as Northern Ireland, outside finance is considerably easier to obtain that in other regions. In fact, the Northern Ireland small firms agency LEDU has had a budget of £25–£30 million per annum in recent years. This would be equivalent to over £1 billion per annum for the United Kingdom as a whole. Since national expenditure on the promotion of small firms is only a fraction of this amount, it can be seen that government assistance to small firms in Northern Ireland is on a generous scale.

Following Reid and Jacobson (1988) we took the view that growth was likely to be associated with a willingness to introduce gearing into the firm (i.e. increase the ratio of debt to equity). Gearing is an automatic effect of taking on debt which increases the risks to the equity holder, but also the potential reward. To gear a small firm the owner-manager must have a strong confidence in the success of the project to which the funds are to be put. Hence, willingness to use debt finance is likely to pick out the more confident and motivated owner-managers. To use debt in significant amounts the owner-manager is taking the responsibility for servicing monthly interest bills. The owner-manager who is most concerned with independence or a 'quiet life' is unlikely to be a large user of debt. To reiterate, we regard the owner-manager's attitude to outside finance as a gauge of his or her motivation to expand the business.

Narrowly defined, equity is money provided to the firm in return for shares. Normally, this is the way an owner of a small firm will provide capital for his or her enterprise. Cash is provided in return for legal ownership of the enterprise. Normally, in a small firm the owner-manager or owner-managers will retain all of the shares of the company. There are two reasons for this. First, and foremost, there is no market for the shares of small companies. It is generally difficult for owner-managers to sell shares to members of the public outside the company. Small companies are very risky, which means that a high return on equity is required. This high yield will depress the price of the equity to a point where it is not worthwhile for the owner-manager to part with ownership. It is not, generally, possible to reduce the risks by careful scrutiny of the company because the costs of this process are high relative to the level of funds being injected. Hence, external equity investment in small companies is rare and will only be undertaken by third parties with special knowledge or interests. The need for information is much reduced if the investor has prior knowledge of the owner-manager. Thus, members of the owner-manager's family or his or her friends may perceive the venture as less risky because he or she knows the capabilities of the owner-manager. Thus, family and friends may provide equity. Venture capitalists may provide equity where the management has a good track record and the business has outstanding growth prospects, but extremely few small firms meet the criteria for venture capital. Public sector agencies, such as LEDU and IDB in Northern Ireland, charged with the responsibility of intervening in the event of market failure, will also occasionally provide equity to small firms although this is not their main role. However, for most firms equity finance comes from the personal savings of the owner-managers themselves (Schluter and Barkham 1985; Barkham 1989).

More broadly defined, equity includes profits retained within the firm. Generally, these are good forms of expansion finance for small firms because they carry no actual interest charge. However, in small firms, profits take time to accumulate and may not be available in sufficiently large amounts at the point at which investments have to be made in order to take advantage of market trends.

The most widely available source of funds for the small firm is debt capital from high street and merchant banks. A problem that small firms often face, however, is that banks provide finance only in the form of an overdraft. Where loans are forthcoming, the banks insist that they be secured on the assets of the owner-manager or the assets of the business. Thus, owner-managers who have property will obtain loans but it is more difficult for those who do not.

Loans of any sort contribute to the gearing of the small firm. Gearing is beneficial to equity holders in times of growth but may be problematic in recessionary periods. One problem associated with gearing is the responsibility the firm has to meet interest charges, whatever the trading condition the firms finds itself in. This research was predicated on the belief that the act of raising finance for the firm is symptomatic of a desire to grow, but this is especially the case with debt finance. Given the potential difficulties that debt finance can create for the owner-manager, there has to be a clear commitment to business development, which underpins the desire for this type of capital.

A final source of finance for small firms is grants. These are most widely available in the economically lagging peripheral regions, which in our study are Wearside and Northern Ireland. However, there are some national schemes which can be accessed by all small firms irrespective of location. Grants are not necessarily 'free' money because they are often tied to specific objectives such as the purchase of capital equipment or the improvement of marketing ability and these may require additional resources from the firm. However, grants certainly do represent finance for expansion at below market interest rates. Thus, in areas such as Northern Ireland where grants are widely available, it is probably true that private sector lending is much reduced and, as a result, it might be expected that the net impact of grants may be less than the flow of public funds to the small firm sector. Nevertheless, recent research indicates that there is an overall net impact (Hart *et al.* 1993a) notwithstanding problems of dead-weight and displacement. Out of the four study areas, it is clear that finance for expansion in small firms is more readily available in Northern Ireland due to the availability of grants.

Our survey investigated whether owner-managers had approached any organisations in the period of the study for the purpose of raising external finance. The answers to this question are summarised in Table 6.4. The majority of firms in the survey (59%) did claim to have attempted to raise finance with most (55%) being successful. The surprise in this table is not that so many did attempt to raise funds, but that such a high proportion did not. In the boom conditions of the mid to late 1980s a higher proportion of owner-managers might have been expected to have been 'gearing up'. The fact that such a large proportion of firms who tried to obtain finance were successful perhaps indicates that the small-firm-capital gap which has received so much prominence in the literature (Barkham 1989) was, with the following caveat, largely filled in the late 1980s. Some sort of capital gap appears still to exist since five per cent of survey companies were unsuccessful in raising outside finance. Furthermore, these eight companies had a good growth record during the study period. However, lenders do face considerable risks of companies failing and in a study of this nature we were not privy to the details of loan applications made and the reasons for the refusal.

Table 6.4. Success and failure in raising external capital

	No. of firms	%
External capital not sought	71	41
External capital sought successfully	95	55
External capital sought unsuccessfully	8	4
Total	**174**	**100**

Source: NIERC Small Firm Growth Survey

The answers to the survey questions on raising external capital allowed us to create two dummy variables: **capfal** indicates firms which have unsuccessfully sought external capital and **capsuc** indicates firms which have successfully sought external capital funding. Both **capfal** and **capsuc** have coefficients which are strong, positive and significant. In other words, growth is stronger in those small firms where the owner has attempted to raise debt finance than in small firms where the owner has been content with internally generated funds. The evidence offers support for the hypothesis that willingness to use external finance is a characteristic of the more ambitious, opportunistic owner-manager and that this ambition is the real source of growth rather than access to finance *per se*.

It is not possible to be exactly sure about the direction of causality and a completely different interpretation of these results is plausible. For example, the direction of causality could be from growth to the desire for additional capital and not the reverse. In this case, fast-growing companies may find it easier to raise external capital and hence be more likely to seek it. We are not in a position to distinguish between these two alternative interpretations although we suspect that **capsuc** and **capfal** represent financial business development activities pursued out of a motivation to grow. Since there is a degree of ambiguity over interpretation, we report the model without **capfal** and **capsuc** in Table A4.2 (p.53). The result of dropping **capfal** and **capsuc** is minimal. The overall goodness of fit of the model is reduced slightly but none of the other variables are affected to any great degree. **Capfal** and **capsuc** appear to be independent of the other variables in our model. It is our contention that they are worthy of inclusion in the preferred equation since they do contribute to an explanation of growth differences between small firms in our sample, which is consistent with other studies and our own *a priori* reasoning.

An interesting feature of the preferred equation (see Table 4.1, p.33) which merits some comment is that the coefficient on the **capfal** variable is greater than that on the **capsuc** variable, indicating that growth is greater in the firms that were refused capital than those who successfully raised it. Two factors have to be borne in mind. First, the number of firms having failed to attract external capital is small and there may be no significant difference between the two coefficients. Second, the refused or unsuccessful firms are likely to be those presenting the banks with high risk projects which by their very nature carry with them high rewards through high growth. The logical response of banks when faced with high risk projects should be to grant loans at a higher rate of interest. However, as discussed in Barkham (1989) banks may find it advantageous to put an upper limit on their loan rates to small firms and to refuse to lend to high risk projects. Banks may prefer the bad publicity associated with loan refusals to the worse publicity that might be associated with 'usurious' interest rates. Since the companies in our survey were all survivors, at least to 1990, we do not observe those firms which raised external capital but subsequently closed. This 'survivor bias' increases the likeli-

Table 6.5. Sources of finance used by small firms

	No.	%	
Bank	63	36	
Finance company	31	18	
LEDU (NI)	31	18	(62% of NI sample)
IDB (NI)	10	6	(20% of NI sample)
Other	5	3	
Own	129	74	
Total	**174**	**100**	

Source: NIERC Small Firm Growth Survey
Note: Columns do not sum to 100% since firms may use more than one source

hood that firms in the **capfal** category were a sub-group of successful businesses among a group of firms with high risk investment projects.

The survey also provided information on the sources from which external finance was obtained by small firms. Table 6.5 shows that own (i.e. internally generated or personal) funds are the most popular source of capital in small firms, which is consistent with other studies (Storey 1994). This is the most easily accessible source of finance for expansion. However, it is surprising to find that not all small firms use internally generated funds. The reason why may be found in Table 6.6 which indicates that the average growth over the period for firms not using own funds is only 6 per cent. Clearly, some firms are unable to use their own funds because they are unable to generate them. The growth rate of the users of own funds is 36 per cent which is close to the sample mean.

Table 6.6. Average turnover growth by category of finance user

	Bank	Finance Company	LEDU/ IDB	Other	Own
Users	29%	50%	43%	-35%	36%
Non-Users	29%	25%	25%	31%	6%

Source: NIERC Small Firm Growth Survey
Note: 148 cases

The next most popular source of funds is bank finance (see Table 6.5, p.93). It is perhaps odd that this number is not higher since most small firms might be expected to have an overdraft. However, it is possible that small businessmen did not include an overdraft in their interpretation of the question. Thus, this variable may refer solely to fixed-term bank loans. From the evidence in Table 6.6 it is clear that the banks do not appear to be concentrating their lending on fast-growth small firms.

Users of finance company funds appear to grow much faster than non-users. This variable refers to the use of hire-purchase or leasing facilities. It is probable that it is the fastest growing companies, which need to invest, that attempt to access this source of finance rather than the direction of causality being the other way.

With regard to the use of LEDU and IDB finance, two factors should be noted. First, the only firms receiving this type of finance are those located in Northern Ireland. Second, these two agencies are not in direct competition. The IDB provides assistance for firms once they grow above LEDU's threshold size of 50 employees. Merging these two sources of finance it can be seen that IDB/LEDU appear to have a good track record in either picking the fast growing firms or, in fact, assisting in that growth (Table 6.6). The issue of causality cannot be fully established and it is possible that both effects are in operation. IDB/LEDU may be simultaneously picking out the best growth prospects for assistance, but are also helping them to grow by offering financial and other assistance. In the period covered by this study (1986–90) there was no evidence to suggest that such a strategy was in operation although the new LEDU strategy (1989–95) does adopt a 'backing winners' approach to public sector support to the small firm sector. Nevertheless, Hart *et al.* (1993a) in a recent evaluation of the performance of LEDU conclude by arguing that surviving small firms supported by the agency grew faster than non-assisted small firms in Northern Ireland.

In the full equation in Table 4.1 (p.33) it is possible that the strong positive coefficient on the Northern Ireland dummy variable is the result of the IDB/LEDU effect. Table A4.2 (p.53) shows the full equation minus the **capfal** and **capsuc** variables but with the IDB/LEDU dummy instead of the Northern Ireland dummy. The IDB/LEDU is significant but less so than the Northern Ireland dummy. Furthermore, substitution of the IDB/LEDU variable for the NI variable considerably reduces the adjusted r-squared of the model. This shows that the Northern Ireland effect is more than simple grant availability. This is not to say that public assistance is not ultimately the root cause of the strong performance of Northern Ireland small firms but it is clear that the strength of the Northern Ireland dummy is not entirely due to the receipt of grants. Chapter 7 explores in more detail regional effects inherent in the variables included in the preferred equation in Table 4.1 (p.33).

It was noted above that there is no market for the equity of very small firms. For this reason owner-managers were not asked specifically about any attempts they may have made to sell equity. However, a question was asked as to whether the owner-manager had plans to sell the business in its entirety or gain a quotation on the Unlisted Securities Market (USM). The USM is generally for medium-sized firms with outstanding track records of profit generation. However, it is the only 'working' market for the equity of small businesses. The results of these questions show that only a minority of owners wished to sell their businesses and only a small minority planned to obtain a stock market quotation (Table 6.7).

Table 6.7. Desire to sell equity

	No. of firms	%
Desire to sell business	24	14
No desire to sell business	150	86
Obtain a quotation	7	4
No desire to obtain a quotation	167	96

Source: NIERC Small Firm Growth Survey

The opportunities for the average small businessman to sell equity are few and far between. A firm has to be of a considerable size and have a strong and consistent profits record for the Unlisted Securities Market or the 'over the counter market' to be an option. Few of our survey companies were of this stature. Similar factors mean the opportunities for sale of equity to venture capitalists are also limited. As a result, the only opportunity for the sale of part of a small firm's equity is a private placing with a member of the general public.

Very few owner-managers had considered the USM and, in the opinions of the interviewers, these tended to be of the 'pipe dream' variety rather than realistic objectives. Rather more owner-managers had considered the sale of their firms outright. This objective tended to be related to the prospect faced by some of the older owner-managers of having no successor to run the firm. Dummy variables based on these questions (see Table 4.2, p.41) added nothing to the explanatory power of the equations and were themselves completely insignificant. For the majority of small firms who wish to grow, debt or grants are the only realistic option for external finance, a fact which is confirmed by the performance of the **capfal** and **capsuc** variables mentioned in the previous section.

Appendix

Table A6.1. Business strategy variables

Strategy and objectives variables
The following variables were based on open-response questions concerning objectives contained in written business plans or defined on an informal basis. The wide variety of answers to this question were categorised:

- dummy indicating business objective to expand
- dummy indicating business objective to maintain existing size
- dummy indicating business objective to improve products or product range
- dummy indicating business objective to improve production process
- dummy indicating other business objectives
- dummy indicating other personal objectives
- dummy indicating respondent stated the growth was an aim of the owners over the period

The following variables were based on questions which asked the interviewees to rate on a scale of one to three the importance of certain objectives concerning growth:

- dummy indicating interviewee stated growth in assets was highly important
- dummy indicating interviewee stated growth in profit was highly important
- dummy indicating interviewee stated growth in profits was highly important
- dummy indicating interviewee stated growth in turnover was highly important

Table A6.1. Business strategy variables (continued)

The following variables were based on the question 'what strategy have you adopted to meet your objectives?'. The wide variety of answers to this question were categorised:

- dummy indicating strategy was to improve production process
- dummy indicating strategy was to improve products or expand product range
- dummy indicating strategy was to improve sales or marketing effort
- dummy indicating strategy was to alter pricing policy
- dummy indicating some other strategy
- dummy indicating strategy to seek new markets
- dummy indicating strategy to improve financial management.

The following variables are based on closed-response questions which required the interviewee to rate on a scale of one to three certain business strategies:

- dummy indicating product development a highly important strategy
- dummy indicating product diversification a highly important strategy
- dummy indicating keeping costs as low as possible a highly important strategy
- dummy indicating producing a high quality product an important strategy
- dummy indicating marketing a highly important strategy
- dummy indicating some other factor a highly important strategy

The following variables are continuous and are based on questions set to check previous questions about strategy:

- number of new products
- percentage of turnover spent on product development
- percentage of turnover spent on process development
- percentage of turnover spent on advertising
- percentage of turnover spent on marketing
- number of trade fairs attended

Further variables based on verification questions:

- dummy indicating research aimed at improving the production process
- dummy indicating that improvements were made in production process over study period
- dummy indicating new plant and machinery as the method of production process improvement
- dummy indicating new staff or training as the method of production process improvement
- dummy indicating reorganisation as the method of production process improvement
- dummy indicating firm actively seeks customers
- dummy indicating agents are the method employed to actively seek customers

Table A6.1. Business strategy variables (continued)

- dummy indicating sales personnel are the means of actively seeking customers
- dummy indicating personal contacts are the means of actively seeking customers
- dummy indicating consultants are the means of actively seeking customers
- dummy indicating tender is the means of actively seeking customers
- dummy indicating attending tradefairs is the means of actively seeking customers
- dummy indicating advertising is the means of actively seeking customers
- dummy indicating some other means of actively seeking customers
- dummy indicating that the firm employs advertising
- dummy indicating that the company employed marketing consultants in survey period
- dummy indicating that the company undertakes market research
- dummy indicating that the company has tried to export
- dummy indicating that the company has entered into agreements with other firms
- dummy indicating that the company has attempted to raise outside capital and succeeded
- dummy indicating that the company has attempted to raise outside capital and failed
- Utton's diversification index.

CHAPTER 7

Regional Disparities in Small Firm Growth

Introduction

The research described in this report was not designed specifically to investigate or to measure differences between regions in the growth of small firms. However, the survey was designed to include a range of locational conditions covering parts of England together with Northern Ireland. Hertfordshire, Leicestershire and Wearside were chosen to reflect the different economic circumstances of the South, Midlands and North of England. It is thus possible to describe the differences in growth between the four study areas and to attempt to account for these differences. This chapter begins by outlining economic conditions in each area. This is followed by a description of the growth rates in each area with an indication of the representativeness of the sample data. The main body of the chapter investigates contrasts between areas in those factors shown in Chapter 4 to be significant influences on growth. The ability of these factors to explain the observed differences in growth is considered in the final section.

The Economies of the Study Areas

Background

The four regions chosen in which to carry out this survey into the determinants of small firm growth differ in terms of geographical location, industrial structure, the traditional role of small firms and the availability of public sector assistance to economic development. The purpose of this section is to present brief regional profiles of the four study areas and to focus on some key economic indicators over the period 1986–90.

Hertfordshire, as a high-cost county with the greatest relative concentration of high-technology industries, forms a distinctly different environment for small firm growth than either Wearside or Northern Ireland. In both of the latter locations operating costs are low by national standards, and government subsidies are more easily available than further south. Against this, both are more remote from the centre of gravity of both consumer and industrial markets in Britain and Europe than is Hertfordshire. Leicestershire can be regarded as intermediate in these respects. It is a centrally-located county within England, but with lower cost pressures than areas closer to London like Hertfordshire. It is also a county with a long and vibrant tradition of small firm activity in a wide range of industries. Its industrial orientation tends to be towards traditional rather than high-technology industry (Table 7.1). Its major industries have been in textiles and clothing, although industry has become more diversified in recent decades.

Table 7.1. Economic Charactistics of survey regions

	Herts	Leics	Wearside	NI
Population (th) 1986	986	874	1135	1567
GDP/Capita (£) 1986	7769	7705	6435[1]	5900
Employment (th) 1987	392.9	361.2	91.8	488.7
Manufacturing Employment 1986 (th)	109.2	136.9	21.9	103.7
of which:				
High Tech Industries (%)	39.9	9.4	13.9[1]	14.3
Small Firms 1986 (%)	26.2	23.0	21.1	25.3

Sources: OPCS, CSO Regional Accounts, Census of Employment 1987, New Earnings Survey 1988
Note: [1] Tyne and Wear

Northern Ireland and Wearside have both experienced a mix of economic and social problems in the last two decades due to a combination of factors which can be summarised as: a peripheral location within the United Kingdom economy, the structural decline of traditional industrial sectors, and, in the case of Northern Ireland, political unrest. Consequently, both areas have traditionally been recipients of public sector industrial development assistance designed to offset the effects of decline and to form the basis for future economic regeneration. Arguably, Wearside may have a slight advantage of being less isolated and having an east-coast location which provides potential access to European Community and Scandinavian markets.

In the case of Northern Ireland, for mainly political reasons, the level of assistance provided to large and small firms is considerably larger than that available elsewhere in the United Kingdom. For example, the Local Enterprise Development Unit (LEDU), which is the government agency charged with the responsibility of strengthening and developing the small firm sector in Northern Ireland, spent an average of £20 million each year (at 1991 prices) during the late 1980s to encourage job creation in small firms. Total expenditure on industrial development and support in Northern Ireland by the Industrial Development Board (IDB), LEDU and other government departments stood at just under £200 million in the financial year 1988–9. Northern Ireland also benefits from granted Objective 1 status in the United Kingdom under the European Community's Structural Fund allocations.

Wearside, situated in the Northern region, has long been eligible for some of the highest levels of regional aid available in mainland Britain. Government Department of Trade and Industry (DTI) regional policy remains in operation, though substantially reduced through revisions in 1984 and 1988. The automatic subsidies have gone with the emphasis now upon selectivity, aiding smaller firms and inward-investment projects from overseas (e.g. Nissan's car plant at Washington). In 1988–9 the Northern region as a whole received £133.7 million in regional preferential assistance. As in the whole of the UK, companies in the region may also receive support for consultancy services and innovation under the DTI's 'Enterprise Initiative', which operates at preferential rates in the assisted areas.

While the late 1980s has seen the decline in importance of regional policy, both financially and politically, urban and local policy has become much more prominent. The Urban Programme, which includes the local authority of Wearside, together with the European Community, has helped maintain and expand economic development policy. Indeed, most of the region, including Wearside, is eligible for assistance under Objective 2 of the Structural Fund allocations. The region has a considerable number of local enterprise agencies supported by local and/or central government and in our study area the Tyne and Wear Enterprise Trust is in operation. The role of the private sector in local economic development has increasingly been facilitated in the locality with the promotion of an Urban Development Corporation (UDC) to cover the riverside areas of the Tyne and the Wear, and more recently with the introduction of the Training and Enterprise Councils (TECs) and the creation of a private sector led organisation called 'The Wearside Opportunity'.

The third study area included in the survey was the county of Leicestershire in the East Midlands region. It was deliberately chosen to provide a contrast to the more peripheral localities of Northern Ireland and Wearside. Leicestershire is an area which is more central to British markets and, apart from a small area in the north west of the county (i.e. Hinckley), lies outside the DTI's list of defined areas for regional assistance. Nevertheless, the county is well served by a network of economic development agencies and programmes operating within the public, private and voluntary sectors. For example, the city of Leicester is designated an Inner Urban area under the Urban Programme funded by central government, while in 1988 a City Action Team (CAT) was formally established in the region which included Leicester. The CAT co-ordinates the multi-million pound inner city programmes of the Departments of Trade and Industry, Environment and Employment.

There are a number of local enterprise agencies (LEAs) in the East Midlands region which offer advice and other support for new and growing businesses. The most prominent one in our study area is the Leicestershire Business Venture. It is financed in partnership by the local authority and the private sector. More recently, the creation of seven TECs in the region as a whole has provided a role for the private sector in local economic development.

Finally, in the late 1980s the local authority in Leicestershire became more active in mainstream economic development activities. These include the provision of financial assistance to start-ups, managed workspace, selective training initiatives and industrial promotion. Overall, it would be true to say that the main characteristic of the range of economic development policies available in Leicestershire is their private-sector orientated approach which stands in marked contrast to the situation in the other two study areas of Northern Ireland and Wearside.

The final study area was the county of Hertfordshire which was selected for the main reason that, being immediately adjacent to London, it was located within the UK's largest, wealthiest and most complex region, and thus would provide an important contrast to the other three areas. This was an important consideration because any model seeking to understand the process of small firm growth must control for the influence of external demand factors reflected in the performance of a variety of regional economies. Although Hertfordshire is largely rural and semi-rural, consisting of a number of small towns and villages, it is also a centre for advanced manufacturing such as the high-technology sectors of aerospace, electronics and pharmaceuticals. Thus, Hertfordshire has a reputation for being one of the most economically prosperous areas in the UK, which, in the 1980s, was reflected in terms of salaries and wages, car ownership rates, house, land and property prices in general. With such an economic profile and reputation it is not surprising to note that economic development initiatives by both the private and public sector were not much in evidence in the county throughout the 1980s. This, again, provides an important dimension to our study in that the performance of the sample of small firms in Hertfordshire does not reflect the existence of a specific policy framework targeted at the local economy. However, it may well be the case that small firms in the county may have benefited from the availability of national schemes designed to promote growth in the small firm sector. For example, it is now widely recognised that the uptake of national schemes such as the Loan Guarantee Scheme (LGS) and the Business Expansion Scheme (BES) have been disproportionately concentrated in the South East region (Mason and Harrison 1991).

Economic Trends in the Study Areas, 1986–90

A further major contrast between the four study areas was in the expansion of their local economies. The latter half of the 1980s, to which the study relates, was one in which the economies of the south of England expanded more rapidly than those further north. This was principally due to the deregulation of the UK financial system over the 1980s. This led to a huge rise in personal debt, mainly in the form of mortgages on homes. The increase in lending was greatest in southern England, where the associated large rise in consumer demand created a major economic boom. The boom spread outwards to the more northerly regions, but in more muted form.

The end of the boom came in 1989 and 1990 when interest rates were raised to damp down the inflationary tendencies which were most evident in southern England. The subsequent collapse in local demand was unsurprisingly greater in southern England, and the more northerly economies slowed down less. The slow-down and recession of the early 1990s affected only the last few months of the target period for this study (1986–90). The virtual absence of recession in Northern Ireland and, to a lesser extent, Wearside, meant that these areas were able to begin catching up on southern England towards the end of the study period. The overall contrasts in growth of Gross Domestic Product were consequently not large but Hertfordshire and Leicestershire expanded more than Northern Ireland or Wearside over the period (Table 7.2).

Table 7.2. Economic growth by region (%)

	Herts	Leics	Wearside	NI	UK
GDP (1986–90)	11.2	13.0	10.1[1]	9.7	12.5
Employment (1987–91)	-1.5	0.4	0.9[1]	7.3	2.8
Manufacturing Employment (1987–91)	-27.2	-13.3	12.2	0.8	-5.7

Sources: CSO Economic Trends
CSO Regional Accounts, Census of Employment 1987, 1991.
Note: [1] Tyne and Wear.

The overall expansion of the local economies, however, masked a very different performance within manufacturing industry. The mid and late 1980s witnessed a reversal of the long-established tendency for manufacturing to expand faster in the southern half of England in the northern half and Wales. The reasons were associated with the more rapid rise in wages and land prices in southern areas during the boom of the 1980s. The huge expansion of office and distributive activities in effect crowded out manufacturing industry from much of southern England.

This pattern is very evident among our four study areas. The most available measure is employment change, and figures are restricted to the slightly later period 1987–91. The inclusion of 1991 exaggerates the growth advantage of the northern areas but even so the contrast is clear (Table 7.2). Wearside and Northern Ireland both expanded their manufacturing employment, while Leicestershire and, especially, Hertfordshire suffered major contractions. Industry in the relatively

Table 7.3. Employment change in study areas, including selected sectors (1987–1991)

SIC Sector	Hertfordshire			Leicestershire			Northern Ireland			Wearside		
	1987	1991	% Change	1987	1991	% Change	1987	1991	% Change	1987	1991	% Change
25 Chemicals	11,393	9,569	(-16.0)	3,750	3,560	(-5.3)	2,620	2,811	(+7.3)	349	306	(-12.3)
32 Mechanical eng	10,236	7,941	(-22.4)	19,630	16,300	(-16.9)	6,970	8,478	(+21.6)	3,610	4,372	(+21.1)
34 Electrical/electronic eng	14,555	11,681	(-19.7)	12,650	13,070	(+3.3)	6,780	8,287	(+22.2)	1,878	1,686	(-10.2)
45 Clothing	1,724	984	(-42.9)	8,030	8,400	(+4.6)	16,710	16,540	(-1.0)	3,272	3,530	(+7.9)
49 Other manufg	1,806	2,418	(+33.9)	1,260	1,010	(-19.8)	4,760	4,994	(+4.9)	130	175	(+34.6)
Total manufg	93,876	68,100	(-27.5)	136,860	118,650	(-13.3)	103,380	104,340	(+4.9)	21,893	25,064	(+14.5)
Total employees (all sectors)	392,986	387,721	(-1.3)	361,200	362,630	(+0.4)	504,130	543,447	(+7.8)	92,721	98,084	(+5.8)

Sources: Census of Employment, Department of Employment

small Wearside economy was greatly assisted by the location of the large Nissan car assembly plant near Sunderland in 1988. Hertfordshire, with a large aerospace sector, was disadvantaged by the beginning of the post-cold-war decline in defence expenditure. These are, however, details overlaid on a strong general tendency for northern areas to do better in manufacturing. Of the 25 best performing UK counties between 1987 and 1991, in terms of employment growth, 17 were in northern England, Scotland or Wales. Of the 20 worst performing counties, 14 were in southern England.

The four study areas considered in this report represent the full range of growth performance. Over the 1987–91 period, Wearside was the fourth fastest growing of 65 UK counties in terms of manufacturing employment. Northern Ireland was ninth. The two areas in southern England were at the tail end of the spectrum. Leicestershire was in 54th position and Hertfordshire was the fastest declining of all UK counties in 65th position.

The strength of the manufacturing sector in employment terms varies greatly between each of the study areas. Using Census of Employment data for 1991, the proportion of employees in the manufacturing sector ranges from only 17.6 per cent in Hertfordshire to nearly one-third in Leicestershire (32.7%). Northern Ireland and Wearside fell between these extremes with 19.2 per cent and 25.5 per cent respectively of total employment in the manufacturing sector. As Table 7.3 reveals, these proportions in 1991 reflect very different trends in the manufacturing sector over the period 1987–91 with both Hertfordshire and Leicestershire experiencing sharp falls in manufacturing employment, while there has been some growth in manufacturing employment in both Northern Ireland and Wearside, with the latter being boosted by the arrival of the Nissan plant.

Table 7.4. Employment by sector 1986

Sector	NI	Herts	Leics	Wearside
Mineral products	4.3	2.1	2.7	6.3
Chemicals	2.2	10.5	2.1	0.7
Man-made fibres	0.7	0.0	0.0	0.0
Mechanical engineering	7.2	9.4	15.5	16.7
Electrical engineering	6.4	18.8	9.3	10.0
Other engineering	17.7	31.3	11.3	23.4
Food and drink	18.4	5.7	6.1	7.3
Textiles	11.6	0.4	26.2	0.5
Clothing and footwear	16.0	1.8	11.8	14.3
Timber and furniture	5.4	4.6	3.1	5.5
Printing, paper	5.3	9.9	5.4	10.0
Other manufacturing	4.9	5.4	6.3	5.2
Total	**100.0**	**100.0**	**100.0**	**100.0**

Source: NIERC Industrial Databases

Table 7.4 presents data on the mix of manufacturing industries in each of the study areas in 1990. These data have been taken from the Northern Ireland Economic Research Centre industrial databases which have been created for each of the study areas. The main points to note are the dominance of the engineering sector in Wearside and the importance of the textile and clothing sectors in both Northern Ireland and Leicestershire. Overall, therefore, all three areas tend to be characterised by the more traditional industrial sectors which stands in marked contrast to the industrial structure of Hertfordshire which is strong in such industries as aerospace, electronics and pharmaceuticals.

From Table 7.5 the performance of the industrial sectors from which the survey firms were selected can be traced over the period 1986–90. The clothing sector declined in all the study areas while Northern Ireland and Wearside exhibited growth in both the mechanical and electronic engineering sectors. Hertfordshire and Leicestershire, on the other hand, recorded a decline or negligible growth in the mechanical and electronic engineering sectors. Both Northern Ireland and Leicestershire portrayed growth in the chemicals sector while in Wearside and Hertfordshire it remained virtually unchanged. Finally, with respect to other manufacturing, this sector expanded in Northern Ireland and Wearside, although in the latter case there were just over 100 employees in this sector in 1986.

Table 7.5. Employment change by sector 1986–90

Sector	NI	Herts[1]	Leics	Wearside
Mineral products	18.7	-51.5	-14.5	-18.2
Chemicals	17.2	-16.0	12.4	-1.9
Mechanical engineering	7.8	-22.4	-8.6	21.8
Electrical engineering	27.4	-28.1	0.7	18.7
Other engineering	-10.3	-32.9	-8.7	-0.5
Food and drink	2.8	-30.6	6.0	-4.5
Textiles	-5.0	17.0	-13.9	13.0
Clothing and footwear	-7.7	-41.0	-8.0	-9.9
Timber and furniture	9.6	-34.4	6.8	19.0
Printing, paper	10.8	-17.2	2.9	15.5
Other manufacturing	18.5	-20.8	-2.9	14.8
Total	**2.5**	**-27.2**	**-6.4**	**5.9**

Source: NIERC Industrial Databases
Note: [1] 1987–91 (Census of Employment)

The performance of indigenous small manufacturing firms in each of the study areas, as measured by employment change, varies quite markedly over the period 1986–90 (Table 7.6). The small firm sector in Wearside and Northern Ireland grew steadily while in Leicestershire there was a decline of two per cent.

Unfortunately, it is not possible to determine to what extent the relatively poor performance of small firms in Leicestershire can be attributed to the initial effects of the economic downturn in 1990.

Table 7.6. Employment growth in small indigenous firms by sector, 1986–90

Sector	NI	Leics	Wearside
Mineral products	18.5	-16.1	3.0
Chemicals	45.7	21.4	1.7
Mechanical engineering	13.2	-5.1	23.2
Electrical engineering	25.4	30.8	34.0
Other engineering	13.2	-6.7	27.2
Food and drink	7.2	0.8	-10.4
Textiles	7.1	-9.5	-100.0
Clothing and footwear	-10.0	-3.7	-29.2
Timber and furniture	1.7	0.5	4.8
Printing, paper	13.7	-3.4	60.6
Other manufacturing	29.1	15.3	59.4
Total	**11.1**	**-2.0**	**18.3**

Source: NIERC Industrial Databases
Note: This data was not available for Hertfordshire

Disaggregated by industrial sector, the pattern of employment change in small firms becomes much more diverse at the regional level (Table 7.6). However, concentrating on the sectors included in the survey, it can be seen that the growth of electrical engineering, chemicals and other manufacturing was common to all the study areas for which data is available. The overall growth displayed in general by small mechanical engineering firms was not replicated in Leicestershire. In clothing there was a decline in employment in the small firm sector in all three regions.

The proportion of small manufacturing firms (i.e. employing less than 50 persons) in the industrial sectors chosen for this study was broadly similar for each of the English study areas (just over two-fifths), while in Northern Ireland it was considerably lower at one-third (Table 7.7). In aggregate, small firms in these sectors grew more rapidly in Wearside and Northern Ireland than in the other two areas. There was also considerable variation in the average employment size of small firms across the study areas with Northern Ireland and Wearside having the smallest at the start of the study period in 1986.

Table 7.7. **Population characteristics of small firms (Survey Sectors Only)**

Region	No of firms	% of Total population of small firms	Employ 1986	Emp change % 1986–90	Average size 1986 (Emp)
Northern Ireland	818	32.2	8,162	31.9	10.0
Leicestershire	884	44.5	12,537	26.4	14.2
Hertfordshire	365	41.9	6,194	19.1	16.9
Wearside	147	46.2	1,882	50.1	12.8

Source: NIERC Industrial Databases

A final element of the discussion on the population of small firms from which the survey sample was drawn is the distribution between the three growth categories selected to structure the survey. Table 7.8 presents data for each study area, and in

Table 7.8. **Population characteristics of small firms by growth category (Survey Sector Only)**

	Fast growth	Slower growing	Static declining	All firms
Northern Ireland				
No of firms	179	266	373	818
% of Total pop of small firms	7.0	10.5	14.7	32.2
% Emp change	195.5	37.4	-21.8	31.9
Leicestershire				
No of firms	111	322	451	884
% of Total pop of small firms	5.6	16.2	22.7	44.5
% Emp change	257.9	33.4	-12.3	26.4
Hertfordshire				
No of firms	28	105	232	365
% of Total pop of small firms	3.2	12.1	26.6	41.9
% Emp change	228.5	30.7	-15.4	19.1
Wearside				
No of firms	33	61	53	147
% of Total pop of small firms	10.4	19.2	16.7	46.2
% Emp change	284.8	38.5	-17.5	50.1

Source   NIERC Industrial Databases

the chosen industrial sectors, on the number of firms, proportion of the total population and the average employment growth broken down by growth category. In each of the study areas fast-growth small firms, defined as having registered 100 per cent employment growth or more between 1986 and 1990, represented 10 per cent or under of the total population of small firms in those areas. There is also a high degree of consistency across the study areas in terms of the average growth performance recorded in each of the growth categories. Nevertheless, it can be seen that fast-growth small firms in Northern Ireland tend to have grown slower than in the other three study areas.

Regional Contrasts in Factors Influencing Growth

In Chapter 4, twenty six variables were identified as statistically significant influences on the growth of turnover in small firms. These included a number of company characteristics, entrepreneurial characteristics and aspects of business strategy. Several of these factors were more in evidence in some of the study areas than in others. These factors could potentially account for the observed differences between study areas in growth of turnover or employment.

Table 7.9. Growth of small firms by region, 1986–90

	Herts	Leics	Wearside	NI	All Areas
Population of small firms in target sectors					
No of firms	365	884	147	818	2,214
Employment growth[1] (%)	19.1	26.3	50.1	31.9	28.8
Sample					
No of firms	42	40	24	41	147
Employment growth (%)	44.1	52.4	64.7	86.6	61.6
Turnover Growth[2] (%)	29.3	48.4	70.9	84.1	56.6

Sources: NIERC Industrial Databases
          NIERC Small Firm Growth Survey
Note[1]: Firms which were operating in both 1986 and 1990, in the target sectors of chemicals, mechanical and electrical engineering, clothing and other manufacturing
Note[2]: Deflated

It should be stressed at the outset, however, that the growth differences between areas, although substantial, were not large in relation to the huge variability between individual firms. The overall average rate of growth in turnover among the study firms was 56 per cent over the four year period, but the standard deviation was 98 per cent and the average growth rate of the ten most rapidly expanding companies was 325 per cent.[1] Within this large range the difference between the sample means for the best performing area, Northern Ireland (84.1%) and the worst performing, Hertfordshire (28.6%), were not huge (Table 7.9). Indeed, they were not large enough to become statistically significant within the regression equations reported in Chapter 4. This does not mean that the differences were not important, nor can we reasonably deduce that the difference between areas observed within the sample were random fluctuations. The evidence of a wider economic contrast between northern and southern parts of the UK suggests a systematic cause. The lack of statistical significance instead indicates that within this group of firms with a wide variation of growth performance, the sample size was too small to rule out the possibility that the geographical contrasts were merely sampling fluctuations.

Northern Ireland and Hertfordshire

To identify those factors which are most favourable in the various study areas, it is necessary to contrast pairs of areas. The clearest contrast is between Northern Ireland and Hertfordshire. Five variables were significantly advantageous for Northern Ireland and six for Hertfordshire. In each case the advantage was statistically significant.[2]

Table 7.10 shows the relative importance of the individual growth variables for Northern Ireland and Hertfordshire. The figures shown beside each variable are the product of the B coefficient and the difference between the regional mean values for that variable in the two regions being compared. These are finally multiplied by 100. They show the variables for which one region may have an advantage over another in these growth characteristics, and their size gives some idea of the impact of each variable within the overall model. The B coefficients are calculated from a variant of the preferred regression equation which excludes the regional and sectoral dummies in an attempt to emphasise the regional differences in the firm, strategy and entrepreneurial characteristic variables in the model.

---

1   The mean for the ten fastest declining firms was a loss of 56 per cent of jobs.
2   Each of the differences in the regional means has been tested for statistical significance. In the case of the many dummy variables the normal approximation to the binomial distribution is assumed and a one-tailed test for a difference in proportions using the Z statistic is carried out. The other continuous variables have had the differences in their regional means tested using a one-tailed t-test. Results are tested at the 0.1, 0.05, and 0.01 levels.

Northern Ireland has an advantage over Hertfordshire in having younger entrepreneurs **(age)**, since younger entrepreneurs tended to have faster growing companies. The average age of interviewee in Northern Ireland was 45, compared with 52 in Hertfordshire (Table 7.11). This difference of seven years is predicted by the regression equation of Chapter 4 to boost growth in Northern Ireland by *8.7* percentage points. The overall growth gap between Northern Ireland and Hertfordshire is 55.4 percentage points. Hence, the age of owner alone can be seen to account for one-sixth of this gap. The relative youth of Northern Ireland's entrepreneurs compared with all other areas may reflect the younger average age of population in the Province. It could also reflect the efforts of the Northern Ireland small firms agency LEDU to encourage young people into entrepreneurship.

Table 7.10. Factors in which Northern Ireland firms have advantages over firms in other areas (Percentage points addition to growth in turnover)

	Herts	Leics	Wearside
Capsuc	2.8	2.3	3.6
Profit	2.0	5.1	
Market	7.5	11.8	1.2
Markres	5.7	10.3	5.7
Age	8.7	2.7	5.5
Diverse		2.2	
Newprod			2.9
Total	**26.7**	**34.4**	**18.9**

Source: NIERC Small Firms Growth Survey

Table 7.11. Average age of owner-managers in survey firms

Northern Ireland	45.3	(1.2)
Hertfordshire	52.4	(1.6)
Leicestershire	47.5	(1.4)
Wearside	29.8	(1.8)
Total Sample	**48.7**	**(1.2)**

Source: NIERC Small Firms Growth Survey

Note: Figures in parentheses are standard errors of regional means. The differences between Northern Ireland and both Hertfordshire and Wearside are statistically significant, as is the difference between Leicestershire and Hertfordshire

Northern Ireland also has a highly significant advantage in marketing function. More Northern Ireland interviewees stated that marketing was an important aspect of their management strategy **(market)**. In addition, more Northern Ireland companies had undertaken formal market research **(markres)**. Together these two variables give Northern Ireland a 13.2 percentage point advantage over Hertfordshire. Marketing has been heavily promoted by LEDU, which provides grants for market research. It seems likely that LEDU's efforts have increased awareness of the importance of effective marketing as well as raising the level of market research. Certainly Northern Ireland's small firms appear to have accepted the message that improved marketing should be a major business strategy. Almost 70 per cent of sample firms in Northern Ireland reported that marketing was important compared to 35 per cent in Hertfordshire and only 18 per cent in the other areas (Table 7.12). Similarly, 39 per cent of Northern Ireland firms had undertaken market research compared with 17 per cent in the other areas.

Table 7.12. The importance of marketing

	Marketing is an Important Management Strategy (% of firms agreeing)	Firms Undertaking Formal Market Research (% of sample firms)
Northern Ireland	65.9	39.0
Hertfordshire	34.9	23.3
Leicestershire	18.4	7.9
Wearside	18.2	22.7
Total Sample	**36.8**	**23.6**

Source: NIERC Small Firms Growth Survey

It should be noted, however, that Northern Ireland firms are handicapped by their high reliance on sales agents to sell their products. Twenty-two per cent of sample companies in Northern Ireland used sales agents compared to 2 per cent in Hertfordshire, 13 per cent in Leicestershire and none in Wearside. The difference between Northern Ireland and Hertfordshire diminishes Northern Ireland's advantage by 3.8 percentage points, and hence detracts from the Province's advantage in marketing. The reason for the greater reliance on selling agents among Northern Ireland firms is likely to reflect their greater distance from markets in Great Britain and the greater time and cost which would be involved in approaching clients directly.

Northern Ireland firms also had a small advantage over those in Hertfordshire due to their greater success in gaining external capital **(capsuc)**. A little over half of the firms in any area used external sources of capital. These included 68 per cent of firms in Northern Ireland and 51 per cent in Hertfordshire (Table 7.13).

There was little difference between areas except for Northern Ireland, where the proportion was significantly higher in the statistical sense. The difference increased Northern Ireland's growth over Hertfordshire by 2.8 percentage points. Again, Northern Ireland's advantage was likely to be due to the impact of government intervention. Government grants for capital investment (as well as Research and Development and marketing) were available from LEDU throughout the 1986–90 period. Until 1989, automatic capital grants were available as an alternative to the 'Selective Financial Assistance' in which form capital grants were available until 1992. Most recently, LEDU has virtually ceased giving grants for capital investment as opposed to marketing, Research and Development, etc.

Table 7.13. Firms successfully raising external capital 1986–90 (% of sample firms)

Northern Ireland	68.3
Hertfordshire	51.2
Leicestershire	55.3
Wearside	45.5
Total Sample	**56.3**

Source: NIERC Small Firms Growth Survey

Note: The Northern Ireland sample proportion is statistically significant in its difference from the other areas

Finally, Northern Ireland firms had an advantage over those in Hertfordshire in being more profit-oriented (**growprof**). More Northern Ireland firms (73.2%) stated that raising profits was a major goal of the company than did firms in Hertfordshire (62.8%). This factor added two percentage points to Northern Ireland's growth. More generally, it is clear that the northern firms (in Northern Ireland and Wearside) were more profit-orientated than those in Hertfordshire and Leicestershire.[3]

In the comparison between Northern Ireland and Hertfordshire the advantage of Hertfordshire firms in having less reliance on selling agents has already been mentioned. The largest advantage of the Hertfordshire firms was the much greater tendency for the entrepreneurs to be members of professional organisations (**proforg**). Indeed, the proportion of Hertfordshire's entrepreneurs in this category at 25.6 per cent was much higher, not only than in Northern Ireland (2.4%), but also in Wearside (9.1%) (Table 7.14). Leicestershire was very similar to Hertfordshire in this respect and the geographical contrast can be seen to be very much north-south in orientation. Firms run by members of professional organisations

---

3 The proportions of firms stating that profits were a major goal of the company were Northern Ireland (73.2%), Hertfordshire (62.8%), Wearside (72.7%) and Leicestershire (44.7%).

grew significantly faster than other firms over this period. The advantage to Hertfordshire over Northern Ireland was 6.8 percentage points.

Hertfordshire entrepreneurs also had a tendency to own more businesses **(othbus)**. Although there were no advantageous links between the various businesses, this attribute was associated with faster growth in turnover. In Hertfordshire, 14 per cent of owners had other businesses. This proportion was similar to Leicestershire (18.2%), but much higher than either Northern Ireland (4.9%) or Wearside (5.3%). We have already noted that Hertfordshire entrepreneurs were older than those in Northern Ireland. Together these factors lead to a picture of more mature businessmen in Hertfordshire with higher propensities to have professional qualifications and owning more businesses. While the latter two attributes were found to boost company growth, greater age was associated with lower growth. A fourth factor was a greater tendency for the sample companies in Hertfordshire to have multiple owners who were an influence on the business **(othbus+)**. Hertfordshire firms were also more diversified with more individual products **(diverse)**, but this was a relatively marginal advantage.

Table 7.14. Firms run by members of professional organisations (% of sample firms)

Northern Ireland	2.4
Hertfordshire	25.6
Leicestershire	9.1
Wearside	26.3
Total Sample	**16.7**

Source: NIERC Small Firms Growth Survey
Note: There is a statistically significant difference in proportions between Northern Ireland and Wearside on the one hand and Leicestershire and Hertfordshire on the other

Business strategy was more orientated towards introducing new machinery to improve production processes in Hertfordshire than in Northern Ireland, an orientation which was found to significantly boost growth. One possibility is that since firms in Hertfordshire faced wage costs 25 per cent higher than in Northern Ireland (see Table 7.1, p.100), their strategy was more concerned with raising labour productivity. However, the difference between the two areas was not large. Moreover, *observed* change in labour productivity (turnover per employee) was less favourable than for Northern Ireland firms, but this may have reflected the impact of slower growth on productivity. In general, southern firms were more likely to introduce new machinery for this purpose (Hertfordshire 72.1 per cent, Leicestershire 73.7%). Fewer Wearside firms did so (68.2%). Northern Ireland, with the lowest wages, had the lowest proportion of all (63.4%).

Taken together the advantages listed above for Hertfordshire firms were estimated to raise their growth by 20.3 percentage points relative to Northern

Ireland (Table 7.15). Equivalently, Northern Ireland firms were disadvantaged relative to Hertfordshire by the same amount. As we have already noted that Northern Ireland's advantages raised growth by 26.8 percentage points (see Table 7.10, p.111), it can be seen that the *net* impact on Northern Ireland of advantages and disadvantages was some 6 percentage points. On balance, these factors thus account for relatively little of the 42 percentage points growth gap between the two areas. Other factors are thus needed to explain the gap. When a dummy variable is introduced into the basic equation for growth in turnover to indicate the difference between the two locations (Hertforshire = 0, Northern Ireland = 1) then this variable is statistically significant, indicating again that Northern Ireland's additional advantage is unlikely to be due to random change. Before discussing the potential nature of the unexplained advantage, the differences in company characteristics and strategy will be examined for the other pairs of areas.

Table 7.15. Factors in which Northern Ireland firms have disadvantages relative to other areas (Percentage points of growth in turnover)

	Herts	*Leics*	*Wearside*
Othbus	3.2		4.3
Prodproc	2.1		
Otherown	2.4	4.3	
Proforg	6.8	6.9	
Agent	3.8		4.2
Diverse	2.0		3.1
Size		3.4	4.2
Founder			6.5
Newprod		11.8	
Margins			2.0
Total	**20.3**	**26.4**	**24.3**

Source: NIERC Small Firm Growth Survey

Northern Ireland and Leicestershire

The list of advantages which Northern Ireland firms possess relative to those in Leicestershire are remarkably similar to those listed above in the comparison with Hertfordshire (see Table 7.10, p.111). Northern Ireland's advantage in attitudes to marketing **(market)** and in market research **(markres)** is larger than in the Hertfordshire comparison. Leicestershire's entrepreneurs were even further behind Northern Ireland than those in Hertfordshire. The difference in the average age of entrepreneurs is, however, less marked than before. The interviewees in the Leicestershire firms at 47 years of age were, on average, two years older than those in Northern Ireland. This gap is small and not statistically significant, but if representative would add *three* percentage points to Northern Ireland's growth.

Northern Ireland firms had a more significant advantage in terms of profit-orientation and were also a little more diversified than in Leicestershire. Like Hertfordshire, firms in Leicestershire were more likely to have multiple owners with professional qualifications. Leicestershire firms in the sample were also one-third smaller in terms of turnover than in Northern Ireland. Since smaller firms throughout the sample tended to grow faster this gave Leicestershire a further small advantage.

The largest measured advantage of Leicestershire firms was in product innovation **(newprod)**. The measured difference was very large (see Table 7.15, p.115). Leicestershire firms reported an average of 7.9 significantly improved products over the four-year period, compared with 2.2 among Northern Ireland firms (Table 7.16). As already noted, we suspect mis-measurement of this variable in the case of the Leicestershire sample, and are inclined to dismiss it as a real advantage.

Table 7.16. Average number of new and improved products introduced 1986–90

Northern Ireland	2.2	(0.5)
Hertfordshire	1.8	(0.4)
Leicestershire	7.9	(1.7)
Wearside	0.8	(0.3)
Total Sample	**3.4**	**(0.8)**

Source: NIERC Small Firm Growth Survey

Note: Figures in parentheses are standard errors of the mean. Interviews in Leicestershire were conducted differently to those in other areas and this may have affected responses to this question

The total impact on growth of variables favourable to Northern Ireland was largest in the Leicestershire comparison. The six statistically significant variables listed in Table 7.10 (see p.111) accounted for 34 percentage points of output growth. Offsetting this were the four variables in which Leicestershire's firms had an advantage over Northern Ireland (see Table 7.15, p.115). Together these boosted growth in Leicestershire by 26 percentage points. The net advantage to Northern Ireland was thus only 81 percentage points out of an actual growth difference of 36 percentage points (see Table 7.9, p.109).

Northern Ireland and Wearside

Most of the advantages which Northern Ireland firms possessed over firms in Hertfordshire and Leicestershire were also in evidence in a comparison with Wearside (see Table 7.10, p.110). Northern Ireland firms again had advantages in being run by younger people **(age)**. The undertaking of market research was also again more in evidence among Northern Ireland's firms. So were positive attitudes to marketing **(market)**, but the gap was less in the case of Wearside firms than for other areas. Wearside firms were more aware of the importance of marketing than were firms located further south. This may reflect a realisation that marketing has to be pursued more actively in peripheral locations. It may also be that development agencies in assisted areas have been successful in persuading firms to take marketing more seriously. Both of these factors would increase awareness of marketing in Wearside, but are likely to do so to a greater degree in Northern Ireland. What was evident was Northern Ireland's greater advantage in conducting market research **(markres)**.

Somewhat surprisingly, Northern Ireland firms had a larger advantage in raising external capital over Wearside than over other areas **(capsuc)**. As an assisted area, Wearside firms would have had access to government capital grants and other financial assistance. They might have been expected to have been more successful in raising external capital than firms in Leicestershire or Hertfordshire.

Finally, Northern Ireland firms had a significant advantage in product development over those in Wearside. On average, companies in Northern Ireland introduced 2.2 significant product improvements over the four-year period (see Table 7.16, p.116). In Wearside the figure was substantially lower at 0.8.

The converse advantages of Wearside companies over those in Northern Ireland overlapped with those already seen for the other areas, but also included new factors. Wearside firms made less use of selling agents **(agent)**, and their owners tended to have more interests in other unrelated companies **(othbus)** (see Table 7.15, p.115). Wearside firms also tended to have a less diverse product range **(diverse)**. Each of these factors boosted Wearside's growth, and reflected weaknesses which characterised Northern Ireland relative to all the other areas.

Wearside companies were also initially smaller than those in Northern Ireland **(size)** which again was an advantage for growth and turnover. More Wearside firms were still run by the original founder, another favourable factor in the growth process.

One respect in which Wearside firms were apparently different from those elsewhere was in the use of price and cost cutting as a major growth strategy. Few firms adopt this as a growth strategy since it is usually seen as a short-term defensive measure which often results in self-defeating retaliation from competitors. Under five per cent of firms preferred price or cost cutting as a growth strategy in the sample as a whole (Table 7.17). However, the proportion in Wearside was over twice as high as in other areas. Although the difference was statistically significant, the small number of firms interviewed in Wearside makes it possible that random sampling fluctuations are causing this result. We can note, however, that the proportion of firms using price/cost cutting strategies was over twice as high on average in the two northern areas (6.3%) as in the two southern areas (2.4%). This may reflect a greater degree of competition between small firms in southern and midland England making price cutting a less attractive strategy.

The overall impact of factors favourable to Northern Ireland in comparison with Wearside amounts to 18.9 percentage points of growth in turnover (see Table 7.10, p.111). This advantage is completely offset by the disadvantages relative to Wearside which contribute 24.3 percentage points (see Table 7.15, p.115). The net effect is thus only 5 percentage points, in Wearside's favour, out of an actual gap in growth of turnover of 40 percentage points in the opposite direction (see Table 7.9, p.109). Clearly these factors do nothing to account for the observed growth differences between the sample firms in these two areas.

**Table 7.17. Percentage of firms using
price or cost cutting as a strategy for growth**

Northern Ireland	4.9
Hertfordshire	2.3
Leicestershire	2.6
Wearside	9.1
Total Sample	**4.2**

Source: NIERC Small Firm Growth Survey

Summary for Northern Ireland

Having compared Northern Ireland with each of the three other areas, it is clear that most of Northern Ireland's advantages are unique to that area rather than being part of a more general north-south contrast within the UK. Most of the advantages appear to reflect the activities of a well-funded and active small firms agency LEDU, which has contact with most of the areas with small manufacturing firms. The pattern of disadvantages displayed by Northern Ireland firms (see Table 7.15, p.115) is more diverse, reflecting the different individual advantages of other areas. Northern Ireland's small firms are less likely to have multiple owners, owners with interests in other unrelated businesses or owners who are members of professional organisations. Each of these is an indication of the nature of entrepreneurs in Northern Ireland. One aspect of behaviour is also clear. This is the disadvantage which Northern Ireland firms have in their heavy use of selling agents.

Wearside compared with Leicestershire and Hertfordshire

In this section we leave aside the Northern Ireland firms and focus on the contrast between firms in Wearside and those in the more southerly survey areas. Within the sample, average growth in turnover was higher in Wearside (43.6%) than in Hertfordshire (28.6%), but similar to Leicestershire (48.4%) (see Table 7.9, p.109).

As argued above, growth in Wearside is likely to be under-estimated. Among the population of small firms employment growth in Wearside was faster than in any other survey area, and twice as fast as in Leicestershire or Hertfordshire.

Two things are striking about those factors in which Wearside firms possess an advantage (Table 7.18). First, the advantages over Leicestershire are much more intense than those over Hertfordshire. In the latter case, what is striking is the lack of any behaviourial or business strategy advantages. Second, the list of advantages relative to Leicestershire is almost completely different from that in the comparison with Hertfordshire. This reflects contrasts between Leicestershire and Hertfordshire firms which will be discussed below.

Table 7.18. Factors which differentiate firms in Wearside from those in Leicestershire or Hertfordshire (Percentage points of turnover growth)

| | *Advantages relative to:* | | | | *Disadvantages relative to:* | |
	Herts	Leics			Herts	Leics
Size	4.5		Market		4.6	
Age	3.2		Otherown		3.9	5.9
Founder	5.0	5.2	Proforg		5.0	5.1
Profit		4.5	Newprod		2.0	14.7
Markres		4.6	Age			2.8
Othbusn		4.1				
Diverse		5.3				
Agents		2.5				
Total	**12.7**	**26.2**			**15.5**	**28.5**

Source: NIERC Small Firm Growth Survey

Compared with Hertfordshire, firms in Wearside have only three significant advantages, each of which is 'structural' rather than behaviourial. These are the smaller initial size of the firm (**size**), the younger average age of owner (**age**) and the larger proportion of businesses still run by the founder (**founder**).

These advantages are offset by a slightly longer list of unfavourable factors. Hertfordshire firms are more likely to have multiple owners (**otherown**), and to have owners who are members of professional organisations (**proforg**). Hertfordshire firms are more likely to state that marketing was an important strategy for growth (**market**) and to have introduced more new and improved products (**newprod**). Once again, the favourable and unfavourable factors largely cancel each other, indicating that the net effect of these variables contributes little to understanding the reasons for the gap in average growth between Wearside firms and those in Hertfordshire.

The same overall conclusion holds for a comparison between Wearside and Leicestershire. The favourable and unfavourable variables offset one another. The list of factors favourable to Wearside is, however, more broadly based when the comparison is with Leicestershire. Wearside firms are again advantaged by being more likely to be run by their founders **(founder)**. Their owners are also more likely to be involved in running unrelated businesses **(othbus)**. Wearside firms are also more profit-orientated **(profit)**, more involved in market research **(markres)**, less diverse in their range of products **(diverse)** and make less use of selling agents **(agents)**.

Disadvantages relative to Leicestershire were that owners tended to be a little older **(age)** and less likely to be members of professional organisations **(proforg)**. Firms were also less likely to have multiple owners **(otherown)**. Ostensibly, Leicestershire's largest advantage lay in a high rate of introducing new or improved products **(newprod)** but, as already noted, this advantage may have been exaggerated by deficiencies in the survey process.

Leicestershire and Hertfordshire

Since growth in turnover displays a north-south contrast, it might be expected that firms in Leicestershire and Hertfordshire would exhibit similarities in their patterns of advantage and disadvantage. The survey results, however, suggest that this is not the case. When compared with Hertfordshire, the Leicestershire firms have few significant advantages. In this respect they resemble the Wearside sample.

The favourable factors for Leicestershire firms are largely 'structural' (Table 7.19). Leicestershire companies are smaller **(size)** than those in Hertfordshire and their owners are younger **(age)**. Both of these characteristics are likely to boost growth. Their only other advantage is in a high number of new or improved products **(newprod)**. As already suggested, we are inclined to suspect the accuracy of our data in this respect and thus to discount this factor.

Table 7.19. Factors which differentiate firms in Leicestershire from those in Hertfordshire

	Advantages to Herts		*Advantages to Leics*
Profit	3.1	Size	3.6
Market	4.3	Age	6.0
Markres	4.5	Newprod	12.7
Othbus	3.1		
Diverse	4.3		
Agent	2.1		
Total	**21.4**		**22.3**

Source: NIERC Small Firm Growth Survey

The disadvantages of Leicestershire firms when compared to Hertfordshire includes attitudes to marketing **(market)**, and a lower level of market research **(markres)** (Table 7.19). They are also more likely to use agents in selling **(agent)**. Together this suggests a particular weakness in sales and marketing in Leicestershire. Firms in Leicestershire are also less profit-orientated in their goals **(profit)**, and their owners less likely to have interests in other unrelated business **(othbus)**. Finally, Leicestershire firms are disadvantaged by the more diverse nature of their product ranges **(diverse)**.

As with the other pair-wise comparisons the impact of advantages and disadvantages tend to cancel out between Leicestershire and Hertfordshire. However, if Leicestershire's large apparent advantage in product innovation is discounted, the balance of advantage would lie with Hertfordshire. Since the actual gap in growth of turnover was in favour of Leicestershire, once again we conclude that these factors do not account for the observed difference in growth.

Explanations of Regional Contrasts in Growth of Turnover

The preceding sections demonstrate that although there are significant differences between small firms across the regions of the UK, the differences identified in this study tend to offset one another. They do not, therefore, account for the observed gap in growth between the survey areas. In particular, they are unable to explain why there was a north-south contrast in growth, or why Northern Ireland should have been the fastest growing area and Hertfordshire the slowest (see Table 7.9, p.109).

Consequently, it is necessary to consider additional factors outside the scope of this study. The most plausible explanation is likely to be the widening gap in operating costs which occurred between UK regions in the late 1980s. The macro-economic circumstances described at the beginning of this chapter led wages to rise more rapidly in southern England than in more northerly parts or in Wales. Similarly, costs of industrial land increased most in southern England. By the late 1980s, the cost disadvantage of southern England had widened to record levels. During the subsequent recession these cost disadvantages have diminished, but during the survey period 1986–90, they are likely to have conferred a distinct advantage on firms operating in the lower-cost locations of the northern half of the UK.

Average wages in manufacturing were traditionally higher in south-east England (including Hertfordshire) than in other regions and the gap widened over the 1980s. One exception was the Northern region (including Wearside) where high-paying steel and chemical industries boosted wage levels. Even here the advantage diminished over the 1980s.

We do not have data on the wages actually paid within the survey firms. In some ways, however, the average wage levels in the local region may be of more relevance. For instance, if small firms are unable to respond to a rise in the general level of local wages, then their quality of recruitment is likely to fall along with the morale and, perhaps, efficiency of their existing workforce. Hence, while observed low wages in a given firm may appear to constitute a competitive advantage, unobserved efficiency losses may be more important if the firm is operating in a high wage area.

By 1988, the gap in wage levels between our four survey areas was very large. The figures for 1988 in Table 7.20 show that manual wages in Hertfordshire were 7 to 8 per cent above the Great Britain average, while those in Northern Ireland were 10.7 to 14.5 per cent below. Hence, Hertfordshire wages were 20 to 25 per cent above those in Northern Ireland. Wage levels in Leicestershire and Wearside were intermediate between these two extremes. The wage-cost penalty for operating in Hertfordshire was much larger in this period than any potential gain in lower transport costs due to location close to major markets. It might thus be expected that firms in Hertfordshire would have low profitability, low levels of investment and loss of market share. In the longer-term only firms with above average levels of value-added per employee (e.g. in high technology-sectors) could be expected to survive under these conditions.

Table 7.20. Wage levels in survey regions, 1988

	Herts	Leics	Wearside	NI	GB (£/wk)
Manual Males	107.0	95.4	96.3	85.5	200.6
Manual Females	108.1	96.0	92.3	89.3	123.6
Non-Manual Males	102.4	91.0	85.5	85.5	294.6
Non-Manual Females	103.4	91.5	91.9	93.3	175.5

Note: Average Wage 1988 (GB=£100)
Sources: New Earnings Survey 1988

Table 7.21. Percentage of firms citing shortage of labour as a constraint on growth

	Not Important	Important	Very Important	Total
Northern Ireland	60	20	20	100
Wearside	84	8	8	100
Leicestershire	70	22	8	100
Hertfordshire	68	16	16	100

Note: Total number of Firm 174
Source: NIERC Small Firm Growth Survey

Despite these cost differences there is little evidence from the survey that firms in the areas of high wage-costs experienced more problems attracting labour. Table 7.21 shows that firms in Hertfordshire showed no greater propensity to cite labour shortages as a constraint on growth[4] than firms in Northern Ireland. Neither was the quality of labour a greater problem for Hertfordshire (Table 7.22). Although there were some differences between survey areas there was no pattern which could be directly associated with levels of wages.

Table 7.22. Percentage of firms citing quality of labour as a constraint on growth

	Not Important	Important	Very Important	Total
Northern Ireland	50	34	16	100
Wearside	40	32	28	100
Leicestershire	58	20	22	100
Hertfordshire	59	25	16	100

Source: NIERC Small Firm Growth Survey
Note: Total number of Firms 174

Industrial rents have always been higher in the South East, including Hertfordshire, than elsewhere in the UK. Rents in this area rose rapidly in the 1980s and by 1988 the rent gap was at a historic peak. The high industrial rents will have contributed to the unfavourable operating-cost environment of Hertfordshire. Firms owning their own property would not be immediately affected, but gains could be made from relocating or liquidating the business if the site could be sold at high cost. Similarly, new or expanding firms would be deterred by high rents and high land costs.

High operating costs affect all manufacturing firms and not just small firms. The widening of the regional cost-gap in the 1980s led to a temporary reversal of the general tendency for southern regions to perform more favourably than northern regions. Since large firms form part of the local market for small firms, the cost advantage to northern areas was magnified by a boost to local demand. In Northern Ireland, for example, two-thirds of total sales of small firms are within the local region (Scott and O'Reilly 1993). It is estimated that a quarter of all sales are to other firms within Northern Ireland. The favourable cost-environment for large firms in Northern Ireland should thus have boosted the size of the market for local small firms as well as directly aiding their cost-competitiveness.

---

4 A more detailed discussion of the constraints on growth within the survey firms is presented in Chapter 8.

The importance of the local demand constraint is demonstrated in Table 7.23 which shows that more of the firms operating in southern or midland England cited shortage of demand as an important constraint on growth. As expected, the area with the lowest proportion of firms citing a demand constraint was Northern Ireland. In principle, a demand constraint may affect fast-growing firms more than their slow-growing counterparts if they exhaust their market. However, it is the areas with the slower growing companies which report shortage of demand as a constraint. Equally, what is reported as a demand constraint may in reality reflect a lack of cost-competitiveness. It is at least plausible, however, that growth in firms in Hertfordshire and Leicestershire was adversely affected by a decline in local industrial customers.

**Table 7.23. Percentage of firms citing shortage
of demand as a constraint on growth**

	Not important	Important	Very important	Total
Northern Ireland	68	18	14	100
Wearside	60	20	20	100
Leicestershire	54	16	30	100
Hertfordshire	25	18	30	100

Source: NIERC Small Firm Growth Survey
Note: Total number of Firms 174

Conclusion

Firms in Northern Ireland and Wearside grew faster over the period 1986–90 than firms in Leicestershire and, especially, Hertfordshire. This north-south contrast was observed whether growth was measured in terms of employment or turnover. It was true for both the population of firms in each area and for the samples undertaken for this study.

A range of significant differences were observed in the factors known to contribute to growth in turnover. Each of the four study areas displayed advantages in some of the variables described in Chapter 4 and disadvantages in others. The overall impact was however self-cancelling and the factors considered in this study did not, in aggregate, account for much of the observed growth contrast between areas. It was suggested that the wide regional differences in costs of land and labour were primarily responsible for the growth contrasts in small firms between areas. These costs widened during the credit boom of the 1980s. Therefore, the discussion in Chapter 4 which sought to model the process of small firm growth does not appear to be potentially helpful in explaining the *actual* regional differential in the growth performance of small firms.

However, this conclusion should not be interpreted as undermining the value of the overall model presented in Chapter 4, but rather re-emphasises the complexity of unravelling the determinants of small firm growth. Our preferred equation in Chapter 4 explained 51 per cent of the variance in growth, while controlling for region. All the regional dummies were positive, and, in the case of Northern Ireland, significant, thus indicating that there were regional factors associated with an explanation of small firm growth. It is simply the case that in the preferred model there were other variables (e.g. **markres**) which were more important. The analysis in this chapter has moved the discussion beyond the parameters of the model to help explain the *actual* differences in growth across the regions.

In conclusion, it is worth re-stating that the study was not designed to investigate the observed regional differences in small firm growth, but rather to assess the importance of factors within small firms to the growth process – namely the characteristics of the owner-manager and business strategy. We have clearly shown the significance of these factors and how they impact across each of the four study areas.

CHAPTER 8

Constraints to Small Firm Growth

Introduction

A number of studies have established that a significant proportion of small firms have growth as an objective but are held back by constraints to growth (ACOST 1990; DTI 1991). These constraints may be either internal to the firm, such as a lack of management time, or external, such as shortages of finance and difficulties in recruiting personnel with the appropriate skills.

Among the survey respondents 121 owner-managers (69.5%) stated that they had a definite intention to grow over the period 1986–90. These 121 respondents were evenly divided between the three growth categories: 39 (32.2%) were fast-growth firms, 41 (33.8%) were slower growing firms and the remaining 41 (33.8%) had remained static or declined. Overall, 93 per cent of the fast-growth firms (39 firms) indicated that they had aimed to grow in the study period, compared to just two-thirds of firms in the other two growth categories. It is thus clear that firms experienced constraints to growth irrespective of the scale of growth achieved in the period 1986–90. The nature and extent of these constraints are the subject of this chapter. It should also be remembered that our sample of firms had been in operation for at least 10 years at the time of interview and, therefore, any analysis of the constraints to growth will not have been inhibited by the difficulties of start-up.

As was pointed out in Chapter 4, an obvious difficulty in any examination of the constraints to growth is the possibility of *ex post* rationalisation by the owner-manager of the survey firm. For example, an owner-manager might state that an external shortage of demand had constrained the growth of the company when in fact the constraint could have been the result of a range of internal factors, such as production difficulties, quality of the product or indeed the price of the product.

Furthermore, there is the added problem that the various constraints may only become operable at a certain growth rate. Faster growing firms will, for instance, be more acutely aware of difficulties of adaptation to rapid change compared to those firms that are growing more slowly. The question of causality is a complex one in these circumstances and it should not be simply assumed that a set of constraining factors determine a particular rate of growth. Nevertheless, the analysis of declared constraints, if carefully interpreted, provides considerable insight into the process of growth in small firms and the nature of policy aimed at stimulating faster growth.

In Chapter 4 it was seen that – even controlling for the effects of sector, region and entrepreneurial characteristics – lack of demand was an important influence on small firm growth. Chapter 7 indicated a degree of regional variation in this factor.

Constraints to Growth

The factors influencing the growth of small firms are many, complex and interrelated. The owner-managers were asked to consider 18 possible constraints and to indicate their importance in preventing the firm from meeting its business objectives in the period 1986–90. The importance of each of the factors was measured on a simple three point scale with a score of '3' indicating it had been a very important influence, '2' important and '1' not important. Thus, the closer the overall mean score for each factor was to 3, the more important the majority of owner-managers found it to be as a constraint to growth. Each owner-manager was presented with a list of possible constraints by the interviewers. It seems likely that this list was comprehensive since no other constraints emerged from the general discussion in the interviews.

The mean scores for each of the potential constraints to growth are presented in Table 8.1. The fact that the highest mean score was only 1.8 indicates that the majority of those firms responding did not find any of the factors listed of great importance in constraining growth. In the light of this result it is perhaps not surprising that in general the 'constraint to growth' set of variables do not emerge as a major influence in the multivariate model of small firm growth presented in Chapter 4.

Before discussing the results in detail there are a number of qualifications that should be noted. First, the low value of the mean scores might result from the fact that the period under investigation (1986–90) was one of overall growth in the UK economy and, therefore, the majority of the small firms in this survey simply did not find themselves constrained in any significant way. Second, as noted above, slow-growing or declining firms simply do not experience the constraints to growth to the same degree as faster growing firms. Therefore, the fact that there were only 42 fast-growth firms (24%) included in the survey might have served to deflate the mean scores for the sample as a whole. Third, it should be remembered that we were not seeking information on the current operating environment of the firm but rather over the specific period 1986–90. Asking retrospective questions in this way runs the risk that owner-managers might forget or otherwise downplay the importance of a range of possible constraints to growth and thus the mean scores do not exceed 2.0.

Table 8.1. Constraints to growth

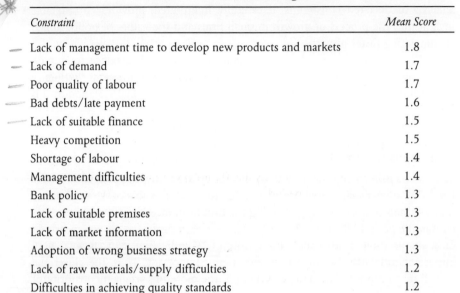

Constraint	Mean Score
Lack of management time to develop new products and markets	1.8
Lack of demand	1.7
Poor quality of labour	1.7
Bad debts/late payment	1.6
Lack of suitable finance	1.5
Heavy competition	1.5
Shortage of labour	1.4
Management difficulties	1.4
Bank policy	1.3
Lack of suitable premises	1.3
Lack of market information	1.3
Adoption of wrong business strategy	1.3
Lack of raw materials/supply difficulties	1.2
Difficulties in achieving quality standards	1.2
Equipment problems	1.2
Lack of finance information	1.1
Lack of product information	1.1
Lack of process information	1.1

Source: NIERC Small Firm Growth Survey

Despite these caveats some interesting results have emerged from the analysis. From Table 8.1 we can see that the most important perceived constraint was a lack of management time to develop new products and markets (mean score 1.8). Forty firms (23% of the total 174 survey respondents) indicated that this had been a very important constraint (score 3) to their growth intentions. This clearly reflects the problems experienced by small firms in the sample run by a single owner-manager who found that a lack of human resources prevented them from taking advantage of potential growth opportunities. However, the extent to which this reflects the difficulties in recruiting appropriate management staff (the external constraint) or the reluctance of the owner-manager to involve others in his or her business (the internal constraint) is unclear from the survey responses.

Lack of demand and **problems with the quality of labour** were also of some importance with each achieving mean scores of 1.7. These constraints clearly indicate that there are aspects of the external environment which had an adverse effect on the performance of some of the small businesses in our sample in the late 1980s. Overall, 42 firms (24%) stated that a lack of demand in their market segment had been a very important constraint to growth while just under one-fifth

(34 firms) indicated that the poor quality of labour had also seriously affected growth (score 3).

The issue of **bad debts/late payment**, which has traditionally been a common complaint of the small business sector, also emerged from the analysis of the constraints to growth in the late 1980s (mean score 1.6). Twenty-eight firms (16%) stated that this had been a very important factor affecting growth in the 1986–90 period. Again this indicates that a major constraint to growth lay, at least partially, outside the control of the firm, and, more importantly, with the attitudes towards invoice payment of the large firms and organisations in the private and public sectors. Furthermore, the role of the banks in this situation has been critical as they, more often than not, are the final arbiters of survival or closure in an acute cash-flow crisis. It is indeed most likely that the onset of the recession in late 1989, towards the end of our study period, had begun to highlight this particular factor even more than usual. Somewhat surprisingly, however, in these circumstances **bank policy** as a factor constraining growth only received a low mean score of 1.3. The intense competition between banks in the late 1980s, and the aggressive lending that this produced, could well explain this finding.

Finally, two other important factors constraining growth can be identified from Table 8.1 (p.128). These are: **lack of suitable finance** and **competition** (both recording mean scores of 1.5). The former reflects the inability to attract the appropriate level and type of finance in order to embark upon projects designed to stimulate growth. This may either reflect a toughening attitude on the part of the providers of finance in an economic downturn (i.e. late 1989–90), or else indicate internal inefficiencies (e.g. a lack of competitiveness or managerial competency) which generally make lenders unwilling to advance the appropriate financial package. For obvious reasons it was difficult to ascertain from our discussions with the 27 owner-managers, who stated that this had been a very important constraint to growth, the precise interpretation of this constraint.

The 22 firms who indicated that **competition** was a very important constraint may well have been accurately describing the strongly-competitive nature of their particular market segment in both domestic and export markets. In other words, they had done everything possible to achieve growth but were simply prevented from doing so by the number of competitors in the market-place. Equally, they may have been seeking, in their response to the question, to disguise the fact that the strongly competitive market-place had exposed some fundamental weaknesses *within* the firm in terms of, for example, management capability, quality of the product, pricing policy or marketing strategy. We have no way of assessing the relative importance of these interpretations at this stage.

The above analysis has underlined one of the major problems for the small firm in achieving growth, namely that of the management resources available to the owner-manager. Allied to the general constraint of **management difficulties** (mean score 1.4) this would tend to point to some sort of growth constraint, not dissimilar to that identified by Penrose (1959), and which points to a general problem associated with the role and competence of senior management in the small firm. Unlike most of the other factors listed, which reflect – on the whole but not exclusively – external factors and influences on the firm, these internal constraints can perhaps be addressed more effectively by a more individualistic (firm-specific) approach to the operation of small firm policy.

Constraints to Growth and Firm Growth Rates

The analysis and discussion on the constraints to small firm growth can be taken further by disaggregating the mean score analysis in terms of the three growth categories used throughout this study: fast-growth, slower growing and static/declining firms. The results are presented in Tables 8.2a and 8.2b.

Table 8.2a. Constraints facing fast growth firms

Constraint	Mean Score
Lack of management time to develop new products and markets	1.9
Poor quality of labour	1.8
Bad debts/late payment	1.7
Management difficulties	1.6
Lack of suitable finance	1.6

Source: NIERC Small Firm Growth Survey

Table 8.2b. Constraints facing static or declining firms

Constraint	Mean Score
Lack of demand	2.0
Heavy competition	1.6
Shortage of labour	1.6
Poor quality of labour	1.6
Bad debts/late payment	1.6
Lack of management time to develop new products and markets	1.6

Source: NIERC Small Firm Growth Survey

Constraints Facing Fast Growth Firms

While it is clear that all respondents complained that **lack of management time** was a constraint to growth, it is also apparent that this was more important in fast growing firms (Table 8.2a). In fact, this was cited as the most important constraint facing these firms. The issue here was the time necessary to collect and analyse market and technological information. There are important policy implications which arise with respect to this group of firms. Attention should be focused on how best to help owner-managers overcome this constraint without creating unwieldy management structures or jeopardising the independence of the owner.

It is also clear that the owner-managers of fast growing firms felt that staffing problems held back the firm's progress. Owner-managers of fast growing firms cited **poor quality of labour** more often than did other firms. Similarly, they also more commonly cited **management difficulties** as a constraint. There was a particular contrast between fast growing and declining/static firms in the frequency with which management difficulties were mentioned. It seems most likely that firms who were not growing were under less pressure to change and hence posed fewer challenges to the capabilities of owner-managers or to the relationships between owner-managers in the case of firms with more than one owner.

Finally, fast growing firms, not surprisingly, experienced more problems with finance. The complaint of **lack of suitable finance** was, as expected, most common among fast-growth firms. Difficulties over **bad debts** were also more common among these firms but the contrast was slight. This is clearly a problem experienced by most firms irrespective of the rate of growth.

Constraints Facing Declining or Static Firms

Some of the problems facing fast growing firms also pose difficulties for all other companies in the sample. However, a **lack of demand** and **heavy competition** were more commonly cited as constraints by declining/static firms than by faster growers. While **lack of demand** may be disguising other difficulties the possibility remains that this was indeed a major constraint retarding the growth of a number of firms. In these cases firms may have been unable to develop new products or new markets to overcome the lack of demand for their main products. Others may have faced temporary or cyclical downturns in demand. What is certainly unclear is the extent to which a genuine lack of demand represents bad luck as opposed to poor judgement or lack of foresight. Answers to such questions were beyond the scope of this study, but there is no reason to believe that, at least in some cases, unpredictable shifts in demand formed genuinely external constraints which could not be overcome in the short period of time covered in this study.

Similarly, in the case of **heavy competition** it was unclear whether this was a subjective judgement (in the sense that almost any competition might be too much). The alternative was an unpredictable increase in competition, which once again could not be effectively countered over a short period of time.

Static or declining firms were also slightly more prone to citing a shortage of labour as a constraint. This could indicate a lack of suitable labour and may well reflect the quality of skills and training in the local labour market. It was, however, the faster growing firms which complained more of the quality of labour, and also of **difficulties in meeting quality standards**. Very few static or declining firms had this problem. This may indicate that their products were of indifferent or unchallenging quality, or, perhaps more plausibly, that they were making fewer efforts to improve the quality of their products.

One possible general interpretation of these results is of cautious and unchanging firms in well-established and competitive markets in which demand for the product was slow growing or declining. Not all static or declining firms would, however, fit into this profile. Many such firms experienced a lack of management time and others may have been affected by genuinely external difficulties such as local labour shortages or unpredictable changes in demand.

Constraints to Growth: the Regional Dimension

To what extent is there a regional dimension to the nature of the constraints to growth experienced by small firms in the period 1986–90? Table 8.3 presents the six most important constraints for each of the four regions. It should be remembered that the mean scores for all the constraint variables were low and, therefore, any regional differences must not be unduly exaggerated. Although there are some differences in the order, there was a general consistency across the regions regarding the nature of the constraints to growth. **Lack of management time to develop new products and markets, lack of demand, poor quality labour, heavy competition** and **bad debts/late payment** were the common constraints in all the regions.

With respect to the relative importance of the constraints, **lack of demand** was marginally more important in Hertfordshire and Leicestershire than in the other two regions. This may well reflect the general difficulty that small firms face in generating sufficient demand for the products in more central market locations. The issue of **bad debts/late payment** was slightly more prominent in Leicestershire than in the other regions, but the explanation for this was not obvious from the survey. **Lack of management time to develop new products and markets** emerged as the most important constraint in Northern Ireland and Hertfordshire. In the case of Northern Ireland this may partly reflect the higher proportion of fast-growth firms in the sample (see Table 8.2a, p.129).

Turning to the constraints which are not common to all the regions, some interesting points emerge. First, **lack of suitable finance** was relatively more important in Wearside and Leicestershire than in the other two regions. This could reflect the poorly developed small firm policy framework in these areas compared to Northern Ireland, or the lack of proximity to the providers of private sector finance when compared to Hertfordshire in the South East region. Barkham (1989), in his study of small firm growth, also uncovered – at least anecdotal – evidence that banks had highly restrictive lending practices in parts of the North East. Second, **shortage of labour** was relatively more important in Hertfordshire than elsewhere, which can be understood in terms of the 'tight' labour markets of the South East in general, and for small firms in particular. Finally, general

Table 8.3. Constraints to growth in the regions

Constraint	Mean Score
Northern Ireland	
Lack of management time	1.8
Poor quality labour	1.7
Heavy competition	1.6
Management difficulties	1.6
Bad debts/late payment	1.6
Lack of demand	1.5
Hertfordshire	
Lack of management time	1.9
Lack of demand	1.8
Poor quality labour	1.6
Bad debts/late payment	1.5
Shortage of labour	1.5
Heavy competition	1.4
Wearside	
Poor quality labour	1.9
Lack of suitable finance	1.7
Lack of demand	1.6
Lack of management time	1.6
Bad debts/late payment	1.5
Heavy competition	1.4
Leicestershire	
Bad debts/late payment	1.8
Lack of demand	1.8
Lack of management time	1.7
Poor quality labour	1.6
Heavy competition	1.6
Lack of suitable finance	1.5

Source: NIERC Small Firm Growth Survey

management difficulties were acknowledged by Northern Ireland firms as being a particular constraint to growth. The issue here was the ability to recruit managers of sufficient experience and competence within the rather 'closed' and 'skill denuded' regional labour market.

Constraints Facing Fast-Growth Firms in the Regions

Table 8.4 presents data on the three most important constraints to growth for fast-growth firms in each of the regions. There is a clear regional pattern to the nature of the constraints recorded by this group of firms. In general, financial constraints were more important in Wearside and Leicestershire than in the other two regions where the constraints related to **labour market issues, lack of management time, competition and lack of suitable premises**. Perhaps not surprisingly, the issue of industrial space was raised by fast-growth firms in Hertfordshire and was combined with the strong threat from competitors. In Northern Ireland, the issue for these firms was one of difficulty in obtaining skilled operatives and management personnel.

Table 8.4. Constraints facing fast-growth firms in the regions
(top three for each region)

Constraints	Mean Score
Northern Ireland	
Poor quality labour	2.1
Lack of management time	2.0
Management difficulties	1.9
Hertfordshire	
Lack of management time	2.3
Heavy competition	1.7
Lack of suitable finance	1.7
Wearside	
Lack of suitable finance	2.4
Bank policy	2.0
Bad debts/late payment	1.8
Poor quality labour	1.8
Leicestershire	
Bad debts/late payment	2.0
Lack of suitable finance	1.8
Heavy competition	1.7

Source: NIERC Small Firm Growth Survey

There is some evidence to suggest, therefore, that whilst fast-growth firms overall do have some difficulty in gaining access to the appropriate finance, there is a clear regional dimension to the problem. Further, more detailed research into the precise nature of the problem in Wearside and Leicestershire is clearly warranted. As noted above, we are much more confident in explaining the *absence* of the problem in Northern Ireland and Hertfordshire than we are in explaining it for the other two regions.

Constraints Facing Declining or Static Firms in the Regions

As Table 8.5 clearly shows, there was one constraint which affected the declining/static group of firms across the regions, namely, **lack of demand**. Labour market constraints and competition constituted the majority of the other factors in Northern Ireland, Hertfordshire and Wearside. Leicestershire was somewhat different in that the issue of **bad debts/late payment** was mentioned along with the **lack of management time to develop new products and markets**.

Table 8.5. Constraints facing static/declining firms in the regions (top three in each region)

Constraint	Mean Score
Northern Ireland	
Lack of demand	1.8
Shortage of labour	1.8
Heavy competition	1.8
Hertfordshire	
Lack of demand	2.0
Shortage of labour	1.7
Poor quality of labour	1.7
Wearside	
Lack of demand	2.4
Poor quality of labour	2.0
Heavy competition	2.0
Leicestershire	
Lack of demand	2.0
Bad debts/late payment	1.8
Lack of management time	1.6

Source: NIERC Small Firm Growth Survey

Conclusion

The analysis in Chapter 4 indicated that in the preferred model the only constraint to be statistically significantly associated with lack of growth is lack of demand. However, an analysis of the perceived constraints to small business development, reported above, is useful because it illustrates the way in which small businessmen operate and gives insight into regional variations in the small business operating environment. Of particular value is the way in which the analysis has highlighted the differences between fast-growth and slower growing companies in the constraints they perceive as important.

Importantly, there is little perception of a capital constraint to growth. This confirms the points made in Chapter 6 about finance and somewhat diminishes the propaganda of small business organisations on this issue. That lack of management time to develop new products and markets is cited by fast growing firms as an important constraint indicates that policy makers should focus on reinforcing successful small firms by providing help in the area of market and product information. Measures designed to improve the effective management of the firm, as opposed to merely seeking to expand the size and scope of the management team, would seem to be of some importance in this context. Access to quality information on new products and markets was seen by growth-oriented owner-managers as critical in enabling them to implement the most appropriate business strategy for survival and growth. Lack of quality labour is a difficult constraint for small firm policy makers to respond to since the answer lies in a general improvement in the education and skill levels of the UK workforce. It is difficult to interpret demand as a constraint, but, as mentioned in Chapter 4, this probably picks up market trends operating at a subsectoral level and indicates that whatever the characteristics of the firm, the external environment is an important influence on growth.

CHAPTER 9

Conclusion

The Regional Context

The growth of small firms is an important issue for economic development. Study after study has shown that small firms have made a disproportionately large contribution to economic growth over recent decades. The motivation for this study is the impact which expanding small firms can make to the development of peripheral regions. In particular, a detailed study of one of Europe's most peripheral regions, Northern Ireland, had shown that small firms were contributing far less to growth than were similar firms in some more centrally located regions. To explain why this was the case required an understanding of the factors influencing the growth of small firms. To our surprise the international literature on this important subject was patchy, and frankly, inadequate. As a result, we designed our own study, the subject of this book, to shed light on the factors accounting for the large differences in growth between individual small firms. This, in turn, was intended to help us understand the lagging growth of small firms in Northern Ireland and, perhaps, also in other peripheral regions.

In one of the swings of fortune which sometimes occur in research, we discovered, again to our surprise, in the course of the study, that Northern Ireland's small firms had improved their growth performance. In the early study (Gudgin *et al.* 1989) Northern Ireland had lagged far behind Leicestershire, the non-peripheral control area, over the period 1973–86. In the current study, undertaken over the shorter period 1986–90, small firms in Northern Ireland grew rapidly, easily outperforming those in the two non-peripheral English counties selected as controls. This intriguing reversal made it even more important to understand the influences on growth, particularly as it opened up the possibility that the improvement in Northern Ireland may have been influenced by government policy, achieved through the very active small firms agency, the Local Enterprise Development Unit (LEDU).

Influences on the Growth of Small Firms

This study of small firms was conducted at two levels. Information on employment growth was collected for several thousand small firms in four areas across the UK. These were selected to include both central areas (Hertfordshire, Leicestershire) and peripheral areas (Wearside, Northern Ireland). A carefully selected sample of fast growing, slower growing, and declining firms was drawn from this database to form the core of an intensive interview survey. In all, 174 firms were interviewed, resulting in a survey base of 240 variables. Of these responses, 138 were judged sufficiently comprehensive, detailed, and accurate enough for a multivariate (regression) analysis.

The selection of variables was based on the three-part distinction introduced by Storey (1994). In brief, the approach distinguishes between the characteristics of the entrepreneur (owner-manager), the salient characteristics of the company (size, location, product group), and the business strategies adopted by the management. On top of these, a fourth set of influences are constraints to growth including both those internal to the company (e.g. management time) and external (e.g. fluctuations in demand).

Particular interest in this study was focused on the characteristics of the owner-manager. This was, in part, because these characteristics were judged to be important, often underlying differences between companies in management strategy, but also because they are highly relevant to policy questions of 'picking winners' or, more prosaically, focusing the limited resources of small firms' agencies on the companies with the best potential to respond.

The approach worked well, and the key result of the study is an equation including 19 statistically significant variables. This equation accounts for half of the huge variation in growth of turnover across the sample of 138 companies. Even over a short four-year period some companies quadruple their size while others shrink by half. Much of this variation reflects random factors that are unlikely to be explicable in a systematic, statistical, fashion. A single equation accounting for half of the between-company variation is certainly better than has previously been achieved. It may well prove difficult to raise the proportion of variation explained much beyond one half, but only future research will reveal this.

Characteristics of the Owner-Manager

The influence of a number of variables in the model describing the characteristics of owner-managers confirmed the view that the characteristics of individuals do play an important role in the performance of the business. The following list of characteristics were significantly associated with faster growing companies:

- **age**, younger owner-managers tended to have faster growing firms

- **shared ownership**, i.e. the presence and influence of other owners led to accelerated growth
- **multi-ownership**, owner-managers with several (related or unrelated) businesses had faster growing companies
- **membership of a professional organisation** by the owner-manager, e.g. the Chartered Institute of Engineers.

Some of the variables are interchangeable with alternative possibilities, but they provide insights, or perhaps glimpses, into the types of people likely to run faster growing companies. These will tend to be younger than average, and entrepreneurial in the sense of aiming to run several businesses – often in unrelated areas. Some aspects of technical competence are directly important, especially when this competence is in applied sciences and associated with professional applications. Straightforward academic qualifications do not clearly enhance growth in the same way as membership of professional organisations. Finally, those willing to work in groups of owners, often with complementary skills, also tend to have faster growing firms.

Business Strategies

The study examined a wide range of business strategies and among these a limited number stood out as being clearly associated with more rapid growth in turnover over the four-year period. These, in turn, can be divided into two categories: business aims and business methods. The business aims were conceptually those in place at the start of the period. However, the survey method meant that respondents were asked at the end of the period to recall what these had been. This may involve a degree of *ex post* rationalisation, but the wide range of answers suggests that this was not so large a problem as to invalidate these variables. Faster growing firms were those in which the owners aimed to:

- **increase profits** (as opposed to turnover, assets, employment)
- **increase profit margins**
- **focus on marketing** as a business strategy
- **improve the production process**.

While these aims might appear obvious, most of them were shared by only a minority of firms. In particular, only a small minority of firms aimed to increase profit margins, but most of those who specified this as a key aim were those with very rapidly growing firms. The aim of improving margins suggests a degree of professionalism not obviously displayed in the majority of firms. The conscious aim to focus on a marketing-led strategy was shared by only a third of companies, but these firms had a high average growth.

The strategies used to realise these aims were similarly varied. Those significantly associated with more rapid growth in output were:

- active engagement in **market research**
- **selling directly to the customer** (avoiding use of selling agents)
- **seeking external capital** (whether successful or not)
- **product innovation**
- **concentrating on a few main products** (avoidance of product diversity)
- **investment in new machinery** as a strategy for improving the production process.

Once again, marketing and selling strategies emerged clearly in the analysis. Those firms which undertook formal market research projects clearly grew faster. At the other end of the spectrum, firms which increased the distance between themselves and their customers, by selling through agents, fared poorly.

Those owner-managers who undertook market research and product innovation tended to be better educated. Often they were graduates. However, it appeared to be the strategy which was of key importance rather than the qualification. For instance, non-graduates, or even those with no formal qualifications, did just as well as long as they engaged in market research and/or product innovation. However, the evidence is that less well-educated owner-managers were significantly less likely to do so. Education thus matters, but in an indirect way, and the disadvantage of poorer education can be overcome by those who adopt similar strategies to graduates.

Company Characteristics

A number of company characteristics including size, age, location, and product group were included within the study – mainly to control for unobserved external influences on growth. Only company size emerged as a consistently significant influence. This accords with many other studies which show that it is more difficult to achieve rapid growth in a larger company. A number of explanations may account for this, but, as a fact of life, it is virtually always present. The only locational variable to remain significant in the multivariate analysis was Northern Ireland. Other locations were not significantly different from one another. Northern Ireland was probably differentiated by its lower production costs and the more generous availability of financial and other assistance from government. Finally, none of the product groups was found to be a significant influence on growth. Firms were as likely to grow rapidly in any one industry as in any other, irrespective of the aggregate growth of the industry as a whole. This result probably reflects the fact that small firms operate in niche markets which are not representative of wide product groups. The product groups would have to be defined very narrowly for them to become influential on an analysis of this type.

Regional Disparities in Small Firm Growth

Although motivated by concerns over regional disparities in the growth of small firms, this study was not specifically designed to investigate growth differences between regions. However, the inclusion of a range of locational conditions makes it possible to describe the differences in growth between the four study areas, and to go some way towards accounting for them. The differences between areas were known to be large using evidence on employment growth from databases which included almost all small manufacturing firms in each area. The interview survey confirmed the regional differences in employment growth and showed that the disparities in growth of output were even larger. Firms in Wearside, and especially Northern Ireland, expanded their output by around 80 per cent, a rate of growth double that in Leicestershire or Hertfordshire. It also quickly became clear that the growth factors identified in this study did not themselves account for the regional disparities. Some of the growth-inducing factors were clearly more in evidence in some areas and not others, but each area tended to have a balance of favourable or unfavourable factors. Any one area like Northern Ireland might have advantages in several factors, and disadvantages in others, and these tended to balance out leaving the area no better off.

For instance, the comparison of Northern Ireland with each of the other three areas revealed a number of advantages. Northern Ireland's chief advantages were having owner-managers who:

- were relatively younger than elsewhere
- attached greater importance to marketing
- had a greater likelihood to undertake formal market research
- had greater success in obtaining external finance
- were more profit-orientated.

The patterns of disadvantage displayed by Northern Ireland firms were more diverse. Small firms were disadvantaged partly because of the characteristics of the owner-managers, and their lower tendency to form teams. In Northern Ireland small firms were less likely than elsewhere to have:

- multiple owners
- owners with interests in other businesses
- owners who are members of professional organisations.

Other disadvantages include:

- the heavy use of agents to sell their products
- a more diverse product range
- a slightly larger initial size.

These advantages and disadvantages tend to affect each other and account, in aggregate, for very little of the growth gap in small firms between Northern Ireland

and elsewhere. The same can be said for comparisons between the other areas. Although there are significant differences between regions in the characteristics of firms, owners and strategies, the differences identified in this study tend to offset one another in every case. Therefore, other factors are needed to explain the *actual* gap in the performance of small firms across the regions.

Why is it, for instance, that Northern Ireland should have had the fastest growing small firms between 1986 and 1990 and Hertfordshire the slowest? The most plausible explanation was likely to be related to the widening gap in operating costs (wages and rent) which occurred between the UK regions in the late 1980s, even though there is little evidence from the survey that firms in the areas of high wage costs experienced more problems attracting labour.

A demand constraint was also identified by more firms operating in southern or midland England. This might itself be caused by higher costs and prices. It might also reflect the poor performance of larger companies in southern England, leading to slow growth in local industrial markets for small firms. The poorer performance of the larger firms was itself likely to be associated with higher costs in southern England during this period.

Constraints to Growth

When asked about the constraints to growth the owner-managers in the survey did not identify any one factor which had seriously impeded firm growth in the 1986–90 period. Lack of demand was the only constraint to emerge from the multivariate analysis of growth, but this only affects a particular group of small firms within the sample.

Differences emerged in the nature of the constraints identified by fast growing firms compared to the group of static/declining firms. The owner-managers of fast growing firms were more likely to cite lack of management time, general management difficulties and poor quality of labour whereas static/declining firms complained of a lack of demand and heavy competition as the constraining factors on growth.

At a regional level there was a broad similarity between the nature of the constraints mentioned. However, some small differences did emerge. Lack of demand was slightly more important in Hertfordshire and Leicestershire than in the other two regions. Lack of suitable finance was cited more often by owner-managers in Wearside and Leicestershire as a factor effecting growth. Finally, shortage of labour was given greater importance in Hertfordshire.

There was a clear regional variation in the constraints facing fast-growth firms. Financial constraints were more important to fast-growth firms in Wearside and Leicestershire. Conversely, fast-growth firms in Northern Ireland and Hertfordshire raised labour market issues, lack of management time, competition and lack of suitable premises as important constraints.

Policy Implications

Economic development agencies in many parts of the world seek to intervene in the private sector to accelerate growth. The intense competition to attract a limited pool of mobile multi-national company projects has led to a focus on indigenous firms. Many of the latter are small firms. Small firms can be helped in many and various ways and most countries have a raft of policies aimed to assist them. In the UK the range of policies to assist small firms began to increase in the 1970s and especially during the 'enterprise decade' of the 1980s. Many policies aim, for example, to facilitate the access of small firms to low-cost capital. Others have eased the burden of regulation. Local authorities tend to concentrate on the provision of inexpensive industrial premises, while many local agencies offer a wide range of support and advice.

Such policies are particularly well developed in peripheral areas of high unemployment. In Northern Ireland such assistance is long established, well financed, and centrally organised in a relatively well funded small firms agency, LEDU. Public spending on small firms in manufacturing and export services has averaged £1000 per annum for each employee over recent years.

The influence of LEDU is likely to be one cause of the fact that Northern Ireland has become characterised by faster growing small firms. This influence may also be apparent in the list of strengths and weaknesses in the previous section. The weaknesses tend to be in entrepreneurial characteristics, which are inherently difficult to influence. In contrast, the strengths are often in business strategies. It is precisely in these respects that LEDU has been active, often providing grants for such things as market research and Research and Development as well as providing advice and creating an ethos of managerial improvement.

The policy issue which stems from this study is whether an improved understanding of company growth can make public intervention more effective, in the sense of either producing faster growth or reducing the costs of intervention. One message which emerges clearly from the study is the importance of marketing and selling methods. This conclusion will be well known to many who work with small firms. This study confirms its importance and suggests that small firms agencies should accord it a key role. The evidence of this study may also be that a cost-effective approach is to support better educated managers since they are more likely to adopt growth-enhancing strategies including market research. This is not, however, completely clear and the opposite conclusion is also worth investigating. In this case, agencies would concentrate on advising less well-educated managers of the value of market research.

The value of product innovation emerges less clearly from the study. This may be because the nature and significance of individual innovations was not measured with sufficient precision. There is some evidence that product innovation accelerates growth, and it seems commonsensical to believe this. However, the evidence is weak and may suggest that the resources available to many small firms for

Research and Development are either insufficient for complete success, or else lead to a depletion of time or resources in other aspects of the business.

Contrary to the general perception among the small firm lobby, there was only partial evidence to suggest that access to capital was a major constraint to growth for small firms. Fast-growth firms in Wearside and Leicestershire appeared to be constrained in this way although the precise reasons were not apparent from the survey and, therefore, detailed policy prescription cannot be made. Policy measures designed to improve the effective management of fast-growth small firms would seem important, given the frequency with which 'lack of management time' was identified as a constraint to growth.

One important application of research on the growth of small firms is in prediction. If small firms agencies are able to predict which firms are likely to grow and which are not, this increases the sophistication of any subsequent intervention. They can choose, for instance, whether to concentrate their resources on a small subset of firms with growth potential. Alternatively, they can focus on those firms which are less likely to succeed without intervention. In either case, the impact of assistance from government agencies may be small or large, and needs to be directly evaluated.

The results of this study should help government agencies and others to identify the firms most likely to grow. However, much further work is needed to test the results in different circumstances. What is also needed next is an *a priori* study which predicts growth using equations like those of Chapter 4, and tests the validity of the predictions. The results of such a study would help to distinguish those statistical associations which are truly causal from those which are merely coincidental.

Appendix

NIERC Small Business Questionnaire

Section 1: Classification and Ownership Details

1. When was this business started?

    Year _____

2. What is the legal status now?

    _____

3. Using revenue generation as the measure, list your products in order of importance.
    Please give the approximate contribution of each to total sales revenue.

    i _____% [   ]

    ii _____% [   ]

    iii _____% [   ]

    iv _____% [   ]

    v _____% [   ]

    vi _____% [   ]

4. a) If the firm is a limited Company: what percentage of the firm's shares do you own?

    % [   ]

    Are there any other major stockholders, and do they exert any influence on the running of the firm? (What kind of influence do they exert?)

    yes / no

    If yes, would you mind if we talked to them?

    If not, who are they, and how long have they been involved with the firm?

    i name _____ age _____ since _____

    ii name _____ age _____ since _____

    iii name _____ age _____ since _____

4. b) If the firm is a Partnership: how many partners are there, what are their ages, and how long they have been involved with the firm? Is there a dominant partner?

    Number of partners   [   ]

    Dominant partner   yes / no

    i name _____ age _____ since _____

    ii name _____ age _____ since _____

5. Do the owners or the partners of the firm have ownership interests in other
    businesses?

    yes / no

    If yes, would you be willing or able to tell us what these are?

6. Do these outside ownership interests present any particular advantages or
    disadvantages to the firm?

    yes / no

    If yes, in what way?

Section 2: Measures of Growth

7. How many people did your firm employ at the following dates? (include management
    and directors).

	MID 1986	MID 1989	MID 1990
FT	[ ]	[ ]	[ ]
PT	[ ]	[ ]	[ ]

8. What was the turnover achieved by the business in the following years (financial year)?

1986	1990
[ ]	[ ]

9. What were the total assets of the business?

1986	1990
[ ]	[ ]

10. What net profit (before tax) did the business achieve in the following years?

1986	1990
[ ]	[ ]

Section 3: Qualifications of Main Decision-maker(s)

This section must include details of the individual or each member of the group running the
firm. (Include 'active' owners and senior managers.)

11. What is the highest qualification achieved by each of the main decision-makers?

    i   name _____qualification _____ course _____

    ii name _____qualification _____ course _____

    iii name _____qualification _____ course _____

12. What qualifications have they obtained while in work? (These need not be work-related but might include technical or professional qualifications)

> Qualification   Date achieved

i   _____   _____

ii _____   _____

iii _____   _____

13. Are any of the main decision-makers members of professional organisations?

yes / no

If yes, please specify:

i   _____

ii _____

iii _____

14. Have you or any of the other main decision-makers ever studied abroad (or outside Northern Ireland)?

yes / no

If yes, where, and for how long? (Please give dates.)

> Institution   Course   From   To

i   _____   _____   _____   _____

ii _____   _____   _____   _____

iii _____   _____   _____   _____

15. Working backwards from the present, including your present post, please give details of your career progression:

	Position	No. of people managed	Activity of firm	Size of firm	Location of firm	Duration of job
i						
ii						
iii						
iv						
etc.						

16. Are there any other senior managers involved in the strategic decision-making process? What are their positions and ages, and how long have they been with the firm?

> Position   Age   Service

i   _____   _____   _____

ii _____   _____   _____

iii _____   _____   _____

Section 4: Motivation of the Main Decision-maker(s)

17. Had you a formal plan for your business in the period 1986–90?

    yes / no

    If yes, could you summarise its contents, and your reasons for preparing the plan?
    (Was it a requirement for obtaining finance?)

    _____

    _____

    _____

    If no, did you have any general objectives for the business during this period? (Was
    there any conflict between the decision-makers over these objectives?)

    _____

    _____

    _____

18. Considering the objectives in the previous questions, what was the company's
    strategy to meet these objectives?

    _____

    _____

    _____

19. Have these objectives been met?

    yes / no

    If no, why not?

    _____

    _____

    _____

20. Did you aim to increase the size of your business over this period (1986–90)?

    yes / no

21. Over the period 1986–90, how important to you were growth in the following?

    NB Please indicate the level of importance on a scale of 1–3
    (1 – not important, 2 – important, 3 – very important)

turnover	[ ]
employment	[ ]
profits	[ ]
total Assets	[ ]

22. Could you realistically have grown faster over the period 1986–90?

yes / no

If yes, why not?

_____

_____

_____

23. Have you ever taken any action to raise capital outside the company?

yes / no

i Institution _____   Result + \ −

ii Institution _____   Result + \ −

iii Institution_____   Result + \ −

24. Has it ever been your objective to go public or to float shares in the business on the Unlisted Securities Market?

yes / no

25. In the last five years, has it ever been your objective to sell the business?

yes / no

If yes, when and why?

_____

_____

_____

Section 5: Business Development Activities

General

26. How many competitors are there for your major product(s) in the principal market you serve?

Product	No. of Competitors
i _____	_____
ii _____	_____
iii _____	_____
iv _____	_____

27. How important have the following been in the survival or growth of your business:

    NB Rank the importance of this on a scale of 1–3
    (1 – not important, 2 – important, 3 – very important)

    development of new products   [   ]

    product diversification   [   ]

    low costs and/or prices   [   ]

    producing high quality product(s)   [   ]

    intensive marketing of product(s)   [   ]

    other factors (please specify)

        i   _____   [   ]

        ii _____   [   ]

Product Development

28. In the past four years have you introduced any new products or made significant
    improvements to those in production? How many? Can you give brief details?

    yes / no

    Number of new or improved products   [   ]

    Details:

    _____

    _____

    _____

29. In the period 1986–90, what percentage of turnover have you spent on developing
    new products? What was the source of the funding?

    Percentage of turnover spent on product development   [   ]

    Sources of funding:

    _____

    _____

    _____

30. How many products have you discontinued in the period 1986–90? What were they?
    Why were they discontinued?

    Number of products discontinued [   ]

        Product   Reason

        i   _____   _____

        ii _____   _____

        iii _____   _____

31. Are any of the following significant sources of information for product development?

NB Rank the importance of this on a scale of 1–3
(1 – not important, 2 – important, 3 – very important)

technical journals   [   ]

trade fairs   [   ]

large firms/small firms (clients, competitors or suppliers)   [   ]

links with education institutions   [   ]

links with government laboratories/agencies   [   ]

trade associations   [   ]

consultants   [   ]

recruiting technical staff   [   ]

Process Development

32. In the past four years, have you significantly improved your production process?

yes / no

If yes:

i   how have you done this (e.g. new machines, new staff, training of staff, reorganisation of work patterns)?

ii how has this been financed?

iii what has been the impact on the business?

iv when did you do it?

Method:

_____

_____

_____

Finance:

_____

_____

_____

Impact:

_____

_____

_____

Dates:

_____   _____   _____   _____

33. In the past four years, have you engaged in research aimed at improving your production process?

yes / no

If yes, what percentage of turnover have you spent?

	1986	1987	1988	1989	1990
%	[ ]	[ ]	[ ]	[ ]	[ ]

34. Are any of the following significant sources of technical information for improving your production process?

NB Rank the importance of this on a scale of 1–3

(1 – not important, 2 – important, 3 – very important)

technical journals	[ ]
machinery suppliers	[ ]
trade fairs	[ ]
large firms/small firms (clients, competitors or suppliers)	[ ]
links with education institutions	[ ]
links with government laboratories/agencies	[ ]
trade associations	[ ]
consultants	[ ]
poaching technical staff	[ ]

Marketing

35. Competitive strategy refers to the main tactics you use to sell your product(s). Two important elements of a sales strategy are price and quality. Could you indicate how important these are to you by placing yourself on the following matrix. Place an X in the appropriate cell.

Product Quality

	Basic Good			Luxury or Sophisticated Good	
	1	2	3	4	5
Low 1					
2					
Price 3					
4					
High 5					

36. Do you actively seek customers?

    yes / no

    If yes, how is this done?

    _____

    _____

    _____

37. What percentage of turnover was spent on advertising budget in the following years?

    | 1986 | 1989 | 1990 |
    | [   ] | [   ] | [   ] |

38. How often have you used a marketing/advertising consultant in the past four years? (Tick appropriate box.)

    Never [   ]   Several times [   ]   An ongoing basis / frequently [   ]

39. Do you use market research?

    yes / no

    If yes, is it done in-house or bought in? How much have you spent per annum in the past four years?

    In-house / bought in _____

    | 1986 | 1987 | 1988 | 1989 | 1990 |
    | [   ] | [   ] | [   ] | [   ] | [   ] |

40. In the past four years, how many trade fairs have you attended?

    Number [   ]

41. Have you had any help from government funds or agencies to improve your marketing?

    yes / no

42. How many sales staff did you employ in the following years?

    | 1986 | 1989 | 1990 |
    | [   ] | [   ] | [   ] |

43. Did you have your own retail or wholesale outlets?

    yes / no

44. Do a small number of important customers usually account for 50 per cent or more of your annual turnover?

    yes / no

    If yes, are these customers the same from year to year?

45. a) What proportion of your output did you sell within Northern Ireland?

      1986   1989   1990

     [   ]   [   ]   [   ]

  b) What proportion of your output in revenue terms did you export (out of UK not just Northern Ireland) in?:

      1986   1989   1990

     [   ]   [   ]   [   ]

NB If company does not export go to 49.

46. How long have you been exporting?

Years   [   ]

47. Was exporting a conscious strategy for the company?

yes / no

48. How do you sell goods overseas?

_____

_____

_____

49. How frequently do employees go overseas on business?

Number of trips per year [   ]

50. Have you made any effort to become an exporter in the previous four years?

yes / no

If yes, what have you done, and how has this prevented you from exporting?

_____

_____

_____

If no, why not?

_____

_____

_____

Section 6: Constraints on Growth

51. Have any of the following, in the period 1986–90, constrained growth in your business?

    NB Rank the importance of this on a scale of 1–3
    (1 – not important, 2 – important, 3 – very important)

    lack of demand for main products/declining markets   [   ]

    shortage of labour   [   ]

    poor quality of labour   [   ]

    lack of suitable finance   [   ]

    bank policy (specify)   [   ]

    heavy competition (home or abroad)   [   ]

    bad debts/late payments   [   ]

    lack of suitable premises   [   ]

    lack of raw materials/supply deficiencies   [   ]

    difficulties in achieving quality standards   [   ]

    management difficulties   [   ]

    equipment problems   [   ]

    lack of management time to develop new products
       and markets   [   ]

    inadequate information on:

            markets (home and abroad)   [   ]

            finance   [   ]

            product technology   [   ]

            process technology   [   ]

    in retrospect wrong business strategy was adopted   [   ]

    NB Please explain in more depth about those you scored three:

    _____

    _____

    _____

    _____

    _____

    _____

52. Has the company entered into any agreements, formal or informal, with other firms (particularly any which limit the size of the market the firm can operate in)?

    NB The respondent may care to consider, as examples, the following before answering:

    i   performance targets set by providers of finance;

    ii licensing arrangements relating to products or machinery;

    iii franchise agreements;

    iv joint marketing, selling or buying arrangements.

    yes / no

    If yes, what type?

    _____

    _____

    _____

53. Have you had any problems in attracting or retaining managers during the last four years?

    yes / no

    If yes, has this constrained the growth of your business?

    yes / no

Bibliography

Advisory Council on Science and Technology (1990) *The Enterprise Challenge: Overcoming the Barriers to Growth in Small Firms*. London: HMSO.

Acs, Z. and Audretsch, D.B. (1990) 'Innovation in large and small firms: an empirical analysis.' *American Economic Review*, September, 78–690.

Barkham, R.J. (1989) *Entrepreneurship, New Firms and Regional Development*. (Unpublished) PhD thesis, University of Reading.

Barreto, H. (1989) *Entrepreneurship in Microeconomic Theory*. London: Routledge.

BDO Stoy Hayward (1995) *Private Company Price Index*, Issue 3. London: BDO Stoy Hayward.

Boswell, J. (1973) *The Rise and Decline of Small Firms*. London: George Allen and Unwin Ltd.

Casson, M.C. (1982) *The Entrepreneur: An Economic Theory*. Oxford: Martin Robertson and Co Ltd.

Chell, E. (1986) 'The entrepreneurial personality: a review and some theoretical developments.' In J. Curran, J. Stanworth and D. Watkins (eds) *The Survival of the Small Firm Vol 1: The Economics of Survival*. Aldershot: Gower.

Chell, E. and Hayworth, J. (1992) 'A typology of business owners and their orientation towards growth.' In Caley *et al.* (eds) *Small Enterprise Developments*. London: Paul Chapman Publishing Ltd.

Churchill, N.C. and Lewis, V.L. (1983) 'The five stages of small business growth.' *Harvard Business Review 61*, 30–50.

Collins, O.F., Moore, D.G. and Unwalla, D.B. (1964) *The Enterprising Man*. East Lansing: Michigan State University Business Studies (Bureau of Business and Economic Research), Graduate School of Business Administration.

Cooper, A.C. and Dunkleberg, W.C. (1986) 'Entrepreneurship and paths to business ownership.' *Strategic Management Journal 7*, 53–68.

Cross, M. (1981) *New Firm Formation and Regional Development*. Farnborough: Gower.

Daly, M., Campbell, M., Robson, G. and Gallagher, C. (1992) 'Job creation 1987–89: preliminary analysis by sector.' *Employment Gazette*, August, 387–92.

Department of Trade and Industry (1991) *Constraints on the Growth of Small Firms*. London: HMSO.

Douglas, E.J. (1993) *Managerial Economics – Analysis and Strategy*. New Jersey: Prentice-Hall International Inc.

Dunne, P. and Hughes, A. (1990) *Age, Size, Growth and Survival: UK Companies in the 1980s*. Working Paper 4, Small Business Research Centre, University of Cambridge.

Evans, D.S. (1987a) 'The relationship between firm growth, size and age: estimate for 100 manufacturing industries.' *Journal of Industrial Economics 35*, 4, June, 567–81.

Evans, D.S. (1987b) 'Tests of alternative theories of firm growth.' *Journal of Political Economy 95*, 657–674.

Gibb, A. and Dyson, J. (1984) 'Stimulating the growth of owner managed firms.' In J. Lewis, J. Stanworth and A. Gibb (eds) *Success and Failure in Small Businesses*. Aldershot: Gower.

Gibb, A. and Ritchie, J. (1981) 'Influences on entrepreneurship: a study over time.' In *Bolton 10 Years On, Proceedings of the UK Small Business Research Conference*, November, 20–21. Polytechnic of Central London.

Gudgin, G., Hart, M., Fagg, J., D'Arcy, E. and Keegan, R. (1989) *Job Creation and Manufacturing Industry, 1973–86, A Comparison of Northern Ireland with the Republic of Ireland and the English Midlands.* Belfast: Northern Ireland Economic Research Centre.

Hall, P. (1985) 'The geography of the fifth Kondratieff.' In P. Hall and A. Markusen (eds) *Silicon Landscapes.* London: George Allen and Unwin Ltd.

Hall, B.H. (1987) 'The relationship between firm size and firm growth in the US manufacturing sector.' *Journal of Industrial Economics 35*, 4, 583–605.

Hart, M., Scott, R., Keegan, R. and Gudgin, G. (1993a) *Job Creation in Small Firms.* Belfast: NIERC.

Hart, M., Harrison, R.T. and Gallagher, C. (1993b) 'Enterprise creation, job generation and regional policy in the UK.' In R.T. Harrison and M. Hart (eds) *Spatial Policy in a Divided Nation.* London: Jessica Kingsley Publishers.

Hart, P.E. and Prais, S.J. (1956) 'The analysis of business concentration: a statistical approach.' *Journal of the Royal Statistical Society 119*, 2, 150–91.

Hitchens, D.M.W.N. and O'Farrel, P.N. (1987) 'Inter regional comparisons of small firms performance: the case of Northern Ireland and South East England.' *Regional Studies 21*, 543–55.

Hitchens, D.M.W.N. and O'Farrell, P.N. (1988a) 'The comparative performance of small manufacturing companies in South Wales and Northern Ireland: an analysis of matched pairs.' *Omega International Journal of Management Services 16*, 5, 429–438.

Hitchens, D.M.W.N. and O'Farrell, P.N. (1988b) 'The comparative performance of small manufacturing companies in the Mid-West and Northern Ireland.' *Economic and Social Review 19*, 3, 177–198.

Humber, S. and Pashigian, P. (1962) 'Firm size and rate of growth.' *Journal of Political Economy 52*, 556–69.

Jovanovic, B. (1982) 'Selection and the evolution of industry.' *Econometrica 50*, 3, May, 649–70.

Kets de Vries, M.F.R. (1977) 'The entrepreneurial personality: a person at the crossroad.' Journal of Management Studies, February, 34–57.

Kirzner, I.M. (1973) *Competition and Entrepreneurship.* Chicago: University of Chicago Press.

Larson, J. and Rogers, E.M. (1984) *Silicon Valley Fever – Growth of High Technology Culture.* London: George Allen and Unwin Ltd.

Leff, N.H. (1979) 'Entrepreneurship and economic development; the problem revisited.' *Journal of Economic Literature 17*, 1, 46–64.

McClelland, D.C. (1961) *The Achieving Society.* Princeton, New Jersey: D Van Norstrand Co Inc.

McKenna, J.F. and Orrit, P.L (1984) 'Small business growth: making a conscious decision.' *S.A.M. Advanced Management Journal*, Spring.

Mason, C.M. and Harrison, R.T. (1991) 'The small firm equity gap since Bolton.' In J. Stoneworth and C. Grey (eds) *Bolton 20 Years On: The Small Firm in the 1990s.* London: Paul Chapman Publishing.

Northern Ireland Economic Research Centre (1992) *Regional Economic Outlook: Analysis and Forecasts for the Standard Planning Regions of the UK. For the years 2000, 2001.* Belfast: NIERC and Oxford Economic Forecasting.

Oakey, R.P., Rothwell, R. and Cooper, S. (1988) *Management of Innovation in High Technology Firms.* London: Pinter Publications.

O'Farrell, P.N. and Hitchens, D.M.W.N. (1988) 'Alternative theories of small firm growth: a critical review.' *Environment and Planning A*, 20, 1365–83.

Penrose, E. (1959) *The Theory of the Growth of the Firm*. Oxford: Basil Blackwell.

Peters, T.J. and Waterman, R.H. (1982) *In Search of Excellence – Lessons from America's Best-Run Companies*. New York: Warner Books.

Porter, M. (1980) *Competitive Strategy*. New York: Free Press.

Reid, G.C. (1993) *Small Business Enterprise: An Economic Analysis*. London: Routledge.

Reid, G.C. and Jacobson, L.R. (1988) *The Small Entrepreneurial Firm*. The David Hume Institute: Aberdeen University Press.

Schluter, M. and Barkham, R. (1985) *Sources and Uses of Capital in Business Start-ups – Results of a Survey to Test the Use of Accountants as a Data Source of the Study of Small Businesses*. Cambridge: The Jubilee Centre.

Schumpeter, J.A. (1934) *The Theory of Economic Development* (trans R Opie), Oxford University Press, Reprint 1969.

Scott, R. and O'Reilly, M. (1993) *Exports of Northern Ireland Manufacturing Companies 1990*. Belfast: NIERC.

Simon, H.A. and Bonini, C.P. (1958) 'The size distribution of business firms.' *American Economic Review 48*, September, 607–17.

Singh, A. and Whittington, G. (1975) 'The size and growth of firms.' *Review of Economic Studies 52*, 15–26.

Smith, N.R. (1967) *The Entrepreneur and his Firm: The Relationship Between Type of Man and Type of Economy*. Illinois: Bureau of Business and Economic Research, Michigan State University.

Smith, N.R. and Miner, J.B. (1983) 'Type of entrepreneur, type of firm, and managerial motivation: implications for organisational life cycle theory.' *Strategic Management Journal 4*, 325–40.

Stanworth, J. and Curran, J. (1976) 'Growth and the small firm: an alternative view.' *Journal of Management Studies 13*, 2, May, 95–110.

Storey, D.J. (1989) 'Firm performance and size: explanations from the small firm sector.' *Small Business Economics 7*, 3.

Storey, D.J. (1994) *Understanding the Small Business Sector*. London: Routledge.

Storey, D.J. and Johnson, S. (1986) *Are Small Firms the Answer to Unemployment?* London: The Employment Institute.

Utton, M.A. (1979) *Diversification and Competition*. Cambridge: Cambridge University Press.

Subject Index

*References in italic indicate
figures or tables.*

Author Index

Regional Policy and Development Series

Series editor Ron Martin, Department of Geography, University of Cambridge

Jessica Kingsley Publishers
116 Pentonville Road, London N1 9JB

Read by Dawn
Volume Two

edited by Adèle Hartley

First published 2007.

Published by Bloody Books®.

9 8 7 6 5 4 3 2 1

Contents

Thanks to Tony Makos, Lara Matthews and John Treadgold for their enthusiasm and imagination.

Adèle Hartley

Sharp Things
Joshua Reynolds

In the ceiling of the subway car, the lights flickered and sparked with each jolt as the car shook from side to side. Shadows swooped and slunk through the car as one end then the other alternated being thrown into semi-darkness by the gallivanting electrical surges. The older man dressed in an assiduously pressed and creased business suit and sitting quietly in the back of the car thought momentarily of one of the old German Expressionistic films of the early Twentieth Century. Slices of light and dark through which the story moved like a fish through a reef.

Louis Roche rubbed his weathered face and tried to ignore the headache clamoring for attention at the base of his forebrain. Too much noise. And the air was too close for him to think properly. He hated New York. America too for that matter. Europe was quieter. Age had brought the Continent a level of civilization, of sophistication that America had yet to reach. And probably never would all things considered.

But he was soon to leave. The job was done. More blood on his hands, but a glass of wine would wash it and the lingering shadows in his mind away. Or at least it had every other time. Roche was a killer, with a killer's dreams that could only be silenced by application of grapes, the more fermented the better. He killed for money, and usually for reasons having to do with money.

Roche's eyes narrowed as he took in the three youths

1

sitting on the opposite end of the car. Urban gangsters with hard eyes and garish clothing of clashing neon and pants that rode lower than could be comfortably worn, at least in Roche's opinion. One of the young men caught his look and glared back, lips curling in a slight sneer. Roche leaned back in his seat and hugged the leather wrapped bundle tighter to his chest before letting it lay across his knees, turning his attention to the others in the clattering car. He didn't need any trouble. Not tonight.

The woman was tall, her jogging suit clinging to her in the appropriate places, her jacket open to reveal a bared midriff, tight muscles all in a row. Roche stirred surreptitiously for a better glimpse. Strong women were his weakness. Well, that and breaking them. She leaned back in her seat, eyes closed and listening intently to her headphones, studiously ignoring the leers of the three youths and the whispered catcalls. Behind her, a man sat, older like Roche, but heavy and thick jowled. His clothes were dirty and worn and the hardhat that sat beside him on the seat attested to the blue of his collar. Still, no one Roche would want to trifle with. He idly flipped through a dog-eared magazine that he balanced on his lap, his lips moving as he read the articles.

A snatch of off-key humming brought his attention round to the vagrant who occupied the left half of the car alone but for his smell. Everyone else, Roche included, had taken seats on the right. The vagrant didn't seem to mind, sprawled out as he was, head thrown back, Adam's apple moving as he hummed to himself and muttered nonsense words, his head lolling around. His eyes were closed and the lids twitched every so often, as if something were pushing at them from within.

Roche shuddered at the thought and shook his head. He shifted the long bundle on his lap and smoothed the leather, feeling the strength wrapped within. The only thing that had never let him down in his life. Of course, the first time it did, he would most likely be dead, but he didn't care to think about that.

'YO! Shut th' fuck up!'

Roche opened his eyes, unaware he had even closed them as one of the youths stood, one brown hand on one of the poles in the center of the aisle to steady himself as he loomed over the humming vagrant. The woman had been jolted awake and was staring narrow-eyed at the youth, but the workman continued to keep his eyes to himself very studiously. Behind him one of his companions shook his head.

'Max leave the fuck-head alone man. He don't even know you're there...'

'Then why's he keep talkin' at me Ritchie?' the one standing, obviously Max, yelled back at his friend. 'You got something to say man?' Max turned his attention back to the vagrant, reaching out for the other man's collar.

The vagrant suddenly opened his eyes and smiled widely. Metal glinted in the flickering lights. Braces, or something like them Roche figured as Max stumbled back a step and the bum sat up. 'I was just trying to tell you a story young man...no need to be rude,' he rasped, his voice gone rough like a bag of rocks in the washing machine from too much booze and too little talking. 'It's a very good story.'

'Fuck your story man and fuck you. Keep talking and I'll pop you one,' Max said matter of factly, one hand patting a bulge under his jacket at his waist. Roche presumed it was a gun. Everyone in America carried a gun.

No sense of style these people. Roche tensed up regardless, fingers deftly untying the bundle on his lap, his eyes never leaving Max. Regrettably, style had little say in where a bullet travelled. And Roche was determined that none would travel in his direction tonight. He had had enough of that for one trip already.

The vagrant, however, was either unaware of Max's gesture and what it implied or was simply unconcerned. Which made him insane. Either way, the next few minutes were going to be painful for someone. 'Really, it's a good story,' he continued, hands sitting limply in his lap. 'You see, I once worked for a carnival. Not one of the big ones, just a small outfit out of Kansas. I was the sword-swallower. I swallowed swords and knives and spears and all sorts of sharp things,' he laughed harshly. 'I liked sharp things y'see.'

'Really? Me too.' The last of Max's little friends laughed, hood of his pullover tight around his baby face as he dug in the belly pocket and pulled out a butterfly knife, its blade snapping open with a wicked noise. The vagrant smiled at the young man and Roche felt the hairs on his neck stand on end.

'I liked them so much, I just kept swallowing them, on stage or not. It was the taste y'see...cool metal sliding down your throat, bitter tasting with a hint of oil and dried blood. I tried rusty things for a new experience, different types of metal. I swallowed nails and tools and razor blades and letter openers and skates and all sorts of sharp things. I was hungry see? More sharpness I ate, more hungered I got for it. Got so I could smell it, smell the sharp things wherever they were hiding. And I ate them all up.' He rubbed at his face with a resigned motion, like a man scratching a phantom itch. Blood trickled down his cheek where he scratched, a slow fat dribbling of thick redness. He didn't seem to mind.

Behind Max, the woman made a disgusted noise, shrinking back in her seat and now even the workman was watching, his eyes flicking up at last from the magazine in his lap. Roche swallowed heavily. He could feel it in the air. Something heavy and dark. A prelude to violence, but on whose part?

A squeal of brakes interrupted the tableau as the train slowed and stopped. The doors hissed open and the sounds of feet slapping cement and voices murmuring over the noise reached them, filling the car. The background music of the subway. It slid a sharp point of reality into the fear gathering in the car. Roche wished someone would get on. Anyone. Anyone who might distract the horrible hum from his story, from his scratching or even distract the bangers from their intended victim. Instead they all held their breath, watching the vagrant watch the people outside. Watching each other watching. Even the gang-bangers. Quiet. Eyes moving, watching. Waiting.

Roche heard metal click somewhere. The train starting up? No. A different noise. Softer. Metal crickets rubbing their steel legs. Edge on edge, like sword blades sliding over one another. He was reminded of the fat little oriental man from a few years ago and the duel they'd had at the top of one of those strange Japanese high-rises, more bill-board than building. He'd moved fast for a fat man.

Just not fast enough.

Roche shook himself as the vagrant threw a smile his way. Between his teeth, there was a glint. Fillings? Roche shuddered. The vagrant looked away and continued his story.

'As I was saying, I ate so many sharp things they pricked my insides something awful. Getting so I didn't even have to look for them no more. They'd come to me, crawling and wriggling across the ground and sliding into me like ticks burrowing into my skin. And then I learned the sharp things...' they got a hunger too.' He chuckled wetly, a thin drizzle of blood leaking out of the corner of his mouth unnoticed as he continued to scratch at his face. 'They hunger for a taste too. The sharp things, they got a life of their own, all cold and not at all like us. But they get hungry like us, want to be used. Want to be loved. They whisper things when they rub together, put thoughts all in my head like hornets buzzing loose up in my skull. They whisper that they need to taste blood...' A spatter of crimson ran down the vagrant's forehead suddenly and something glinted in the wound. As he took his hand away from his cheek, the fingers of his hand the color of fresh roses, the skin pulsed and squirmed as if things were pushing at it. Roche was reminded of wasps getting ready to leave a nest, or ants boiling up out of a hill.

'Oh that's it man!' Max yanked at the pistol in his waist-band, but before he could pull it free the vagrant's hand clamped down on his wrist. Max screamed like a girl and the bum let him go to fall backwards to the floor of the car. Roche suppressed a gag as he saw the thin red lines, almost like five deep paper cuts on Max's wrist, begin to bleed. On the tips of the vagrant's fingers, several sharp somethings glinted in the light of the flickering bulbs overhead.

'Sharp things got a hunger, and I'm all full of sharp things so I got it too I guess. I gots to let them out or they'll eat me right up and no sword-swallower worth his salt can let the sword swallow him, no sir,' he hissed, his words like a blade over a whetstone. And on his cheek, the wound he had dug opened like the petals of a flower and the sharp tips of several carpenter's nails poked through. He coughed and several razor blades and shards of metal flowed out from between his lips like glittering vomit to tinkle and clatter on the floor. Things poked and slid from out of his face and on his hands, his fingertips bulged like overcooked sausages, splitting to allow knife blades and razor hooks to come into the light. 'I gots to let them all out...'

The woman screamed, clambering over the seats behind her in an effort to get away, the hard hat just ahead of her, reaching for the door to the compartment behind the one they were in. He wanted to follow them, but Roche couldn't look away. He recognized the smell that had surrounded the vagrant now. It was the smell of dried blood and rust. Of weapons never cleaned. The vagrant didn't speak anymore, indeed couldn't, his throat bulging as something uncoiled in his gullet and rose to the surface.

Max squealed as he wriggled away, clawing for the gun in his pants with his unwounded arm. Ritchie and the nameless butterfly knife–carrier rose with startled oaths, Ritchie pulling his own piece with a speed that belied his looks. The .38 he produced spat once, twice and the vagrant stumbled, whipping his head around to grin and his mouth opened wide, so wide, and he spat a stream of blood and ten penny nails and screwdriver tips into Ritchie's face. Ritchie fell back into his seat, eyes big, hands fluttering in surprise to touch the new extensions in his face, now little more than a ruin. He shrieked and twitched, the hot smell of urine filling the car.

Roche flipped away the leather bindings on the bundle in his lap to reveal the sheathed sword, the slender curved katana that had served him well in his profession for so many years. The only thing he had ever truly loved. The only thing he could depend on. He rose out of his seat, adrenaline thumping in his veins as he grabbed the hilt and drew the blade.

Butterfly knife jabbed at the vagrant who spread his arms wide, letting the blade pierce his chest. As the young man struggled to pull the blade loose, the vagrant placed his hands around his head like a priest preparing for benediction and pushed his hands together until they met in the center of the boy's skull, slicing through muscle and bone and meat like a hot knife through butter. Gray sludge pooled around his fingers as he let the flopping body fall, the knife folding into his chest and disappearing with sickening pop of displaced air. His hands looked like freakish, multi-limbed insects as he turned, metal edges sparking against each other and the steady drip, drip, drip of blood running down his arms.

As Roche started forward, Max pulled himself up on his elbows and fired wildly, the bullet catching the vagrant in the eye, throwing him backwards. The youth pulled himself to his feet, using the seat at his back for leverage, and aimed the pistol in a shaky grip for another shot. But the vagrant surged forward in a blur of metal and darkness, jaws opening wide, knife blades and stickpins protruding out of his gums, nestling between his yellow crooked teeth. He closed his mouth with a snap and Max howled, his gun-hand gone in a fountain of blood and splintered bone and then he became quiet as the vagrant slapped a hand over his head and tore his face away like a toddler tearing apart tissue paper.

It was quiet then, but for the panting of the two behind Roche, still struggling with the door, making animal sounds of fear as Roche stepped into the aisle, his sword catching the light as he held it up slanted crosswise in front of him in a classic defensive position.

The train went clickety-clack and the lights dimmed and grew strong again. They'd missed the next station. An announcement blared over the speakers, incomprehensible. Roche thought he picked up something about linework. It didn't matter. Nothing mattered but the thing advancing slowly towards him, steel teeth shining as it grinned at him.

'What are you?' Roche whispered. The vagrant cocked his head, tongue rubbing idly at pieces of Max meat caught in his extra steel teeth, his one good eye shining madly.

'I don't rightly know anymore,' he replied softly. 'Just hungry I guess. They've about hollowed me out, the sharp things. Takes more and more to fill me up. They'll be looking for a new home soon I expect.' He started forward, sharp things clicking and scraping in his skin as he rattled towards Roche.

Roche looked back at the woman and the workman. 'I'll hold him for as long as I can. Get out,' he said curtly, and then he spun to meet the first lunge of the vagrant. His sword lashed out and blood flew. Or something like it. Roche fought with a killer's skill, his swordplay learned from a dozen masters over three decades.

He had fought in two wars and several so-called police actions and he had killed more men than he saved. Louis Roche was a murderer a hundred times over, a man born to kill.

But the vagrant was a monster.

Every cut he made, every slice into his opponent's flesh allowed more metal to fall to the floor or splatter towards him. Nails, blades, wire bits, pitchfork tines, hairpins, fishing hooks. Roche was breathing hard after a few minutes, sword flickering out in trembling hands to parry lazy slashes or to ward off a snap of grotesque jaws.

He danced out of the way of a clutch by sharp fingers and brought the sword down on the vagrant's arm, slicing it clean off at the elbow. All at once, as the vagrant fell back, a veritable flood of metal burst out of the stump, spraying the back of the car. The air screamed as it was sliced in a thousand and one spots.

Roche fell, razors and other things less identifiable embedding themselves in his up-flung forearms and chest and groin as he fell to the floor of the car, his sword sliding away. Behind him, as his sight grew red he could hear the gurgling screams of the other two passengers as they too fell beneath the shining sharp edged 'blood' of the vagrant, torn apart even as the door to the next compartment finally slid open.

Roche slumped between seats and rolled onto his stomach, trying to lever himself up despite the intense pain.

The vagrant lay still and somehow shrunken where he had fallen, in a pool of thick blood that looked somehow diseased and rotten. Around him lay his precious sharp things, rolling to and fro in the movement of the subway car, clattering and making a racket.

Then, as his eyes flickered, the sharp things began to squirm towards him like worms.

'They've about hollowed me out...they'll be looking for a new home soon I expect...they'd come to me, crawling and wriggling across the ground and sliding into me like ticks burrowing into my skin...they get hungry like us...want to be loved.' The vagrant's words filled his mind, pushing through the cloud of pain, echoing and re-echoing. He could feel the ones already embedded in his arms and stomach beginning to work their way in, sliding deeper and deeper into the meat of him and Roche grunted in pain.

But he didn't begin to scream until he heard his own sword begin to slither towards him.

Between The Screams

Brian G Ross

I was fourteen when the Midnighters sent me out on my first rape. My first time. It was hers too, but I popped her cherry all over the alley just the same. Looking down, when the moonlight found me, I saw a flash of red. At first I thought she'd cut me as she'd been thrashing about like a rabbit in a trap. It wasn't until I'd cracked her head on the corner of a garbage can — one, two, three times — that I realised the blood belonged to her. By then she was dead anyway, and it didn't matter much anymore. Flecks of brain, like purple boogers tangled with my pubic hair, but my cock was still hard.

So I finished the job, then the boys took me out for a burger to celebrate.

Finally, I was one of them.

The cops in this dirty town know about our little games, but they never come after us with badges or batons. Too many skeletons. Too many closets. If you have a big enough torch, you can see right into every one.

We are sleeping dogs to them, and if we happen to wake up from time to time, so be it. They take the rough with the smooth. Likewise, out of what passes for respect amongst us, we leave them alone. Nobody gets hurt, and the world keeps on turning.

Every now and then a fresh face comes along — wet behind the ears and eager to please — and tries to make a name for himself by stepping out of his jurisdiction and tagging one of us. They're easy to spot. They've got the shiny shoes and the starched collars, and that new recruit smile yet to be dissolved by the darker side of their job.

They pick us up for swiping a case of beer, or mugging some old broad — lame shit like that — but we let that slide. We don't take retribution on the rookies. That's like candy from a baby. They get one chance — one heads-up. Then, as far as we're concerned, they ain't rookies anymore, and anything we give them, they have coming.

But three years is a long time to live on the edge of society. Soon enough you start looking over your shoulder and waiting for the hammer to fall, to drive you into the ground like a railroad spike.

All the bad stuff I've done — the blood, the screams, God, those screams — it's all piled up in my head like bricks. And even on the tips of my toes, day by day, it's getting harder to see past the nightmares.

There are nights I can't sleep; when my sheets are soaked with sweat, and tangled with the memories of the terrible things I've done. I can't deny my past, but likewise, I can't go on this way either.

I think the only thing that makes sense is to stop, turn around, and hope you can find your way back again.

All I have to do is tell The Master.

The warehouse on the corner of Park and River is where it all goes down. It was abandoned by a local paper supplier a few years back when they went tits up. They moved out, we moved in. Sometimes, if you listen carefully, you can still hear the echoes of days gone by — the forgotten whirr of photocopiers, the glug of the water coolers, shit like that — but most of the time it isn't so quiet. The atmosphere is tainted, you know, like spoiled meat. Spend enough time in here and you feel it. It creeps all over you. In the silence, the air shrieks, because the walls remember, even when nobody else does.

I stand before The Master; feet together, hands steel-bound behind my back, naked as the day I was born. With us, you go out the way you came in. That's just one of our rules. It's crazy now, but at the time it seemed to make perfect sense.

The Midnighters — about twenty strong — form a half circle around me. Bad news and baseball bats, that's what they are. Their stink is thick in my nostrils. It is my stink, and now I must leave it behind.

I fall to my knees when The Master asks it of me, and keep my eyes on the floor until he speaks. I focus on a crack in the concrete and imagine slipping through it and away. He asks why I have petitioned for this audience, his voice like thunder in the emptiness of the warehouse. I swallow hard. Saliva cuts my throat like a razor.

'I want out.'

The crowd moves in. They can sense blood, even before it flows.

'Out? You are asking to leave the Midnighters?'

'I don't want to be a part of this bullshit freak-show anymore.'

A murmur washes over the crowd as The Master throws me a misplaced smile. He is older than me — one year, maybe two — but the lines on his face tell a longer story. His teeth are either yellow or missing, and his breath smells like the last girl he fucked. The cuffs eat into my wrists.

'You know where the door is,' he says finally, motioning to the exit with his head and his hand. 'Any time you want to leave, be my guest.'

It takes most of my strength to keep from laughing. My first step towards the door would also be my last. I'd have a knife between my shoulder blades within seconds.

'This bullshit freak-show, as you call it, raised you from the gutter, made you a man!' A dozen heads snap up and down in agreement like string puppets. 'Where's your loyalty? Where's your goddamn respect?'

I shrug and my chin falls onto my chest. The memories of the last three years weigh heavily on my heart. 'I'm tired of the games. Tired of the running. Tired of acting like a fucking monkey all the time.'

The crowd is getting restless behind me. I can feel their rank breath on the back of my neck like a herd of bulls waiting for the red rag to drop. 'I'm resigning my position. I nominate Franko. He's had his eye on my seat since Christmas.' I flash him a smile, but from the throng of the crowd he pretends not to notice.

'You resign,' The Master warns, 'and with that you lose your power to nominate.'

I lift my head and smile right back at him. 'I know how this works.'

The Master nods sagely. 'The board shall decide these matters, Trevor.'

Throwing my real name in there is the ultimate humiliation. There are a few sniggers, but The Master raises a hand and they are stilled.

The silence brings with it a flash of understanding, and there is a trace of sadness behind The Master's eyes. 'Are you sure you want to go through with this?' For a finger-snap I can almost see myself getting out of this, but then he continues and that moment is gone. 'This is the only chance you get.'

'I've had enough,' is all I can think to say. I struggle with the cuffs but they are cinched close to my wrists.

'Very well. Bring in the subject!'

At the far end of the warehouse, strangled screams zap through the night. Two masked teenagers — Midnighters I have probably helped raise — drag a naked girl towards them and towards us. She doesn't look a day over fifteen.

Their leather-gloved hands are under her armpits, and her bare feet scrape along the concrete like dead meat. Her skin has been flayed and she bleeds from a dozen sores all over her torso. Ribs stand out like tent-poles under her skin: it's been days since we've fed her. Around her pubic area are the first sprouts of womanhood. If she is lucky, she won't live that long.

The Midnighters drop her to the ground in front of me like a sack of garbage, and The Master nods to signal their dismissal. They slink away like oil without meeting my eyes.

After a moment the girl lifts her head from the concrete. Threads of red snot stream from her burst nose. One of her eyes is purple and bloated.

Joanne.

She stares right through me, somewhere far away from the brutality she has experienced at our hands. A quiet lake, a roaring fire, a summer meadow. Perhaps, if her mind is able to escape these horrors, there is hope for her yet. I can only pray that we have afforded her that much, but I guess I'll never know for sure.

I remember the day we grabbed her, in the tunnel behind the school. I knocked out two of her teeth with my elbow, blackened her eyes with my fist and violated her with a syca-more branch; all while her classmates skipped home for cookies and TV, and the setting sun danced golden diamonds in the snow. It was a beautiful afternoon. The blood came in warm spurts. It tasted like hot milk.

'This is the bitch!' In that moment, everything stops. Even Joanne blinks out of her reverie, and all of a sudden she is back in her own personal Hell. 'You have five minutes, Trevor. Beat the bitch, and, in return, The Midnighters give you freedom. Should the bitch beat you however, then freedom is hers, and you will perish in her place.'

Even before he has finished I am nodding. I know the game, and the sick rules we play by.

The Master yanks her head towards his and now speaks with almost fatherly tenderness. 'Honey, this is your lucky day. All you've got to do is, blow this punk away — ' he arches an eyebrow ' — and you're home free.'

Looking at her now, I can't remember if her name is Joanne or Jessica or maybe something else entirely. It scarcely matters though. She spits out another tooth and it bounces along the concrete like a grisly tic-tac.

'Midnighters, escort the subjects to The Chamber!'

The naked girl shrieks defiantly as she is pulled onto her feet again, but has little strength left after many hours of rape and torture. Most of the struggle remains locked in her throat.

With a fistful of blonde hair he pulls her along the ground, ignoring her gurgles and groans. At first she tries to walk with him but soon, with most of the fight torn from her, she collapses in a heap, and lets him drag her dead weight to The Chamber. Her once baby–smooth ass is now blistered and scarred where we have abused her.

The second Midnighter pinches the nerve at the base of my neck and, with his other hand in the small of my back, marches me forward.

I turn to him, but don't recognise him behind the plastic Halloween disguise. 'You put your hand there and we better be dancing.'

An ironic smile scratches across my face. He doesn't miss a beat, nor does he bend to my silent struggle. I have trained these boys well.

The Chamber is the last place a lot of our girls ever see. It is stark white — except for the dried blood and shit that smears the walls like finger-paints — and the brightness still hurts my eyes, even now, after all this time.

An electric fan spins high above in the rafters, circulating the stench of death on whispered wings. Whoop-whoop. The smell almost overpowers you. It knocks you back, like heat from a furnace.

A black bra hangs from one of the fan's metal blades, tantalisingly out of reach. Even from here I can see the crusts of blood on it. I forget which of our girls it came from. There have been so many over the years.

'Five minutes, girls,' I hear The Master say as we are tossed into The Chamber. 'Clock's ticking.'

My head bounces off the floor as they close the door behind us, and through purple stars I stare at the cold concrete walls. I have led many here and pulled their rotting carcasses from the room after the maggots and the flies have feasted. A dozen battered faces trip through my mind.

The girl who starts with a 'J' picks herself up — tears standing in her eyes — and scrambles towards me, her starved fingers reaching. I try to pull away but her desperation is greater than mine.

'Look, you don't have to do this,' I tell her as she stuffs my lifeless cock into her mouth. 'You really think those assholes are going to let you walk away from here?'

She ignores me and moves her lips and tongue quickly, but after a minute of nothing she sighs and slows her pace. Finally, with some effort, I manage to free myself from her mouth.

The girl gulps for air. 'If I don't do this they're going to kill me!' She pulls my hips back towards her and talks around my cock, like a kid eating a candy bar. 'If you don't cum, I'm going to die! Do you understand that?'

'What's your name?' Her tears fall freely now. She is weeping red rivers, but barely makes a sound. 'Hey!'

I hawk some saliva from the back of my throat onto the girl's face. Surprised, she pulls away quickly, her broken teeth grazing my cock as she does. I wince.

She wipes the taste of what she is doing from her mouth and drops her head. 'J-Jennifer.' Her voice is a hiccup. She sits in a growing pool of her own blood. 'Jennifer Barnes.'

'Well Jennifer Barnes, you know, they're going to fucking kill you anyway, whether I cum or not. You want to drag me down with you as well? Fine, but whatever happens, in a minute-and-a-half those assholes are going to come in here and tear us apart, so you can either carry on sucking my dick, or you can go through that door back there — ' I point behind me ' — go along the corridor, take a left, and get the fuck out of here while you still have the legs to do it.'

In this girl's fresh tears I can see the first buds of hope. After everything she has been through, sometimes all it takes is a well-placed smile to convince someone of a happily ever after that was never really there in the first place.

The crowd outside are baying for blood — whose, didn't matter. Louder now. In a matter of seconds this room will be crawling with them.

'It's the only chance you've got,' I say.

'What about you?'

'I'm dead anyway. Go, right now! First on the left and don't look back.'

She doesn't wait for me to tell her again. She tears away towards the rear of The Chamber like a cartoon, on legs that are barely able to support her, babbling incoherently all the while. I hear a thank-you in there, I'm sure of it. But don't thank me yet sister, because some nightmares follow you home.

When she finds the door it smacks off the wall as she pushes through it. The sound reverberates around the warehouse, and all at once I don't hear the Midnighters counting down the seconds. All of a sudden an army of feet are heading in the other direction. A moment later the alarm sounds. Jennifer's job is complete.

The Midnighters move in a pack like the wild dogs they are. They cut the alarm and chase the breach and, using their distraction as my camouflage, I walk out the front door and into the fog of the early hours. Behind me I hear Jennifer — as loud now as any girl we have ever snared — pleading first for help, then for mercy, then for death. I wasn't lying to her — not then, at least. Those guys will rip her apart, one limb at a time.

I know that one day they will catch up to me, because in the end we all reap what we sow. I don't know the details, but it's coming, as surely as the next sunrise. Tomorrow, next month — one day when my back is turned, or when my eyes are closed.

The hows and the wheres are not important, but every minute I have, I owe to that girl who starts with a 'J', and her willingness to trust the guy who caught her, raped her, and eventually, wasted her.

I smile as I hurdle the fence and fade into the blackness.

There's no escape.

Not from The Midnighters.

Pebble Toss and Dare

Bradley Michael Zerbe

Beyond the dead-end on Maple Street the grass grew in brown, saucer-shaped clumps. Litter drifted about in the leaves. Remains of the sixties — cigarette butts, rusting cans, bottles, and here and there the eye of a marble glinted like a dead child winking up from the grass. I hated that place.

Pebble Toss and Dare was the name of the game. My brother John and I couldn't get enough of it. First we rode out to the last house on Maple Street. Then we parked our bikes and picked up some choice stones from the gutter. We always spoke in whispers as we waited for the sun to set and the prickly longing of the game to summon us — the dare called to our bones and flesh. I was too young to understand.

The rules were easy. We took turns throwing stones down the street, daring each other to run and fetch them. A simple act, and then we would step ten paces closer to the end and repeat the process. When the scene around us became scary and those bone-chillin, piss-your-pants willies crawled up our arms and down our backs, that was when the game turned truly grand.

Every time the sun faded behind the trees an army of those bastard willies poured from my ten-year-old gut and attacked me. The stars above twinkled like fireflies and laughed, warm summer breeze smelling of stale creek mud and decay. And then the boys appeared and watched us. Very likely it was these young devils that bullied us to the dead end in the first place.

Sitting on their pads of brown grass, they seemed to possess qualities beyond that of mere ghosts — showing us cruel tricks by floating detached limbs into the sky and flipping their skin inside out leaving a veiny mess. And what chilled us deep inside was the fact that they wanted us to join their ranks; I could sense this plain as day, as though they each had a tiny strand of my guts wrapped around their pinky fingers, as they wound me in closer for the kill.

I repeat: those willies were bastards; one glimpse and I was outta there in high gear.

But not John. He always threw his remaining rocks at the boys first. He never told me why, and I never cared to ask. Throwing stones was his way of dealing with the unexplained, I suppose. But where he found the courage to stand those extra few seconds was beyond me.

Soon we'd be peddling home as fast as our grimy legs would go — two scared shitless speedsters out of control. Then it was wash-up time, suppertime, and bedtime. This was the order of our lives, that is, until this one extraordinary time when we both went too far and the game was changed forever. Actually, Pebble Toss and Dare came to an end that night, at least for me. And of course the game had to end on some lousy condition.

I threw the stone and made my dare. John retrieved it, barely winded at all. We moved closer to the end, our shadows growing longer behind us, the breeze drying the salty sweat on our lips.

John threw his stone, and it landed a few feet from the dead end.

'I dare you, or you must clean my room for a month.'

'That's not fair!' I kicked the gravel. 'You never gave me

one this hard before. What gives?'

John shrugged and crossed his arms.

'It just happened, alright? A dare's a dare.'

And he was right. I could either get the stone, or pay his price. So I ran.

Ten more steps and I would have had it. The stone would have been in my fist and I would have raced back dare in hand. But those bastards came — knees wobbled. The boys sat on the dry grass watching us like a gang of country hoodlums with jack shit to do.

I put on the brakes and slipped. They laughed as I went down, the thin gravel tearing a hole in the seat of my shorts. All six of them laughed. Could have been more. The fat one was the easiest to pick out because his belly jiggled. The smaller one by his side stuck out a forked tongue and whipped me off with both hands.

'Come on Jim!' my brother shouted.

I jumped up and ran away as fast as I could, my dare unfinished and lost. I was an undeniable chicken. This unfortunate blunder had happened before (you know who to blame), and as before, I would pay the price.

'One month, Chicken Jim,' John said as I stopped beside him.

'They were t-there,' I said as I tried to catch my breath.

'I didn't see none, Chicken Jim.'

'They laughed at me, and the fat one tore off his nipple and and...I got scared.'

I rubbed my arms, hair standing up straight and cold and prickly.

'Didn't I teach you not to be a scaredy chicken?' He poked me in the forehead — I hated when he did that.

'Well, why don't you...'

I decided then to double dare him. Don't get me wrong, I loved my brother. But I was mad. He had no right to toss the pebble that far so late in the day.

'I d-double dare without a c-care, John.'

'What did you say?'

'I double dare without a care,' I said quickly and looked at my feet.

Those bastards in the pit of my stomach had fallen silent. My anger did them in.

John turned and faced the end of Maple Street. Darkness was nearly upon us, and I hoped that this would help him decide to turn down my dare. For a few small seconds while fate forged a new pair of shadow dice to roll, I was in the clear. But then John shook his head and made a condition. If he completed the dare now, we would be even.

'I'm using my condition. Whatever I do, you must do. If I pick up the stone, you must do the same. And if I step on the grass, you must step on the grass.'

'But you can't John!'

He turned and spat. Then he poked me in the forehead and ran, his features pale and courageous in the spook-laden light. Near the end he slowed, and then his shadow picked up the stone. He turned and threw it towards me, and it landed near my feet. Then John calmly walked to the end and stepped onto the grass. My heart sank as his form disappeared in the shadows — no willies — full-blown terror!

'John! Get back here so we can go home!'

No answer.

What would they do to him, I wondered?

'John! John!'

Tears streamed from my face. I thought about leaving. I couldn't leave. It was all my fault for double daring him. I should have just let it go. I —

'I'm waiting, Jim. I used my condition, remember?' my brother called from the darkness.

In my mind I saw the mean one pull his fleshy nipple

from the wad of fat in his hand and reach back to hurl it.

'Let's go home John, I'm scared!'

'I'm waiting, Chicken Jim.'

I walked over to the stone. John was right. A condition was a condition, no getting around it. Only one a year, no more or you reneged. Why John had to use his on a double dare, I would never know.

I picked up the pebble and tossed it. The spooky sound of it landing sent those bastard willies into action like hitting an ON switch.

'I dare ya, Jim!' my brother shouted.

I wiped my face with a sleeve and ran. Stupid conditions.

Fireflies danced above as the wind rushed past. My vision blurred, body tingled. My legs pumped up and down as I pretended I was racing home on my bicycle. I leaped off Maple Street into the arms of my brother. He hugged me and set me down. Then he took my hand and led me through the grass over to the others.

The game had been a farce, a cruel ploy aimed at tricking us into joining their ranks. Realizing this made me cry. Pebble Toss and Dare. A game for dead boys. A game for stupid dumb dead boys who don't know they're dead. I cried until the fat one (named Judd, I later learned) pushed me down and sat on my head and farted.

As a leaf falls fluttering to land upon the crumbling cement of our prison, so did one hundred years flutter past before our eyes. No more grass. No more Maple Street. Just overpass 139 with our ghostly legs dangling off both sides. What stayed with us, the thing that never quite left, was the game. They called it something different these days, but it was still the same old Pebble Toss and Dare. Rocks were still rocks. Kids still got those bastard willies. And I guess us dead boys still looked spooky and wild when the sun went down.

I stood and stretched. A milky fog rose from beneath the pass as yet another rainy day approached its end. But we didn't mind the rain; it was the smell that bothered us. Mix the swampy shit stink from below with car fumes, and you got one big headache. I yawned and slapped a handprint on a car window as it zoomed past. New Ford Mustang. Blue.

My brother stood at the edge of the overpass. Probably scaring some kids again. Some things never got old.

'Get back here, John,' I called. 'He's not gonna do the dare. He's too chicken.'

A pale boy with red hair stood crying in front of him. He wore a shiny white suit, and his feet were naked and blistering. John had already swiped his sunglasses, a move that could only make it harder to get him. I stepped closer to listen.

John had his arm around the boy and a tight grip on his shoulder, an undeniable chicken if I ever saw one.

'Let me explain one more time,' John said. 'I throw the stone, you go get it, and then you get your sunglasses back. Sound fair?'

The boy shook his head no, and I agreed with him. There had to be a catch if John was involved.

'Well that's the way it's gotta be. Ready?'

'Condition, please.'

John's jaw dropped. That was a word from a different time, a strange life, so long ago. How could this carrot top know what a condition was? John took a deep breath and smiled.

'Name your condition, buddy.'

'I go get your rock, and then you must take me home. That's my condition...please?'

John shrugged. 'A condition's a condition.'

He reached back and threw (a palm-sized chunk of concrete, smooth on one side and jagged on the other) and I ducked out the way. The rock passed through Billy, who wasn't paying attention, and sailed down the road before bouncing off the passenger door of an old Volkswagen Beetle. White. Antique plates. I hated those cars. Then it rolled to a stop three-quarters of the way across the pass.

'I dare ya, carrot top!' John shouted, and all the boys turned to look.

The redhead's face went white as those bastard willies rushed him. He pointed.

'I see them, in a row on each side.'

'You wanna go home, kid? You made a condition, so do the dare, now!' John screamed and surprisingly, the kid ran.

The heads of the boys swiveled as he passed them. Halfway across Judd came from out of nowhere and tackled him. Then he sat on the poor carrot top's back and flattened him out.

'You're never leaving, pumpkin head! Never!' Judd shouted as he jiggled his fatboy tits and laughed.

John winked behind his new pair of sunglasses as he walked past me. Another one in the books. I shook my head. Not much changed around here. But then again, every time I caught a side view of Judd, I swore the dead boy had grown fatter.

My one thousand and twelfth birthday passed like any other, but lately the world below was changing crazy fast.

Six hundred and thirty four of us lay on the pedestal of a roof overlooking the remains. Luckily, the cloud of human shit smoke, as we liked to call it, which now blocked all of the sun's natural light, had moved above us. This had been a cause for celebration because for a few centuries we couldn't see squat. But then we looked around and asked the question: what happened?

Below us the streets and buildings crumbled with age and neglect, lit only by murky manmade power that resembled swamp gas. And everywhere we looked, fat, slothlike beings roamed, or should I say, oozed, back and forth. Grimacing and identical, it was hard for us to believe that their gluttonous bodies contained any trace of the human life we once knew. The scene was mind-blowing, hardcore sci-fi, and most of us cried.

This was worse than standing at the dead end on Maple Street all those years ago, waiting to play the dead child's game. The world had filled with that brown grass, existing in saucer-shaped clumps, and litter — only worse. This was worse than before. Before there had been hope.

Those old bastards spilled from their hiding places once again, and we clung to each other in despair.

Baby Steps

Scott Stainton Miller

The day looked funny. Sort of gray. Usually in Autumn things were clear and cold and good. Not today, although everything was in abundance: falling leaves, blue skies, the usual feeling of change. But it didn't look right. The air, the sky, the grass, everything. It crossed his mind that perhaps it was because he was getting older, but he rationalised that any jading or dimming down would happen at forty or fifty, not seventeen. Which is what Henry would be at precisely 2:28 this afternoon. He felt good about it. It sounded sexy. Seventeen. Still young, but not a kid and a whole world away from eighteen, which loomed to him like thirty did to people panicking in their twenties.

Eighteen sounded like responsibility.

Seventeen sounded like a last shot at enjoying life and the limited amount of freedom that came with it. And, fingers firmly crossed, at fucking too. He listed his accomplishments mentally as he walked.

Three handjobs.

One blowjob.

Much in the way of kissing, a long list tarnished somewhat by the slightly, and some cases vastly, suspicious quality of some of the girls. One of whom, a skinny, nasty thing, had had to leave school because of the bun growing conspicuously in her super-efficient oven.

'Yuch,' he said to himself.

He was walking around his suburb, attempting to shake out the strange feeling of disquiet he'd woken up with and which hadn't been helped by the odd tenebrous quality that the light had. He should have been feeling good. School was closed and would be for the next two days. The boiler had broken, freeing all the captives, and then the janitor had died, freeing everyone; a heart-attack in the gym hall.

And at 2:28 he'd be seventeen.

'Huzzah.'

He stopped. The man down the street, the one his father referred to as That Dimwit, was nailing another poster to a tree. He waited until the man had finished and walked away before he approached the tree. It was a different poster for the same thing. His daughter was missing. She'd been missing for nearly three months. The photograph was in colour now, but it still provoked the same shameful reaction in Henry; she was ugly. And he hadn't liked her. He didn't even feel particularly bad that she was missing either. Which was the most shameful thing about it. But then he hadn't known her, had barely spoken to her. The impact on his life was zero.

He watched the father walk away, stopping at all the trees that grew out of the pavement to nail down another futile poster.

'Poor guy,' he said aloud because he felt that the scene deserved a compassionate comment and that was pretty much the best he could come up with.

The kitchen stank. His mother stood pouring bleach into the sink. She lifted her head as he came in but didn't turn around.

'Have you been pouring bacon fat into the sink-hole?' she asked.

'Uh, no. I haven't.'

'When you make yourself bacon do you...'

'I grill it on silver-foil and then I ball up the foil and put it in the bin, yes.'

'Really? You don't just tip out all the fat into the sink?'

'No.'

'Because it cools in the pipe, congeals there and then rots.'

'I know. I don't do that.'

She didn't say anything else. Just nodded to herself and poured boiling water into the sink-hole.

He smiled widely, baring all his teeth, and then walked up the stairs to his room, whistling Happy Birthday.

He sat on his bed and contemplated masturbating, but decided against it. There had been a couple of close calls recently, with his mother either walking in before the finish or after. He'd managed to pull his jeans up and his t-shirt down in time, but she'd looked at him oddly each time and he didn't want the act and her appearance to somehow become linked, so he'd been doing it less and less and only at night.

Sighing, he looked out his window. That Dimwit had walked in a complete circle and was now in his street, nailing posters to trees.

He closed his eyes and listened to the thunk of the hammer and decided that the day would now not be redeemed. And he was right. His father came home late while his mother barely said two words to him all day. His presents too had been disappointing; a book he'd read already and vouchers for a store he never shopped in. For the final nail, his mother had announced that they would be entertaining the neighbours tonight.

After dinner, he went up to his room and stared at the ceiling, unable to focus on any one thought.

*

He sat at the top of the stairs and listened. It was midnight and he couldn't sleep because of the chatter coming from the living room. So he got up, sat near enough to hear and hoped that he'd soon be bored enough to try for sleep.

It was his father that was doing most of the talking.

'I hate That Dimwit. But, you know, it is a shame. What happened to his daughter. Emily I think was her name, wasn't it? I never read the posters... Yes, Emily. Anyway, it's a shame.'

Ian Donaldson, the dick from next door who frowned at Henry whenever he could, chimed in.

'She probably ran away. Is there any more wine?'

'No, I don't think she ran away. It feels like something bad has happened, don't you think? There's a funny feeling in the neighbourhood.'

'Mmm. Do you mind if I...Ah, thanks.'

Henry heard the sound of a cork being popped. Ian Donaldson had very florid cheeks. He was probably just here for the booze. Which Henry could understand. His wife Elaine was a solid gold cunt. Henry would be drunk all the time too if he had to admit in public that the cold, sneering bitch was his wife, the woman he had volunteered to marry and multiply with. Not that they had multiplied. Her vagina probably crunched up his weedy sperm like caviar.

Henry's mother piped up. 'Yes, I think she's dead. It's been a while now. Three months, I think.'

'No,' said Mr Donaldson, 'I don't think she's dead. I just don't. I mean...'

'Oh, she's dead. I don't know how she died, but I know she died. I can feel it. Her father probably did it. Got sick of her. Resented having to raise her. She seemed like a disappointment, didn't she? Didn't she, John? Seemed like he didn't love her, and who could blame him? I mean, did you ever see her? Such a stupid girl. And ugly too.'

Mrs Donaldson threw in her tuppence worth.

'I wouldn't know about that. I don't like that man, but I'm sure he loved her. Why else would he spend so much time nailing up those awful posters?'

'Maybe he wants people to think he's grief stricken when he's really jumping for joy.'

'Oh, come on...'

'Sorry. I'm just kidding. She is missing and it is terrible,' replied his mother.

Henry stood up, disturbed, and went back to bed. At around two o'clock he awoke to the sound of tapping. He looked out the window. That Dimwit was hammering posters onto trees. Hammering them over the ones he'd already put up that day.

Henry exhaled, reached under his bed and pulled out his one tired old porno magazine and tried to masturbate, but every time he came close to having an orgasm he thought he could hear his parents creeping around, so he stopped and lay awake until morning.

Gray light. Another boring morning. He got up, got dressed and left the house without seeing either of his parents and walked to the park to smoke.

It was seven in the morning. The park was empty, save for the occasional dog-walker and he sat on the swings, self-consciously smoking a cigarette and wondering why anybody smoked. He coughed and spat and resolved to get to the bottom of the mystery by finishing his cigarette and enjoying it.

He did so and walked along the path adjacent to the burn,

whistling. He looked hard at all the bushes, hoping to find the girl's body and be a hero.

'Nope. No corpses for me today,' he said and stopped. There was a foot sticking out of the sewage pipe that opened into the burn.

'Oh fuck,' he whispered, his heart beating faster and faster.

Slowly, he walked up close to the large, rusty black pipe and peered in. The foot led onto a leg, the leg to a body. It was naked and female. There were flies all over it, buzzing in the pubic hair, rubbing their hairy legs together and walking around on the flesh, which, he saw, was greenish white and flecked with muck. There were deep looking gashes on her thighs, which were splayed. He tried not to look at the vagina.

Shaking, he backed away from the pipe and, filled with the sudden certainty that whoever had killed her was still here, he broke into a run.

It wasn't her. It wasn't Emily. Nobody knew who it was.

The school remained closed and wouldn't open again for another week. A curfew was imposed.

The police questioned Henry. Had he touched anything, seen anything else that might be of help, no matter how trivial? They didn't seem terribly interested in his answers. When he asked if they thought it had anything to with Emily they told him that they were doing all they could to find her and asked was she a friend. Yes, he lied and they patted him on the shoulder and told him to go home and to get in touch if he remembered anything else.

His mother drove him home.

'What did it look like?' she asked after ten minutes

of silence.

'Dead.'

'How awful. Did it smell?'

'Only when I got close. The burn stinks anyway...I just thought it was the burn.'

'How awful.'

They arrived back home and he went up to his room and spent a horrible afternoon trying not to think about anything, but his mind kept returning to the body, the way the legs were spread, the frilled edges of the scores on its thighs, the flies rubbing their hands together.

It was three in the morning. He woke up when his dream turned ugly. Something had been tapping on his floorboards. He sat up. He could still hear the tapping. He went to the window and peered out the curtain. That Dimwit was walking from tree to tree, nailing up more posters. He was crying and talking to himself. Suddenly he stopped and looked up at Henry's window. He waved and smiled and held up a poster. Henry closed his curtain and lay back on his bed. He hadn't realised, but he had an erection. He closed his eyes and started to masturbate, and when he came it was hard and painful and seemed never to end.

'What were you doing last night?'

His mother stood at the breakfast table watching him eat. She had been staring at him for a good few minutes before she spoke.

'What do you mean?'

'I mean what were you doing last night... I could

hear you.'

He didn't know what to say. There was something about the expression on her face that was causing him to remember something. He wasn't sure what and so kept quiet. Finally, it returned to him. He must have been about ten. His mother stood by his bed, holding a pair of his pyjama bottoms inside out. The crotch was stained with silvery white streaks. He didn't know what they were. Her eyes were very wide. She held out the pyjama trousers and said 'Stop it. Just stop it.' He nodded, ignorant, and said that he would.

She looked just like she did that morning.

'What were you doing?'

'Mum, I was sleeping. I don't know what you want.'

'Footsteps. Footfalls. I heard you thumping around.'

'Oh... Oh. The guy down the road was nailing up posters at about three this morning. I heard him and looked outside. Poor guy.'

'He's an idiot. His lawn is dying. His daughter is ugly.'

'I know, I know,' he agreed, too quickly. She narrowed her watery blue eyes and looked at him carefully.

'Something....smells in here,' she said and fetched the bleach. He left her there soon after as she stood there, her back to him, pouring the entire contents of the bottle into the sink.

He decided to take the bus into town, spend his vouchers. He sat on the top deck near the back, which, he quickly realised, was a mistake, that was where the bad boys sat. On cue, two of them got on and started to walk towards him. They sat directly behind him and lit up a joint.

He didn't want to move, so he sat there, concentrating on not appearing in any way concerned. There was a tap on his shoulder.

'You go to my school.'

He turned around. He'd never seen them before. They probably never went to class.

'Uh-huh,' he said and turned around.

'You found the body. Didn't you?'

He turned around again and looked at the other boy. His hair was bleached and shaved up the sides. He had terrible black-heads, dead eyes. He disgusted Henry.

'Was it naked?' asked the boy, smiling.

Henry nodded.

'Did you see its pussy?' said the boy. His friend started giggling.

Henry nodded and breathed heavily through his nose. He wanted off the bus, but the next stop wasn't for a while.

'What did it look like? Did you get a hard-on?' asked the boy.

'It was purple,' said Henry. 'There was blood all around it. The thighs had big holes in them. Finger marks.'

The boy shut up and stared at Henry as if he wanted to kill him. Nothing was said for the rest of the journey.

Henry's father sat in his favourite chair and smiled at him as he came in.

'Be nice to your mother,' he said.

'What?'

'Be nice to your mother. She's in a funny mood and I want a quiet life.'

'Ok.'

'Good boy,' said his father and smiled.

Henry paused.

'Are the Donaldsons coming over anytime soon?'

His father laughed and shook his head.

'Oh, Lord no. Never again.'

He nodded gratefully, went to bed and thought about the boy on the bus. About the questions he'd asked. They were so specific. Like he'd known what to ask in order to bother him. He turned on his side and tried to sleep.

He was beginning to drift when he heard the tapping again. He got up and tip-toed to the window. That Dimwit was out again, nailing more posters over the ones he'd probably only just nailed up that day.

He held his breath and watched him. That Dimwit stopped and turned round and Henry thought he was going to wave at him again, but he didn't, he just stood there, looking directly at the house. After a minute or so, he waved at someone and started to walk over. He stood on Henry's lawn and held up a poster. His face broke into a wide grin and he stepped forwards into the shadow cast by the house and out of sight. Henry stood there for a good few minutes, but nothing more happened and he went back to bed.

'Fucking weirdo,' he murmured and then drifted off.

His mother sat at the breakfast table smiling. Henry watched her for a minute and then entered the kitchen. She looked up. Her eyes were watery and red-rimmed.

'I heard you again.'

'Sorry.'

She just looked at him.

'That guy was out again last night,' he offered.

'I know. I had to go and speak to him.'

'What did you say to him?'

'I told him that I was sorry about his daughter,' she smiled. 'Sorry she was so stupid and ugly.'

Henry stopped in his tracks and swallowed.

'Just kidding,' she said and grinned. 'I told him to go and get some rest and that if I saw or heard anything I wouldn't hesitate to call him, morning, noon or night.'

Henry smiled and decided to skip breakfast.

'What is that?' asked his mother, not looking at him or expecting a response. She just cocked her head and started sniffing the air, a look of total disgust playing across her face.

Henry couldn't quite figure out what seemed unusual. Then he realised. That Dimwit was nowhere to be seen. School was still closed and he found that without it, he didn't quite know what to do with himself. He never called his friends and he found that he didn't miss them. He didn't even think about fucking anymore and usually that was all he thought about. He seemed to have drawn a blank with each morning and embraced it. But, however dimly, and quite unrelated to the body, he still felt unsettled. The days still looked gray, dusty, as though there were no more new days to be had, and the old ones were being re-used.

He stood in the centre of the street and looked around for him.

Nothing. No one. The posters on the trees ruffled in the wind.

He walked on and found himself at the park. He considered walking along the burn again. Maybe he'd find another body. Emily's this time.

He sat on the swings and smoked instead. As usual it was disgusting and he ground it out halfway.

'Got any cigarettes?'

He turned around. The boy from the bus was standing

behind him, his giggling sidekick beside him. There was a girl there too, holding onto the boy. It took Henry a while but he realised it was the girl, the pregnant girl, he'd kissed. She looked at him blankly.

'Last one,' he said and turned back around, started swinging. The boy grabbed the chains from behind and stopped him.

'Was it fuck,' he said.

'Are you the father?' asked Henry, pointing at the skank.

'Yep,' said the boy, smiling. Henry thought of the child growing up in their care and felt a sudden surge of anger. He bit his lip.

'Looking for more naked ladies?'

Henry smiled and pulled a cigarette out of his pocket. He lit and dragged on it. The boy smiled. Henry smiled. And then, he put the cigarette out on the boy's face. He hadn't even thought about it and as he was doing it, it didn't seem like a big deal. He felt like doing it and so did it. The boy screamed and held his hands to his face.

'Bastard!' he seethed. Henry stood up and walked towards him. The skank pulled the boy back and screamed at him.

'I know where you fucking live!' she shrieked. Henry wanted to punch her in the stomach until she miscarried.

The sidekick stood there, mouth open. Henry moved towards him and he flinched. The boy was walking around in circles, holding his face and shouting threats. But he didn't come any closer to Henry who eventually just walked away, his mind already moving on.

He decided to go to bed. There was nothing on television and his parents seemed to be in an odd mood. He started up the stairs when his father called him back down.

'There's a couple of kids outside our house. Teenagers. Do you know them?'

He went to the window and looked through the blinds. It was the boy and his skank. They sat on the opposite side of the street, partially hidden by the trees that lined the edges of the pavement.

'One is this pregnant girl that used to go to school. The guy is just an idiot. They're not friends.'

'Uh-huh, and why are they sitting there watching our house?'

'I'm not sure.'

His dad looked at him and smiled. He looked highly amused.

'You really don't know?'

'No.'

His father nodded.

'I see. And this pregnant girl... Is it yours?' he chuckled softly and raised his eyebrows.

'No, dad. It's not mine.'

A thump sounded out from somewhere in the house. His father paid it no mind, just kept staring at him, smiling.

'What was that?' asked Henry.

'I don't know. Ask your mother.'

'Where is she?'

'In the cellar,' said his father, a barely suppressed chuckle escaping his throat.

Henry emitted a nervous little snort and stood silent, listening. Another thump.

'Seriously, what is that?'

'Ask your mother,' he whispered.

Henry moved past him and headed towards the kitchen. The cellar was a dark, unpleasant place that Henry had been in twice in his lifetime. It was where they kept the

Christmas tree and any unwanted bric-a-brac they couldn't bring themselves to throw away. It was small and spidery and never part of his thinking. It could only be accessed through a small wooden door next to the steps leading up to the kitchen. He walked down the steps and stood outside the door. There was a light inside. He opened the door. The smell hit him immediately and he gagged.

His mother stood under the single bare light-bulb, her back to him. There was something at her feet.

'What is it, Henry?' she asked.

'Dad wanted to know what the noise was.'

She nodded slowly. Henry felt sure she was smiling at something funny.

'He knows what the noise is,' she said.

'I don't.'

'Oh, I think you do,' she said. She still hadn't turned around. The shape at her feet moved.

'...What's that?' he asked.

She turned around. She was indeed smiling.

'Have a look,' she said and moved aside.

Henry stepped in, the smell somehow not as foul to him anymore, and bent down to take a look. It was a large burlap sack. He opened it up. Emily was inside, a rag in her mouth. Most of her hair was missing, torn out at the root. She was filthy and bony. When she saw him she started wriggling wildly.

Henry stood up quickly, hitting his head off the light-bulb, which popped, leaving them in a darkness that was almost unbelievable in its totality. He felt his mother's hands at his neck, her breath on his face.

'Do you like your birthday present?' she asked.

Henry couldn't answer her, her hands were tight around his throat.

'Do you like your birthday present?' she hissed.

41

He nodded. He could feel Emily writhing against his ankles.

She squeezed his throat and kissed his cheek. It was the first time she had ever kissed him and the strangeness of it somehow scared him even more than the fingers on his Adam's apple.

'What do you say?' she whispered, then let go of his throat. Emily was thrashing now, ceaselessly beating against his legs. Instinctively, he kicked at her and she let out a shocked, broken little whimper. He kicked again, his crotch getting hotter with each kick. He kept kicking until he felt something hot and wet against his thighs. It felt amazing, like never before. He breathed out and shuddered, his mind awash with colour.

His mother touched his shoulder and told him to go and get ready for bed. School started tomorrow. The softness in her voice almost made him cry, but he didn't. He stayed strong.

'Tell your father to come down when he's ready,' she said. Henry nodded and, in a daze, wandered back into the house.

His father still stood by the window. He smiled at Henry.

'Mum says to go down when you're ready.'

'Great. Thanks, Henry.'

They stood silently for a while, just standing there. Henry's father motioned with his hand to the window.

'They're still there, you know. Are you sure they're not friends? They might like to come in.'

Henry smiled slowly and nodded his head.

'I'll go and see,' he said and as he walked he could feel himself growing hard again. He opened the door and waved at them.

The Skin And Bone Music Box

Andy P Jones

Awooden soldier cartwheels through the air. Mediter-
ranean sunlight flashes across the smooth lacquered
surface of his immaculate uniform: red tunic, black
trousers and miniature buttons of real brass. The toy soldier's
arms flail spastically as he twists and spins through an open
window.

Marco, sitting cross-legged on the floor, unfolds his
chubby limbs and crosses the room towards the window. He
walks slowly, picking his way through a graveyard of wood,
clay and tin. Dead toys that other boys and girls would have
cherished. Toys reduced to splinters and shards by a child
who treasures nothing because he can have anything.

Marco looks through the high church window onto the
roofs of the hovels below. The peasants pay gruelling taxes
to his father, obey the laws born of his shifting whims, and
live in fear of his brutality. Marco is only seven years old, but
he already understands that one day they will do the same
for him.

He tilts his head downwards and inspects the shattered
wooden body on the flagstones beneath his window. From
a less lofty perch, Marco might notice that the fallen hero's
painted smile is fractured into a grimace. Denied this irony,
he is, nevertheless, amused by the miniature carnage. Marco
chuckles.

Rosa sings. Her voice glides through and around the wood and sackcloth stalls of the marketplace. Fatherless, and with a Mother too frail to labour and too crippled to whore, Rosa sings for both of their suppers. Brown, silk-smooth hair clashes with her coarse rags.

In this village raped by taxes, charity is as rare as manure from Marco's headless rocking horse. This is a hand-to-mouth community. And a broken widow and her malnourished child don't have able hands to offer. But they still have mouths to feed.

One of these mouths, however, is more than merely hungry. It shapes notes so pure they shimmer in the fetid air. Rosa sings melodies that float above the fog of harsh voices and violent smells. This barefoot child who never asks, who always smiles. This waif with an angel in her throat. She brings something to the market beyond price and barter. And so, anything they can't sell, they give to Rosa. The stone bleeds, but it's not good and it's not enough. And this pale girl who floats crystal song above the cesspit will soon die of starvation.

Marco hates the market. The reek of poor people disgusts him. But Marco wants toys. He plucks a glass apple from one of the stalls, and the trader holds his breath as the boy watches his own bored reflection swim across the smooth blue-green glass.

Rosa's gift whispers in Marco's ear. His face softens, his brow unfurrows. Marco carefully, respectfully, replaces the glass apple. He walks towards the beautiful weave of pitch and tone.

Marco is a full year younger than Rosa — not that you would guess as he stands, enchanted, before her. An ever-full belly and a head spewing over with arrogance add to the boy what poverty takes from the girl.

Marco raises a fat finger and points at the music box made entirely of skin and bone.

We recognise this view. A high, arched window frames a brown collage. Small squares of wood and straw squeezed together above the heads of the men, women and children who stagger through life in this dusty manor. The vista is partially obscured by a shining head of shoulder-length, chestnut hair.

We recognise this voice. Languid, serene, perfect.

Marco turns his back on the window and faces into the room. His features are twenty years older now; precocious contempt has hardened into handsome malevolence. He regards his reflection on the surface of a blue-green glass apple and hurls the brittle fruit across the room.

The apple explodes against a wall, radiating fine shards of glass onto Rosa's head. Rosa doesn't flinch, she simply halts her song.

Time has changed her too. Her body has filled out, but it is soft and doughy. The muscles in her useless legs, too badly broken and too crudely set, have long since wasted away. Blood seeps from a thin cut in her forehead, but her scarred face no longer feels pain.

Rosa wipes the blood from her eye and sings the first high, clear note of a different song. Her mouth is twisted but her voice remains true.

Marco turns back to the window.

Hostage Situation

Joe L Murr

Trent Gulo almost walked straight back out of the bank when he saw the queue. More than twenty people were waiting their turn, half of them senior citizens. This was bad. They always wanted to chat to the tellers about their grandchildren, cats, and incontinence. He'd be here for God knows how long.

Patience, he told himself. He needed to deposit the cash he'd got for plumbing services rendered, two hundred and fifty dollars in small bills, and do so today. Otherwise his rent check would bounce. Nosy landlords were the bane of his existence.

He got in line behind a fat man in denim overalls. Sweat beaded on the porker's bald spot. The pinkish scalp reminded Trent of roasting ham. He had a sudden urge to stick a fork in it and call it done.

Already he felt like a coiled spring, and he was getting tenser by the minute.

'Goddamn,' he muttered. People like him shouldn't have to wait in line. He deserved preferential treatment. Clenching his teeth, he tried to wait like a good consumer. To while away the time, he thought about how he'd boil and season the head of the pretty young thing he'd killed yesterday.

Five minutes later, he'd barely advanced a few feet and two soccer moms joined the queue. One of them had a baby in a backpack. It started crying. Someone should smother it.

Snap its neck. Anything to shut it up. That would be so easy.

He wondered how much more of this he could stand.

'Goddamn,' he said again.

The fatso turned and gave Trent a broad smile. 'You said it, brother.' He wiped his forehead with a paper tissue. 'Must be something wrong with the air conditioning. Can't get worse than this, eh?'

Trent bored into his meek brown eyes. 'I have no interest in having a conversation with you.'

'Jeez. Sor-ree.'

Trent glanced back at the doors of the bank. Outside, cars streamed by, windows flaring white with reflected sunlight. Three men came into view, backlit by the harsh flicker. At the doors, they halted for a few seconds to pull something onto their heads. Trent suddenly knew that this was not his day.

'God damn.'

The trio marched in. Stockings disfigured their faces. One of them was a giant, over seven feet tall. He carried a gym bag and a sawed-off shotgun. The other two drew pistols.

'Everybody down on the floor now!' the giant shouted.

Trent complied immediately, thinking, How many times have I heard that line on TV?

Around him people shouted and screamed. He wished they'd just shut up and get on with it. The sooner the robbers got what they'd come for, the sooner this would be over, and the less the chance of bloodshed. Didn't they understand that? Of course they didn't. They never did. Many were the times he'd whispered, 'Hush, hush, this won't hurt.' He never meant to hurt them. But their fear always excited him and he could no longer control himself. Even now he felt the thrill surge through him. He looked at the mascara tears tracking down the faces of the prone soccer moms and thought of sharp implements.

'That's right,' the giant said, 'on the floor.'

The screaming died down to sobs and oh my gods. Even the baby went quiet.

'Cover them, Crosby,' the giant said. Trent twisted his head around for a clear look. Crosby was the beefy guy wearing a Metallica T-shirt and combat boots.

'Yeah,' Crosby said.

'Stills, start at that end.'

'Gotcha, Nash.' Stills was decked out in a tie-dye shirt and ragged jeans. Under his pantyhose, round glasses bulged like goggles.

Nash the giant and Stills walked out of sight. Trent was facing away from the counters and didn't think it would be a good idea to antagonize Crosby by turning around for a better view. He could hear well enough what they were doing.

'Fill the bag.'

All right. Five minutes, and they'd be out of here. He began to rehearse his statement to the police. Nothing he said should arouse any suspicion. As he thought of what he'd say, he listened with mild amusement to the soccer moms weep and the fat man on his other side gasp and whimper.

The baby began to bawl again, but Trent didn't mind too much now.

A few more minutes, and it would be over.

Then he heard the gunshot and knew that that wasn't the way it would play out.

A man groaned in pain. A second later the sawed-off boomed. Someone hit the floor with a squelch. A fresh chorus of shrieks and whimpers erupted. Trent's nostrils quivered. There was blood in the air.

'Stills, you okay?' the giant said.

'Gutshot me, man.'

Crosby ran out of view, shouting, 'Motherfucker, mother-fucker!'

Trent had to see what was going down. The scent of blood made him abandon his caution. He curled up into a ball and then squirmed around.

Stills was leaning against the counter, hand on his stomach. A dark stain spread on the tie-dyed shirt and down his thighs. A man in a cheap suit twitched on the floor, face torn open to the bone. The revolver in his hand clattered against the tiles.

'He ain't dead,' Crosby said.

'He is now,' Stills said, and raised his pistol. He squeezed off three rounds. The first got the twitcher in the chest. The other two went wide. A grandma howled in pain, clutching her shattered wrist.

'Fuck,' Stills said. 'Sorry.'

'Let's go,' the giant said. He retrieved the bank guard's gun.

Crosby helped Stills stand up straight. 'Hang in there, buddy.'

The giant slung his gym bag and an almost empty Hefty bag on his shoulder and followed Crosby and Stills to the door. 'Everyone, stay down!'

Trent exhaled. Well, that was that. Until the police came, he'd just lie on the floor and enjoy the sobbing and the heady smell of fear and blood. Although he had an urge to crawl over to the dead man and tear into his flesh, he didn't have to do that, and he wouldn't. He could keep himself under control. He wouldn't get the bloodlust, not here, not now.

He stretched out and tried to relax.

Then he heard the sirens. Crosby, Stills and Nash crashed back in. Stills dropped groaning to his knees. Blue and red lights flashed through the doors.

'God fucking damn,' Trent said.

The fat man rose to his feet and made a run for it. Something must've snapped in him. The giant gave him the other barrel and his belly burst in a welter of gory blubber and he slumped.

Yummy.

The baby's screams went up a notch.

The giant reloaded. 'The bitches with the baby,' he said. 'Get up.'

No response.

'I said get up. I'm sick of listening to that noise. You hear me?'

The soccer moms finally got up. Trent watched with interest. It was about time they did something about the baby.

'Go,' the giant said.

They shambled to the door.

'Go out, then stop. Sit on the sidewalk. If you try to run, I'll waste you, got it?'

'Please just let us go, please.'

'Got it?'

The women did as they'd been told and sat down on the sidewalk. Red and blue washes of light haloed their hair.

'Crosby, keep them in your sights.' The giant took out a cell phone and dialed. A moment later, he shouted: 'No, I won't "please hold", I'm robbing a fucking bank here. You hear me? Goddamn. They put me on hold.'

Just then a phone rang behind the counter.

'Pick it up,' the giant shouted.

A middle-aged teller answered it. 'Yes? Yes, he's here. Sir? It's for you. The police.'

The giant marched over to the counter and took the phone. 'All right, this is the situation. We have hostages. You see those two ladies outside with the baby? They move, they die. You guys do anything, they die. Don't talk back. We want a car and a doctor, okay? In half an hour. If it takes longer than that, people will die.'

He hung up.

'Bad scene, man,' Stills said. He sat against the wall in a spreading slick of blood. He clawed his shirt open and inspected his chest. 'Oh crap, I think I can see a piece of gut hanging out.'

Trent smacked his lips. This was going to be torture.

And if it dragged on for too long, he wouldn't get to deposit his money on time. The rent check would bounce. He'd have to call his landlord and explain. How infuriating. He hated to draw attention to himself. Never give anyone a reason to remember your face.

It suddenly occurred to him that the situation might turn out even worse. What if he got shot and ended up in the hospital? If he were out cold for a couple of days, his landlord might enter his apartment to find out why the rent hadn't been paid. The bastard would snoop around and find all his pretty things.

His fists clenched. He growled involuntarily.

'What the fuck is that?' Crosby said.

Oh Christ, he thought. I'm getting the bloodlust.

He closed his eyes tight and tried to think nice thoughts. Discipline. Back down in daddy's cellar. That'll learn you to keep still.

But he couldn't stop growling. Adrenaline surged in his system. It took all his self-control to stay on the floor. He bit his hand. Pain was good. Causing pain would be better. No, he must not, not where people can see. He tried to ride it out.

Two pairs of shoes squeaked up to him.

'It's him,' Crosby said.

The giant said, 'You ever see someone having an epileptic fit?'

'Nah.'

'Me neither. What the hell's wrong with him?'

'Maybe he forgot to take his pills. Or something.'

'Whatever. Grab him, we're tossing him out.' The giant raised his voice: 'Lady, call that number the cop left, tell him we're releasing a hostage.'

Trent was hauled up. Cigarettes and beer stank up the robber's skin, but at this moment even that wretched aroma was enough to make Trent salivate. He needed somebody's flesh.

'Jesus,' Crosby said, 'he's vibrating like a jackhammer.'

'His mouth's foaming, too. Maybe it's rabies.' The giant cackled. 'Don't let him bite you, man.'

Crosby frog-marched Trent towards the door. The blood-lust was peaking. He could no longer resist it. He unleashed it. He jerked himself free and spun around.

Close up he could see Crosby's eyes through the panty-hose. They were dull and stupid and now widened with belated surprise. Trent slammed his forehead right between them. There was a crunch and Crosby staggered back, hands cupping his nose.

The giant raised the sawed-off. Trent grabbed Crosby by his shirt and flung him towards the giant just as both barrels went off. Crosby folded in two like a collapsible chair.

The giant cracked the shotgun open. Trent howled and rushed him. The giant tried to sidestep out of the way but lost his footing on the bloody floor and fell. Trent followed him down and hammered his head against the floor until he went still.

One more to go, no time to savor the carnage. Kill first, feed later. Trent rolled off the giant and turned to face Stills — but the man wasn't there anymore. A blood trail led from the wall to the door. He advanced at a crouch, his only thought to pull the fucker's guts out with his bare hands.

Stills was kneeling on the sidewalk, his back to the entrance. He pointed the pistol at the baby. A police bullhorn squawked protest.

Trent went through the door as silently as he could, trying to bite back his growls.

'Get me a car now!' Stills shouted, his voice cracking as he tried to compete with the baby's bawling. 'And a doctor! I've been gutshot, man!'

Trent closed in and seized Stills's pistol arm. The gun went off into the air. He twisted the arm down over his knee. The pistol clattered to the concrete. He followed that with a jab to Stills's belly. The man screamed. Trent took the pistol and shot him under the chin. The back of his head splattered apart.

They were all dead now. Trent's bloodlust surged to an almost unbearable peak. There was only one way to satisfy it. His attention focused on the dead man. He was only semi-aware of noises and activity around him. He dropped the pistol and bit down into the corpse's cheek. He started gnawing. Blood erupted into his mouth. His fingers sought the bullet hole in Stills's belly. He'd claw it open to get at the goodies within.

Moments later he was yanked up. A prize morsel of cheek dropped from his lips. He stared in uncomprehending fury at the men in blue who surrounded him. He hit them, tried to bite them, tried to struggle free, but they were stronger than him. Something struck his head and he blacked out.

When he came to, he found himself in the back of a police car. It was moving. He was handcuffed. Steel mesh separated him from the two officers in front. He remembered that he'd done a bad thing in public. The thing to do was to act perfectly reasonable. They'd have to let him go.

Trent said, 'You can let me off at the next intersection.'

The driver's eyes met his in the rearview mirror. 'Can't

do that, champ. You got a bit carried away there.'

'It's just that I need to deposit some money. Or my rent will be late.'

He could already see his landlord unlocking his door.

'Not gonna happen. You'll be spending some time under psychiatric observation.'

Looking through all his stuff.

'You know, Mr. Gulo,' the other officer said, 'you could've been a hero if you hadn't...snapped.'

Finding his pretty things.

'Goddamn.' His fists clenched. He began to growl.

Rite of Passage

Ken Goldman

'... we're captive on the carousel of time. We can't return we can only look behind from where we came...'
The Circle Game, Joni Mitchell

Tuesday, July 27 4:37 p.m.

They stood on the long elevated walkway near the center of the Jerome Avenue overpass, five kids thoroughly bored with the nothingness of a hot summer's day. Far below on The Cross Bronx Expressway the afternoon rush hour had begun, and the rows of traffic moved like sluggish snakes.

The older boy of sixteen with the blotched coffee-colored skin was called Speed, his name memorialized in a tattooed snake-like 'S' that crawled up his neck. Taller than the others and significantly uglier, he studied the noisy flow of motor vehicles before reaching his decision. He turned to look at the untested kid with the faggoty name of Eugenio, the name probably a result of his being raised in a home filled with girls. A more suitable moniker could be worked out later, assuming this neophyte didn't turn candy-assed during the next few minutes.

'Think you got the stomach to do what I tell you, new boy, no questions? You made of the real stuff? Enough to do what I say right now, hey, new boy?'

For no apparent reason the others seemed to look up to Speed. The fat kid was Mateo — rechristened 'Brute' — whose only discernible talent was his ability to fart on demand. Rumor had it the chubby kid's own initiation had involved a freckled little girl from St. John's Elementary and a pink pair of Barbie panties which he had kept inside his pocket since that day. He always laughed dutifully at Speed's jokes, while the Corteza twins, Buzz and Kink, remained respectfully silent, careful never to contradict or offend with an opinion. Speed wasn't their leader; that was someone older named Carlos Sanchez whom Eugenio wasn't supposed to meet until later when the other 163rd and Ogden boys agreed it was time. But Speed conveyed his own unpolished brand of menace, and he didn't give a rat's turd about what answer he received from the new kid. This induction rite was just another way of passing the time. He could have just as easily asked the recruit if he felt like running down to old man Duster's store to pick up a container of water ice and some soft pretzels for him and the others. Given the heat of the afternoon, that wouldn't be such a bad idea.

Speed's question to the young Ogden-Boy hopeful was, of course, academic. If Eugenio hadn't the stomach — more precisely, the gonads — to prove his mettle, he wouldn't be here. The new kid understood this and so did the others. Still, the ritual played out according to the rules.

Eugenio's smirk proved a sufficient reply.

'Okay, then. First stranger comes through the overpass gets some serious damage done, don't matter who ...' In a self-conscious stew of Hispanic attitude and Scorsese-speak that he had copped from Carlos Sanchez, the tall boy addressed the others. But Speed's eyes never left Eugenio's. '... Don't matter who crosses. We hit, we run. We're talkin' whoever... nun, cowboy, or the Mayor, our new pal here gon' to lead the way, maybe get us some pocket change. New boy's gon' to show us what he's got inside him. You still in, new boy?'

'You feeel like eeeting my sheeet, new boy...?'

Eugenio again kept his response minimal, but secretly he waited for this moment. He flaunted the switchblade he had concealed inside his jeans for the occasion, snapping it open for effect. The polished steel glimmered in the sun.

'I'm in.'

Nods of silent approval from the twins. Brute looked to Speed before committing himself to a response.

Speed's expression revealed nothing of the wheels turning inside, however slowly. Because the new kid's bit of showmanship seemed to work on Kink and Buzz, Brute ventured his own awkward smile towards the recruit. Rules established, the five waited.

An elderly white woman appeared from the Deegan Expressway side of the overpass. She looked confused, as pasty-faced old crones always seemed. Stopping in her tracks she stared at the five youths loitering on the walkway. She would have to maneuver herself past them if she intended to visit the borough's east side. Eugenio figured the shriveled old bag was taking inventory of the situation, probably considering whether the trek across might be worth the potential danger for a lousy carton of skim milk. Like a wary animal she stepped forward once, hesitated, then spun around when a 'D' train passed nearby. Eugenio half expected the jumpy bitch to sniff the air for the scent of a predator.

Some internal warning system must have kicked in because grandma disappeared the next moment. Eugenio would never have admitted it to the others — he did not admit it even to himself — but he felt relieved the withered old prune had decided against journeying across the overpass today.

Some little kids approached from the west end, two boys and a red-haired girl. She was dressed in denim shorts and dirty T-shirt exactly like her male pals, except hers had a Ricky Martin iron-on, the same one Eugenio's ten year old sister, Lucinda, wore and would probably keep wearing until it rotted.

The kids paused. Maybe one of them had second thoughts about the lengthy trip across the overpass. One boy whispered to the other, the girl giggled, and all three ran off in the opposite direction. Eugenio had no idea what had just transpired among them, but he felt certain the five Ogden Boys' presence on the Jerome had something to do with their altered plans too.

During the next ten minutes no one approached the walkway. Although the sun would set in a few hours, the heat felt more scorching now than it had at noon. The five waited in silence, their dark eyes shifting from the east side entrance to the west. A pedestrian entering either end of the walkway required several minutes just to arrive at where they stood, and the relentless heat did not make the wait pleasurable.

'The first one,' Speed had said. 'The first one who comes over...'

Eugenio spotted the dog sooner than the others. It seemed too handsome an animal to be a stray. Panting in the heat it sniffed its surroundings as if trying to locate something familiar. The others had been watching the walkway's east end, but the yellow labrador approached from the west. Although moving in hesitant stop/starts he was almost halfway across before Speed spotted him too. Eugenio did not consider the dog's advance worth mentioning.

Speed thought otherwise.

'Well, well... What have we here?' Speed crouched to one knee and called to the animal. 'C'mere, boy... You lost, eh? Hey, big fella, you lost?'

Although large, the dog did not appear very old. With an almost puppy-like shyness, tail wagging, he inched toward the group. The lab must have somehow become separated from his owner which probably explained why he seemed so trusting. Eugenio felt something heavy sinking deep inside his gut. He suddenly needed to spit out more words than he had spoken all afternoon.

'The first one that comes over... nun, cowboy, the Mayor... the first one...'

'He's got a collar, Speed... see, it's an expensive harness collar, too, not a choker. Good lookin' dog like this got to belong to someone who's got some green. That means a reward. And he's wearin' a license. That proves he's — '

Speed clearly wasn't interested in money honestly earned and didn't bother investigating the canine's credentials. Likely he just wanted to wrap up the afternoon's ceremony to get out of this heat. He led the animal by its collar closer to Eugenio. When the dog followed willingly, the kick–boxer inside Eugenio's gut again sprang to life. The kid never really believed Speed wanted him to cut some poor white lady's throat just to gain admission to their exclusive little street club. But a dog was only a dog, after all. It mattered little how expensive an animal he seemed. What mattered now was how easily the moral considerations of Eugenio's initiation rites could be readjusted. That opened up shitgobs of new possibilities.

Brute spoke up. 'Christ, he's shakin' all over. He's lost, all right. This is one scared mutt.' The twins decided to have themselves a look too. For a moment the bad-ass veneer the four had worn all afternoon disappeared, and they were just some kids trying to calm a gentle and frightened animal.

But Speed wasn't drawn in, absorbed in studying the expressway below while considering exciting new possibilities for goosing up the day's roster. The traffic feeding out of the Grand Concourse and the George Washington Bridge had picked up. It was coming at a good clip now, a damned good clip. Eugenio felt uneasy about what his pimpled mentor might be thinking. Reading the tag hanging from the lab's collar seemed a lame attempt to buy some time, but he could think of no other way.

'Dog's name is Buddy. Says so right here on — '

Absently he stroked the dog's muscled haunch, and the animal's shaking subsided a bit. Another tag dangling from the lab's neck caught Eugenio's eye. But Speed already had turned his attention back to the others.

'A slight change of plans, startin' now. I'm askin' our good pal Eugenio here to demonstrate those balls of steel he assures us he has.' Smiling through crooked yellowed teeth, he set a bead on his recruit. 'So, new boy? You think you own a pair?'

'You theenk so, keed, hey...?'

A chorus of blaring horns from the Interstate screamed inside Eugenio's brain while Speed waited for his answer. When no answer came he went for the face-to-face.

'You hear me talkin' to you? You need me to spell it out? Or is that blade in your pocket just for show and tell?'

'Speed, look... I'm not gon' to hurt this dog, okay? Jesus, man, read what's on his collar. Tag says he's a 'companion' dog. This is a seein'-eye dog some poor blind bastard must've lost, for Chrissakes! His leather strap here's been torn off. I won't cut this animal, Speed! I won't!'

Speed's face exploded in a full grin that resembled a mouthful of chipped crockery. His expression remained in place like a fright mask while the snake on his neck sprouted purple veins.

'You think I want you to slice up your little perro friend into burger bits with that fuckin' toy you're carryin', Eugenio? No, man. I got more heart than that, and a whole lot more sense. I don't see no 'vantage to leavin' a blood trail for any local badges, even if it's only a dog's.' He studied The Cross Bronx below.

'Traffic down there's all of a sudden movin' like a sonofabitch so late in the day, don't you think? Heat must be sendin' folks home early, hey?'

Eugenio tried to keep his voice steady. He couldn't.

'Speed, listen...'

'— No, you listen, you soppin' load of chickenshit! This ain't about some piss-assed oral exam. This mutt's goin' over the side, new boy. If you don't do it, I will. And if I do it, you can kiss your Ogden-Boy tomorrows good-bye and go back to playin' with your sisters. Time's come to see what you're made of, new boy.'

'... load of cheekensheet... keees good–bye...'

Eugenio looked to the others hoping to spur a sympathy vote from any of them. The twins' faces had returned to stone. Only Brute looked as if he might protest, but instead he chewed his lip and said nothing. From kids like Brute any show of dissent proved too tall an order.

If only one of them said something, stepped forward to take his side, protested that this was a dangerous and crazy thing to do, totally crazy and so fucking wrong...

No one did. So hot... too hot to think clearly... too damned hot to know the right thing to do... too hot to even think at all...

Eugenio didn't think. He acted. He pulled the lab tightly against his chest.

'You touch this dog, Speed, and I'll kill you.'

The youth had not marked the time of day he uttered those words. He did not own a watch. There would have been no need to check the hour had he worn one. But at exactly 5:13 p.m. on this summer afternoon Eugenio Ramos Tourlitos was about to enter the most significant moment of his life.

Tuesday, July 27 5:09 p.m.

Dr. Adam Hampel thanked God he had fixed the BMW's air

conditioner last weekend. After another ten–hour shift he could never have manipulated the Z3M Roadster through this cross-town traffic in such heat. From the speakers Linda Ronstadt was finishing the last bars of 'You're No Good,' and those lyrics might summarize Jeannie's sentiments if he didn't arrive home soon. He tried changing lanes, but that made no difference at all.

The time had come for some damage control. He pressed the cellular's speed dial, hoping when he walked through the door an hour late his beautiful enraged wife would not feel pissed enough to use his steak dinner as a shot-put. Fortunately traffic ahead picked up beneath the Jerome Avenue overpass. With luck the 240 horses beneath his hood could make New Rochelle before his young bride dialed her lawyer. The phone rang once.

'Adam?'

'Three words, babe... Emergency cardiac infarction. George Clooney wasn't around and there was only me in the E.R. You want the long version, or should I just cut to the "I'm sorry" part and stop for flowers?'

Jeannie managed a stony silence, but she wasn't very good at maintaining her pretence.

'Damn you, Adam. I was going for an all-out tantrum here, so don't you get charming on me. Dinner will be ruined again, of course.' She added a carefully measured but ineffective pause. 'Just hurry home, okay?'

'Sure thing, babe. Maybe if I can jog it from here, I can make it...'

This would have been Hampel's clever rejoinder as he began the last thirty seconds of his life. Instead he had opportunity only to utter 'Sure thin — ' before his brain registered the large tumbling object as something alive. The plummeting creature appeared above his field of vision, kicking at the air. It came flailing at him like a furry cannonball that shattered the vehicle's windshield. Still kicking it struck the surgeon square in the face with the force of a dropped anvil. In a flashfire of pain lasting only a millisecond his cheek bones splintered. Hampel's head snapped backwards with a crack like dried wood as his neck bone detached from his body and the world went black.

'Adam...? Are you — ?'

The BMW ricocheted off the guard rail, careening into the center lane. Still bleating Jeannie's voice the cellular bounced across the dashboard until its casing shattered. The sports car spun out, tossed about like a crimson pin ball. It collided with an eighteen–wheeler hauling produce to New Haven, the thick crush of metal echoing clear to the Concourse. The weaving truck spilled several hundred Jersey tomatoes onto both sides of the roadway sending the small Beemer through the guardrail into the opposing traffic. It struck broadside a southbound school bus returning to St. Michael's Academy in Perth Amboy. The surgeon, never one to wed his Armani to a seat belt, catapulted from his vehicle. He skittered head-over-wingtips across the highway like a skimming stone, coming to rest balls up in the spilled tomatoes that smeared the highway like a great parmigiana.

The chain reaction began. Veering out of control the rammed bus rolled over, concluding for thirty-three girls and two nuns an otherwise exhilarating summer session at a Connecticut presentation of Shakespeare's 'As You Like It.' Tearing a great swatch through the traffic the school bus bludgeoned the guard rail, which sheared it in two. Several girls hung in misshapen contortions from the windows above the St. Michael's logo, their uniforms and faces reduced to red smears.

Scattered about the highway like abandoned dolls more schoolgirls lay in twisted heaps surrounded by 'As You Like It' playbills. Some twitched as if they had been spread on a skillet. Most lay still.

Amid the debris of flesh and metal a bloodied labrador retriever moaned, barely breathing near the tangled steel that had been a red sports car. The injured animal crawled whimpering and crab-like on its belly, then lay motionless on the blistering asphalt.

Tuesday, July 27 3:48 p.m.

In the world whose boundaries bordered 163rd and Ogden Streets, from the old fruit and vegetable markets beneath the elevated trains to the ten-acre tract of weeds at Vyse Street, there was no one in the South Bronx who did not know Carlos Sanchez. But a reputation in the borough did not come easily. Every day you had to earn the right to others' respect, and you had to demonstrate that nothing could stand in your way from doing exactly what you wanted. Those on the outside might shake their heads and question the logic of what seemed senseless acts of violence or cruelty. The world beyond the barrier didn't understand. It was not about hurting anybody; it was never about causing pain or misery. Such things were by-products of an on-going process, a means to an end.

The blind black man entering Joyce Kilmer Park at 3:48 on July 27 would serve that purpose. Carlos and two of his friends had been watching him for almost an hour as he walked with his companion dog in the cool shade of the elevated trains. Occasionally he stepped into a store for a cold lemonade or a piece of fruit while he mopped the beads of sweat glistening on his dark skin. He had not quite reached his elderly years, and the tacky straw hat he wore made no fashion statement. But judging from his neatly pressed Bermuda shorts and well-scrubbed seeing-eye dog, he was in no need of a tin cup. Possibly the blind stranger lived in the reconditioned condominiums across from the Bronx Mall. There was no way to determine anything certain about him other than he was sightless and did not appear wanting for cash.

But that was enough.

The youths followed a half block behind, watching him as the guide dog led its master safely along the paths into the park. Once inside, Carlos and his two friends closed the gap. The heat of the late afternoon had kept the benches of Kilmer Park completely empty. This worked to the boys' advantage.

Uttering the simple commands of 'Forward' and 'Stop,' the man located a water fountain. From his pocket he pulled a collapsible dish. He placed it on the ground to offer his canine companion a cool drink in the shade and a brief respite from the day's oppressive heat. The dog, in a demonstration of canine etiquette, waited for his master to sit on the bench.

Smiling, the man gave the labrador a reassuring pat on his head. Once satisfied that he could safely turn his attention to the water, the dog lapped gently at the dish.

Carlos watched this, and kept his voice low.

'Moose, you stay on the path, see if anyone comes. Antony, you're with me.' He pulled out a knife as they approached the park bench. This would be one of Sanchez's easier hits, almost not worth the trouble in such heat. But such were the rites even when the sweat poured from your brow. Your personal worth was continually subject to judgment, and nothing would be gained by turning away from an opportunity once it presented itself.

'A hot day, yes?' Carlos remarked to the man on the bench. 'Muy caliente, as my friend here would say.'

'Muy caliente,' Antony repeated to inform the blind man that Carlos had brought company.

'That's quite an animal you have there... yes, quite

an animal.' Carlos reached to pat the yellow lab. When it growled at him, he pulled his hand quickly back.

'My dog won't hurt you, young man, but you ought not do that, touch my dog, you know. It tends to distract Buddy from his job, you know...' The man's voice revealed his discomfort over the intrusion.

Carlos saw no reason for small talk in such heat. He shifted himself to the bench's other corner. When the kid spoke again the blind man jerked at the sound of his having moved closer. Sanchez pressed the side of his knife's blade hard against the man's cheek and talked close to his ear.

'Can't say I know a whole lot 'bout these seein'-eye mutts, mister. Tell me. How distracted would ol' Buddy be if I used this shank to cut your fuckin' throat right now?'

The blind man did not demonstrate as much fear as Carlos would have liked.

'Listen, young man. I don't have very much money — '

'We'll start with your watch, then. Hold it out for my friend, will you?' He slapped the cold steel blade against the man's cheek.

'My watch is in Braille... It won't be of any use to — '

'— Hey, you blind fuck!' Antony interrupted, taking the timepiece and holding it up for Carlos to inspect. 'Did anyone ast you t' talk?'

Carlos studied the watch in his accomplice's hand. The blind fuck was right. It was a useless piece of shit. Antony tossed it into the bushes.

'Your wallet!' Sanchez said, trying to keep his voice reasonably calm. He crouched to stroke the dog's head again, hoping to dissuade it from suddenly tearing his lungs out.

The blind man held out a thin and tattered wallet. Carlos took it, not surprised that he found less than thirty dollars inside. Now he was genuinely pissed. He wasn't going to walk away empty-handed.

The dog was sharp and seemed to sense Carlos's anger. Panting with the heat, the yellow labrador again expelled a low rumbling gurgle despite Sanchez's vigorous strokes. Carlos pulled away, looking over at Moose hoping he had not seen.

'Tell your mutt to stay calm.'

The man hesitated, then spoke softly. 'It's okay, Buddy. This young man isn't going to hurt us. There's a good dog...'

His voice sounded convincing enough, but the animal's growls persisted as a low guttural sound deep inside its throat. Sanchez took the gamble and slowly cut the leather strap of the harness collar. He pulled at the lab gently, but the dog resisted, refusing to budge from the blind man's side. Its teeth were sharp enough to make Carlos uncertain he trusted the labrador's stubborn protectiveness.

'You're one smart fuckin' pair of eyeballs, huh, boy?'

Antony saw Carlos cut through the dog's harness. From his gate-keeping position on the path Moose looked behind him and saw it too.

'Jesus, man! I wouldn't do that...'

Moose caught himself. He knew that Carlos Sanchez did what he did because he felt like doing it. No further explanations were needed.

The blind man sensed the sudden slack in the dog's short leash.

'What in the name of — ?'

'Make this dog move, mister,' Carlos said. 'You make this fucker move away from you now!'

The man on the bench held fast to the leash with both hands although the strap was attached to nothing. A bitter smile bordering on defiance smeared across his face.

'He won't do that. It's called intelligent disobedience, young man, a concept I'm fairly sure is beyond your grasp. It's part of his training. He won't budge if he senses danger to me, not even if I tell him to.'

'... a concept beyond your grasp...'

Carlos heard only the put-down. This meant the man had upped the ante beyond the basic grab-job Carlos had anticipated. But this was okay, this was just fine. Carlos lived for new challenges. He would show this guy something about intelligent disobedience.

'Antony, pull that trash bag out of the can and bring it here. Better get a second one too. Our pal Buddy looks like a double-bagger. Maybe even three.' He turned back to the bench. 'Not smilin' now, are you, motherfucker?'

Carlos wondered if the man might suddenly panic and shout for help, but luckily he was too smart for that. He remained silent trembling on this park bench like he had a bad case of the shivers despite the infernal heat. Probably he was hoping these damned kids were pulling some thoughtless prank and nothing more serious than that.

Carlos felt uncertain how far he wanted to take this. He had already committed to forcing the plastic bags around the helpless pet, maybe hauling the struggling animal a few blocks away. Later he could set the animal free without looking like his spine had turned to putty. This was a shitty enough thing to do to a blind guy just because the man had given him attitude, and a terrible and shitty thing to do to the dog that was probably the poor fuck's only friend. The blind guy would get his dog back somehow, someone would find it, Carlos assured himself. Ditching the guide dog was only something to fill the time on a hot day when you were so fucking bored you could bust. That the man was black didn't even enter into it. Hell, the man had dissed him in front of his friends, so it was really a question of honor, and Carlos really had no choice. This made the act almost okay and not so shitty. Almost.

How much harm, really? In an hour someone would find

the dog. Life would go on like it always did, and the others would tell yet another story about how Carlos was just being Carlos.

How much harm, how much, really?

While Sanchez held the labrador down, the words repeated silently inside him.

'Just Carlos being Carlos...'

He tried not to think about his actions as he and Antony forced the thick trash bag over the kicking dog's head.

It was 4:02.

Tuesday, July 27 8:23 a.m.

The day did not officially begin until the phone call came.

'Eugenio, your sister is on the phone!'

He always picked up the receiver with the same words, but he waited until he heard his mother hang up before he spoke them.

'So, Loosey-cinda, they make you a nun yet?' Eugenio waited for the familiar giggle that always came. He missed hearing her laugh ever since she had left for the summer.

'Twelve Hail Marys for giving your sister lip,' she said. 'So, how you doin', Eugenio? Are you being good?'

'Ogden boys don't need to be good, 'Cinda. Just have to be cool.'

His sister went silent. Eugenio knew what that meant.

'Is that thing today,' she finally asked, 'that initia — initiati-a — ?... What do you call it?'

'Initiation. Yeah, it's today. You goin' to tell Mom?'

More silence. Then, 'Maybe I will... Maybe I should do just that...' For a ten year old, the girl could turn suddenly serious so damned fast.

Now Eugenio laughed. 'Then maybe I should take your Ricky Martin CDs and use them for Frisbees, eh?'

The familiar part of the daily ritual returned now, the almost religious moment that included turning on Lucinda's boom box. They didn't allow music where she was spending the summer, and this part of the morning phone call had become mandatory for his kid sister.

'Maybe I won't let you hear it this morning,' Eugenio teased. Not 'till I hear you say something nice about my new friends, Lucinda Marina Tourlitos!'

Lucinda knew when diplomacy was called for. To hear Ricky Martin every morning she would lie through her teeth.

'Ogden boys are sooooo nice... cute an' sexy an' smart an' soooo good-looking, and... and... did I already say sexy?'

'Okay, okay, no need to overdo it,' Eugenio said, unable to stop himself from smiling. 'And now, ladies and gentlemen...'

He snapped the 'PLAY' button of the boom box picturing the delight on his sister's face. Together they sang the familiar chorus.

'Up-side in-side out... Livin' la vida loca...'

The brother and his young sister continued singing even after the recording ended. The routine never varied, yet the laughter always came.

This was always the best moment of the day.

Tuesday, July 27 5:13 p.m.

'You touch this dog, Speed, and I'll kill you.'

... and at exactly 5:13 p.m. on this summer afternoon Eugenio Ramos Tourlitos was about to enter the most significant moment of his life.

No other time existed but this moment. There were no yesterdays or tomorrows to concern him, because whatever choices he made after today would be measured against what he did right now. It all came down to a kind of chain reaction, an unfolding of events like the demonstration of toppled dominoes he had once seen at the mall with Lucinda. Today he had been like one of those dominoes set into motion by the others.

Eugenio understood what he had to say. He hoped his voice would not reveal any uncertainty because he felt anything but certain of his next words.

'You don't come near this dog, Speed. I'll do this myself.'

He could almost hear Lucinda, lecturing to him, 'Eugenio, Eugenio, what were you thinking? Why would you want to do such a terrible thing?'

But Lucinda wasn't here now. His little sister had got it into her head that some day she wanted to be a nun, and she was spending her summer at that parochial school in Jersey, a place just over the bridge called St. Michael's in Perth Amboy, and she was off today with the nuns seeing some bullshit Shakespeare play in Connecticut.

Lucinda wasn't here now, and the yellow labrador was.

Eugenio tried lifting the animal, but the guide dog proved too heavy for him alone. Brute stepped forward to assist, and together they managed to clumsily raise the animal above their heads to the edge of the screen mesh rail of the overpass. The labrador, although terrified, struggled but did not bite, did not even try. Gasping for breath, Brute stepped back. This moment belonged to Eugenio alone. Speed and the twins watched without saying a word.

But Lucinda would not remain quiet.

'Eugenio... Eugenio... what were you thinking...?'

Below and less than a block away the yellow school bus was nearing the underpass, but the boy's mind was elsewhere. Eugenio hoped the others did not notice him look away as he heaved the kicking dog over the side...

Fat Hansel

David Turnbull

When Gretel arrived at her brother's house, hot and bothered from her long journey, she found him sprawled out on the fireside rug. He looked as vast and immobile as the proverbial beached whale. Gretel inhaled a sharp intake of breath, well and truly staggered by his astounding girth. In the seven or eight months since she'd last paid a visit he'd piled on the pounds.

His face looked like an over-inflated balloon, cheeks so puffed out and swollen they almost consumed his sunken eye sockets. His belly drooped around him like colossal hunks of flaccid blubber. His upper arms were the size of ham thighs. His fingers were as stout as pork sausages. It was impossible to tell where his monstrous legs ended and his gargantuan buttocks began. His shirt and trousers were like huge canvass tents; still they strained at the seams. Around him the furniture was dwarfed by his immense presence.

'Come in,' he'd called out when she'd knocked on the door, clutching the letter he'd sent to her. She had picked her way cautiously through the discarded rubbish that had piled up in the gloomy, ill-lit hallway. When she entered the front room Hansel adjusted the pillows that were propping up his engorged head. He looked up at her and smiled disarmingly. His bulldog jowls shuddered.

'So what happened?' asked Gretel.

'Like I said in my letter,' replied Hansel, 'she's gone.'

Gretel edged her way around his huge frame and eased herself down into an armchair. 'Gone where?' she asked.

'Gone for good,' came Hansel's terse reply.

'And the baby? My precious nephew? Little Hans? Where is he?'

'Gone with her.'

'Why?'

'We argued.'

'About what?'

'Three guesses.'

'Your weight?'

'She called me fat.'

Gretel raised her eyebrows. 'She had a point.'

'It's not right to mock the afflicted,' complained Hansel, groaning as he shifted position again. 'I have a medical condition. You know that more than anyone.'

'That's as may be,' said Gretel. 'But you're not going to tell me that all of this started because Helga has the audacity to state the patently obvious.'

'She tried to put me on a diet,' whined Hansel. 'She wanted me to eat lettuce and radishes and pickled gherkins — I'm not a rabbit!'

'Maybe she was trying to act in your best interests,' suggested Gretel.

'I don't like that kind of stuff. She did it to provoke me. I like bratwurst and roasted belly pork and schnitzels cooked in butter and strudels with brown sugar and double cream.' He began to salivate and lick his lips. 'You don't want to know how horrendous my appetites have become, Gretel. You really don't want to know.'

Gretel sighed. 'It was eating that kind of stuff that made you like this in the first place.'

'Don't you start on me now,' moaned Hansel. 'I would have thought that if anyone would understand my predicament it would be you!'

'If you're in a predicament,' said Gretel. 'It's one of your own causing.'

'It's not,' snapped Hansel. 'It's post traumatic stress. You were there. You know what that old witch was going to do to me.'

Gretel clicked her tongue loudly against the roof of her mouth. 'You have to move on. That was years ago. It's all in the past.'

'For you maybe. But not for me. I think about it all the time. About how she locked me in that cage and stuffed me with food to fatten me up. About what she was planning to do with me when I was good and plump.'

'So you binge out and make yourself even fatter to help you forget? That makes no sense what so ever.'

'It makes me feel better,' said Hansel.

Gretel sniffed the air. A meaty aroma came drifting in from the kitchen. 'Are you cooking something?' she asked.

'Some stock for broth,' replied Hansel. 'A meat pie for my lunch.'

Gretel sighed again. Louder this time, shaking her head in despair as she did so. 'So you can get up off your backside then? You are able to look after yourself? Particularly when it comes to food I suppose?'

'I'm not a complete invalid,' said Hansel, sounding hurt. 'I just need a bit of help to tidy the place up. But if it's too much to ask...'

Gretel rose to her feet, rolling up her sleeves. 'So it's going to be just like the old days is it?' she harrumphed. 'Me cleaning and scrubbing, while you stuff your face?'

Gretel got stuck into the kitchen. Two weeks worth of

greasy dishes were piled up in the sink. The rubbish bin was overflowing with dried up potato peel and mouldy cabbage hearts. The table top was caked in glistening, fatty grime.

Hansel was up on his feet now. She could hear the floor-boards in the front room groaning under his weight as he blundered around with the feather duster she had forced into his clammy hand. She suspected that the only reason he'd been lying on the floor when she arrived was to make himself look pathetic enough to elicit sympathy from her.

Hansel was good at eliciting sympathy.

Everyone sympathised with Hansel. Poor Hansel, locked up for all those months, nearly roasted alive, almost eaten for supper, practically sliced and diced and devoured.

What an ordeal.

Such torment and tribulation!

Poor Hansel.

Poor, poor Hansel!

What about poor Gretel?

No one ever thought to ask how she felt. All those months on her knees, up to her armpits in soapsuds, scrub-bing the witch's floors from back to front and front to back. The old hag was never satisfied. There was always some sort of criticism belching out with the foul breath from her snag-toothed mouth. 'You've missed a bit,' she'd cackle.

Or: 'Are those dirty streaks that I see?'.

Or: 'Is that a footprint over by the door?'

Or: 'Is that a hand print by the cooker?'

Damn the pus-filled boils on her hoary old face!

And through it all Hansel would be sitting pretty in his cage, stuffing his face with honey cakes and fondant fancies. Licking his fingers one by one. Picking bits out of his teeth. Belching and farting.

Suffer?

When did Hansel ever truly suffer?

Were his knees bruised and swollen? Were his finger-nails splintered and bleeding? Were his hands afflicted with dermatitis and eczema? Did he survive on runny gruel and dried bread crusts? Did he sleep on wet straw on the scullery floor?

The sound of bubbling and hissing from the direction of the stove interrupted her thoughts. Hansel's stockpot was coming to the boil. Wrapping her hand in a towel she lifted the lid. Delicious smelling steam engulfed her face. She gazed down on the translucent amber liquid that bubbled scrumptiously over meaty bones and hunks of onion and carrot. Her stomach rumbled as she set the pot to simmer.

Hunkering down she opened the oven doors and marvelled at the wondrous pie that sat there, slowly crusting golden brown, in a large oval baking dish. She sniffed at its appetising aroma and smacked her lips, resisting the temptation to sneak a pinch of the buttery pastry. Her big brother might be a fat, lazy attention–seeker, but boy could he cook!

Hadn't it been Hansel's culinary skills that had won Helga's heart in the first place? Hadn't he wooed her with gastronomic dexterity? Although she was as skinny as a sparrow Helga had a healthy appetite. And despite what Hansel said about her she was good for him. The best thing that ever happened to him in fact.

Helga had relatives in the village. They would know where she had gone.

Gretel decided to go down there and confront them first thing in the morning. Gretel fancied herself as the peace-maker. She was sure that things were not beyond repair. Besides there was her nephew, Little Hans, to consider. She would force Hansel and Helga to consider him too. Put the little one first. Get them back together for the sake of the boy. Leave things to develop from there.

That decided she gave Hansel's stock a vigorous stir with a wooden spoon and licked away succulent juices that splashed onto her fingers.

A few minutes later Gretel returned to the front room to check on Hansel.

She found him on the floor again. This time his back was propped against the wall. The feather duster was propped up beside him. His legs were splayed wide so that his belly rested massively between them like a mountain of molten lard. He wiped his sweaty forehead with a grimy handkerchief.

'Hard work this housework lark,' he said.

Gretel cast a critical eye around the room. Dust motes shimmered in the shafts of mid-morning sun shining in through the window. The ashes from the previous night's fire were still cold and sooty in the hearth.

He hadn't exactly knocked himself out.

'Maybe if you had done a bit more housework,' she said. 'Helped out a bit around the place, Helga would still be here.'

'I doubt it,' shrugged Hansel.

'You might have shed a few pounds into the bargain,' said Gretel.

'I doubt it,' sighed Hansel.

'Your problem is you lack motivation. Don't you miss Little Hans? Don't you want to make the effort to get your son back?'

Hansel looked up at her with a despondent expression on his face. 'You should know better than anyone how difficult it is for me to exert myself too much.'

'Not this again,' Gretel muttered to herself.

'You know what it was like for me in that cage,' Hansel continued. 'There wasn't enough room to swing a cat. The bigger I got the less room there was. My energy was drained. It made me all stiff and lethargic.'

'Poor you,' sneered Gretel.

Hansel was on a roll. 'I had nothing to do all day but think and eat and think and eat. And you know what I mostly thought about?'

Wearily Gretel slumped down into the armchair once more. 'Surprise me,' she heaved.

'I thought about what the witch was going to do to me. I thought, how come she wants to eat me when she's got all this food? She can't be hungry. It must be the taste then. There must be something really special about the taste of human flesh. And I wondered what it would taste like...'

He shook his head ruefully and his cheeks wobbled.

'Did you ever have terrible thoughts like that, Gretel? Did you ever wonder what human flesh might taste like?'

Gretel felt her face flush red. Her heart was thumping in her chest. For some unfathomable reason a trickle of sweat traced a cold finger down her spine. She sprang to her feet, avoiding Hansel's eyes.

'I have to get on,' she blurted. 'I haven't got time to gab all day. And neither have you!'

Gretel busied herself with the dirty dishes, crashing them loudly back and forth from the sink to the drainer in an effort to drown out the ideas and notions that were filling up her head. Had she ever thought such terrible thoughts? Back then, long ago, in that creepy old cottage, had she wondered what it might feel like to close her teeth around muscle and flesh.

Perhaps she had?

There was so much of the experience that seemed lost to her. Some things were as clear to her now as the day they happened. Like endlessly scrubbing the floors and polishing the kitchen worktops. Other recollections were extremely hazy. For example how long had they actually spent incarcerated by the old hag? Hansel said a few months. To Gretel it seemed much longer.

There was a huge, disturbing gap in her memory. The period from the time they kicked the witch into her own oven and slammed the door shut till the time they stumbled back into the village all ragged and dishevelled was a complete blank. An empty void where somehow it was as if she'd blinked out of existence for however long it took them to find their way home. Sometimes she lay awake into the early hours of the morning straining to remember.

She'd spoken about this to Hansel on many occasions, hoping that something he told her might spark a light in the total darkness that cloaked the entire incident.

'We were lost in the forest for a long time,' Hansel would say. 'We walked in huge circles. We slept in gullies and ate nuts and roots. We cried endlessly. We hugged each other for warmth and comfort. We were like wild things by the time we found our way out. Our clothes were in tatters. Our bodies were all punctured and bloody from the thorn bushes.'

Try as hard as she might Gretel could remember none of it.

So maybe once in a while, back there in the witch's cottage, she had wondered just what it was that drove the old woman to imprison children and fatten them up for the oven. And perhaps, like Hansel, she had considered what it might taste like?

She thought about it now. The very notion made her gag.

The smell of the broth and the meat pie seemed to close in around her like a malevolent mist. Her stomach turned and she felt the colour draining from her face. She clutched the rim of the sink to steady herself.

'Hansel!' she called out, as much to regain control of her senses than anything else. 'Hansel! I hope you're not shirking again!'

Gretel fled the kitchen and found her way down the creaking stairwell to her brother's basement. Here were all the accoutrements of the laundry room. A scrubbing board and a mangle. Chunky blocks of green soap. Scouring brushes for grimy collars. Starch for clothes that were Sunday best.

On the wall above the deep stone sink hung a family photograph from the day that Little Hans had been christened. Hansel and Helga smiling broadly. Helga seated with Hansel standing slightly to her back. Little Hans wrapped in a white blanket, nestled in Helga's arms. Hansel gazing adoringly down on both.

The proud parents.

The loving family.

That was what Gretel had to focus on. It was down to her to bring the three of them together again. Leave the past to moulder and decompose like the dead thing that it was. Concentrate on the future. After all the past could not be changed but it was entirely possible to direct events towards a future goal.

She turned her attention to the mountain of dirty washing that lay on the basement floor. As she had suspected Hansel had just dumped everything he'd worn over the last two weeks down here in anticipation of her arrival. She listened to see if he was moving around upstairs. Not a sound. He was probably slumped back down on the fireside rug, yawning and scratching his fat behind.

This is it, she thought. If I don't get Helga to come home, this is me for the rest of my life. I'll be stuck here, running around after Hansel. It'll be just like the witch's cottage all over again. Me scrubbing floors while Hansel stuffs his face and grows more and more obese by the day. Only this time he'll be trapped inside a cage of his own making. And I'll be trapped right here with him!

She glanced up at the photograph again. Helga had a delicious beauty about her. Her blond hair hung in plaits around her shoulders like corn sheaths. Her eyes were as green as gooseberries. Her cheeks were like rosy apples. Her lips as ripe and red as plums.

Some said she was far too good for Fat Hansel.

Not Gretel.

I'll bring you home, she vowed. I'll stick around till you persuade Hansel to get his eating under control. We'll work out an exercise plan for him. We'll sit out in the garden while he chops wood and does all the chores he never got round to in the past. You'll drink fresh lemonade and I'll bounce Little Hans on my knee.

Her attention returned to the pile of dirty washing. Clicking her teeth and sighing with irritation she set to work separating the whites from the coloureds. Hansel's clothes were gargantuan. She very much doubted that she'd be able to fit more than two items on the washing line at a time.

They reeked of his sweat and were crusted with bits of foods that had dribbled from his gluttonous mouth. One shirt in particular was so stained with splatters of gravy or sauce or something that she'd have to leave it so soak for days. She looked at the cuffs and groaned. They were caked in the stuff.

It was then that she noticed the chopping block in the

corner. Its wooden surface was stained the deepest red. She walked over to it and picked up the meat cleaver that lay on top of it. Bits of fat and gristle were congealing along the razor sharp blade. Tiny splinters of bone fragment were lodged in the cracks of the chopping block's furrowed surface. Crimson splatters of blood fanned out across the wall.

What had Hansel slaughtered here? Something big. A deer perhaps, or a wild boar? Hansel was no hunter. How had he managed to catch such a thing, let alone drag it down here? She thought of the stockpot bubbling on the stove and the meat pie baking in the oven. Her greedy brother could obviously muster a considerable amount of energy when it came to filling his belly.

She picked up the meat cleaver and sniffed the blade cautiously. It smelt sweet and salty. She felt sure that it wasn't venison or pork, but the smell was familiar. Once, long ago, she had experienced something similar. She took another sniff and pondered.

Then slowly her memories unfolded before her, multiplying like the vicious rash of some rampant infection. Terrible memories of her last moments back there in the old witch's cottage.

The crone had been kicked into her oven and the door slammed shut. Her ear splitting screams had fallen silent and had been replaced by the crackle and hiss of roasting flesh. She and Hansel had been crying in each other's arms, stumbling towards the front door of the cottage, when the aroma hit them. The delicious smell of meat basting in its own oily fat. They froze in their tracks. Gretel looked at Hansel. His eyes seemed crazed and haunted. His lips gleamed wetly. Not a word passed between them as they turned on their heels and went back to the kitchen.

Still without a word Gretel had opened the oven door and Hansel had hooked the witch's charred, smoking carcass out onto the kitchen floor. She was no more recognisable as a once living thing than a stuffed turkey would be on a Christmas Day table. Her creamy translucent juices oozed out onto the terracotta floor tiles.

It was Hansel who tasted first. Leaning down he took a pinch of crispy flesh between his thumb and forefinger and popped it into his mouth. He quivered. His eyes rolled back in their sockets. He rubbed his oversized belly.

'Yum,' he sighed. 'Good.'

He took another pinch of meat and held it out to Gretel. After a brief moment of procrastination she closed her eyes and leaned forward. It felt like Manna on her tongue. She had not tasted meat for so long. She chewed it and savoured the texture between her teeth. And swallowed and felt the warm, masticated chunk slide down her throat like honey.

She looked at Hansel and he looked at her. They both looked down at the roasted witch. In the blink of an eye they fell upon her. They fed in a tumultuous frenzy; clawing and tearing and shredding.

Hansel was just plain gluttonous. Gretel was half-starved. Survival, she told herself. I'll die if I don't eat. I'll never make it back out of the forest. But all the time as she chewed on the fat and gnawed on the bones, her mind was filled with a guilty thought that repeated itself over and over and over.

'I've never tasted anything so good in all my life!'

And when it was over. When all that was left on the floor before them was the rib cage and the spine and the witch's scalded and blistered head. When they both sat there covered from head to toe in grease and crumbs of crackling, burping shamefully. That was when the disgrace of what they had done drove them screaming into the forest.

There in some shady hidden gully they had wiped the memory of the incident from the disturbed recesses of their minds.

Till now!

Gretel looked again at the chopping block and the meat cleaver. She looked at the bloodstains on the block and on the wall. She looked with fresh eyes at the stains on Hansel's huge shirt. In a blind panic she fell to her knees and rummaged through the laundry pile till her hands came upon the items she had dreaded finding. Helga's shredded dress and the blue blood-soaked blanket that had belonged to Little Hans.

She looked once more at the picture that hung above the sink. Was that really adoration in her brother's eyes? Or was it something else? Something closer to avarice?

She heard him now in the kitchen above. The floorboards bowing as he plodded towards the stove.

'Let me be wrong!' she cried out loud as she dashed for the stairs. 'Oh please let me wrong!'

The stockpot was still simmering away on the stove. Her hands trembled as she picked up the cloth and lifted the lid once more. Luscious steam engulfed her like a humid shroud. She looked down into the bubbling, churning cauldron and her eyes acknowledged what they'd denied when she'd first caught sight of them. Finger bones! Tiny bleached finger bones, bobbing around on the scummy brine of the stock.

Gretel's hand went to her mouth. Her heart clattered against her chest.

'Little Hans,' she whimpered.

Her legs felt as if they were about to collapse under her. She steadied herself against the stove. Hansel's words came banging back into her head. 'You don't want to know how horrendous my appetites have become. You really don't want to know.'

Nearly two weeks! That was how long he had claimed since Helga left with Little Hans. What else had he created and devoured in that time? Schnitzels? Peppered Steaks? Bowls of goulash? Fat links of sausage? A meat pie?

A meat pie!

Gretel pulled open the oven doors. Warm aromatic air wafted out and caressed her face like some hideous seductive wraith. The shelf was empty. She heard the chink-chink of cutlery coming from the front room.

'Hansel!' she cried. 'Hansel! Don't you dare!'

When she barged into the room Hansel was balanced precariously on a dining–chair that was almost completely swallowed by his bloated posterior. Before him on the table sat the pie; golden brown and steaming. A huge wedge of it had been transferred onto his dinner plate. He was chewing voraciously. A trickle of glossy brown gravy was dribbling over the undulating ridges of his innumerable fleshy chins.

Gretel's mouth began suddenly to salivate. She was horrified and disgusted with herself. She felt her insides twist with a spasm of ravenous yearning. Her lips smacked guiltily. Free at last from the constraint that had been forced upon it by her subconscious mind, her hunger became as horrendous and uncompromising as that of her insatiable brother. It was like a curse. She would never be free of it. Nausea washed over her and made her giddy. Nonetheless her stomach rumbled with callous expectation.

Hansel looked up. His eyes had that crazed and haunted look about them. 'Yum,' he said. 'This is good!' He stabbed at a chunk of meat with his fork and held it out to her. There were little creamy flecks of fat buried within its deliciously layered texture. It looked as if it would just melt on your tongue.

'Want to try some?' asked Hansel.

Gretel swallowed hard. She opened her mouth to speak. The reply hung on her lips for a long, long time.

Childhood

Morag Edward

'**M**ummy, mummy,' Ben whispered. There was no response. He tried a slightly louder 'Mummy!' but she just started to snore.

His mother's maternity leave meant she stayed at home with him now. Ben had been delighted with the changes to his daytime routine. It was a shame daddy still went to work, but at least he came home for tea and helped Ben make pudding. Chocolate pudding was the best, especially for whoever got to lick the bowl it had been mixed in.

Ben played with his train set on the cool flagstones of the kitchen floor and mummy continued to doze in the chair by the Aga. After a while he became restless again and prodded her fat foot to try to waken her, but only gently. She slept on.

Ben decided to make the most of the situation and go exploring on his own. It was almost like playing hide and seek and mummy did have her eyes closed, so it really was almost the same. He went into the hallway and glanced at the cellar door. Ben knew that on the other side of the door were flights of steps leading down into the depths of the house.

There were all sorts of things in the house that were off-limits to Ben, including the kitchen if unsupervised, the computer and piles of neat paperwork in the study, the medicine cabinet in his parents' bathroom and the ladder to the attic. Of them all, the cellar was the one that fascinated Ben the most. Everyone knew that the entrance to fairyland was underground.

Ben's parents had taken in a lodger who was staying temporarily in the comfortably converted cellar. Ben liked Uncle Joe and was glad that he'd come to stay. Ben knew that he wasn't supposed to go down into the cellar and disturb Uncle Joe, or leave toys lying around outside the cellar door. Those were the house rules, and Ben was usually quite a good little boy. This didn't stop him trying to sneak a peek through the open cellar doorway when Joe was heading in or out, just in case he could see a flash of tiny iridescent wings in the background.

Ben loved adventure stories about hidden tunnels and buried treasure and magical lands and little creatures like fairies and pixies that played in the garden. He also listened to the scary warnings about bad men and talking to strangers and what happened to little boys who played with sharp things, hot things and things they had been told not to touch. He preferred the stories about fairies and pixies living at the bottom of the garden. He'd drawn endless pictures of them for mummy, daddy and Uncle Joe who said they had put the pictures up at work so they could look at the drawings while they were away from him and so that everyone could see how talented their little boy was. Ben's own bedroom was papered in drawings of the small winged creatures and his obsession showed no sign of fading.

Ben and his mother often had their own adventures in the garden searching for the little magical people, but so far they hadn't been able to find any of them. Mummy wasn't very good at bending down to look under fallen tree trunks at the moment but she was useful for checking the high-up places. A chattering bird bouncing on a branch, butterfly wings catching the sunlight, large insects buzzing past, leaves suddenly rustling on a still day, sounds from the undergrowth, all had Ben pointing eagerly and rushing to investigate.

This morning he and his mother had left the fairies and pixies a gift of leftover chocolate pudding to show that they were friendly, and that Ben was looking forward to meeting them. Usually they left dandelion heads, pine cones or daisy chains, so today's pudding was a treat. He'd made sure the piece of pudding was neatly laid out on a low branch and when they'd returned after lunch to check on progress, it had all gone! Ben was so excited he'd sent his mother investigating every high part of the bushes and garden wall while he crawled around the undergrowth calling out to the pixies. He was a child who didn't talk much, in fact he was usually very quiet, but when it came to communicating with the little people, Ben was vocal. The extensive garden search and subsequent clean-up was possibly why his mother had so disappointingly fallen asleep now.

Ben could never say what made him dare to open the cellar door that afternoon. He had just been playing, crawling quietly around the hallway, following the pattern of the old floor tiles, but then he reached up and fiddled with the door handle, it turned, and he discovered that the door was unlocked. He paused to see if the sound of his guilty fast-beating heart had woken his mother, but she snored on, her vast expanse of stomach rising and falling rhythmically. Ben opened the cellar door and reached up on tiptoes to flick the light switch on. He looked at the flight of stairs leading down into the cellar.

'Don't go down into the cellar, its Uncle Joe's room now,' that was one of his parents' rules and he could still hear it dimly, but that was a hard thing to remember now that he was standing there actually looking down the well-lit cellar steps with growing excitement.

The little boy stepped down each stair with difficulty because they were large and his legs were short, and there did seem to be an awful lot of steps. There were two short flights down with a turn in the middle where they changed direction. From the top step he hadn't been able to see down further than this mini-landing with its potted fig tree. Once there he stopped and from this leafy vantage point, Ben surveyed the forbidden land.

The cellar had several windows along one long wall, all up near the ceiling. There were two huge bookcases stacked full of old books; an enormous desk and a large comfortable-looking chair by it. He couldn't see round the corner to the en-suite bathroom but he knew it must be there. Ben had been allowed to play with the tiny sample tiles the decorator had left behind. At one end of the cellar were Uncle Joe's bed and a chest of drawers. It was while Ben was looking at the bed and thinking about how neat it was and wondering if mummy made Uncle Joe make his bed too, that he noticed there was something odd hanging on the wall above the pillows.

Ben stared until he remembered to breathe again, but couldn't go any closer to look at it because he couldn't actually move. Uncle Joe had found a pixie and nailed him to the wall on two crossed pieces of wood to display him as though he was one of the hunting trophies grandpa had in the dining room of his house. But this wasn't a deer head; this was a little man, one of the magical people from the bottom of the garden. Ben felt so horrified he couldn't even scream. The fairy, or pixie, the little boy wasn't sure which, but the figure had a tiny beard and long hair so was probably a pixie, had been stripped down to a little twist of white fabric round where his underpants should be, and there was blood on him, blood on his forehead and on his side and on his hands where the nails were holding the arms

outstretched, and on his feet which had been nailed together at the bottom of the vertical piece of wood.

The little boy finally managed to move his head and
wrenched his gaze away from the sickening sight. He
focussed again on the big desk and saw this time that there
was something hanging on the wall above the desk too, and
it was another little man, just like the first and nailed up
to another wooden cross, and almost naked, and bleeding,
another dead pixie. How many more had Uncle Joe caught?

Were there any left in the garden? Had he hunted them
all down and killed them all? No! Ben's heart broke apart
and the terror, the sheer horror of his appalling discovery
finally reached through the shock and let him struggle to his
feet and run. He ran as fast as he could back up the stairs and
out of the bad man's cellar and into the hallway, safely back
into the hallway where he slammed the cellar door closed
and fell onto the floor screaming and howling and shaking.

His mother had woken up at the sound of the screams
but the little boy was oblivious to her as she rushed to scoop
him up and clutch him to her to try to quell his agonies.

'Ben, Ben, my baby, what's wrong, what's wrong, my
poor baby, shush now, shush.' She held her son tightly and
rocked him.

By the time Ben's father and Uncle Joe managed to get
back home from the office, the doctor was gone and Ben
had been sedated. He was laid out on the sofa in the sitting
room, with his swollen blotchy face resting on his mother's
lap as she stroked his hair and murmured comfortingly to
him. Ben was still awake but he seemed to be calm, though
he twitched from time to time. Their doctor had been at
a loss to explain the trauma as there had seemed to be no
physical cause and Ben's mother hadn't been able to shed
any light on a fright he might have had, as though any fright
could have made him so inconsolably broken. She was just

relieved that he seemed to have calmed down, finally. Ben's father and Uncle Joe rushed into the sitting room to see what had happened. The little boy took one look at them, focussing on the man who had been out hunting his beloved garden pixies. Ben started to scream again, and scream, and scream.

As the days passed, many adults talked to Ben. They tried comforting him, cajoling him, begging him and at one point just shaking him and yelling at him, but it became clear that he could not or would not talk. Eventually they agreed that it would be best if Uncle Joe moved out until Ben's problems had been sorted. Now Ben only screamed in his sleep, which seemed to be an improvement. His mother didn't leave his side but every day he just sat at the bottom of the garden quietly crying.

'Come on Ben, don't cry laddie, what must the fairies think? You'll be waking them all up,' attempted his mother as she sat beside him with one arm around his trembling shoulders. This prompted a fresh wave of howls and hysteria, which just added to the mystery and his mother's anguish.

The child psychiatrist decided that Ben was having anxiety issues about his mother's physical changes, and that perhaps he had some sort of exciting new form of pre-emptive sibling rivalry. He put Ben on medication so the adults were able to feel more reassured and worry a little less. Ben never spoke or smiled or drew pictures of pixies and fairies any more, but at least he didn't seem so loudly distraught and inconsolable. Some days he didn't even venture to the bottom of the garden but just sat at the kitchen window, dumbly staring into space.

After a few heavily sedated weeks all round and one dramatic rush to the maternity ward, Ben got a baby sister. The nervous adults were enormously relieved to discover that this event didn't set the little boy off again. In fact, Ben seemed thrilled and eager to sit by her cot and watch over her. He'd whisper to her even though he still wasn't talking to anyone else and he stood protectively by her when visitors came round to admire her. He brought her little presents of dandelion clocks and old pinecones every day, which he left on the floor by her cot. Ben adored his little fairy sister and she in turn would giggle and gurgle happily when he was around her. It was proving to be such a successful relationship that Ben's medication had been stopped. He still wasn't his old self, but something good seemed to be happening, and the whole family felt able to look to the future.

Then Uncle Joe came to visit the family, and brought each child a gift. He'd really missed Ben and was looking forward to meeting the new baby girl. He had remembered that Ben's most favourite things in the world were pixies and fairies, so had brought him a small painting of an enchanted land full of the little people, and a tiny realistic doll dressed as a fairy for the girl. The little girl herself was already dressed as a fairy, in a tiny sparkly pink dress and crumpled pretend wings. Ben waved a little fairy wand at his baby sister and she tried to grab it from him. She was fast already!

Ben's mother led Uncle Joe through to the children. 'Ben, look who has come to see you!' she exclaimed, 'are you going to show Uncle Joe his new baby niece for mummy? There's my good boy.'

As Uncle Joe approached the children. Ben turned round to see that awful man coming towards him and his fairy sister, holding out another of his dead fairy trophies and reaching out to get the baby girl this time. The fear overwhelmed him completely. Before anyone realised what was happening, Ben screamed and tried to drag the baby out of her carrycot, away from the man and to safety. Ben pulled at her by one of her tiny little arms and the new screams of the baby girl accompanied those of her terrified big brother.

The carrycot toppled over and as the baby hit the floor there was a cracking sound.

Ben's hysterics stopped after a few days but he still seemed unable to speak, and so it was decided that he would be placed in a children's clinic. Uncle Joe knew of one run specifically for emotionally disturbed children who needed to have a break from their families and be looked after and helped back onto the right path by professionals. This residential clinic was funded by the church, but the focus was on non-denominational medical care with first-class paediatric specialists for the children's problems. It had an excellent reputation and sounded as though it really might be able to help Ben.

They quietly drove Ben to the home, through the huge ornate gates and past the monkey puzzle trees. They parked outside a lovely old gothic building, where some of the staff members were waiting for them.

'It looks like a fairy palace!' Ben thought as he stared up at the turrets and the mossy gargoyles round the roof. He clutched the broken fairy wand he'd hidden in his pocket.

The adults got Ben out of the car and into the wheelchair one of the nurses was going to use to get him safely to his new bedroom. He thought the nurses looked funny, like penguins in their black dresses, thick black cardigans buttoned right up to the neck and black and white headcloths.

'This is one of the nuns who will be looking after you,' said his father with an encouraging smile.

'Call me sister,' the friendly penguin woman said as she helped Ben into the wheelchair.

'My sister,' whispered Ben. His mother flinched. She

would go back to the hospital to be with her baby daughter once Ben was safely installed in the clinic.

Gravel crunched underfoot as the nun turned Ben's wheelchair to face the dark gothic building, and began to push him towards the entrance.

Like Snow

Brian Richmond

The dead people did not appear suddenly. Slowly, ever so slowly, they began to emerge from the background like pictures in a darkroom. Some of the townspeople glimpsed them at this early stage but most of them said nothing. They would rub their eyes, look away, tell themselves there was nothing there. Well, there couldn't be anything there, could there? That shape behind the branches in the park...That face outside the tenth floor window...

Danny, being nine years old, was not so logical. The sound of his parents arguing downstairs came up through the floor and woke him. As usual, he put the pillow behind his head then pulled it round over his ears. Lying there, he thought he glimpsed something in the moonlight. When he stared at it directly, it disappeared. But, glancing from the corner of his eye, he made out a curve here, a line there. At first, he wasn't afraid. Then his mind seemed to sift and arrange these disparate elements, forming them into the vague shape of a standing man.

Danny leapt from the bed and hurtled down the stairs. He was so quick that his parents barely had time to stop shouting before he came into the room. The echoes of their anger seemed to still reverberate in the air so that the silence hissed. Danny flew right into his mother's arms and she knelt down to enfold him, glaring over his shoulder at her husband. The shaking boy told them about the shape but, of course, they called it a nightmare. However, his mother said he could sleep in with her that night. Daddy would take the spare room. Just until Danny settled.

But Danny didn't settle. He insisted he could still make out the figure, even in daylight. His parents dismissed this but, in their guilt, felt unable to force the issue. The boy stayed in with his mother at nights and, although dad was supposed to be sleeping in the spare room, Danny heard the subdued murmuring of the television throughout the small hours. The bedroom that had been his refuge was now a place of fear for him. Walking along the landing he would dash past the door even though it was kept closed. His parents tried to urge him to go in, telling him there was nothing to be afraid of, but Danny saw the outline growing stronger and, as time passed, his parents changed. They no longer brought him in, no longer denied that anything was there. They, too, seemed to hurry past the closed door with averted eyes.

Then, of course, the other dead people became visible, all over the town. In homes, offices and factories, in shops and streets and playgrounds, they coalesced. Not that they were ever truly solid. You could always see through them. Yet they were not blown or dispersed by the wind. In fact, they did not move at all and, certainly, no one ever heard them make a sound. Although they were clothed, it looked as if they wore shapeless, blanket-type material that draped over their bodies. They were old and young. Many people found the babies the most disturbing of all.

Their gradual appearance helped. If they had manifested themselves suddenly, chaos would have resulted. As it was, people did refuse to go into the places where the dead people — as they were now being called by almost everyone — had appeared. The worst sensation was that of going to, say, a rarely used cupboard, opening it and finding one of them there.

However, as time went by and in the manner of such things, people became used to them. After all, they didn't do anything, they were just there. The child who first ran through the strange figure in the playground was undoubtedly brave but, once others had seen he came to no harm, it soon became a game. Motorists routinely drove into them, then watched them shrink behind in the rear-view mirror. Rooms, quickly abandoned, gradually came back into use.

Speculation continued: scientists, priests, UFOlogists, all had their theories. They were the ghosts of the departed although, despite careful scrutiny of old photographs, paintings and records, no connection could be found between the dead people and the spaces they inhabited. They were energy imprints which changing atmospheric conditions had made visible. They were the signs of the coming apocalypse. They were, simply, dreams.

Camera crews came: at one point, it seemed as if everyone in the town was interviewed. Clusters of people were to be seen standing around the dead, measuring, sampling... all without success. The dead people could be captured on camera but the sampled air was just air. Spectroscopy detected nothing. When they first appeared, it was thought the dead would tell us everything. They turned out to reveal nothing. And the scientists and the film crews left the town while the evangelists and the spiritualists and the UFO enthusiasts stayed.

Like the rest of the town, Danny eventually became accustomed to his strange presence.

He even moved back into his room, although his father stayed in the spare bed. The dead man, whose image had first so frightened the boy, became just another aspect to his life and far from the most frightening one at that.

In fact, there was a certain kudos in having an apparition in your room. Classmates came round to play although Danny eventually stopped this when they started using the dead man to practice their Power Ranger martial arts moves. It was stupid but he felt punching the defenceless figure to be cruel, disrespectful.

Like the others, Danny's dead person appeared expressionless. Yet, looking closely at him, Danny sensed a sadness there and, maybe more than that, a kind of sorrowful sympathy. Although his parents weren't religious, something in the face reminded him of a picture of Jesus he'd seen in some book.

On those nights when his parents' shouting woke him, he found it comforting to see the dead man there. He took to speaking to his spectral roommate, telling all the things he couldn't share with his friends or his parents. The dead man never blamed, never judged, just always listened.

More than ever before, Danny's room became his refuge. He would sit on the floor and draw or read his comics and not feel lonely. There was no need to risk his mum's sudden bursts of temper or, much more frighteningly, her tears.

Then, just as suddenly and inexplicably as they appeared, the dead people began to fade.

Most people were glad. The ghosts — if that's what they were — had gone from frightening, to familiar, to annoying. A resentment began to build against them. Who were they? What did they want? Why didn't they just leave us alone? People sometimes swatted at them as they would at a smoker's fug, seeking to dispel them. It began to feel as if the townspeople were under surveillance, as if these unblinking figures were not just watching, but judging. Not everyone saw compassion in their eyes. Some saw condemnation, regret, warning. They didn't do anything, so what use were they? Why couldn't they just go?

Danny didn't share this sentiment. At first, he pretended

nothing was happening and, because the disappearance was slow, he was able to maintain this fiction for a while. When the shouting woke him, he could still count on the man to be there, constant, unchanging. Yet, as time went on, the truth became harder and harder to deny. All over town, the apparitions were fading.

Mummy and daddy sat him down and told him that dad was going to be staying somewhere else for a while. They stressed how much they both loved him. That nothing was his fault. That grown-ups sometimes needed time apart to think about things. Danny ran to his room and wouldn't come out. Eventually he opened the door to a promise that dad would take him to the park.

It was autumn. Tendrils of mist draped the bare trees like Halloween decorations. The playground in the park was empty, swings swaying in the bitter breeze. A dead person was there, an old woman, staring off over the top of the roundabout. She was fading like the others, almost gone but given extra definition by the misty air.

Danny walked over to her. He stood in front of her and looked into her eyes. They didn't return his gaze, just kept staring in that familiar unblinking way. Danny reached out to touch her but his father called: 'Danny! What are you doing? Leave her...that...alone!' Danny was shocked to hear tears in the thickness of his father's voice.

That night, when Danny climbed into bed, the dead man was almost gone.

Remembering how the mist had seemed to emphasise the lines of the woman in the park, he ran to the bathroom, picking up a white plastic container of talc and carrying it back. He poured a mound of powder onto the palm of his hand then blew it gently towards the dead man. Little specks of talc whirled in the air and Danny told himself the outlines of the face and body solidified somewhat.

Comforted, he climbed back into bed and fell into a restless sleep. He dreamt but forgot his dreams as soon as they ended.

When he awoke, the dead man was gone. Crying, he ran in to his mother and leapt into her arms. She held him close. 'Is he ever coming back?' Danny sobbed. Mummy squeezed him tight. 'I don't know,' she said, her own voice breaking, 'I don't know...'

In his empty bedroom, a thin scattering of talc lay on the floor. It looked like snow.

Like snow.

Adultery

F R Jameson

She lay her head on his chest and tried not to think of his wife.

He fiddled with her hair and stared at the wall ahead, already thinking of elsewhere and other things.

Apart from their breath the room was quiet. The sunlight shone though the curtains, lying them out in a haze of grey.

It was she who interrupted the silence. She always — despite wanting to keep him — opened her mouth and sent him away.

'What time do you have to get back?'

'Soon I guess. I've got to go to the office to pick up some stuff, and then — well, I think there's plans later.'

'Right.'

'We can stay a while longer though.'

'Oh. Good.'

She'd learnt to love and hate at exactly the same time. She was still pressed naked into him, but was filled with such quiet rage. She knew it was pointless articulating it. The afternoon would just end badly — screaming, yelling, him storming off. She'd think she was right, but tomorrow she'd crumble and call him. Even though she was the person wronged, she'd end up bearing the apology.

And so she stayed silent, hidden away with him on a sunny afternoon. Lovers, friends — looking forward to a quickie and another goodbye.

There was a grunt behind them, female and sexual. They both stared at the bare wall beyond the headboard, as if they'd be able to peer through it.

'Looks like someone has the same idea we do,' he said.

'That's what hotels this cheap are for, darling. Anybody checked in now is busy humping.'

The woman next door cried again. A high pitched yelp, enjoying the most pleasurable pain.

'Do I sound like that?' she asked.

It was one of their jokes that the little moans she'd thought were contained in her head were actually loud and projected.

'No. Yours are more prolonged.' He laughed.

The woman next door yelped again.

'I wonder what he's doing to her,' she said.

'How do you know it's a he?'

'Oh don't do that,' she said. 'Please keep your adolescent thoughts to yourself — please. Let's assume it's a man and a woman. Do you hear anything except her? I don't. I can't even hear the mattress, and if they'd been next door while we were doing it they'd certainly have heard the mattress.'

'Maybe their mattress is better.'

'Oh come on, how many times have we been to this dump? Have we ever had a good mattress? Do you really believe that the only good mattress they're hiding from us?'

'It's the best I can afford babe,' he said. 'It's the most I can spend without — ' he always hesitated to say his wife's name ' — noticing.'

The woman cried again and then gave a quick, harsh sigh.

She raised her head from his chest and studied that wall hard.

'Are we sure she's okay?'

'She's fine,' he said.

'That didn't sound like she was having fun.' She was whispering now.

He whispered back. 'Maybe that's just how she sounds. Maybe it's S and M and he's tied her up in some ridiculous position. Maybe he's stubbing cigarettes out on her. I'm sure she's fine and enjoying it and is a consenting party.'

The next cry was long, the clear sound of pain in her larynx. It shuddered the wall. There was a gasp, where she tried to draw air to the base pit of her lungs, then another elongated scream.

'She's fine and enjoying it and is a consenting party?' she asked.

He was looking over his shoulder, concern now on his face. He let go of her and for once she didn't try to hold onto him. He picked up the glass from the bedside table and placed it to the wall.

He stood at the wall for a long minute, trying to hear the happenings of the next room. Finally he let go and stepped back. He smiled at her reassuringly.

'Whatever's going on,' he said, 'it's stopped.'

Her next cry was awful. The word 'No' ripped from her stomach and dragged out so that the last of the syllables barely had the air to carry them forth.

He dropped the glass and it shattered on the floor. He leapt to the bed, to save his naked feet from the broken shards. He clutched her. One arm carefully around her waist, the other jammed over her mouth.

They sat there, wrapped into each other, desperate to not even breath. They could hear each other's heartbeats and both seemed far too loud.

They heard a step in the next room, shuffling and light, so they could only just pick it out. It made its way slowly to the wall, and then smacked itself into it. It didn't gently place its head there, it thumped it. It made sure that —

if there was anybody in their room — they knew it was listening.

They thought they could hear breathing in the next room. They thought it came from just the other side of the wall. They thought it was an incredibly angry breath.

They didn't know how long they sat like that — listening to being listened to. Tears rolled down her face; his were bottled up.

Neither of them was sure they heard it creep away from the wall. The step was too light, too delicate. They only knew — absolutely knew — the next time the woman screamed.

'Be quiet,' he whispered. 'If I let you go, please don't make any noise.'

She nodded and he slipped his hand from her mouth. Her gaze turned to him and sailed over his feet, he grabbed his hand back to her mouth just as she was about to scream. His toe was sliced open and blood was seeping across the white sheets.

'It's okay,' he whispered. 'It's just a cut. That's all. It doesn't hurt, it's not going to kill me. Please don't make any sound — you can't make any sound, he can't know we're here.'

The woman's next cry ended in a whimper, her strength ebbing away. They heard her sob, weep in pain and fear. There was a slap and then silence.

He let her go and sat back to the headboard, clutching a pillow case to his toe.

'What are we going to do?' she asked.

'I don't know.'

'Ring the front desk,' she said. 'Tell them. Get them to come up and stop it.'

'Yeah.' He picked up the phone. 'Surely somebody else must have done this. It's so loud. How can we be the only people to hear it?'

'How many people do you think are in this shithole?' she asked. 'If it's only us and there's no one in that corridor then we have to do it — please.'

There was another cry, the longest yet. It got choked in her throat, like she was being made to swallow it back down.

'Hello. Hello. Hello,' he said. He pushed the receiver down a couple of times and said 'Hello' again in his loudest possible whisper.

He looked at her. 'It's not working.'

There were a series of yelps — short, sharp articulations of suffering.

She pushed herself as far away from the noise as she could. He stayed by the wall, one hand with the pillow to his foot, the other holding that broken telephone.

'What are we going to do?' he asked.

'We have to go to the front desk, call the police — save her.'

He stared at her.

'I don't know if I can do that.'

'What?'

'If we call the police we can't just slip away before they get here, we'll have to be here when they arrive.'

'What?'

'We can just send the front desk up here,' he said. 'We'll check out, tell them something is happening next door and get them to come up.'

'But they might not do it straightaway. She's going to die in there. We have to get the police.'

The woman whimpered, as if being touched by something dreadful.

He sat on the bed, still with the phone, still with the pillow, his eyes squeezed tight.

'If we get the police we have to stay and talk to them,' he said.

'So?'

'We'll have to give our real names. We can't be Mr and Mrs Smith anymore.'

'So?'

He hesitated. 'Mary will find out.'

She stared at him. 'What?'

He put his foot to the floor, gazing nervously in case he pierced it down onto broken glass.

'Don't you see?' he whispered. 'I've got to think of that. It can't get out, us being in this hotel. I'd lose everything. I have to think of that — we have to think of that.'

'What?' she said. 'That woman is going to die!'

'Not if we work fast. I'll check out, you run to the phone box. They'll never identify us — never. She'll still be alive and we'll be okay too.'

There was another scream, then another, then another. It sounded like she was being ripped apart at the throat.

'No,' she said. 'We can't do that.'

She got up and started to swiftly — clumsily — put her trousers on.

'I'm going to run down and tell them,' she said. 'I'm going to get them to come up, call the police. Can't you hear her? We have to stop it now.'

She pulled her trousers on and started to fumble with her blouse. He leapt across the glass at her. She staggered backwards to the wall, he dropped to the bed.

'What are you doing?'

'Let me go first, let me get out of here. I'm sorry, but it's got to be this way. I can't be caught here.'

'She's going to die! Is your wife so important you'd put her above this?'

There was another scream, the most tortured yet. A scream that grabbed hold of their innards and yanked them around. It was drawn out, terrifying — final.

He clutched his hands to his head, tears blinding his eyes.

'Oh no!' he cried.

And they heard that step again — the light, shuffling step — and simultaneously they realised how loud their voices had got.

They looked at each other — too scared to scream, whisper or breathe — just nervous eyeballs peering at nervous eyeballs, a trembling apparent on both their skins.

The step moved away from the wall and they heard the door next door open. The corridor had thicker carpet and it was harder to hear, but they knew which way it was coming.

He sat on the bed — naked, shivering, bleeding. She stood — hastily dressed, tears running down her petrified face. They waited, apart.

It — whatever it was — lingered for a moment in the empty corridor. Beyond that was a deserted staircase and floor after floor of vacant rooms. The lobby was a long way down now, too far for anybody to hear anything.

There were three heavy knocks on their hotel room door.

Gristle

Stephen Roy

'I'll have another package soon.'

Ponyboy mouthed the words as he typed them. The chat room was double password protected and known to but a few well-connected aficionados.

'The next auction will be held within three days.'

Three separate responses popped up within moments. Each expressed the almost palpable level of interest he'd grown to expect from his customers. One of the regulars, a guy by the name of Johnny-Cake, admonished him to pay more attention to specified desirable attributes; height, weight, hair color.

'I know what I'm doing,' Ponyboy said harshly, then reiterated the standard terms of sale, cash on delivery.

He signed off and headed out to another day on the job. His irritation dissolved at once into a smile as he thought of the new plasma TV he'd picked out. This commission would cover the cost nicely.

If it wasn't for the way he made his money, Eddie 'Ponyboy' Hatch might have been any twenty-something slacker. Most nights he stayed up until dawn. He played video games non-stop, ate junk food, drank Red Bull and vodka and he seldom dragged his ass out of bed before noon.

What set him apart, what made him unique, was his profession. Eddie Hatch stole children. The world was full of careless kids and there was never a shortage of rich men with twisted desires. He gave little thought to those kids. What happened to them wasn't his concern. He just did his job. Three or four times a year he'd take a road trip, snatch a kid, find a buyer and deliver the goods, all within a couple of days. The money was amazing.

Eddie rolled into Collinswood, Illinois a couple of hours later. He'd found the quiet, out of the way Chicago suburb on Mapquest.

'What the hell did people do before the Internet?' he wondered out loud. Easy research, no faces, phony identities, just Ponyboy, a name he'd taken from an old movie called 'The Outsiders'. As he remembered, the real Ponyboy hadn't stolen children but it didn't matter, Eddie wasn't much for details. The movie's title had been spot-on, though. Eddie had always been an outsider himself, ever since those painfully lonely two and a half years at River Mill High in Fort Wayne. The lost look he saw in the mirror was what he looked for in others.

Scrawny, with little facial hair and a lot of pimples, the child thief could easily pass for fifteen if the lighting was right. Give him twenty minutes in a mall or a movie theater or a park and without fail he'd find the one kid who didn't belong. He could always spot the outcasts.

He conducted business from a white panel van. From the outside, it could be any painter's ride, a passing flash of anonymity you'd never remember. Inside though, was a different story. The average painter never thought of such a dizzying array of electronics, two laptops, WIFI adapters, a wireless router, a couple of digital video cameras, everything a budding salesman needed for success.

Eddie also kept a small supply of Amyl Nitrate handy. Once he made an acquisition, he'd usually slip the kid a little happy juice to mellow him out then find the nearest wireless network. Almost every coffee shop carried them now.

Just park in back, flip on the switches and let the bidding begin.

'There's my boy,' Eddie whispered as he tracked his prey while finishing a large Dr. Pepper.

He'd spent ninety minutes watching 'The Ring', a pop out of the shadows kind of flick from the corner of his eye. Mostly though, he'd been searching for a new package among the fifteen or so afternoon patrons. Eddie spotted the kid in the sixth row as soon as the lights came on. Eleven, maybe twelve, blond hair, pressed jeans, shirt buttoned up to his neck. He'd been sitting alone and his faded blue eyes were drawn into a wary glance.

'You know, I nearly frosted my shorts when Samara crawled out of that TV,' Eddie said as he edged beside the boy. He had a 'Gee whiz, wasn't that cool' tone to his voice that a lot of his overly young friends found comforting. The kid relaxed in measure but his eyes still carried a look Eddie knew well, a look kids sometimes got when they didn't know what load of crap the world would dump on them next. That look said the boy could be taken.

'Y-Y-Yeah, I've seen it five times already and it still creeps me out.'

'A stutter,' Eddie thought. 'The profile just keeps getting better.' Eddie knew a lot about nervous ticks and annoying speech impediments and all the other geeky habits that often resulted in an ass–whipping at school.

'My name's Eddie,' he said extending his hand.

'P-P-Petey,' the kid said looking up hopefully and almost smiling as he found a friendly face. Sometimes that's all it took — a friendly face.

'Shouldn't you be in school?'

'D-D-Ditched it today. Had a test. Didn't study. You won't tell will ya?'

Bing. Chalk up another score.

'No sweat, dude. I ditched classes plenty when I was your age.' He had, too. Hung out alone, just like Petey.

'Hey, you want to grab a slice of pizza before you head home?'

'D-D-Don't know. Maybe I should just stick around here.'

'Come on. There's a place down the block. We can be back in twenty minutes.'

The kid thought it over for a moment but any residual anxiety melted at the prospect of a new friend and a slice of pizza. 'S-S-Sure, but I gotta be back in a half hour to meet my uncle.'

'Done. My ride is out back.'

Eddie always parked behind the theaters. No one paid any attention back there.

'You want a coke on the way over?' he said as they climbed into the van. The juiced soda waited in the cup holder. Petey gulped it down without a pause.

'T-T-Thanks. Hey, you got some awesome stuff back there.'

The stutter started to get on Eddie's nerves, only the first word of each sentence. It didn't matter much. Petey would be quiet soon enough.

'Yeah, that's my gig. I'm a web developer. I work projects all over town and I never know what equipment they'll have, so I bring my own.'

'Cool.'

'Why don't you go on back and check it out while I drive to the pizza place?'

It took exactly six minutes to get to the Starbucks he'd scouted out earlier. The sign out front advertised free WIFI connection. Eddie parked in back and crawled into the business end of the van. He signed on, set the camera and had his requisite three bidders in no time.

He turned to find Petey curled into a fetal position, facing the van's wall. Normally Amyl Nitrate made them drowsy, but sometimes it knocked them out cold. Eddie made a mental note to use less next time. Bidding jumped when the kids were awake.

'Come on little buddy, it's time to get up.'

Petey moaned, stretched his legs, straightened his back then issued a sound from deep in his throat. Low, almost guttural, it could have been the sound of snoring, but it wasn't.

'Wake up, Petey and smile for the camera,' Eddie said as he grabbed the kid's arm and rolled him over. 'Daddy needs a new pair of ...'

Eddie 'Ponyboy' Hatch never got a chance to say the word shoes and the last two things he ever saw were faded blue eyes without a hint of humanity and an impossible collection of teeth. The van rocked back and forth briefly then settled on its springs and had someone walked by at that moment, they'd have heard the sounds of a good meal.

In time and more the young boy stepped into the sunlight, picking absently at his teeth. Petey was a good name, but it wasn't his. His real name couldn't have been pronounced by the likes of Eddie Hatch.

His face mellowed with the satiated smile of a full stomach. Though young by the standards of his clan, he'd honed his skills well. He'd seen Eddie Hatch as an outsider before the movie ever started. He knew at a glance he could be taken.

As always at such times, his uncle's image rose in the boy's mind, deep blue eyes, the shadow of his bushy brows, brilliant white teeth and his lessons, repeated endlessly until they became second nature.

'They know us not boy, for we are beyond their imagination. Vampires, werewolves, incubus, they've created a thousand foolish and fevered stories, all in a sad attempt to deny a more painful truth, that there is, in fact, a higher step on the food chain.'

Living at the periphery of man's understanding and the shadow of his fear, his kind aged slowly and ate only what was needed to cull the herd.

'The world is our table, boy,' his uncle would say. 'But they must remain passive. They'll stampede if they suspect. Look for the outcast, the outsider. He will not be missed.'

The boy ambled drowsily down the busy afternoon road and to the world he appeared a child of eleven in need of an afternoon nap. The sun glimmered off his sandy blond hair and his eyes, pale blue and wary, scanned the horizon as he quickened his pace. His uncle waited. He didn't want to be late.

Back in the parking lot, he'd left behind a nondescript white van full of electronics and a mystery. Nothing remained of Eddie Hatch, nothing save an insignificant spill of blood and some gristle.

The boy never liked gristle.

And Then...

Kim Sabinan

The torturer snapped his fingers.

A Candle for the Birthday Boy

Christopher Hawkins

The kid was turning six, and he was missing the whole thing.

Not that it mattered to him, Nate thought. What did six-year-olds know about what it took to throw a party this size, about what it cost to keep over a hundred kids full of cake and punch when the guest of honor was off hiding who knows where? What did he care that they were all waiting, waiting for him to come outside and open the presents that their parents had spent far too much money on in hopes of impressing his old man? The party was almost over, and the guest of honor couldn't even be bothered to come out of the house.

No, that wasn't fair. Danny was only a kid, after all. He shouldn't have to worry about things like money and all the pressures that came with it. Besides, Tabby was the one he should be angry at. He hadn't seen her all day either, and she was supposed to be responsible for half this mess. He had counted on her to be here, to fill the glasses with punch, to cut the cake and pretend she cared about the kid. A few of the single mothers in attendance noticed her absence, or at least sensed it in his thoughts the way sharks smelled blood in open water. The quick among them were all too happy to step in, the whole time casting sidelong glances at him that said that they'd be willing to take over for Tabitha at more than just the cake table.

As much as he wanted to, as much as he saw her absence as the excuse he needed, he felt guilty for being mad at her. This whole thing, this party, had been her idea, and as soon as she'd brought it up, he'd wrapped all his hopes around it. It was the first time in the eight months they had been together that she had shown anything better than disdain for the little boy, and he was not about to let it slip away. Nate had seen the way she looked at him sometimes, with that absent, almost vacant stare, like she was looking at an animal she'd just as soon put to sleep. He had wanted to see this new offer as a gesture, as a sign that she had accepted the boy, that she was willing to take the two of them as a unit, and see herself as part of a family.

Now, he wasn't so sure what he wanted. She had had everything ready by the time he was out of bed. The thoughtfulness, the sheer amount of selfless activity, was so uncharacteristic of her that he should have suspected it right away. She had clipped down the tablecloths and stocked the plates. She had filled the punch bowl and covered it with plastic wrap to keep out the bugs. And though the idea of assigned seats evaporated once the children arrived, she had even taped down place cards.

And, of course, there was the piñata.

She had tied it to a tree near the center of the yard. It hung there, big and garish, an eyesore in the shape of a bloated sheep. Alternating bands of green and yellow worked their way forward from its rump, culminating in a grin and cartoon eyes that were far too big for the proportions of its head. It was hideous, but she had insisted upon the thing, telling him that it was a birthday tradition in her family.

There was that word again: family. She had used it expertly, wielding it like a weapon pointed straight at his heart. He'd wanted to object, but she had played him and she had won, just like she always did.

A fat child stalked by the cake table, drinking what must
have been his fourth cup of punch. He walked by the piñata,
eyeing it hungrily. He and the other children were restless,
hopped up on sugar and anticipation. Nate wished, not for
the first time, that Sandra was there. Sandra would have
known what to do. Sandra would have been able to keep
this party from disintegrating into a riot. Sandra would have
been able to make her son, their son, show up for his own
birthday.

But Sandra was in Colorado. Nate had seen to that. He
had driven her away and replaced her with a pale imitation.
A younger imitation, to be sure. One that looked better in a
black, see-through nightgown and knew a few extra tricks
between the sheets. One who scared him sometimes with
the feral look that seemed to come over her like a storm
when he least expected it. One who had once taken a carving
knife out of the kitchen drawer and pointed it at his throat
from across the room.

At the end of the lawn, the magician he had hired for two
hundred dollars an hour was twisting balloons into shapes
while a crowd of distracted children sat bouncing their legs
on the grass. Their mothers stood behind them, forming a
corral with their bodies and trying to not be too obvious as
they checked their watches.

He tried to picture Sandra, working the crowd, engaging
the mothers as only another woman with children could. He
tried to remember her walk, the way she moved. He tried to
picture her face, but all he could see was Tabitha, that wild
animal look in her eyes as she screamed at him, screamed
threats and obscenities that made his muscles tense and his
cheeks turn hot. All he could see was her lithe form blocking the doorway as he tried to walk away, a mist of spittle
and dark intentions spraying from her mouth like venom
until finally his hand rang across her face and left her eyes

wide with silent shock.

But that was weeks ago, one shameful moment best left forgotten. He had wanted to end things with Tabitha then, just call it off and send her packing, but she had thrown herself into the planning of the party with such enthusiasm that he all but forgot about it. She had meant for him to forget it. He wasn't naïve enough to believe otherwise and he wasn't naïve enough to believe she had forgotten his part in it either. But he had seen such sincerity in her actions, a genuine wish to make amends that he could not refuse. Only now, alone among all these people, did he begin to see the cruel joke she had played on him.

He handed another cup full of punch to a young girl who took it and turned away without saying a word. She had to stop to let the fat kid by as he shouldered across her path. Nate had the kid figured right away: awkward, spoiled, a bully in training. His route took him in long, leisurely arcs around the piñata, circling it like a hyena stalking a wounded gazelle. He tried to look disinterested, all the while alternating his gaze between the stick, left tantalizingly against the trunk of the tree, and the one person in sight with the authority to keep him from picking it up and bashing the hanging prize to papery bits. Nate met the kid's gaze with a silent warning, and watched him skulk away to join the others.

He cast a glance back at the house, hoping that his son was somewhere inside, just pouting over his mother. He tried not to listen to the gnawing animal in his gut that told him he wasn't. Tabby was gone. That much he was sure of. Knowing it should have left him relieved, after everything, so why was the thought mixed in with so much dread? She wouldn't take the boy with her. She hated Danny. He knew that now. She hated Danny almost as much as Nate realized she had grown to hate him. Would she take Danny just to get back at him for what he'd done? Was she even capable of something like that?

Again, the feral face returned to him, the knife flashing beneath it in the dim glow of nighttime. Oh yes, came the answer. She's capable of that. She's capable of all that and worse.

He turned back to the piñata, that grinning monstrosity that seemed to taunt him with the punch-line of a joke that it wasn't willing to share. He looked at the wide, hemp rope tied around its middle, and only now noticed that it was tied like a noose.

He looked across the crowd of children, touching every face with his eyes, hoping with growing panic that the next one they fell upon would be the face of his boy. One by one he passed them, and with each one he felt a tingle rise higher up his spine and tighten across his scalp. How long had she been gone? Five, maybe six hours at most? In that time she couldn't have gotten far. He had to call the police. He would call them and they would find her. They would take her away in handcuffs and the boy would come leaping into his arms. They would lock her away and the two of them would be free and he would call Sandra and they would start all over again.

He put a hand on the table to steady himself. A fly landed on his knuckle and he paused to bat it away. He couldn't call the police, not yet. What if Danny was just hiding after all? What if he was just playing a game of hide and seek with some of the other kids and hid so well that they lost interest and stopped looking? He knew the thought was stupid, but it calmed him anyway. He couldn't call the police until he was sure, and before he could be sure, he had to go back into the house. Someone else could watch the party. The party could go straight to Hell for all he cared, as long as he found the boy.

'Hey! Put that down!'

Nate turned to see a woman in a red dress taking the fat kid by the arm. Was she his mother, or someone else's mother? Nate didn't care. The stick was in the kid's hand, and now he dropped it to the ground and stomped away. High above the scene, the piñata grinned.

How long are you going to wait? it seemed to say. How long before you go back into the house and find out what you already know? Tabby's gone. Long gone. But the boy might still be there, somewhere. She wouldn't have taken him because she hated him even more than she ended up hating you, but that doesn't mean you won't still find him there, in the house, left someplace where it won't take you too long to stumble across him.

A breeze kicked up, brushing another fly past his nose. The leaves in the tree swayed, but the piñata was like an anchor at the end of its rope. That insane, wide-eyed face still pointed right at him, right past him to the house. Go on, he heard it say in Tabitha's voice. Go back to the house. Go back and see what I've left there for you.

More children swarmed the punchbowl, helping themselves now that Nate was no longer keeping up. He barely noticed them. His eyes were fixed on the piñata, on the wicked grin that still seemed to be keeping secrets.

'Here, let me help.'

Nate heard the voice, but it wasn't until he felt the hand gently taking the ladle away from him that he actually turned to see who had spoken. He didn't know her name, but he recognized the windblown blonde hair that spilled out from dark roots to her shoulders. She was pretty in spite of her hair, and she didn't have a wedding ring. None of the mothers here seemed to have wedding rings. He would have noticed the expectant smile on her face, but he was looking past her, at the house.

'Could you...' he began. The sentence didn't have an ending that would make him seem anything but crazy. Could you call the police? Could you send everyone home so I can hunt down my mistress? Could you keep the children out of the house in case my son is lying dead inside?

'I just need to go check on something,' he said finally. 'In the house.'

'I'll be waiting,' she said, and he would have picked up on the flirtation in her tone, maybe even enjoyed it, if she hadn't sounded so far away. He moved past her, more conscious with every step of the cartoon eyes that bored into his back. That piñata, that monstrosity, would be watching him the whole way, never wavering, never moving, not even swaying in the wind.

The thought stopped him, and he turned. As if on cue, the wind kicked up again. Paper plates tumbled off tables and napkins took wing. Leaves swayed back and forth, moving with the air.

The piñata didn't budge.

Once again he started toward the house, this time determined to make it there without looking back. Tabitha had hung the piñata there to unnerve him, to make him panic. He wasn't about to let it do either of those things. The house was where he needed to focus. The house was where he needed to be. He couldn't let the image of the thing's grin cloud his thinking. It was paper, that was all. Paper and paste in the shape of an animal.

But if it was just paper, why didn't it move with the wind? If there was only candy inside, why did it need such a thick piece of rope to hold it in the air?

In the distance behind him, he heard a commotion that made him stop again. The house was close now, less than a dozen yards and he would be inside. Still, the upraised voices made him all the more certain that he could not go inside, that he wasn't running toward the things that he dreaded discovering, but away from them.

The children were running now. He could see them at the edges of his vision. He turned his head to watch them, knowing why they were running, and knowing where their paths would all meet. Their mothers chased them, but they couldn't keep up. They called out, but the children did not hear.

The fat kid had the stick. He swung it in wide scything motions so that no one dared get close enough to take it away from him. Mothers shouted, but his eyes were fixed on the prize. The children crowded around, just outside the reach of his swing as he brought the stick up and over his head. A scream welled up in Nate's throat but couldn't find any breath to carry it.

The piñata grinned in triumph as the stick struck home.

The thing bobbed on its rope like a man dropped from a gallows. A cloud of flies scattered, only to close back upon it as the fat kid hefted the stick for another swing. The children held their breath, waiting to see what would spill out. Nate held his breath, too, knowing all too well what it would be. Already he could see the dark stain where the stick had cracked the paper, spreading out across the green and yellow in a blossom of brownish red.

Again, Nate tried to scream. He found his feet moving again, and all his breath seemed to be used up in the motion. The fat kid was grinning now, almost frantic. He held the stick above him like an executioner's axe, and Nate could see now that the edge of it was thin and sharp, like a blade. His eyes were wide, his teeth set, and in his features Nate could almost see Tabitha laughing at him.

Then the stick struck again, and the piñata spilled its contents in a slush upon the ground.

The children tensed for an instant, ready to pounce.

Then they stopped. Their shoulders drooped as they saw the glistening aftermath at their feet, and instinctively, they stepped away. Mothers stood behind them, their mouths hanging open. The fat kid dropped the stick, and looked down at the blood that covered his shoes. In the crowd, one of the children started to cry.

Nate staggered to his knees at the edge of the gore, and though grief filled his chest the way the heady scent filled his nostrils, all his mind could do was to ask itself over and over what he was going to say. What would he say to the children who stood slack-jawed, to their mothers who looked at him with accusation in their eyes? What would he say to Sandra when he told her what he had allowed to happen? Most importantly, what was he going to say to Tabitha once he got his hands around her throat?

The head of the piñata dangled above him, still grinning, still hanging from the end of the rope. It dripped out the rest of its contents in a steady rhythm upon the grass. How could there be more of it? he thought. There was already so much on the ground. There was too much. There was far too much.

Then he looked at what lay in front of him, really looked for the first time. There was a liver, too large, like a half-inflated beach ball. There was a length of tripe, and a smashed, spongy mass that might once have been sweetbreads. A pig's head lolled on its side, severed by the butcher's saw just below the jaw line. Its feet poked up at odd angles from piles of meat and bone. In the middle of it all, soaked through with blood, was a pair of Danny's overalls.

Nate looked up at the grinning head of the piñata, and through his tears, he began to laugh.

'Daddy?'

He turned, and Danny was there. He stood, whole and alive. The sun shone bright upon his dark hair, and he was smiling. Then he saw the tears in his father's eyes, the mass of meat and entrails beyond him. His face fell, and his body began to shake. Nate pulled him close, and held on as hard as he could.

'Daddy...'

'It's all right, son.'

'Aunt Tabby told me to hide in the house. She told me to wait until the piñata broke open, and then I could come out.'

'I know, son. It's all right.'

The boy's voice was quickly turning to sobs. 'It was a joke, daddy. I didn't know what was inside. Aunt Tabby told me that it would be funny.'

'Aunt Tabby was wrong.' She was wrong, all right, Nate thought. When he finally caught up with her, he'd make sure she knew just how wrong she had been.

'I'm sorry, daddy.'

Nate held the child out at arms' length. 'It's not your fault, son.'

Tears began to dry on the child's cheeks. 'You're not mad?'

'I'm not mad.'

Danny's mood seemed to change on a dime, and a smile spread across his face. The others seemed on their way to forgetting, too, because Nate could hear the sounds of nervous conversation beginning all around him. He would make them understand that none of this had been his idea, that Tabby was the one to blame for all of it. He would clean up the mess, then he would call Sandra and tell her he was sorry, sorry for everything. He would ask her, he would beg her, to come back from Colorado, so they could be a family again. She would come back, and everything would be all right.

'Can I go play now, daddy?'

Nate ran his hand through the child's hair, gaining strength from the warmth that he felt there. 'Of course you can.'

Danny turned and was off as if nothing had happened. He snagged a cup of punch from the long table as he went, and the other children trailed off to follow. Nate looked up at the mothers who remained near the piñata, and he was pleased to see that the looks on their faces were ones of sympathy, and not accusation. Perhaps everything really was going to be just fine.

He stood and walked back to the punch bowl, basking in the sense of normalcy he felt as he took his place behind it. Some had spilled in the commotion, and the puddle was finding its way onto the grass in small drips. He'd clean it up later, he thought. He'd clean everything up later. He threw a napkin down at the edge of the table to stop the dripping, and only then did he notice that in the middle of the sticky pool lay a crowd of dead flies.

Across the yard, Danny ran in a circle with his friends. They stopped running, and he raised the cup to his lips. Nate felt all his fear and dread return as if they had never left, and he cried out to his son to stop him.

But it was too late. The cup was almost empty, and all around him, children were starting to fall.

The Door

Suzanne Elvidge

Behind him, her door slams shut, final, unforgiving, cutting off all chances of return. He is in the street, on the street in fact. All his belongings are still in her cupboards, her wardrobe, on her shelves. Not even a credit card in his pocket — his wallet and car keys are still in the jacket slung familiarly over the back of her chair. He does not want to return to her, at least not tonight, not until the hard words they shared have lost some of their edge.

The sun, harsh, pitiless, glints off the wing mirrors, windows and door handles of the cars parked down both sides of the narrow road. In the distance, he sees the vaguely familiar face of a neighbour. He raises his hand cheerily and sets off purposefully down the street, as if to get a paper, as if being the wrong side of a slammed door is the most natural thing in the world.

The argument was devastating in its finality, and has left him alone and friendless in a place he came to only for her. He revisits the fight racing in his head. The stupid, pointless fight that started over something and nothing, he can't even · remember what. An imagined slight, or forgotten washing up, the matter of day-to-day domesticity. But as fights increasingly did, over the dying days of their relationship, it descended into a battle over his distance, her dependency, the shadows in his childhood that more and more invaded his waking and sleeping hours, his guilt and loss over something he still cannot remember.

He becomes more and more frantic, tasting her taunts in his mouth and spitting out the bitterness of the phrases until he can no longer differentiate between the reality of the fight and his frenzied imaginings. The few people treading the narrow pavements edge away from the pale-faced beautiful youth whose lips drip vitriol — a tragic Ophelia drowning in tears.

He wanders for a couple of hours, getting further and further entangled in the back streets of the strange northern city where he arrived only recently. In his distress and confusion he becomes more and more lost, and as the sun drops lower towards the horizon, the Victorian redbrick terraces in the narrow roads start to look menacing, with hard eyes of window glass and doors set in gaping toothless mouths.

He decides that he has at least to retrace his steps, to find a way out of the city, to hitch to somewhere he knows, where he has some friends. But he realises in his misery he has wandered aimlessly, and has no idea how he has got to where he is. He walks down the darkening, narrow streets, and his heart and his footsteps start to beat harder and faster.

He no longer recognises anything and his anger quickly turns to fear. And then, looking up ahead, he thinks he sees a corner he almost remembers. His heart lifts, he laughs with relief, and breaks into a run. But when he gets there, he realises that it is only familiar because he was there half an hour earlier. Gasping, his heart pounding inside his ribs, he turns blindly round a corner. He finds himself in a dead-end alley enclosed by dark, windowless buildings and ending in a brick wall, broken only by a door.

The door is painted green, a sickly, weeping green, and the paint is oozing and blistering. The surface of the door around the handle is splintered, as if someone tried to break it down, escape through it, away from the alley, but it remains shut. Someone failed. The broken wood, once raw, is discoloured and darkened by the passing of winters. No one has set foot in this alley for many years. No one has troubled its darkness. Until now.

He turns to leave the alleyway — this, obviously, is not a way out of the hated city. But... the entrance to the alleyway seems to have disappeared. He is trapped in a box of red brick walls, caught between the blankness where the entrance used to be and the door at the end of the alley. He looks to the sky, now completely dark. He howls in child–like fear. And somewhere in that cry is a sound he recognises from within himself and from a long-hidden past. He stops, and hears another sound from that same hardly recalled past. A choking wet sound. And a called name, his name, the one he no longer uses but had never known why until now. He begins to remember.

And so does it. In the depths of the alleyway, in the dark, oily shadows of a storm drain, it stirs and shifts in the darkness. It groans and rouses, disturbed by his movements. It is awake. And can now see how to escape.

And so, behind him, from the drain, he hears footsteps. The tap of heel-toe echoes, a hard, clipping tap, the sound of a child's party shoe on stone flags. And he spins around. There is no one there. In front of him, the door. Behind him, blocking his retreat, between him and the now blocked–off entrance, the footsteps. Which is he more afraid of? And the footsteps get closer, seem to bring with them the sound of water and mud, and he thinks he sees something in the shadows, something reaching out to him, something with a child's shape. And he half-remembers a reaching hand, just before it disappeared, and he decides.

Panic-stricken now, he runs toward the door and snatches for the door handle — he will run anywhere, try anything to get away from the dreadful sound of the approaching, invisible, damp footsteps. The door opens easily, on hinges oiled and cared for. As he steps quickly inside, over a scattering of small bones on the moss-encrusted ground, the door slams shut behind him. The second door to slam behind him this day. But this time he breathes a sigh of relief as the sound of the footsteps is blocked out.

He is standing inside a beautiful living room. His feet sink into plush, velvety carpet, and on the far wall, a fire burns merrily in a well-blacked grate. Light pours in from behind him, a full, rich, mid-afternoon sunlight, and glints off the fire irons and gilded picture frames. His shadow stands out black on the carpet before him. The wood of the furniture glows the deep, rich brown of long cared-for timber. He feels a sense of comfort, of reassurance, almost as if he has come home. He turns round and the sunlight from two immense picture windows drenches him, bringing tears to his eyes and making him blink. The door now has a glass pane in it, and through it he sees a path leading down through a beautiful garden to a lake. He walks to the door and places his hands flat on the glass, feeling the warmth of the sun against his chilled hands. Down by the lake, a child laughs, and seeing him at the window, she waves and beckons him out, a pretty blonde girl in a white frock and shiny black party shoes. He recognises where he is, remembers this place from his childhood and feels a wave of comfort. This is followed by a chill watery wash of fear. As he reaches out to turn the polished brass door handle, words of warning on his lips, icy teeth of cold bite down into his bones, and the sun ahead of him and the fire behind him winks out. The lake is the last thing to disappear, its surface rippled as if by a thrown pebble.

He spins round, and the carpet and fireplace have gone, with piles of mouldering furniture where before has been luxury and beauty. He turns his head slowly, his body frozen in terror, and the old door is there again in a blank wall, and the footsteps echo once more in his ears. This time they are almost at the door. And he feels guilt from a half-forgotten aftermath of a child's mistake; guilt for the mistake and guilt for the forgetting.

The door creaks open, perhaps it never fully shut, but he isn't there to see it. He runs, dodging piles of broken furniture, scattering decaying books for girls and boys and fading children's toys. As he darts from one room to another, he catches momentary glimpses of rooms he remembers. A brightly lit dining room and a cosy kitchen, in between a stinking bathroom, a misty damp sitting room, a dark bedroom with a rotting child-sized bed. And always, the wet tapping of the footsteps. Just as he sees the polished wood front door, he trips on a doll's pram and falls, hitting his chin hard on the cold black and white floor and sending a jar of pain throughout his body. As he scrabbles to find his feet a tendril of wet cold, a child-sized hand, wraps around his ankle and he smells the damp stench of stagnant water and weed, and he knows who it... she... is.

She pulls him back down and he feels the chipped and cracked marble tiles of the stinking hallway scraping his belly. His fingernails scratch and scrape at the floor, trying to get a hold as he is dragged further back inside the house. His nails broken and his fingertips bruised and bloody, he finally catches hold of the edge of a broken tile. Stopping with a jolt that almost tears his spine apart, he wrenches his leg free, leaving skin and sock and shoe in the clutches of something he doesn't even want to see. He hurls his scream-ing body at the door, leaving a bloody bare footprint on the stained marble, and falls out of the door into an unfamil-iar, well-lit street. When he turns to look back, he sees only an ordinary redbrick terrace, with the light of a television flickering out from behind well-kept curtains, a cat asleep on the windowsill, nothing like the house he has emerged from, the house that somehow he has just visited, the house he had forgotten but that is now seared into his brain. But that house was far away and a long time back.

He waits a moment, wondering what to do, and the footsteps begin, a quiet tapping ringed with water, becoming louder. And so he starts to walk away and the steps quieten. With a silvery scar winding around his leg up to the knee and a shuddering limp, he heads towards the bright lights of the main road out, and leaves the city, alone and penniless, hitching lifts on trucks and in cars with only the few drivers brave enough to take a one-shoed, wild-eyed and silent young man with a cast of grey in his hair, dried blood on his chin and lines etched deep in his cheeks like tribal scars. In the new city he listens for footsteps, and eventually he hears them, very distant and quiet and he remembers the house. When they get too close, he moves again. And again. To another city, another town, another village, it doesn't matter which, and the footsteps go away. For a while. For a very little while. But then they start again. Each time they find him a little more quickly, they are a little louder, bring a little more dampness with them and come a little closer.

He disturbed something in that alley. The girl, the memory, that belonged in his past, he has helped her to escape and she is still looking for him. And one day, because he stays somewhere a little too long, perhaps the footsteps will get a little too close...

Sally

Patricia Russo

So why did I save Sally, you ask. That's certainly a fair question. A lot of people would have walked right past her. You've seen that happen, I'm sure. I know I have. Thousands of times. People just don't care about other people. I mean, not really. Well, I'm different. That's just not the way I am.

For example, I knew you wanted to talk as soon as you came in here. Most people wouldn't have seen that. Or, if they had, they wouldn't have cared. They would have ignored you, just let you sit here with your coffee and your loneliness and that brick you get in your chest on bad days like this one.

Tea? Fine. Tea, not coffee. Now listen, listen a minute. I was telling you about Sally. You know Sally, of course.

Sure you do. Believe me, you know her. She comes in here all the time. Dark hair, real long, almost down to her butt. Until she cut it off, I mean. Almost has a crew-cut now. Used to have that pain in the ass dog that tried to bite everyone? Lives over on Seventh. Works on the stock crew down at the super-center.

See, you remember. Okay, you want to know why I saved her when she didn't want to be saved. Like I said, it's a fair question. Aren't we all autonomous adults, you're thinking, with rights and everything, the right to decide shit for ourselves, isn't that what dignity and freedom are supposed to be all about? And I agree with you there, I really do. I thought about this a lot, in Sally's case. Turned it over and over in my mind. But the thing is, she asked me for help, even though she denied it later.

Of course you know what she did, how she came running out of her building and tried to throw herself in front of a speeding car. That happened at the beginning of the year. If it wasn't January 1, then it was close to it. Happy New Year, yeah? Of course Sally's been on the edge for a long time now. One of the marginal people, you know. Just barely scraping through each day. Socialization problems, or maybe it's basically screwed up brain wiring. She has boundary issues, big time. Talks nonstop, can't tell no one is paying attention. Thinks the universe revolves around her, that whatever she cares about at that particular second has to be of overwhelming interest to everyone else. She sits too close to you, too, gets into your personal space.

Right. There's lots of people like that.

Well, when she ran out into the street that time, screaming about the demons in the walls and the monsters in the toilet bowl and the fanged cockroaches swarming out of the microwave, all that crap, her friends laughed at her. I mean, there they were, holding her back, holding her down, practically, and laughing at the same time. I didn't laugh. Later, when she told me about what was going on in her apartment, I listened without judging, which is what she needed. See, I'm good at that, listening. It's a skill I have. That's why people want to talk to me all the time, because I know how to listen without making them feel like I'm looking down on them. Almost every day some crazy smelly bastard or some psycho chick latches on to me and blabs out their life story, yaks both my ears off, I'm telling you. I don't mind, though. I help a lot of people. I guess I've accepted it as my purpose in life.

So Sally, after her friends stopped her from throwing herself under the wheels of some asshole's SUV, and then laughed and basically demeaned her, she found me. This was in January, only a couple of days later. Miserable weather, you remember. It snowed for days and days, no let up at all. It was like the end of the world, almost.

It's not the end of the world, though, until it is the end of the world. That's what I always say.

Huh? No. It's not a joke. More like a...motto. Get it?

Okay. So there I was in the snow, all miserable and minding my own business, and Sally comes up and grabs my elbow and says, 'There's nothing wrong with me, you know. I just don't want to put up with it any more.'

Now, when someone announces there's nothing wrong with them, just flat out of the blue like that, you can bet that savings bond Grandma gave you for your tenth birthday that you've been keeping tucked between page 286 and 287 of that copy of 'Gravity's Rainbow' you bought in grad school and never read that something's wrong with them. You can count on it.

'Put up with what?' I asked Sally. It was obvious that she wanted to talk.

'The way I have to live,' she said. She'd put a coat on, but hadn't bothered with a hat, or gloves. Or boots, either. She was standing in the snow in flip–flops. Her toes were all curled and blue. 'Some people wouldn't mind, sure. Fuck, some people would probably get off on it. But I can't stand it. I want it to stop.'

'Is this about the cockroaches?'

'The cockroaches are the least of it.' She ran her hand over her bristly hair. Her fingers were blue, too. 'The cockroaches are just a, you know, symptom.'

'Because you can force the landlord to call an exterminator. You've got rights.'

'It's not about the cockroaches.'

Of course it wasn't. The cold must've been freezing my brain cells, because it took me halfway to forever to figure out the reason Sally grabbed my elbow on the street. I bet you're way ahead of me here, right? You know what she really wanted.

Thinking about it now, I realize that was the first time I saved Sally. If I hadn't taken her back to her apartment, she might have stayed out there in the cold and the snow until she got sick, or even until she died. You can die real fast of hypothermia, and she was certainly dressed damn suicidally.

At her building, on Seventh, she didn't want me to come inside. Or that's what she said. She didn't mean it, of course. I walked her in, and I walked her up the stairs. Then, at her door, she didn't want me to come inside her apartment. So she said. 'It's bad,' she said. 'I mean, really.' That's when she told me everything, and I listened, without judging.

It all started a few weeks after she moved in. First, unexpected and unexplained sounds. Sounds that were out of place, as she put it. Tea kettle whistles, canary chirpings, bike-bell ting-a-lings. Usually these sounds would intrude in the early morning, while she was doing something perfectly ordinary, like making the bed or looking for the pair of spare shoelaces she was sure had to be somewhere in the back of the drawer. Then came the smells — humus-rich mud, grammar school paste, weed-killer.

'I should have known then, with the weed-killer, that this wasn't going to be fun at all,' she said.

The visual, and physical, intrusions arrived shortly thereafter. Disemboweled kittens rolling across the floor, chewing on their own entrails. Flames jumping out from under the sofa to crisp up the mail, a magazine, a peanut butter sandwich. Sally couldn't leave anything on the coffee table any more. Floods in the middle of the night, sometimes water, sometimes blood, sometimes urine, sometimes a liquid she couldn't identify, washing across the floor — only a couple of inches high, but still. Disturbing.

Telling me this part, somewhere around here, she started to cry.

Elephant heads with three horns pushing out of the drywall and leering at her. The scented candle her ex had given her a week before they broke up splitting itself like an amoeba, and the daughter-candles splitting and splitting again, so that there were now at least a dozen or two of the lavender monstrosities cluttering her shelves. They had learned how to light their own wicks, as well. The pipes in the bathroom and under the kitchen sink growing luxuriant black beards. The refrigerator door acquiring pockets, or pouches, somewhat like a possum's.

'It's not right,' Sally sobbed. 'I didn't choose to live this way.'

Most of us don't, though. Choose the way we live. But you gotta make the best of it, you know? Because what else can you do? Take you, for example. You're what, three hundred, three twenty? You got to live with that, and everything that goes with it. That guy over there with the butt-ugly face — he's got to live with that. I bet it's no goddamn picnic for him, either.

'I want out,' Sally said, but she didn't really mean it. Doesn't really mean it. She's meeting me here later, by the way. That's why I was sitting over there by the door. Actually, she should have been here by now. I told her six. I don't know what's keeping her. She's a little bit of an airhead, you know? I'm not being mean, now, she admits it herself. I guess the time's gotten away from her, again.

Her apartment? Yeah, I've been inside. It's all true.

Yes. All true.

I'll introduce you to Sally when she shows up. Oh, that's right, I forgot, you know her. Well, when she comes, tell her you want to see her place. She'll pretend to be shy about it at first, but she'll let you come over. She just says she can't live with it — I mean, that's what she was saying, that she couldn't live with it. Which is silly talk, pure and simple. Just ridiculous.

The other day, when she —

Ridiculous, because of course she could live with it. Can live with it. Conjoined rabbits scrabbling under your bed isn't going to kill you. It's just not. I mean, is it? Sand pouring out of the electric sockets won't kill you. Come on. It won't. Windowpanes sprouting scales and fins and flapping against the frames like dying salmon isn't exactly pleasant, but unpleasant is not same as fatal. You following me? Sometimes you just have to be rational about stuff, and deal, you know? Just cope. Like a damn grownup.

You'll see, when Sally comes. I helped her understand all that, the other day, after I saved her. Saved her again. She admitted I was right, and I give her a lot of credit for that. It's one of the most common failings of humankind, not admitting when someone else is right. So, after I took the gun away from her —

Oh yeah. Only a twenty-two, but still. Now, if Sally had truly been serious, she wouldn't have pulled that stunt out on the street. She'd have done it at home, inside, where no one could see her, or stop her. Not that anybody did try to stop her. You know how people are. No compassion, no fellow feeling. I did, of course, but that's just the way I am. So after I took the gun away, I sat her down on the steps — yeah, this was outside her building — and we had a good long chat. In the end she couldn't defeat my logic. Oh, she tried at first. People do. They get defensive, want to justify themselves, when they know they're wrong. Sally came out with some story, how the mushrooms that were growing on the vacuum cleaner were making so much noise singing French punk songs she couldn't concentrate enough to load the gun, so that's why she had to go outside, but she realized what a lame excuse that was. Then it was the same old rigmarole about how she didn't want to live, et cetera, et cetera, yadda blah yadda. In the end I almost had to twist her arm to get her up the stairs.

No, she did agree with me. I said almost had to twist her arm. I didn't literally twist her arm, come on. I'm not a violent person. Haven't you ever heard of a figure of speech? I only pushed her a couple of times. Not hard. Not hard. And anyway, it was for her own good.

You shouldn't believe everything you hear. I know who it is, too, who's going around talking shit about me. It's Sally's ex, isn't it? No? Bullshit. He's always hated me. Now he's telling people I hit Sally, shoved her, beat her up the stairs, practically, and kicked her through the door. And slammed it shut behind her. You can smile, nobody's saying this crap about you. Nobody's going around the whole damn city lying about you. Bullshit you didn't smile. I'm sitting here across from you, I'm staring you in the face. Goddammit, I hate when people lie just for the hell of it. I can't fucking stand it.

Sally went back into her apartment of her own free will. I shut the door behind her, yes, because she was a bit distracted and forgot, but I didn't slam it. Shut it a little fast, maybe, because some of the gut-trailing kittens were scrambling to get out, but I did not slam it.

Okay. As long as we've got that cleared up.

She should be here soon. Damn, but she's late. I told her,

meet me at the coffee shop at six, and she promised, right before she went back inside her apartment. I figured I should do a bit of a follow-up, you know? Make sure everything was okay. Like they say, you save someone's life, you become sort of responsible for them.

You know what? It just occurred to me. I bet she's late because she's buying me a present, a thank-you gift kind of thing. Wow. She doesn't have to do that. Though it's really nice of her, don't you think?

No, you don't need to go. There's no one waiting for you at home. Ah, cut it out. Haven't I proved that I can see right through your bullshit? You live alone. You haven't had a date in nine years. There's no ice cream in your freezer, but you're going to get yourself a couple of half gallons at the convenience store when you leave here, but you're not going to leave here yet, because you want to meet Sally. I mean, meet her again. I told you, I know these things. I can read people. Not that I'm trying to take credit for that. It's just the way I am.

A talent, yes.

Of course I still have the gun. With me? Naturally. If I left it at home, somebody might break in and steal it, and then there'd be one more firearm in the hands of a criminal. People don't think about that when they buy guns, but they should. A lot of the guns on the street are stolen from law-abiding citizens. A lot. You didn't know that, did you? Folks need to be more responsible, that's what I think. We wouldn't have so many problems today if people were more responsible.

Like Sally, keeping me waiting like this. Keeping us waiting. She's not being responsible. I'm a very responsible person myself, as you've certainly noticed. And punctual. You could set your watch by me.

No. You do not have to go to the bathroom. You haven't

even finished your coffee. Sorry, tea. Gotta be ice cold by now. Waste of money, if you ask me. Ordering something you're not going to finish, but hey, it's your wallet. Though I would have thought you'd economize more, with that crappy part-time bank teller's job you got.

Sally's making me wait because it's more dramatic. She likes drama. And her friends are so dumb they fall for her act all the time. I bet if her friends heard the way she was carrying on the other night, they'd all have had heart attacks on the spot. She's really immature, you know. Craves attention. I knew she was just trying to get me to go back and pay some more attention to her. Some people are like that. Attention whores. But I'd already spent hours with her, and saved her life to boot, and enough was enough, you know?

So immature. Screaming fit to wake the blessed mummified dead. I ask you. Is that the way a grown woman should behave? I think not.

I'm glad you agree with me.

She screamed and screamed and screamed. I thought she'd never quit, never realize her ploy wasn't working. I thought she'd scream until fricking daybreak. I stood on the sidewalk and timed her. Eighteen minutes and forty-three seconds. Sheesh. Can you believe that? I bet when she woke up the next day, her throat was sore. Heh. Remind me to ask her about that, when she finally deigns to show up.

Let me order you a fresh coffee. No, it's no bother. Truly. I insist. I know you'd like a fresh cup — dark roast, sweet, no milk, right? Right. See, I know these things. You don't really like tea. See? I knew that. You know some things, too. Yeah, I think you do. You and I, we're pretty compatible. You quit the knee-jerk bullshitting, we'll get along really well.

Here comes the waitress. Oops, not supposed to call them that. The wait person. I think I'll have another cup myself.

I can't wait until Sally gets here, can you? So much to talk about! You have your story you want to tell. And Sally's going to bring me a present and thank me. The three of us will have a great time. Oh, yes. I'm sure of that. I have absolutely no doubt about it at all.

You're sure of it, too, aren't you?

See? I knew you were.

Fingers

Jamie Killen

Monday

K eith did not notice at first that something was wrong.
He awoke to the shrill beep of his alarm clock only
a foot or so away from his ear. Without opening his
eyes, Keith swatted at the machine with his left hand until
the noise stopped. He rolled over, pulled the blanket over his
head, and savored the five minutes of extra rest the snooze
function allowed him. When the alarm went off for the
second time he turned it off and stumbled blearily toward
his apartment's tiny kitchen. It was when Keith reached
to turn on the coffee-maker that he noticed his finger was
gone.

For a moment he stared, convinced it was an illusion, a
trick of the light. But no; where his little finger had been
attached to his right hand there was only smooth, unblem-
ished skin.

Trembling, Keith touched the area with his left index
finger. He felt no pain; there was just a faint tickle when his
fingertip brushed the light hairs that grew there, like the
hair on his knuckles. He slowly squeezed his hand, made a
fist, wiggled the remaining fingers. When he closed his eyes,
he could feel his little finger moving with the rest of them. It
was only by looking at it that he could tell it was gone.

Keith realized he was murmuring to himself. 'Shit, shit,

oh, Jesus, shit...' He reached for the phone, nearly dropped it, and punched the 'Talk' button. He stared for a moment or two, wondering who he should call. Hands shaking, Keith managed to dial the first number that he could think of.

'Come on Petra, Jesus, pick up, please pick up.'

'What?' Petra's voice, bleary with sleep, snapped at him through the phone.

'Petra, you have to come over here. Now. I think I have to go to the hospital.' Keith tried and failed to keep down the hysterical note in his voice.

'Ok, slow down. What happened?' Keith hadn't been sure at first why he chose to call Petra, of all people. Now he remembered the countless times his sister had taken control and turned into a problem-solver during moments of crisis.

'My finger's gone.'

Silence. 'Gone? You mean you cut it off?'

'No, no, it's just gone, it disappeared like I never — '

'Keith, calm down. Breathe. Are you bleeding?'

'No.'

'Ok, I'm coming over. Don't move.' She hung up without waiting to hear his reply.

During the twenty minutes it took Petra to reach Keith's apartment, he sat on his sofa, sneaking the occasional peek at his right hand. He thought about calling the school to tell them they needed to arrange for a substitute, but knew they would ask why he couldn't come to work.

Keith leapt up and opened the door before Petra had finished knocking. With a baggy sweatshirt over her tiny frame and her short black hair in disarray, his sister looked about twelve years old. Her expression, however, made it clear that she was in full warrior-woman mode. 'Are you ok?' she demanded.

Keith held up his right hand in reply. Petra's eyes widened and her own right hand flew up to cover her mouth. 'Oh,

Keith...' she breathed. 'How did it happen?'

'I don't know. I woke up and it was like this.'

Petra reached out as if to touch it, then pulled her hand back. 'Right. We're going to the emergency room.' She helped him find a pair of shoes and led him to her car, hand on his elbow. Under other circumstances Keith might have shook her off and told her not to mother him, but now he appreciated the contact. He caught a glimpse of himself in the side mirror as he climbed into the car; his skin looked chalky white, there were dark circles under his eyes, and his hair stuck out almost as much as Petra's. He could not recall ever looking so bad.

'Don't worry, Keith.' Petra shifted into reverse and looked over her shoulder. 'We'll figure this out.'

It took three hours of waiting and Petra threatening to sue before Keith saw a doctor.

'Now, you have something wrong with your finger, right?' The man flipped through some papers on his clipboard.

Keith crossed his arms, freezing in the paper gown he had been told to wear. 'Yeah. It's gone.'

The doctor's eyes moved to Keith's hands. 'You mean that one?'

Petra muttered something under her breath. Keith ignored her and told the doctor what happened. The man spent a few moments looking at Keith's hand, prodding and squeezing where the finger had been. Finally, he stepped back and glared at Keith. 'Look, there's no trauma. No scar tissue. This looks to me like a birth defect.'

Petra leapt to her feet. 'What? Listen, I'm his sister, and I can tell you he was born with all ten fingers. I mean, Jesus, you don't really think we could have gone twenty-six years without noticing, do you?'

'Digits cannot just disappear. I don't know what you're up to, but it's wasting my time. You can talk to a psychiatrist, if you want.' The doctor looked down at Petra with disgust.

'Keith, get dressed. We're going to a different hospital,' Petra said, staring at the doctor. 'This guy's useless.'

Two hospitals and eight hours later, Keith told Petra to take him home. 'I'm sick of this.'

He expected her to argue, but she just rubbed her eyes. 'Fine. But I'm not leaving you alone, ok?' They left the emergency room and walked toward the parking lot.

Petra sat still for a moment, frowning, before turning on the engine. 'I just don't understand it. That X-ray looked like you never had that finger.'

Keith nodded, afraid his voice would break if he tried to speak. The last doctor had taken an X-ray of his hand. There was no trauma, no broken bones, just a blank space where his finger should have been. It looked as if his finger had been erased.

Back at the apartment, Keith flopped onto the sofa while Petra perched on the arm of a chair. 'Can I use your laptop?' she asked.

'Yeah, why?'

'I'm gonna look for a specialist. These ER guys don't know what they're talking about.' Petra moved to the breakfast nook, cleared away a stack of papers, and opened the laptop.

Keith laughed. 'A specialist? They have specialists in mysterious vanishing finger disease?'

'Don't be a jerk. It might be something new. They didn't know what AIDS was for a couple of years after it showed up.'

'Jesus, Petra, you're supposed to be making me feel better, and you have to go and talk about AIDS?'

Petra swivelled around to glare at him. 'I'm not saying you have AIDS, dipshit. I'm saying maybe there's a new disease that makes digits, I dunno... Atrophy.'

Keith jumped up, crossed the room, and held his hand directly under his sister's face. 'It didn't fucking atrophy, Petra. It was there yesterday, now it's gone. Name me one disease that does that. Go on, name one.'

Petra grabbed Keith's shirt and hauled him down to eye level. 'Calm. The fuck. Down.' She released him and turned back to the laptop. 'Go take a nap. I'm going to do some research, then I'll make dinner.'

Petra shook Keith awake several hours later. Two plates and a steaming pizza box sat on the coffee table. 'How do you feel?' she asked, opening the pizza box and pulling out a slice.

'Ok. Did you find out anything?'

She shook her head. 'Only that you can find some truly amazing smut by googling "disappearing fingers".'

'"Smut"? You sound like Mom.' Keith sat up and reached for some pizza. 'How about doctors?'

'Oh, that's the good news. I made an appointment for you tomorrow with this orthopedic specialist. I talked to her and she seemed really — ' Petra cut off.

'Really what?' Keith asked.

Petra stared, wide-eyed, at Keith's right hand. He looked down.

His ring finger was gone.

⁂

Tuesday

Neither spoke on the way home from the orthopedic specialist. Keith knew from the way Petra's hands clenched the steering wheel that she was furious. It had been more of what they had encountered the day before. The woman had explained in a slightly patronizing tone why they must be mistaken, why digits could not simply vanish without a trace. They had received yet another referral to a shrink, this time a specialist in body image disorders.

Back at the apartment, Petra brewed a pot of strong, black coffee. Each sat on one of the barstools next to the kitchen counter.

Petra started to say something, then abruptly cut off.

'What?' Keith asked.

'Nothing.'

'No, really, what?'

Petra looked away. 'I was about to say you should try to get some sleep. Stupid. Sorry.'

'Why does it happen when I go to sleep?' Keith whispered. 'Why does that matter?'

The panic hit fast and hard. Keith buried his face in his hands, not wanting Petra to see him cry. She silently put an arm around his shoulder while he gasped and shook, which only made him cry harder.

After several minutes, Keith wiped his face and took a deep breath. 'Whew. Sorry. Shit, that was weird.'

'No it wasn't. Quit being such a guy, for God's sake.' She cleared her throat. 'Anyway, we don't know sleep has anything to do with it. Could be anything.'

Keith looked down at his coffee. 'Listen, thanks for being here. I know it's not a good time.'

'Shut up, man,' Petra murmured.

'Seriously, don't you have to work today?'

'They can handle things without me for a few days. Besides, I have some vacation time coming.' She looked at his hand and bit her lip. 'Is it true, that thing they say about phantom limbs?'

Keith grimaced. 'Yeah. It feels like they're moving on their own.'

'You mean like, independently?' Petra asked, frowning.

He held up his hand. 'Yeah. It's getting worse. At first they just felt like my fingers always did, but now it feels like they're twitching.'

Petra looked like she was about to say something, but instead rose and went over to the laptop.

For the rest of the day, Keith tried and failed to get any work done. He paced the apartment, drank coffee, and stared at the TV without paying attention to what was on. Petra emailed a dozen medical professionals in four countries. She scanned a few message boards relating to rare illnesses before quietly searching on websites relating to the paranormal. She felt like screaming in frustration; there was nothing that sounded like Keith's condition.

'Petra, give it a rest,' Keith called over his shoulder. '"South Park" is on.'

She stared at him. 'Are you serious?'

'Hey, just because I'm scared stupid doesn't mean I can't be bored, too.'

'Oh. Ok. Can't do much until one of these guys emails me back, anyway.'

They ate a dinner of leftovers and watched TV for several hours, Petra getting up to check her email every ten minutes. When Keith felt his eyelids begin to droop, he switched off the TV and turned to Petra. 'Do me a favor, would you?'

Petra yawned. 'Sure.'

'I can't stay awake any more. When I go to sleep, would you watch me for a while? These two both disappeared when I went to sleep. Maybe if you're watching...'

Petra saw the fear in her brother's tired eyes. She smiled. 'Sure, bro. I wasn't planning on going to sleep right now anyway.'

Keith lay back on the sofa and dozed off almost immediately. Petra stayed in the armchair, eyes locked on her brother's right hand. After Keith had been asleep for ten minutes, Petra got up and grabbed a book out of the bookshelf. Once she had made sure he was still intact, she curled up in the chair and tried to stay awake by reading. She glanced up each time she turned the page.

It was when Petra reached the bottom of page 37 that something happened. She looked up, expecting to see Keith unchanged. This time, the middle finger of his right hand began to move strangely, twisting and spasming. Petra froze. It spasmed twice more, then began to withdraw into Keith's hand. First the knuckle pulled into Keith's palm, then the fingernail. Finally, smooth, normal skin closed over where his finger had disappeared.

Petra realized that she was hyperventilating. She felt a scream building in her chest. Clenching her teeth, Petra forced herself to take deep, even breaths. She gripped the arms of the chair and closed her eyes, unable to look at her brother's hand. Once she was certain that she had gotten herself under control, Petra shook Keith awake.

Wednesday

'This is ridiculous,' Keith muttered, eyeing the priest as he moved around the apartment.

Petra privately agreed, but tried to look cheerful. 'Maybe there's something to it.'

'I haven't even been to Mass since I was fifteen.'

'Me neither.'

The priest finished reciting his prayer and turned to the siblings. 'Well, I've blessed everything here.'

'Is there anything else you can do? Splash holy water around or something?' Petra demanded.

Father Jacobs shrugged. 'Look, Petra, I don't know what one is supposed to do in a case like this. I think Keith needs a doctor, not a priest.'

Keith sighed and turned away. 'We're trying,' Petra told Father Jacobs, 'but no one believes us.'

'I'll make some calls, tell them that I can testify his hand didn't always look like that.' The priest's gaze drifted to Keith's hand. He was barely able to stop himself from shuddering. 'I'll pray for you.'

Thursday

Petra awoke to the sound of Keith pacing and muttering. 'Keith?' she asked, sitting up and peering over the back of the sofa.

Her brother moved back and forth in his little kitchen, crossing the floor in three steps. Petra heard him whispering to himself, his voice fast and agitated. Keith's left hand clutched a cup of coffee and he tapped the ceramic absently with his index finger.

Petra stood and moved cautiously toward the kitchen. 'Keith, sweetie? Are you ok?'

Keith looked up at her. His eyes were so bloodshot they seemed almost entirely red. His black hair looked greasy and he had three days' worth of stubble on his face.

'What if it keeps going?' he asked.

'What?' Petra touched his arm to stop the pacing.

'What if it keeps going? What if it doesn't stop with my fingers? What if it keeps going until I'm gone?'

Petra looked at the wild-eyed expression on her brother's face and tried to calculate how long he had been awake. More than thirty-six hours, at this point. 'Keith, that won't happen. That doctor in Germany is supposed to call back, she seemed to think she could help.'

Keith laughed. 'Petra, come on. A doctor can't fix this.' He held up his right hand. 'You know what this feels like? They're reaching. All the ones that are missing, they're reaching for something. Every time someone comes closer to me — you, Father Jacobs — they stretch and reach for you like they're hungry. I hate it.'

Petra turned away so he wouldn't see the tears in her eyes. 'It's late. You've been awake for way too long.'

'I'm not sleeping.'

'I know. Keith, I promise you, I'll find a way to fix this.'

Keith smiled sadly at her and said nothing. Petra tried to think of something else to say, but gave up and went back to sleep.

Friday

Keith woke up to the sound of Petra screaming. His first thought was that he had accidentally dozed off and lost another finger during the night. He lifted his head from the kitchen counter so fast he nearly fell off the barstool. Petra stood in the middle of the kitchen. She no longer screamed, but instead gasped, 'Oh no, no, no, no...' over and over again.

Keith stared at his sister's face, afraid to look at his hand. When he finally did get up the courage to look, he screamed louder than Petra had.

Keith's index finger and thumb had not changed during the night. Where his other three fingers had been, new ones had grown. But these were not his fingers. Twice as long as any normal human fingers, they were slick, gnarled, root-like things, bone white and each tipped with a jet-black nail. They scuttled across the countertop toward Petra, dragging Keith's hand behind them. He pulled back and, with effort, dragged them back toward himself. They stretched to their full length, grasping and straining. Keith felt their rage and frustration flow up his arm and throughout the rest of his body.

'Petra, get a knife,' Keith said.

'What?' Petra yelled.

'Get a knife now, damn it!'

Without taking her eyes off Keith's hand, Petra opened a drawer and rummaged around until she found a carving knife. Keith gripped his right wrist with his left hand. 'Ok, cut them off.'

'Keith, no, we should go to the hospital.'

'Do it now, Petra, for Christ's sake, do it now...'

Petra looked into her brother's terrified eyes, nodded once, and lifted the knife. The fingers, as if sensing what was about to happen, squirmed from side to side. Petra silently aimed, counted to three, and slammed the knife down.

The first chop severed the middle and ring finger, leaving the little finger hanging by a strip of flesh. Rather than the gush of blood Petra had expected, the stumps just oozed a black, oily fluid. A smell of rot and waste filled Petra's nostrils and made her gag. She took a deep breath, lunged forward, and sliced off the rest of the little finger.

The severed digits jerked once or twice, then lay still.

Keith jumped up and backed away, holding his mutilated hand out in front of him. He stared at the things that had been attached to him. There was something so wrong about them, so much worse than any deformity he had ever imagined.

Petra still held the knife as though she expected the fingers to come after her. 'Does it hurt?' she asked quietly.

Keith looked at his hand and nearly vomited. 'No. I can still feel them, though. I think they're angry.'

'What do we do with these?' Petra asked, gesturing at the remains.

'Burn them.'

Petra thought about protesting. When they found a doctor, they might need them for tests, she wanted to say. Maybe someone could dissect them and figure out what they were. No, she decided. Keith was right. They had to be destroyed.

'Ok, stay here,' she said. 'I'll take care of it.' She found an empty coffee can and used the knife to sweep the fingers into it. 'Got any lighter fluid?'

'Under the sink.'

Keith sat on a chair and waited for Petra to return. When she did, she wordlessly pulled a first aid kit out of the cabinet and set about bandaging Keith's hand. 'They're not bleeding,' he protested.

'Infection,' she replied shortly.

After he was bandaged, Petra leaned back and closed her eyes. 'I went down the street to that park and burned them there. They went up like paper. They just shriveled, no bones left, nothing.'

After a moment, she asked, 'Want me to call Mom?'

'No.' Keith shook his head. 'She can't help and all it would do is scare her to death.'

Petra nodded, obviously having reached the same conclusion. 'I think you're right about this being something a doctor can't help us with,' Petra said slowly. 'There's this place in New York that investigates paranormal phenomena. I looked at their website yesterday. They seem pretty scientific, not these stupid New Age types. What do you think?'

Keith looked at the floor. 'Can't think of anything else to do.'

Petra got up and went to the computer. 'I'll go book our flight.'

Saturday

Keith stood on his apartment's tiny patio and looked out over the city. He never went out on the patio during the day, when all he could see was the smog hanging over downtown Phoenix. He enjoyed being there after dark, though. There was something soothing and almost hypnotic about staring at the lights in the distance.

He grimaced as his phantom ring finger made a sudden movement. Keith knew his finger was nothing more than a stump wrapped in gauze, but he could still feel it stroking the metal of the patio railing. He felt it wanting, struggling to escape.

'What do you want?' Keith whispered.

To his shock, something answered.

'We want in.' It was not so much a voice as a hiss. It sounded as though it came from right next to his ear, but Keith somehow knew that no one else would be able to hear it.

Keith clenched his teeth and gripped the railing with his good hand. 'In where?'

'Your world.'

Keith swallowed, not sure he wanted to ask the next question. 'Why me?'

The thing paused. When it spoke again, its voice held nothing but contempt. 'Why not you? You're a door. Any human would do.'

'Fuck you,' Keith whispered.

It snarled. 'When we get out, we're going to tear that bitch sister of yours into pieces. We can't wait.'

Then, for the first time, Keith was awake to feel one of his fingers disappear. He gritted his teeth and forced himself to stay quiet, certain that if he started screaming now he would never stop. He kept his eyes on the city lights while the thing's fingers grew to replace his own. Standing perfectly still, Keith let them flex and move. They skittered across the railing, through the air, over Keith's body.

As the things explored their surroundings, Keith made a decision. It became clear exactly what had to be done. This wasn't just about him anymore. Slowly and calmly, he turned and walked back into his apartment.

Petra heard a door slam and opened her eyes. 'Keith?' She squinted at her watch in the dim light. 5:45.

Keith moved through the living room and into the apartment's small hallway. He held a paper sack under his arm. His right hand was swathed in gauze and tape.

Petra sat up as Keith shut the bathroom door. 'Keith? Where did you go?'

Silence. Petra went to the kitchen and turned on the coffee pot. She rinsed a few bowls and set out a box of cereal.

After five minutes had passed, she tapped lightly on the door. 'Keith? Are you ok?'

The door opened. Keith gestured for her to come in. Petra frowned. 'Did you put on more bandages?'

Keith didn't answer. Instead, he picked up a pair of surgical scissors and began cutting away the tape. Petra took a step back. 'What are you doing?'

'Look.' He unwound the last of the bandages and held up his hand.

'Oh, Jesus...'

The fingers had grown back, just as large and horrible as they had been the day before. His index finger had been replaced by one of these new digits as well. All four of them extended toward Petra, almost as if they were sniffing the air. Then they lurched toward her with such force that Keith's arm was pulled along with them for several feet. Petra scrambled backwards until her back hit the wall.

'It's spreading, Petra. It's going to keep spreading. And when there's more of it than there is of me, well...' He jerked his chin toward his hand. 'I won't be able to control it.'

'What is it?' Petra whispered.

'I don't know. Something trying to get through from somewhere else.' Keith rummaged in the grocery bag.

'We're going to New York today. They're expecting us. They'll know what to do.' To her own ears, Petra's voice sounded weak and scared, like a little girl's. She stared at his hand, amazed at how ridiculous Keith's normal, human thumb looked next to these other things.

'No. I know what to do.' Keith pulled a bungee cord out of the sack and wrapped it tightly around his wrist.

'What? What are you doing?'

Instead of answering, Keith smiled sadly at his sister. He wished he could spare her this, but he needed someone here. 'Love you, sis. Remember to burn it.'

Petra saw Keith pull the meat cleaver from the grocery bag. Using all his strength, he laid his arm flat on the bathroom counter. She had time to scream Keith's name and to take one step toward him before he swung the cleaver into the flesh of his wrist. Blood, real human blood, poured out onto the white ceramic tiles. The thing that had once been Keith's hand fell into the sink. Keith shrieked and cursed in pain, slumping to the floor. Petra stood still for only a second before she bolted for the kitchen. She ran back carrying the phone in one hand, the bottle of lighter fluid and box of matches in the other.

Sunday

Petra glanced at the clock above Keith's hospital bed, then once again counted his fingers. Nearly twelve hours of sleep, and still no sign that it had spread. She even counted his toes just to be sure.

Tilting back in her chair, Petra closed her eyes and let herself drift off.

When she woke up, it was to the sound of her mother's voice. 'Oh, Keith! Petra, wake up.'

Petra opened her eyes and sat up straight. 'Mom, hi.'

Her mother gently stroked Keith's forehead. 'What happened?' she asked without looking away from Keith's face. 'The nurse said something about an accident, but she wouldn't say what it was, and — '

'Mom, Mom, he's going to be fine. That's what's important.' Petra wondered what she should tell her. It had been easier with the paramedics and police; she had simply told them that she had found Keith like that, and she didn't know what had happened. The things that had replaced Keith's fingers had burnt to nothing easily enough, leaving only his thumb and what remained of his palm. She and Keith would have to come up with a story after he woke up, but she decided not to worry about that yet.

'But I just don't understand how it could have happened. I mean, if he was around some kind of machinery or something I could see it, but in his apartment? How did you — ' Petra's mother looked up and gasped.

Petra frowned. 'What?'

Her mother's eyes looked not at Keith, but toward Petra.

'Oh, Petra, sweetheart,' she breathed, 'how did you lose that finger?'

Trick or Treat?

Clare Kirwan

'That isn't real blood, is it?' said her mum.

'Course not!' said Sally, hugging her witch's cloak around her.

'Look at the state of you! I warned you about messing about with the other children. That stuff might never wash out. And why are you shaking, child? It's not that cold out. And what's the matter with him?'

Sally didn't answer. She just gave a warning look towards Ben, who shrugged and shuffled his feet and carried on picking bits of pocket fluff off a lollipop that looked like a pumpkin.

'I'll clean him up.' Sally didn't want her mum to see. She pushed Ben, with sticky hands, towards the stairs. 'Come on, let's go and get changed.'

At the top of the stairs she pulled him into the bathroom and locked the door. It felt impossibly safe in there, breathing the familiar smell of shower gel and toilet duck. She gripped Ben by the shoulders. The black and white makeup had run and smeared across his face where he'd been crying.

'You must never say anything to mum about this. Never!' she hissed at him.

'Get off!' he squirmed away. 'You've got blood all over you.'

'Well turn the tap on for me!' she snapped. He reached across her, his hands very small and grubby.

The water ran as red as raspberry crush, pink splashes clinging to the sides of the basin. She scrubbed her hands with the nail brush, then rinsed the brush under the tap and swirled water over everything to wash it away. Then she examined Ben — making him take off his stupid skeleton top so she could rinse the shoulders where she had shaken him and then putting it over the towel rail to dry. He watched in silence, his bottom lip starting to quiver again.

'It's alright, Ben. It'll be alright. But we mustn't say anything. This is our secret now, okay? It's really important.'

Ben nodded slowly. His ribcage looked as fragile as a bird's, the bones and veins showing through delicate skin. She wrapped him in one of the fluffy blue bath towels that Uncle John had brought with him — the ones they weren't supposed to use.

'I'm frightened,' he said.

Sally wanted to say: So am I. She wanted to wrap herself in the other towel and for them both to sit down on the bathmat with the coloured fishes on, under the big light, and stay there for a very long time. But instead she said: 'There's nothing to be frightened of. Go and put your pyjamas on.'

He hesitated. 'I want to stay here with you.'

'You can't!' She opened the door and pushed him out. 'Mum'll be up in a minute. Ask her to read something to you.' She gave a final shove and shut the bathroom door quickly behind him.

Beneath the cloak, her dress felt tacky. She pulled it off and flung it in the sink, and the water ran even darker. Her stomach heaved and she tried not to think about the eyeball mallows and the chocolate bats they'd be given by old Mrs Harris at number 11... just before it happened.

Sally shuddered, feeling for a second as though she was

back out there near the alleyway where the street light was broken, feeling the sudden blast of chill air that had made her turn in time to see the black shape moving in the darkness. It moved in such a strange, deliberate way. Why had she just stood there and waited for it to reveal itself? No — she hadn't just stood there, but had moved towards it with no idea why.

The bathroom radiator clanged cheerfully, but her skin had tightened with gooseflesh. She climbed into the shower and stood under the gushing head of it without moving, mesmerized by the scarlet spinning down the plughole. She closed her eyes.

'I'm not a witch.' She whispered. 'I'm not witch.'

The man had said she must be — she was dressed like one. His voice was soft, but his eyes bored into her as though he was actually touching her, and she'd wanted to run away, wanted so much, but she couldn't move. He smelt overpowering, or was it his voice? Old and sweet. He had been tall, so tall, or was it that she had fallen? And he had caught her, lifted her up as though she didn't weigh anything at all. And Ben's tiny face, staring at her as though from a long, long way away.

Bang, bang, bang on the door.

'What are you doing in there? Sally?' Mum's voice dragging her back ... from where?

'Just a minute!'

It was all such an effort. She felt so heavy and so light. It had been so hard to get up again and stand swaying in the sudden blaze of moonlight, and Ben, his face streaming with paint and tears, pulling her with his small hands. She held him until he was as calm and dazed as she was, his little body, so like a bird.

She dried herself carefully, and brushed her hair in front of the mirror. Her face was pale — like someone else's face.

She pulled her hair back from her neck to examine the two small wounds — round and deep but strangely painless. She had stopped bleeding.

She came out slowly.

'Are you finished? You're a dream walking, you are!' Her mother's voice was raw in her ears. 'Are you hungry?'

'Yes,' she said, softly. 'Yes, I am.'

Feeder

A C Wise

I t had started with such a simple thing.

'Would you run out and get me a pint of ice cream?'

Just a simple question. He could see her in his mind now as she asked it; sitting on the couch with her legs tucked under her, the TV glow casting her in a snow-cold light that made everything look slightly unreal. It had been raining and he pointed to the downpour as a reason not to go, but she had turned to him with puppy-dog eyes and a little smile.

'Please?'

Her eyes were limpid pools in the flickering light — now mauve, now blue, now gray. The light also made her look softer; her hair and the gentle curves of her body. She looked vulnerable and it had been like a magic spell. After all, need can be a very powerful thing.

'Look at you; you're just skin and bones! Don't you eat at all anymore?'

His mother's words echoed in his head as he lay at the foot of the stairs, gazing up their length at the long climb.

'I'm fine, ma.'

Then he had been. What would she think if she could see him now? He smiled, a humorless smile curtailed by a wave of pain. It shot through him and he gripped the bottom stair, panting shallowly through gritted teeth.

Phantom pain, only an illusion, it wasn't real. He repeated the litany, waiting for the ache to subside. After all, how could a limb hurt when it wasn't there?

'At least let me make you a couple of sandwiches for the road...'

'Shut up, Ma,' he told the carpeted step in front of him. When he craned his neck upwards he could see her standing there, arms crossed, lips pressed into a thin line.

'Go away,' he told the eyes; bright with disapproval bordering on disdain. She shook her head at what her son had become; her phantom form dissipating. Just another illusion.

'I'm fine.' He scowled at the place where she had been, but then his expression quickly melted into a grin. 'I got my girl to take care of now.'

Pain washed through him once more and he was dizzy, tasting bile at the back of his throat. He could feel sweat beading, cold on the back of his neck and he rested his forehead against the rough carpeting before him.

'Clara.'

He whispered her name aloud, his knuckles white and bloodless with the force of his grip. He could see her; not as he could see his mother, but in his mind's eye. And he could feel her too. He could feel her waiting for him at the top of the stairs. He could feel her need.

'Do these jeans make me look fat?'

On the bed, reading a magazine, he did not look up.

'No, honey, you look fine.'

'Really?'

She turned to him, need clear in her eyes. Even in the room's dim light they were shining. She needed his approval, needed him to tell her she was still beautiful — if only to him.

He looked at her then, really looked, as if for the first time. It had been her figure that had first attracted him. He had no interest in those waif-thin, starved-looking women who glared at him from billboards. He wanted a woman with some meat on her bones and he had found her in Clara. He knew other men would never look at her the same way he did, he knew she was safe from their lustful gazes — she was something he could have all for his own.

He rose and crossed the room to her, putting his arms around her so she was pinioned between them and looking directly into his eyes.

'Of course.' He smiled and leaned to kiss her gently on the forehead. 'You'll always be beautiful to me.'

It was just a subtle emphasis, the slightest trick of the tongue and worry hovered in her eyes.

'Really?'

'Really.' He smiled; the reassurance to bind her to him.

Her face flooded with gratitude, melting beneath his gaze.

'You're so good to me. I don't know what I would do without you.'

What would she do without him? The thought made him ache, more than his phantom limbs. Tears sprung up in his eyes, just thinking of Clara without him. They had been through so much together, especially in the last few days. She was so vulnerable and without him, she would be utterly helpless, utterly alone.

Outside the wind howled and shook the walls. Frozen flakes of white drove against the windows and chill air screamed as it tried to find its way through cracks and under the door. Snow piled in drifts, high-reaching, to touch the windows and seeking to go higher still. How many days had they been stranded, storm-bound within these walls? He had lost count.

Trying to think made his head ache, made him remember the gnawing hunger — as cold and sharp as the howling wind — and made him remember the phantom pain radiating from the place where his legs had been.

He reached for the step above him, ignoring the pain. He had to get to Clara; he had to take care of her. She needed him. Gripping the next stair, he dragged himself slowly upwards, stopping, sweating and panting again with shallow, rapid breaths.

It was not the phantom of his legs that ached now, but the stumps where they had been. Twisting around he saw their scabbed ends, poorly healed. Black blood crusted and clotted the wounds, which were beginning to stink — like rotten meat. But for Clara, it was worth it — she was worth anything.

Clinging halfway up the stairs, sick with pain, he closed his eyes and thought of her. Her image flickered against his closed lids. He saw her on a night like this, rising ponderously from the bed and making the floor boards groan beneath her. It was near midnight and he had rolled to watch her standing in the cold, snow-filled light.

Her pendulous breasts sagged to her bulging stomach, which in turn spilled to meet the thickness of her thighs. The thin material of her nightgown strained as it stretched across her ample buttocks. There were dimples where her elbows had been and her face was a moon that she turned to him; her eyes bright in the dough of her cheeks, liquid and smiling.

Her need for him was so much greater now and thus so much greater was his love.

'Where are you going, honey?' he murmured, still sleepy.

'I can't sleep. I thought I would just get a little something. I know I shouldn't...'

She wheezed a little, even standing still. He rose.

'Don't be silly. You lie back down. I'll get you something.'

'Are you sure?' Her face flooded with relief and gratitude.

'Of course, honey, anything for you. You just relax and don't worry about a thing. As long as I'm here, you'll never have to worry about anything ever again.'

'I'm coming, Clara,' he whispered, opening his eyes.

He reached for the step above him. His fingers were claws gripping the stair. His arm was stick-thin, his skin translucent and he could see the blue veins circling the bones just beneath the surface. His mother was right; he couldn't remember the last time he had eaten.

He watched Clara eat instead and that was food enough for him. He brought her things. He brought her anything she asked for; he brought her things that she didn't ask for — anticipating needs that she didn't even know she had.

Like now. She hadn't called for him, but he knew that she needed him and that need drove him on and gave him the strength to keep climbing. On the landing he rested again. The scabs on one of his legs had opened, bringing fresh blood pulsing sluggishly to the surface. When he looked behind him he could see a sickening red trail staining the pale green of the carpet.

He turned away, focusing on the last few steps. Though his wasted muscles trembled, he pulled himself the rest of the way and then lay panting on the hall floor. He could see the door now; open just slightly, the flicker from the light of the small battery-powered TV spilling out towards him.

'I'm coming, Clara,' he whispered, pulling himself forward.

The wind rattled the walls and he felt the cold seeping up through the floor and into his bones. He thought of Clara, thought of all the times he had driven in sleet and rain and swirling snow to bring her buckets of fried chicken, pints of ice cream, a dozen donuts — whatever she might be craving. The thoughts kept him warm.

He thought of the way her waist had steadily thickened, straining the limit of her jeans. He thought of the way her legs had swollen, the gentle curves softening further and further until they lost all definition. He remembered when her legs had begun to ache, the bones straining under the masses of her flesh, until she couldn't even get out of bed anymore.

And faithfully he had continued to bring her things, continued to feed her and reassure her that she was still beautiful. Her eyes would well up with tears and she was so grateful; clinging to his hand, fairly weeping, overwhelmed by his love for her.

He sighed and the pain receded. He reached for the door. He thought of the fear that had been in her eyes when they had first realized that they were snowed in and the power was down, and then when the food in the fridge and freezer began to spoil. She had clung to him, sobbing.

'I'm so hungry!' she had moaned. 'What am I going to do?'

Her pleading eyes were liquid light; so full of need, so full of fear. At first he had been afraid too, but his fear had melted away in the face of her desire. She was counting on him, relying on him and who else was there? No one. In her whole world, there was only him.

'Clara?' he called softly, not wanting to disturb her as he pushed open the door.

The only light in the room came from the flickering of the little TV, resting on Clara's stomach. Above it her moon-round face was relaxed, slack even. Her eyes were like two pools of ink, almost lost in the rounds of her cheeks which pushed up towards her forehead. Her neck had been swallowed long ago; her shoulders rolled and quivered and from there down it was one great mountain of flesh, rippling and flowing to dominate the bed.

She was a mound of shadows, fold upon fold. The bed had given way beneath her long ago, the legs splintered, the mattress bowed to touch the floor. Around her great bulk the sheets were stained with blood; as black and crusted as the blood adorning the stumps of his legs.

'Clara?' he called softly, pulling himself forward.

The light on her face was pale fire and shadows clung to her. Her chest rose and fell steadily and he could hear the whine of her breath moving in and out between parted lips.

'Clara?'

He moved closer still, catching the edge of the bed's cover to pull himself up to her. With the movement, something heavy slipped from the bed and fell with a sickening thud to the floor beside him. A bone, long and slender and picked clean of all meat, lay gleaming in the same light that lit Clara's features. Phantom pain shivered the length of his phantom limbs, but before it could get a hold of him Clara turned and her features washed with a new light as her eyes rested on him.

'There you are!' she exclaimed, with a soft rubbery smile. 'I was starting to worry.'

'Don't worry, now. I'm here.'

He pulled himself up beside her and her features relaxed once again. Pressing close, he draped his arm across her bulk, pillowed on her great breasts, just beneath her chin. The bed stank of blood and other things beside, but he blocked them out, focusing on Clara.

The wind howled outside, but he wasn't the least bit cold. At first he had been afraid, but he had learned not to be afraid any more.

This time, he imagined, he wouldn't even feel the pain.

Urbane

Frazer Lee

Jennifer examined the bone-saw through tired, aching eyes.

Drifting off momentarily, she stared at the sticky red residue clinging to the sharp teeth of the circular blade. Tiny fragments of bone and grue glistened in the overhead lights. Drip-drip, went the tap. Plink-plink, went the surgical steel table as the water droplets parachuted down onto its smooth surface. They made little clearings in the river of blood there, then mingled with the trails of red and swam steadily downstream toward the plughole's abyss.

'Wanna get pizza? Or are you gonna cosy up with John Doe over there all night?'

Jennifer snapped out of her trance.

Her colleague, Bill had already scrubbed up and was ready to go. And he was asking her out again. Jennifer was never quite comfortable being asked out over the dead bodies in the morgue, especially by Bill. He had funny, creepy eyes. Or maybe he just looked at her funny. Either way, he wasn't going to get a look in.

'No thanks Bill,' she heard herself say, 'I'd better clean up and get going. I'm meeting a friend tonight.'

Bill made a joke about her having a life, leered at her in that disconcerting way of his and (praise the lord) left. Jennifer set about bagging up the body of her John Doe and washed down the table, ready for tomorrow's cadavers. She didn't dislike doing autopsies; it was kind of therapeutic to her. No, it was just that there were so damn many this month.

The New York night was freezing cold and loud as hell. Just the way she liked it. She breathed in the sulphur of the air hungrily. Heading home, Jennifer stopped off at the store to grab a snack and some body spray.

As she showered, Jennifer realised just how good she was feeling about tonight's date. Hospital orderlies weren't usually her type, but this young British guy definitely had something about him. He was charming, witty, and urbane. Yes, he was handsome and just a little bit mischievous around the eyes. Not like yucky Bill, oh no. He had a cool name too — it had made her laugh when he introduced himself as Geez. Like 'Jeez?' she had said. And he had laughed too. This was all very encouraging; the sex would be great. Yes, he'd do.

Pausing to check her reflection in the side window, Jennifer stepped into the cab. As it trundled along to the club, she sniffed her wrists. The body spray was a little acrid, but musky enough to disguise the stench of latex gloves and chemicals from her busy day. She settled back and enjoyed the ride. Despite her tiredness, Jennifer was feeling good about herself. She felt like having a drink and dancing.

Hot white searchlights pierced the night sky above the club. Massive fiery letters spelled out 'EVILUTION' above the entrance. A crowd of revellers lined up impatiently outside the doors. Jennifer paid the cab driver and took in the scene for a moment. So it was a rock club. This was going to be one hell of a party.

She clutched her invite and, ignoring the queue, held it out to a huge, monolithic doorman. He looked like he had been forged from granite and wrapped in layers of beef. His hands were bigger than Jennifer's TV set. Suddenly, he

smiled. She had an invite — she must be somebody important. And as he ushered her inside, seeming to shrink by
a few feet as he did so, Jennifer really felt like somebody
important. The collective gaze of the revellers, all lined up
in the cold, seemed to be one of searing envy. And she had
to admit; she liked it.

Inside, the music was deafening. As Jennifer entered the
hot maw of the club, her mouth opened in wonder at the
sheer size of the place. Massive sculptures of intertwining
bodies snaked upwards from floor to ceiling, framed by giant
red velvet drapes. A balcony, like a pulpit in this cathedral
of sweat and noise, overlooked the huge dance floor. Behind
it, coloured light fizzed and swirled through a vast stained
glass window.

Geez was waiting for her at the bar. He looked great. His
hair slightly ragged, and his suit like something from an
experimental Japanese movie. This was certainly a change
from hospital orderly garb, to Jennifer's delight. He ordered
her a large vodka tonic — her favourite drink. When she
insisted on paying, he laughed and said she could get the
next round. So British.

After a couple more stiff drinks, they hit the dance floor.
The music was heavy, rumbling and sexy. Jennifer got into
it immediately. She felt great, and Geez was keeping up with
her. As their bodies brushed together, she could feel the electric effect he was having on her. She felt more intoxicated
as they danced. The music slowed and she allowed Geez to
place his hands on her as they danced. He stroked her face
and caressed the small of her back. Then, he licked his finger
and placed it inside his pocket.

Drawing his finger out, Jennifer saw the little dab of
white powder on its tip. She giggled tipsily, mesmerised by
the powder's iridescence beneath the club lights. 'Well, why
not?' she thought. It had been a long time since she had

done anything so naughty. Since her med school days in fact, and they were a distant memory.

Jennifer sucked on Geez's finger hungrily. The drug cascaded down her throat like popping candy, shocking her instantly with its effects. This wasn't coke, or any other drug she'd dabbled with. As her body numbed pleasantly, Jennifer could only manage to mouth a single word.

'Wow.'

Geez threw back his head and laughed merrily. Then they kissed. The lights whirled and the music seemed to bleed warmly into Jennifer's ears, the very floor beneath her feet grew soft.

As the song finished, Geez whispered desperately into Jennifer's ear. She wanted him too; it was true. He led her away through the crowd. There was a place they could go, where no one would disturb them.

Unseen by the revellers, a man stood watching from the pulpit balcony high above, immaculately dressed and older than anyone in the club. Puffing on a fat cigar, he smiled dryly through the smoke — his eyes following Geez and Jennifer's progress across the crowded dance floor.

Kissing and laughing as they went, the lovers crashed through a fire escape door and down a stairwell into the gloom beneath the club. The light was scant, coming as it did from emergency lights in the stairwell. A slight exhilarating chill gave Jennifer goose bumps. Groping under Geez's shirt, she felt his nipples stiffen too. As he pushed her gently against a wall, Jennifer's eyes searched the darkness for clues.

'Where are we?' she asked, breathlessly. Her voice echoed as she spoke. Wherever they were, it was a large room of some kind.

'Underground car park,' mumbled Geez as he kissed her neck, 'It's disused, no one ever comes down here anymore.

Well, no-one but us perverts...'

She laughed. As his fingers penetrated her clothing, Jennifer gave into her hunger completely. The drabness and detritus of the working day were falling away utterly, the darkness of the subterranean car park replaced by a brilliant white light as she closed her eyes. She could feel the drug Geez had so kindly administered really kicking in now. It was astonishing. Piercing dots of sharp crystal joined the whiteness in her mind's eye. Geez parted her legs and spread her arms out by her side so that she formed an X against the wall. She drifted almost out of her body and into a reverie — a place where every nerve ending was numb with love and desire. Whatever Geez was doing to her, she never wanted it to stop.

Suddenly a light exploded in her face, blinding her. Someone had thrown a light switch; dozens of strip lights buzzing into life. Her eyes were open, but her vision was blurred and distorted. Distant shapes teased her with their oblique forms. She squinted, and saw what looked like Geez standing in front of her. He was not alone. Others stood around him in a little group. She could not move her arms and legs.

The onlookers stood politely and waited as Jennifer's vision returned to her. She became all too quickly aware of a strong smell pervading the damp cold air of the car park.

Blood. Her own blood.

Panicking, she tried to move. Her arms were somehow glued to the wall above and behind her. Fear rising into her throat, Jennifer craned her head as far forward as possible. Her vision snapped into focus revealing the source of the sanguine smell. Geez had certainly had his way with her.

Jennifer's belly was wide open. Careful incisions had been made to reveal the pulsating organs beneath the folds of her flesh. These folds had been stretched out and pinned back onto the wall, so her abdomen looked like an obscene fleshy umbrella. Her intestines were clinging on for dear life — any further movement and they would surely spill onto the cement floor. Her wrists had been nail-gunned to the wall.

She gagged and swallowed hard. Strangely, the musk of the body spray was suddenly pleasing to Jennifer. The drugs were obviously still doing their job.

Looking beyond Geez's little group, she could see the shapes in the distance more clearly. Stretched between each concrete pillar of the underground car park was a human body, pinned out as she was, forming Xs as far as the eye could see. Some were quite fresh and others were horribly decomposed, their flesh livid and yellowing under the fluorescent lights. More John and Jane Does than she had ever operated on at the hospital.

Jennifer tried to scream as the group approached her, but no sound would come. The distant rumble of the nightclub music dared her to make a noise.

At the head of the group was the cigar-smoking man, studying her with idle amusement just as he had on the balcony. He took one last puff of his cigar before nonchalantly tossing it away. Behind him, Geez and a few other striking urbanites smiled at her sickly. To them, she was a work of art. Eviscerated.

'Who are you?' croaked Jennifer, pathetically.

'We are the Urbane,' came the old man's reply as he entered her, 'and we must feed.'

Then the wanton rushing of the others. Teeth and claws snapping and twitching as they devoured her slick, wet organs.

Drip-drip went her blood.

Plink-plink as it joined the dark crimson pool beneath her feet.

Harvest

David Dunwoody

Gabe washes his vehicle's tires and windows every morning. It's an exhausting and fruitless task, but — well, it's something to do and, more importantly, it looks nice when he drives into the city center. His homestead is another story altogether. Gabe lives on the eastern perimeter of Potter Parish, his bedroom window looking out on sun-baked steel and concrete: the Wall, topped at 300-yard intervals by watchtowers, curls of barbed wire jutting from the cement at random points. He lives in the house his father built, a modest 5-room ranch surrounded by overgrown grass. The acres behind the house have become a wasteland of rust-eaten farm machinery, dead tools lying on dead earth. Gabe worked the land once but has given himself over to other pursuits. More precious pursuits, in his humble opinion.

Once finished cleaning — the dust will attack in clouds as soon as he drives off, oh well — Gabe goes inside. The screen door claps at his back with warm familiarity. Since his wife passed on, Gabe's life has been solitary. A bag of fresh lemons lies in a sink with half-melted ice; fishing a clean knife from the cutlery drawer, he tears the bag open. She always made lemonade on blazing hot days like this, but now he handles all the chores, and it makes him appreciate her all the more. Gabe slices into a lemon. The smell fills his nostrils, delicious. His son used to do chores too, helped with the farm work, but he'd gone off with the rest to be killed by the Others. That was before the Wall. Before everyone realized they could never win, only hide.

He works in the kitchen until early afternoon, then drops ice cubes in the pitcher of the lemonade. Stirs in a bit of sugar — rare commodity these days, but he only uses it for drinks. Gabe takes the pitcher out into the dry Texas heat.

One of the guards hollers from the nearest watchtower. Gabe smiles and waves; it's hard to tell who it is from this distance, but it sounds like Toby. He opens his mouth to —

No, Toby is my dead son. That's Lucas up there.

The guard climbs down a ladder inside the perimeter. 'Gabe, I saw you sweating out there all morning. You didn't have to do this.'

'It's nothing.' The old man shrugs inside clothes that seem to grow bigger every day. 'You all spend every day sittin' up there, you deserve something better than hot water.' The appreciation in Lucas's face is genuine. He empties his canteen and fills it from the pitcher. 'You take care of yourself, Gabe.'

'Oh. Yes.' Gabe had hoped for some conversation, but the boy has to get back in the tower. Offering a parting wave, Gabe heads back to the house. Grass bends and crunches under his shoes. It's damn hot today; it'll be good to spend a few hours indoors, finishing off the lemonade.

Stepping through the back door, Gabe sees his son standing in the kitchen. No, it can't be, but nothing else makes any more sense and he fully believes that Toby has returned home, right up until the thing steps into a ray of sunlight and Gabe sees through dust motes its sunken pallor and the hunger in its milky eyes.

It is upon him then. Gabe's head bounces off the floor and into the shockingly powerful grip of the thing, the

Other. It straddles him, and pus runs in rivers from a ruined mouth as it makes some inhuman, godawful sound. Then it dashes his skull against the floor.

The dead man had climbed the wall at a point several yards north, where the guard on duty made a habit of filling his canteen with homemade vodka and passing out. Many times before, in the middle of the night, the dead man had scaled the wall for a quick peek before dropping back into the brush. Today, in broad daylight, it has come over.

Self-sustenance is the singular purpose in this wretched thing's existence. That means feeding, and feeding, and feeding. But meat is scarce in the badlands. Still, the dead man, moving alone, had eaten enough to rejuvenate its soft tissue, to stir activity in its putrefied brain. And it thought. It thought that there must be a better way to eat. So it had crept outside the Parish's walls for days, hunkered down in the grass, eyeing the watchtowers. At night, it stole glimpses into the meat's world. And it had seen something, something startlingly familiar, something that awakened dim memories in the recesses of its mind...

Then it had a plan.

Now the dead man fishes through Gabe's pockets. It desperately wants to feed but time is running short.

It finds what it needs and creeps out the front door.

Scarlett is the last out of her classroom, as usual. She refuses to leave her desk until she's finished drawing her garden. Every colored pencil in the box has been worn to a nub over the course of the week; golden tulips fringed with violet push out from behind huge pink blossoms that endlessly rain petals. Having never seen any plant more vibrant than a dandelion, Scarlett paints this garish rainbow from her imagination. The second nudge from her teacher gets her to finally pack it up and hurry out.

Billy's waiting by the exit, backpack swinging in a bored

arc. 'C'moooooon,' he drones as Scarlett races down the hall.

Outside the buses are lined up, five of them serving the Parish. This is the only elementary school in town. It's a place where parents can send their children to mimic the life before, to experience some semblance of the normalcy that was stolen away before their birth. Billy is Scarlett's best friend. They board their bus together, casting a suspicious eye toward the new driver. Soon they'll be back home in the apartment complex and Scarlett can show Mom her garden. It's what she wants for her twelfth birthday. Not the entire thing, just a few flowers to sit on the windowsill. The gold and purple ones.

'I had to miss recess,' Billy mutters as they locate a vacant seat in the back. 'I know.' Scarlett tries to mask her resentment. She'd spent the whole period waiting for him by the monkey bars. 'It's James Schumer's fault,' Billy continues. 'He called my grandma a rotter. Right in front of Mister Beasley, and he didn't even do anything!' Billy's grandma had died from cancer the month before. She wasn't infected. She just went to Heaven like regular people. Jimmy Schumer is a prick (a word we don't say, Scarlett) anyway. (I know Mom, but it's true.)

Scarlett's dad is a rotter. Was. They burned him a long time ago, so long it seems more a dream than a memory.

PPO Wolff has seen his share of violence. Inside the Parish, assault is always a first-degree felony, and rape a capital offense; yet somehow, that doesn't stop some. Wolff is a constant witness to the enduring vices of men.

He patrols the northeastern quadrant with PPO Trejo. From the hospital in midtown to the patches of expired farmland on the east Wall, it's a varied beat bringing him into contact with dozens of people every day. Gabe Hiller is one of his favorites. Approaching Gabe's house, he doesn't think much of the front door hanging open. Then Gabe's name, on his lips, turns to a glob of saliva that lodges in his throat.

The old man's on his back in the kitchen, visible through the front hall, and is clearly dead. The amount of blood pooling around his head is obscene. For a moment, Wolff can't even approach him. Trejo sweeps past and kneels beside the corpse.

'Careful!!' Wolff violently clears his throat. He reaches to his hip for the machete hanging there. Trejo's hands freeze on Gabe's chest; with deliberate slowness, almost as if diffusing a bomb, he pulls back. 'I don't see any bites,' Trejo breathes. How could he in that mess? Wolff steps lightly forward, watching for any movement. Clothes aren't torn, no obvious flesh wounds — no signs of feeding. It looks like most of Gabe's brains are on the floor anyway. Jesus, he's dead. Just plain dead.

But it's Trejo who vomits at the realization. He spins to avoid the body and hits his partner's shoes. Never seen a normal death before. 'Who — who would do this — just kill someone?'

'They might still be here,' Wolff whispers.

Trejo looks to the back door, two running steps away. 'I'll get the guards.'

'No. They'll lock down the Parish. Even if we tell them it wasn't an undead they'll quarantine us.' As he speaks, Wolff glances down the hallway to his right and checks the other rooms. 'No one's here. We have to — '

A cold, small seed of horror in the pit of his stomach erupts. Tendrils of ice freeze every bone in his body. He drops to rifle through Gabe's clothing. 'Keys...' He gasps. 'Oh, God!'

'What is it?' Trejo looks again to the exit.

'His bus wasn't outside. It's gone.' The chill is paralyzing now. 'C-call the school.'

Most people refuse the security of the walled cities. Unthinkable, perhaps, but something stubbornly and stupidly romantic in the human spirit won't be caged. So they live a nomadic existence on the outside, where they almost certainly die of infection. It takes weeks, sometimes months to progress through a still-living body but the free-rangers don't burn their infected; right to the bitter end, they pray over them, pray to the God that checked out over a century prior.

So what makes it worth the hardship, the slow death, the swelling of the ranks of the dead? Scarlett's mother could never answer the question, but Scarlett knows. She dreams of unfettered fields, forests, natural gardens bursting with colors she's never seen. Jostled awake in her seat, she watches the colors dissipate before her eyes and from her mind.

Billy's inking his backpack with a felt-tip marker. 'This driver sucks,' he says loudly. Those within earshot laugh in agreement. They're moving pretty fast now. The floor vibrates under Scarlett's feet and she imagines the entire thing might come apart around her if their speed increases. 'Hey,' a kid up front yells, 'that's where I live! Stop, you're supposed to stop!' The driver doesn't respond, doesn't even glance in the mirror. The faces of the children become confused, worried. Scared. Someone else shouts at the driver to let him off. Scarlett's apartment building whisks by. 'STOP!' Billy jumps to his feet and is thrown back down. A girl begins to cry.

Hurtling onto a side street, the bus leaves asphalt and bounces the panicked children over an uneven dirt track. Tree branches scrape the roof and sides with high-pitched squeals like the shrieks of bats. Scarlett clings to the seat in front of her and closes her eyes. If she only sits quiet and makes herself invisible, it will be over. If the sobbing and screaming will only stop, then the bus will stop too and it'll be as if nothing ever happened. In her mind's eye she sees Dad, bound and bathed in flames; and the cacophony of cries around her is her mother's anguish.

It pumps the brakes in time with the gnawing of its stomach. Each distended sore in its belly is a slavering maw; the screaming of the children, the salty scent of their fear, excites it further.

No more waiting. No more hunger.

Stopping, rising, turning, it reveals itself.

The first thing the principal asks when Wolff and Trejo reach the school is, 'Do the guards know?'

'It's a stolen bus, ma'am. Gabe Hiller's. Now what number is it?'

'132.' She stammers. She'll be on the radio as soon as they depart, Wolff knows, but at least they'll have a bit of time before the Parish goes into lockdown. Time to find the kids before security protocol leaves them stranded with a murderer. Gabe wasn't fed upon, Wolff assures himself. It's a man we're after, a maniac to be sure but a man that can be reasoned with and, if necessary, killed. He starts the patrol car.

'He didn't go back the way he came. He'd want to take them somewhere isolated, right? Let's try the southern storehouses. Right Trejo?'

'I don't know.' Trejo's squeezed himself against his door as if he wants to be as far from Wolff as possible, far from this chase. He doesn't trust instinct. He wants to call the guards.

'We CAN'T!' Wolff barks.

Red. A tableau of dripping crimson, running darker as it makes its way down to collect in syrupy pools. The woods are all sun-streaked greens and browns but Scarlett only sees and feels and tastes red. In her eyes, her mouth, between her toes inside shoes that beat the earth with spongy noises. The tree branches are no longer bats' claws but the scrabbling fingers of the rotter. All she can remember is being knocked down, as the others crowded into the back of the bus; the emergency door was rigged shut, wouldn't open; then red red red. (Your clothes, honey. They're ruined!)

Billy. Billy, never again. Not Mom either. And no more drawings, not when her hands will never wash clean. A roar like thunder fills her ears and makes her head swim. Still she runs.

(I'm sorry about my shirt Mom, and I lost my backpack, but it's not my fault. I'm the only one who made it to the front door and if I'd gone back I would have SEEN.)

Far too late, Scarlett realizes she's fled in the direction the bus was facing — deeper into the woods.

And she looks back.

The trees in the afternoon sun are strangely menacing, gnarled arms blocking her in. They are alone, though — no blood-caked nightmare pursuer in sight. He's back at the bus, isn't he, with Billy.

Can she risk turning back and trying to find the road? Is it any safer out there? Somehow she's sure that the rotter has her scent in its nostrils and will come for her, will find her anywhere. She continues into the woods. They can't last forever. There's always a wall.

Red-black-red-black. Impact. Dizzying blur gone in a sobering WHITE flash. Sounds from the past and present collide as they reverberate around Wolff's skull: Trejo's voice merged with groaning steel merged with a jackhammering heart.

The car landed right side up. Wolff shakes droplets of blood from his head and pieces together the crash. There was a tree in the road, is that what it was? He slaps Trejo's shoulder with a still-tingling hand. Guy's out cold. Pulse is good though; unbuckling himself and leaning over, Wolff spies a gashed robin's egg on his partner's temple. 'Shit.' He pulls the keys from the ignition and climbs out.

Just off the road bedside a wooded area, several felled trees have been set upright against a concrete abutment. They're lazily lashed together with rope, making it easy for one to have been knocked loose. That's not what stops Wolff in his tracks.

It's the tire treads veering past the abutment into the woods, cutting a violent swath away from the road.

Car's crippled. Trejo might have internal injuries. It's over; undead or not, Wolff has to call the guards on this, yet his boots stay rooted in place, eyes probing the wound cut into the trees by what could only be the stolen bus.

Make the call, then head after the bus. It's that easy, easy, easy, shake yourself awake, make the fucking call! Why are we running into the woods now, buddy? Because those kids are in there somewhere screaming, buddy, they're pissing themselves and screaming their little throats raw. Some sick fuck from right here in the Parish, BUDDY, was willing to kill for those kids, and what he wants from them is worse than death.

Wolff's left ankle nags at him. He pushes harder with each step, pain for fuel.

There's the Wall. Its slate-gray surface is deceptively cool-looking. Scarlett nearly runs right into it; thrusting out her palms, she gasps at the heat emanating from the concrete. The blood on her skin and clothing is saturated with sweat. She wipes her dirt-gummed hands on the back of her shirt and glances over her shoulder.

The rotter is atop her.

Its knee drives into her chest, and the undead stumbles right over Scarlett into the Wall. Its sleeve catches on a snarl of barbed wire and tears open — no, not its sleeve but the very flesh of its arm, ripping like wet paper. Scarlett backpedals, trying to catch her breath. Her heel snags on something and she spills over the ground.

Pulling free, the rotter turns. She can't tell whether or not the blighted orbs in its head are fixed on her. Head to toe it is drenched in her classmates' blood. A gruesome question crosses her mind: isn't he full yet?

It staggers forward. Scarlett looks down to see what tripped her. It's a hole ringed by a steel lip. It's a sewer.

(Maybe he can't climb, maybe he won't follow, please don't let him!)

She goes feet-first.

It's upon approaching the bus that Wolff finally knows how terribly wrong he was.

The windows are painted crimson from within. The odor hits him with a force as if the bus itself had rolled onto his body. Coupled with the sick ache of realization, Wolff is driven to his hands and knees, dry-heaving over the gore-matted grass. And still he must go inside. He must.

He braces himself against the side of the vehicle. Its door hangs open. Silence inside; drawing his machete, he edges closer, trying to tune out the rustling of the trees.

The rustling of the trees in the still air.

Wolff spins around. Where's it coming from? Straight ahead. His hand closes like a vise around the machete handle, but it doesn't stop him from trembling as he steps away from the bus. There are no shapes discernable in the foliage. No movement. The rustling is more distant than he first thought. Is it the undead, its belly heavy with meat, fleeing toward the south Wall? Is it the children? He nearly calls out to them.

He has to pursue the noise but he must look in the bus first and make sure he's not deserting any survivors. With the hope of life waiting to be found, Wolff steps in. It's almost like stepping into the ruptured bowels of a great worm.

He lurches, grabs for a dry surface to steady himself and finds none, falls flat in the aisle. Floor, seats, ceiling are all greased with innards. Jesus, this was a rapture, a feast. The gluttonous thing devoured the sweetest meat and cast the rest aside. A red lump, scant inches from Wolff's face, is a discarded head. His guts churn with nothing in them and only flecks of spittle escape his mouth as he retches to the point of near-blindness.

Still heaving, Wolff hurls himself from the abattoir and into the woods.

An unfamiliar sensation — pain — radiates through the dead man's legs when it hits the tunnel floor. Waning light fixtures bolted to the ceiling create rippling patterns in the waste water at the man's feet. It studies patterns. It knows which way she ran.

Tunnels extending beyond the Wall have been sealed off save for tiny grates, so Scarlett's escape route is severely limited. There must be a passage branching off that goes back into town...she splashes along frantically. Wishes Mom could reach down and pluck her away from this, into her bed, wishes she could relax her throbbing limbs against her mother's warmth. (It's not your fault, baby. He'll never find you here, you'll never see a rotter again.)

The dead man tongues the back of its teeth. The tang of blood in its mouth does nothing to quell its hunger, nor does the pulp filling its stomach and throat. The girl is near and she belongs to it. This pursuit has spent enough of the rotter's energy already. It quickens its pace.

She thinks of her garden, not the one on paper but the real one that must exist somewhere out there, a place where the dead can never go. Again she thinks how wonderful it would be to plant those lovely flowers on the windowsill, a barrier against the things that took Dad and Billy. The sewer is rank and colorless. No protection here.

Scarlett hits another bricked-up wall. Dead end this time.

There's a manhole overhead, its ladder extending only part of the way down, just beyond her reach. She jumps desperately at it. The noise doesn't matter anymore. He's already closing in.

Rounding a corner, it sees her. She leaps and leaps and leaps and salts her meat with terror.

A cry ricochets off the walls; the dead man turns, and its vision is bisected by the machete cleaving through its skull.

The blade stops midway through the rotter's head. Wolff tries to yank it out. Stuck fast. The rotter grabs his arms. 'Get ouuuuuuuuuut,' Wolff hollers at the girl over the croaking sounds of the undead. It lunges at him, but the protruding machete handle keeps it from finding purchase in his flesh. The croaking is incessant, brain mutilated and misfiring. Ruddy teeth gnash at Wolff who cannot shake free of its grasp. He can't reach the machete either. And the girl is standing frozen at the end of the tunnel.

He leans back, trying to throw the rotter off balance, and they both go into the water. 'RUN!!!' He bellows.

Scarlett watches the rotter writhe atop the policeman with a blade jutting out the back of its head. She can't help but she can't leave. She can't let it out of her sight, lest it spring on her again when she least expects it. (Please kill him!)

The policeman yells again — this time in pain. He and the rotter rise in tandem and stumble toward her. She cringes, is bowled over, and the pair smash through the brick wall.

Wolff lands on top of the undead. He grabs the machete again and puts all his weight on it. It sinks down like a lever, separating the rotter's upper skull from its jaw. Rancid bile and child-meat spew forth. This time, the stench knocks Wolff clean out.

He awakens with his face half-submerged in sewage. Wolff jerks up, spits and sees the dead rotter there. 'Dead,' he whispers.

They went right through a section of wall sealing the Parish's sewer system. Better call the guards on this one. Wolff snorts loudly, trying not to laugh. He calls, 'Little girl?' She appears to be gone. Thank God. And there's a ladder right overhead that will take him out of this hell.

'Ohhhh...'

He looks down at the back of his hand and studies the bite. Went deep. Deep enough, anyway.

'Oh.'

It happened in the car accident. Yes.

Wolff repeats it over and over again in his head, a mantra. If he says it enough, it'll be true. As if nothing ever happened.

Several hundred yards down the tunnel, Scarlett finds a ladder she can reach. It takes all of her strength to move the cover aside, but she manages it enough to slip out into the sun.

Before her is an expanse of waist–high grass. At her back, the Wall. The Parish. Mom too, but she'll think Scarlett died on the bus. She'll be better off; Scarlett imagines it would almost be worse for Mom to spend the rest of her life wringing her hands over her almost-eaten daughter, than lying awake with a new nightmare to haunt her. Now she can move on, like with Dad. That's what the girl tells herself.

The Proposal

Charles Colyott

There are no words for the emotion I see behind her eyes. Equal parts hatred, gratitude, confusion and fear; I'd like to imagine there was love there too, but there isn't and there never will be.

You'd think I'd be used to this by now.

You'd be wrong.

If you were to listen to Evie or Phillip, her idiot lover, I'm the villain here. That's what's wrong with this damned country. You make a deal, you're supposed to honor it. You don't back out or sneak around trying to screw the other party.

Oh, sure, but I'm the bad guy.

Dear little Evie knows just how bad I could be, though. She sees it, feels it, hears it. If I don't start liking the way of things very soon...well, they'd be sorry.

I don't want it that way.

I never wanted it to be that way.

I really did love her from the very first moment I saw her. Who wouldn't have? She was so beautiful, so alive. And when she walked past me, and the honeysuckle scent of her skin numbed my nerves and made my legs wobble, I couldn't help but wonder about her vibrations, her wavelengths. The music of her laughter filled me with such a profound faith; in her perfection, she was proof of something beyond us all, something real and true. Sure, all the other idiots on campus were staring at her perfect ass, or wondering what it would be like to touch her.

She did touch me, even though her flesh never so much as brushed against mine.

I loved her — then and now — on a level most can never ever know.

It was for her, and only for her that I offered to help...

Phillip. What sort of man with any spine whatsoever is named...Phillip?

The emotions in Phil's eyes, as I hum softly alongside Evie's pale neck, are much easier to decipher. He hates me, but he needs me. He's smart enough to know that much, at least. That, and that he could never stand against me.

I love the irony.

Phillip was the starting quarterback during senior year; I am a scrawny anemic freak. Before Evie, my only association with Phillip involved him calling me a retard and crushing my hearing aids beneath his five hundred dollar Italian loafers. Even without my leg braces, I would never have been able to fight him, not physically. He was one of the most popular guys in school, and I was the guy nobody wanted to make eye contact with, as if my disabilities were somehow contagious.

Evie, though...she never treated me like I was any different.

I've never understood how such a wonderful creature could stand being with such a cretin. I suppose, from a high school perspective, Phillip was a kind of god. He had it all.

But who holds all the cards now, eh Phillip?

As my lips mutter soft breaths along her collarbones, I allow myself a smile.

He hates this.

He hates that I am seeing her like this, that I am touching her like this, so intimately. I know Evie, body and soul, far better than he ever will, and that kills him a little. Well, it's time he learned that life can be cruel.

I watch his fists clench and unclench and I smile.

Try it, kid. I double dog dare you.

She twitches, and I can feel the waves of her first breath ripple throughout my body. The sounds I breathe along her breastbone and stomach are not words. They are, I suppose, the literal language of love, of god.

What the Hindu sought in the crafting of mantra, I have mastered.

What the occultists and kabbalists attempted, I have perfected.

All matter is energy, and all energy is merely a vibration, a waveform... And in those vibrations, I have found The Sound.

Everything I have ever done — the cochlear implant prototype I patented in high school, the landmark acoustical protocols I introduced in college, the nights of ayahuasca madness in Rio Branco, the Darshans in Calcutta — has led me to this work.

I spied it in the works of Abramelin, Bardon, and Crowley.

Everything, even the Bible, echoed what I knew...

In the beginning was the Word, and the Word was God. Take away the idiotic interpretations and the meaning is simple — sound is the basis of it all.

That first night, in the rain, I asked Phillip what he was willing to do, to give, to have her back. There'd been an accident, he said. A deer bolted in front of the car, Evie swerved, and they'd rolled off the embankment.

I asked him again.

He just stared at her; her purple and black swollen throat, the swelling around her eyes and cheekbones. I slapped him — something I'm very proud of — and told him to put her in the car.

And I made him an offer, a proposal. His love would live again, but she could never be his. From that day forward, she would be mine.

That was the idea, anyway.

I gave her my breath, my vibration, my sound. I sang away the swelling, the bruising, the death, and gave her life... my Evie.

She wouldn't speak to me.

Wouldn't look at me.

Phillip. That fucking Phillip. He'd told her.

She wouldn't be a kept woman, she said. I told her it was all she'd ever been. She slapped me and walked out.

The next time, I shackled her to the bed. I didn't want to.

She'd been out jogging, apparently, and a mugger stabbed her through the heart. Phillip, naturally, came to me.

I whispered The Sound, my lips a hair's breadth from her split sternum. The wound knitted together, leaving no trace. I could feel a shuddering breath, and her heart began to beat — I felt it in time with my own.

Again, there was the look. She saw the shackles and spit curses at me.

She wouldn't eat or drink.

She called me a monster.

Eventually, when it was clear she'd rather die again than live with me, I unlocked her. She went to Phillip, who kissed her and touched her and started to cry. He said he thought he'd never be able to hold her again.

I could taste the bile in my throat.

This was the way it went for a while. Poor, poor Evie would fall victim to the world, heroic Phillip would sacrifice all for his lady love, and me, well, I would love her back to life.

And her hatred for me only grew.

When I give her The Sound, worshipping her as she deserves to be worshipped, she looks down on me in disgust like any goddess would.

I believe in her still.

Phillip stands back, watching. I actually catch him checking his watch.

Sorry if I'm keeping you from something important, asshole.

When Evie opens her eyes, she sees she is bound again.

This time I refuse to let her go so easily; sooner or later she has to see. I try to speak, but she cuts me off. 'Fuck you,' she says. 'Just let me go, you bastard.'

Phillip makes some sort of crack, and now it's my turn to clench my fists.

Because I love her, I set her free.

Evie steps down from the bed and starts for her lover.

'Isn't it strange,' I manage before my voice cracks, 'that so much tragedy could happen to one girl?'

She stops, and, for one moment, I think she might turn.

She doesn't.

She never does.

Not when I told her that their 'accident' didn't involve any deer. That her car was strangely unmarred.

Or when I reminded her that she's never gone jogging in her life.

'Do you know what it was tonight?' I ask. She actually looks at me for a moment.

As the tears burn my cheeks, I say, 'Tonight it was suicide. Yeah, apparently you were so fed up with life that you shot yourself in the back of the head...three times.'

She looks to Phillip, who pulls her in close and holds her tight. His eyes say who holds the cards now, bitch?

'Evie... please?' I say, but they turn and leave.

At the closing door I scream, 'One day I won't do it, you know... I won't.'

But they, and I, know that I will.

I always will.

Guts

Gavin Inglis

Sylvester sat alone in the windowless bathroom, under the ugly shaving light, and fought constipation.

The corners of the floor and the dirty recess behind the sink were lined with a bleary gloom. It was after three a.m. and his flatmate was staying over at the girlfriend's. Sylvester heard only the slow drip from the bathtub cold tap.

He bent forward, his face hot, head aching with the effort, but it was nearly there: one solitary shit, dense as a rock, on the very verge of being expelled. He could feel it, lodged right in his sphincter, ready to leave but at the last awful point where he seemed to have nothing to push with. He tried to relax the muscles while still keeping up the pressure.

Then it tickled him.

Something brushed lightly against the skin where his buttocks came together. The surprise was enough. He felt a contraction and the shit squeezed that final distance, dropping free into the pan. A wave of relief slid over him and he reached for the paper. He wouldn't be passing any more for some time.

Sylvester stood up and turned to examine his twenty-minute excretion. His hand froze.

The shit had sunk to the bottom of the white bowl, tinted yellow by the light and the urine in the water. Dark and compact, it was ringed by an indentation where his muscle had gripped. But that wasn't the sight that held him paralysed, staring at his own waste.

A white string poked from the shit, five or six centimetres, weaving around in the water. A second, short length trailed from the opposite side.

There was a worm in his shit.

His hand snapped forward and pulled the flush lever. Water cascaded around the bowl, stirring the waters and obscuring the sight. Too late he realised he should have kept it; got somebody to identify it. But the waters slowed and cleared and the evidence was gone.

A worm. Anything but a worm.

Gingerly, he wiped. Little came off on the tissue. Sylvester remembered his bodily unease of the past few days: stomach pains he associated with the constipation; a bubbly rash on his legs and back; sweats and anxious moments at night when his throat seemed to constrict and breathing was a struggle. Until now, they had seemed small, disconnected things. He had visited the doctor that very afternoon.

His GP was a pale man, with little hair and a propensity for gazing out of the surgery window. He had examined the rash and talked in soothing tones about dry heat and mild eczema, the time of year, hydrocortisone clearing it up. Then he had explored Sylvester's anus with a gloved finger and recommended a box of Bran Flakes.

Sylvester hadn't mentioned his trouble breathing at night; it seemed a vague, dreamlike thing. Now he recalled something in his throat, about two weeks ago. He had coughed up what he thought was rice or a piece of noodle, some undigested legacy of a Chinese takeaway. But there had been no such takeaway.

Now he made the connection. The thing he had coughed up then had looked exactly like a smaller version of the worm in his shit.

A younger version.

Two weeks ago.

Terror blasted through Sylvester. Not worms — he stumbled out of the bathroom, naked from the waist down. His briefs and trousers he left crumpled on the floor. He ran for his bed and slipped under the duvet, where he curled up and began to shiver. The picture of the worm was still vivid in his mind, stretched through his shit, white and wriggling.

Sylvester pulled the cover over his head and huddled, trying to eliminate the image. What his mind found instead was a party, two or three weeks ago.

It had been yet another art school thing, in a flat off Byers Road. He had been drunk and at his most vulnerable: surrounded by attractive women, one week after his split from Jen. Seven days alone after two and a half years of mutual comfort and regular sex.

An acquaintance had been drinking something unusual with two girls in velvet. Sylvester rolled over to investigate.

'Mezcal,' Mark was saying. 'It's from Mexico. Each bottle's got a worm in it. It's a sign that the drink's good quality. There has to be a high enough percentage alcohol to preserve the worm.'

'I heard that was tequila,' said one girl.

'I heard that was bollocks,' said the other. 'A marketing gimmick.'

'It's good luck if you get the worm in your shot,' said the first.

'It's bollocks,' said the other.

'It makes you virile,' said Mark. 'And here's a man who needs both luck and virility. How's it hanging, Sly? Want a mezcal?' He poured a shot for Sylvester. A little object dropped through the golden stream. 'And there you have it.'

Sylvester looked at the glimmering liquid, both disgusted and fascinated. The little ridged brown worm was curled at the bottom of the glass, drifting with the booze. 'Don't you ever swallow the worm by mistake?' he said.

'You're supposed to,' said Mark. 'That's why they put it in. It's an acquired taste.'

'I'm not very keen on worms.' He wrinkled his nose.

'Are you...frightened of them?' It was one of the girls. She had striking, pearly blue eyes rimmed thickly in black, curtained by chocolate red hair. She mesmerised him.

'Not frightened,' he lied, 'but I don't want to eat one.'

'Is it the way they wriggle?' she persisted, with an evil, flirtatious twist of the tongue. 'Or the way they burrow?'

'It's an agave worm,' Mark said, reading the bottle. 'It lives in the plant they use to make the stuff. There are probably dozens mashed into the drink. It's not like it's an earthworm.'

The girl leaned closer to Sylvester. Her companion smiled. Those eyes were locked on his.

'Feel your fear.' Her breath was warm on his face, her words theatrical. 'Grasp it and stare at it until you see every detail. Slowly embrace it and take it inside. Only by overcoming your fear can you grow stronger. If you give in, it will consume you forever.'

Sylvester didn't want to eat the worm. Yet the girl was intimately close. He felt heat in his lap. She seemed excited by the situation. And being single had given him an urge to test his boundaries. He lifted the glass into the light.

'It's cloudy,' he said. 'Is it supposed to be?'

'No...' said Mark.

'Don't avoid it. Show us your guts.' The girl waved a black-nailed hand past his face. 'Do it.'

Like an idiot he drank the stuff. It was warm and smooth. The girl smiled as he took the worm into his mouth. 'Warrior,' she said as he swallowed.

And within three minutes she and her companion had

departed for another conversation.

The worm nestled between Sylvester's gum and lower jaw. It felt fragile and moist. Surreptitiously he spat it into his hand and dropped it into an ashtray, shivering at the touch of it.

But the shot had been cloudy.

Sylvester trembled again beneath the covers as he remembered. He threw them back and made for the living room, gathering his trousers on the way. Ice slid across his skin. Before pulling them on, he inspected the insides for worms.

His heart pounded. It was four in the morning and there was nobody he could call. But he did have a computer. He searched the net and found pages on mezcal and tequila. There was nothing about worms like these. But he found a page using the words 'Mexico white worm'. The shakes seized him as he read:

Ascaris Lumbricoides ... adult females reach 20–49cm in length ... light infections do not usually cause symptoms. Serious disorder may be caused when the burden amounts to 100 worms or more ... the resistance of Ascaris eggs to chemicals is almost legendary ... infection occurs when embryonated eggs are swallowed with contaminated food or water.

Contaminated food or water. Sylvester's stomach tightened as he scrolled down to a black and white image. A pair of adult hands supported a huge clump of what appeared to be beansprouts. This was an incidence of Ascaris removed from the intestine of a two-year-old child. It had been a terminal infection.

The word terminal hung there on the cold screen. Sylvester felt terribly small and alone. But there was more:

...larvae may become lost ... downstream wandering can lead to the anus ... upstream ... the larvae may wander into the brain.

He was sick at last, suddenly, turning his head aside from the computer. Four weak spasms dribbled down the wallpaper. He sucked in breath.

And saw two worms the length of his finger among the vomit. One peeled off and dropped to the ground.

Sylvester fled from the computer, back to his bed. He twitched beneath the covers. His head itched all over. His stomach pulsed. He scratched at his back, his legs, thinking of the things exploring his body, wandering through his tissue. He couldn't run from the house. He couldn't go anywhere. They were inside him.

He bit his thumb hard and fought the rush of fear. In the morning someone would be able to help. Somebody had to know what to do. He tried not to think about his dismissive GP and the waiting lists for specialists.

He closed his eyes but now he could see them, burrowing, worming. He tried to think of something, anything else, but there was only the wriggling of the idiot white shapes through his insides, each one stuffed with tiny eggs, ready to burst.

Then he remembered. At the back of the bathroom cabinet was a dusty box of industrial strength painkillers left over from his flatmate's rugby injury. Sylvester staggered through and scrabbled for the box. Toothpaste and aftershave tumbled to the floor. It was important not to think too hard about what he was going to do.

There were fourteen pills left. The box listed their use-by date as a year ago.

He took them all. It required two glasses of water.

Then he went to his cutting tray, fitted a new blade to his

scalpel, and took it to bed.

After a while, the ceiling went fuzzy. Muffled rain tapped the window. Grasp it and stare at it until you see every detail.

In time, his limbs became heavy. He sank further into the bed. Slowly embrace it and take it inside.

Sylvester was dropping off to sleep. He blinked and pulled down the duvet. The air was cold on his skin. Turning on his bedside lamp, he brought it close to his stomach, and tried to steady his hand.

He gritted his teeth and made the incision, shuddering with the pain. Blood spilled out, a red ocean flooding across his stomach and legs, soaking into the sheets. He drew the scalpel further. The fat peeled apart. He had to saw at the muscle, screaming now. Blood covered him.

Sylvester felt faint. Something further was in the way and he pushed the scalpel in, feeling the surface give and puncture. He discarded the scalpel and pushed his slippery fingers into the cut. He smelt incontinence, the reek of his own bowels.

Through the agony, he managed to reach down, fascinated at touching his own insides. His hand found a mass of coiled organ and slowly drew one strand out. It seemed an alien thing, thin yet packed full. It was hot on his palm.

The room was slipping away, but Sylvester kept pulling, easing the section of intestine out through his amateur incision. If he phoned for help, the first thing they would do was put it back inside. There was no point in being frightened now. He had to get them out.

Black layers smeared in from the edges of his vision. He reached for the scalpel and as he tilted towards oblivion, he slit the damp tube and parted it.

A choked mass of spaghetti filled it to bursting point.

The Night Animals

Scott Stainton Miller

They'd gone to bed early, hoping to make love while they had the chance. Both of them were tired and sad, and neither felt like it, but they knew they had to re-start otherwise the absence would become the rule and not the exception. So they'd made love, skipping foreplay, relying on good old-fashioned Vaseline, which Ben always thought of as cheating, and...it had been good. A nice re-introduction. They'd always sworn not to lapse into the Parent Thing, and up until now they'd managed quite nicely, even through all the nightly screaming that babies excel at, a role theirs had enthusiastically embraced. They'd endured it, and kept up the fucking and the general enjoying of each other that eludes too many and which had imposed a constant kind of weariness in many of their friends and acquaintances.

Yet, now that their child, Francis, was five years old, polite, intelligent and well behaved, they'd somehow let their responsibilities towards him pugilise their responsibilities towards their marriage. It was as though they hadn't avoided the deluge, but had simply confined it for a while and it had swelled and swelled throughout the years until eventually it had broken open and flooded through their home.

They'd talked about it, assigning blame to their jobs, to each other's newly short tempers, but mostly to Ben's mother, who had recently devolved into something of a child herself.

'Now we have two,' Elizabeth had said and Ben had agreed with her in his mind, yet had angrily scolded her for it at the time.

But they'd weathered the early years, which were surely harder to surmount than this; a mellower, less hysterical period, and they both told each other that they were entering a new phase of life.

They kissed, he turned out the light and they rolled into their sleeping positions. A small cry sounded out from Francis's room and Ben raised his head, alert for more, but none came and he drifted off.

He awoke at three in the morning.

He sat up in the darkness and glanced at Elizabeth who was snoring gently by his side. A cold feeling of dread slowly began to spread through his stomach and he wondered if he'd had a nightmare, yet he couldn't remember dreaming. There was something familiar about the feeling, the quickness of it, and his mind began searching itself for a memory. Something about night-time as a child. He shivered and was about to lay back down when the phone started to ring. The feeling in his stomach deepened and he felt a strong urge to go to the bathroom. Elizabeth sat up, glanced at the glowing red digits of the bedside clock and turned on the light.

'Ben?' she said, he nodded and stepped from the bed. His steps increased in speed as he moved through the darkened hallway and down the stairs to the kitchen. He picked up the receiver and before he could speak, a small whimper at the other end cut him off. A thump came over the line and he could hear panicked breathing.

'Hello?' he whispered, suddenly feeling foolish. He should just hang up. It was probably just a prank.

'Get away!' shrieked a voice on the other end and he almost dropped the receiver.

'Mum?' he asked, his heart now racing.

'Get away! Go away!' she screamed. He flinched. He'd never heard such fear in somebody's voice. His chest tightened. Someone must be in the house with her. Someone who intended her harm.

'Mum, call the police! Put the phone down! Put the phone down!' he shouted, again feeling foolish. He had no idea how to react to this or what might actually be happening.

A sharp thunking noise came over the line and he heard her voice getting further and further away. She kept repeating the same thing; 'Get away! Get away!'

She must have dropped the phone.

'Shit!' he cursed. He shouted as loud as he could for her to put the phone back in its cradle, but it was futile, he knew she couldn't hear him. Large thumps and bangs sounded out, mixing in with her panicked 'Get away!'s. He put the phone on the kitchen surface and called for Elizabeth. She was already coming down the stairs, pulling her robe together.

'What...' she began and he cut her off.

'Where's your mobile?' he asked, panicking horribly.

'Um, it's in the bedroom, what's...'

He ran past her, past Francis who was standing wide eyed in his bedroom doorway, and into the bedroom. Her phone was on her makeup desk and he grabbed it and dialled 999.

'What service do you require?' asked the operator.

'Police!' he blurted and then waited with an increasing feeling of terror to be connected. Seconds passed, Elizabeth appeared at the door. He held up a finger and waited.

'What is the emergency, please?' asked a voice, male, expressionless.

'It's my mother. There's someone in her house. Please go there, please,' he babbled.

The voice on the other end remained even. He asked him where she lived, he told him and was assured that a car would be sent there as quickly as possible. There were more questions but Ben hung up and ran down to the kitchen, Elizabeth following him. He picked up the phone and listened. He could hear his mother crying and whimpering somewhere, the loud banging noises almost drowning her out.

'Mum, I'll be there soon, ok?' he said, paused as if expecting an answer and then handed the phone to Elizabeth.

'What's going on?' she asked.

'I... don't know,' he said, running his fingers through his hair. 'Someone's in the house with my mother, I think. She called and then dropped the phone... I can still hear her.'

She stared at him, pale.

'I called the police, but I'm going to drive there anyway.'

'It's an hour away,' she said, heavily.

'I know how fucking far it is,' he muttered, ashen. 'Will you keep listening, please? She might come back on,' he said.

She held the phone to her ear and listened, the colour draining from her face as the noises grew louder and the panicked crying turned into sustained, horribly shrill screaming.

There was no sign of the police. He swore loudly and pulled up in front of her house. She still lived in the house he'd grown up in, right, he thought, in the middle of fucking nowhere. He shook his head and tried to feel angry, but all he felt was scared. He resolved to move her into a home when this was over. If it isn't over already, he thought and then chastised himself. For all he knew she could simply have been sleepwalking, which she was prone to doing, and to performing odd tasks while doing so. He'd forgotten about this in the first rush of panic and he now clung to the idea as he walked up the stairs to the front door. He glanced at the handrail he'd had fitted along the stairs. She was getting so terribly old. He tried to think about the matter of her age, about the burden she'd become, anything but the reason he was here.

He stopped.

All the lights were off. Even the porch light, which automatically switched on when motion was detected.

He fumbled his keys out and tried to unlock the door. His keys wouldn't turn. It was already unlocked. Swallowing hard, he pushed it open and stepped inside. There was a strange smell in the air. He sniffed and instantly shallowed his breath so he wouldn't inhale too much of it. He reached out for the hall light-switch. Flicked it. The dark stayed so. Of course, he thought and stepped further into the hallway, listening hard for even the slightest of sounds, but it was hard, his blood was pounding.

'Mum?' he called.

Nothing.

'Mum?'

He made towards the stairs that led to the first floor. His foot creaked on the first step.

'Mum?'

The house suddenly came alive with noise. The stairs shook as though someone was stamping on them. He was surrounded by bangs and thumps and in the centre of it all was the sound of his mother's screaming. Panicked he raced up the stairs, clumsy in the darkness, and he mis-stepped, sprawling hard across them, breaking a front tooth as his face smacked hard against the top step. Blood burst from his lip, hot and strong smelling and he screamed in pain, novas of pain swirling in front of his eyes.

'Mother!' he roared and the noises stopped. The bulb in

the hall began to fizz and blinked erratically into life, flickering horribly but casting a dim illumination throughout.

He could see his mother's feet sticking out of the cupboard adjacent to the stairs and, stumbling, he ran down to her.

He crouched and opened the cupboard door wider. His mother sat there in her night-gown whimpering, face red and streaked with tears. He lifted her up and out and held her. Without pausing he strode to the front door and stepped outside. Dim red lights were strobing along the trees that lined the small dirt road leading to the house.

'Fucking finally,' he hissed. But the lights stopped and he was left there in the darkness, his mother crying in his arms like a baby.

'I'm afraid your mother has had a stroke.'

Ben sat on a gurney, his lips and jaw swollen and he stared at the doctor as though he hadn't quite heard right.

'A stroke?' he asked.

The doctor, a young, bored looking man, who'd grown cold the instant Ben had refused treatment for his tooth, nodded and exhaled.

'Yes. A stroke. A mild one, but still, you know, a stroke. She's not terribly coherent and has clearly been hallucinating. But, this will pass. She'll have some trouble with her memory and she may take some persuading that she was imagining whatever it was she was imagining. But, be patient.'

Ben nodded. 'When can she leave?'

'I'd say in a day or so. She'll need some care for a short while...'

'She'll live with me.' Ben interrupted.

The doctor nodded and puffed out his upper lip as if to

communicate his strong desire not to be there.

'I think I'll take some pain-killers now.' said Ben. The doctor nodded and went to fetch a nurse.

When he arrived home, Elizabeth had already left for work. He'd called her from the hospital and told her everything was fine and explained about the stroke, she'd told him she loved him and that everything would be ok. He'd nodded, said goodbye and settled into the hard plastic chair in the waiting room, too worried and nervous to go home. He wanted to stay and wait for his mother. He was scared. The stroke explained away her behaviour. But it didn't explain the noises. Part of him wanted to forget about them, dismiss it as disorientation brought on by panic; the hectic rush of his blood. While another wanted to fixate on them to the exclusion of all other thought. This was the successful part.

'Is she here?' asked Elizabeth. He nodded and gestured upstairs.

'She's sleeping.'

'How is she?' she asked but Ben heard it as 'How long will she be here?'

He paused for a beat and then smiled. 'Fine. She'll be here for a little while, I think.'

She nodded and Ben felt unnaturally angry with her, couldn't help thinking that everything about her was at that moment grotesque with insincerity.

He closed his eyes and told himself he was just tired. And troubled. His mother hadn't been making any sense at all. The doctor had warned about her not being herself, about her mind reorganising itself. But he hadn't said anything about the periodic bouts of hysteria and babbling. She kept repeating things too, disturbing things that he knew had no basis in reality. He ascribed it to the stroke, not fooling himself even slightly.

'Where's Francis?' he asked.

'He's at my sister's, I told you that yesterday.'

Ben nodded. 'Isn't he... worried? About his granny?' he asked.

Elizabeth looked at him oddly and he wondered irritably what she was thinking.

'Are you ok?' she asked.

He sighed and answered her honestly. 'No. I'm tired. I'm upset. And... I'm pissed off. I called the police again to ask why nobody was sent and you know what they did? They put me on hold and I got disconnected after a few minutes. Twice.' He smiled coldly. 'And I have this feeling I can't shake. It started the other night, like I'm about to remember something. Something important.'

She grimaced and hugged him and amazingly he felt a little better.

'I'll go see her after I put this stuff away, ok?'

She kissed his cheek and moved to the counter, lifting up her shopping bags to unpack.

'Elizabeth? You heard the noises on the phone didn't you?'

She pursed her lips and nodded.

'What do you think that was?' he asked.

'I don't know. Maybe she was making the noises. Or... maybe somebody was in the house. You said the door was unlocked.'

'Maybe. It wasn't her, though. It was coming from everywhere. And they happened when I was there... I didn't see anybody.'

'Mm. Has your mother said anything else?'

He nodded slowly.

'What?'

'She,' he laughed, not remotely amused '...she said Dad was in the house with her. And her brother.'

Elizabeth raised her eyebrows and sighed.

'That's...That's really creepy,' she said. 'But, look, she was just hallucinating. It's common, you said so yourself, some even smell things that aren't there. She was probably just lost in memory. Don't you think?'

He nodded. And then shook his head.

'Actually, I don't know. The noises were so loud they shook the stairs. I fell,' he said and bared his teeth, the crooked remains of his right front tooth glinting at her.

'Well, Ben, it wasn't ghosts, ok. You spook easily and it wasn't ghosts. Maybe it was her boiler. She's had problems with it before, it can make a racket. Which you know.'

He smiled and nodded: 'An answer for everything.' He grinned widely and licked at the splinters of his tooth.

'Nope. Just common fucking sense.' she muttered and went back to unpacking.

He stared at her for a while and then stood up. 'I'm going for a nap.' he said and waited for her to respond. When she didn't, he kicked the stool against the counter and bounded up the stairs two at a time.

Yawning, he pulled off his t-shirt and headed towards their bedroom. His mother was in the guest room. He stopped. He ought to check on her. She was zonked out thanks to some interesting sounding medication, but it couldn't hurt. He tip-toed to the end of the hall and pushed the door open.

His mother lay on the floor, wrapped in a blanket. Dread filling him, he bent down beside her and listened for a heart-beat. His dread faded as it sounded out, strong and fast. He lifted her and grimaced. She'd soiled herself. He lay her on the bed and went back downstairs.

Elizabeth had finished unpacking and was now starting on dinner. He coughed and she turned around, a look of sour expectancy on her face.

'I need your help,' he said.

'Oh yes?'

'I just checked on her...she's messed herself.'

'And?'

'I can't clean her.'

She raised an eyebrow.

'I can't clean her, Elizabeth, it's hard enough seeing her like this, I don't want to be wrist deep in my mother's shit,' he said, his voice hardening on each word.

She cursed and shook her head disgustedly.

'We need to put her in a home. Now,' she hissed and stomped past him up the stairs.

The sun had gone down early and the air was grey with dull, dying light. Elizabeth was in bed even though it hadn't even turned nine. He sat in the lounge, his mind finally blank.

The occasional scuffling noise came from the floor above, nudging against his consciousness, but he resisted the urge to ascribe it to anything other than the good old, reliable house sounds.

He turned the television on and fell asleep soon after.

He awoke to see his mother standing in front of him, back-lit by the blue light of the television. All he could make out were the lit edges of her nightgown, the rest was a blur of shadow.

A small chittering noise arose and the tv blinked off.

'Are you ok?' he asked, rubbing his eyes.

She snickered and he followed the faint white blur of her nightgown as she walked away from him. He stood up, eyes still adjusting to the dark, and followed her. The overhead light switched on and he saw his father standing at the foot of the stairs, dressed in the black suit they'd buried him in, his moustache and comb-over still as slick and black as he remembered them. He cried out and staggered back. Somebody grabbed him from behind and whispered in his ear; he started and turned around, his brain frozen with shock. It was his uncle. He too looked exactly as he had when he was alive, clammy and ill, bald-head too white and sheened with small beads of perspiration. He smiled those teeth, horribly yellow from smoking, and nodded slowly.

Ben shook his head. His uncle's face darkened and he moved towards Ben, fingers crooked and twitching rapidly against his sides. Ben closed his eyes, not wanting to see. A tremor of disbelieving fear suddenly rose through him, shaking him free, and he screamed and screamed until Elizabeth bounded down the stairs shouting for him to stop.

He opened his eyes and groaned. His mother sat propped against the wall, mouth slack, eyes rolled back white in her skull, a puddle of urine spreading from between her legs.

'Oh, no,' said Elizabeth, hugging him tight. He wanted to explain to her that he wasn't screaming for his mother, but he found that he couldn't stop shaking long enough to speak.

The ambulance arrived and the futility of it almost made him smile. They lifted her onto a gurney and covered her and were gone in less than ten minutes. Elizabeth was already crouched at the urine stain, scrubbing. He sat and watched and waited until finally she finished and sat next to him on the couch.

'I'm sorry, baby,' she said. 'Do you think it was another stroke?'

'No,' he stated.

'What then?'

He looked at her for a good long while and then decided to just tell her.

'My father was here. And my uncle.'

She let out a small laugh of disbelief, not cruel, but surprised. She shook her head and touched his cheek.

'Baby, no. You didn't. You dreamt it. Your mother told you she saw them and you dreamt it.'

'Elizabeth...'

'No. This is terrible and I am not going to just agree with you and say yes you saw some ghosts. Your mother just passed and it was horrible...for both of us. You need to start missing her and thinking ahead.' She kissed him. 'Don't confuse your dreams with reality, ok? You're tired and sad and that's all you're doing.'

He looked at her and nodded.

'Good,' she said. 'And your mother creeped me out too with all that talk, I wasn't having the nicest dreams either...' she began.

'Wait. What? What talk?'

'Just what she said to you. When I was...when I was cleaning her, she said that your dad and her brother were coming... But, I know she was just talking about death. I think she knew she was going to die. The stroke just made her express it strangely.'

She kissed him and stood up.

'Do you want me to call your aunt in the morning?' she asked.

'No. No, I'll do it,' he said and smiled weakly.

He remained where he was, watching the sky lighten.

✳

He thought about his father. His appearance hadn't impacted on him quite the same as his uncle's, but that was hardly surprising. He'd barely known the man. His uncle however had always been vivid in his mind from an early age. His mother had loved the vile man as she should have, but had always seemed slightly wary of him, more than a sister ought to. Even his mother's younger sister Jean, someone who Ben had long thought of as a rock, seemed afraid of him.

Ben had always hated him.

That slick bald-head, those yellow teeth. The smell of him. And the old books he carried around with him that smelled almost as bad as he did.

This had been problematic since he'd been more of a constant in Ben's life than his father, who was frequently away from home, attending to various business contacts. Uncle Bill stayed over a lot, always sleeping in the cellar, a detail that had caused Ben a lot of sleepless nights as a child; the image of his uncle, crawling around in the dirt, in the dark like some kind of night animal.

When he'd been found dead in the forest nearby, his body propped against a tree, Ben had felt nothing but relief.

His father had hanged himself shortly after in a hotel room.

That too had inspired little in the way of grief.

This was the first time since he was a child that he'd even thought about them. Thanks mum, he said and shook his head, forcing a laugh. He'd decided that he had been dreaming, that you lived and you died and the worlds of both never met.

He straightened his tie and stood. Everyone was assembled in the living room, sharing awkward small talk and waiting for the hearse. The coffin stood at the back of the room, ominous and avoided.

It was time. He went downstairs and watched the men carry the coffin away.

He sat in the car with Elizabeth and his Aunt Jean. Nobody spoke until after the burial, exchanging brief words of grief and hope before checking that everyone knew the way to the hotel.

Ben said nothing.

His Aunt smiled at him as they got back in the car and he held her hand. Elizabeth had taken a taxi back to her friend's house to pick up Francis, who they'd decided shouldn't attend the actual funeral, but the wake, they'd concluded, was ok.

Jean gripped his hand and sighed.

'How are you doing?' asked Ben.

'Fine. Fine. What about you?'

Ben nodded, his lips pressed together. 'I'm ok. I could have done without seeing her...the way she died.'

Jean squeezed his hand and smiled. 'I understand,' she said. 'Did you see your father?'

The blood drained from Ben's face and he cocked his head. '...What?' he asked.

'Did you see your father? And your uncle, did you see him?'

Ben couldn't speak. She was being so matter of fact.

'I...' he began.

'You did, didn't you? They'll still be in your house, you know. I'd be careful,' she smiled. 'Well, we're here. See you inside.'

He just stared at her as she got out of the car and entered the hotel. He didn't even hear the driver asking him if he shouldn't be inside with the rest of the mourners.

✳

Ben stood at the entrance to the bar they'd hired, looking for Jean. He couldn't see her.

'Fuck,' he whispered.

'Nice.'

Elizabeth stood behind him, holding Francis's hand.

'Hey,' he said, pleased to see his son. He bent down and hugged him, asked him how he was doing.

'I'm sad,' he said simply and Ben felt as though to start crying would be never to stop.

'Me too,' said Ben and something in his voice made Elizabeth take note.

'I'll go and take him to see my parents,' she said and squeezed his arm. He nodded and continued to scan the room. Jean stood at the back, staring at him. He passed through the crowd, and headed straight for her.

'Are you going senile?' he snarled.

She smiled and shook her head. She was clearly drunk. He snorted and nodded irritably.

'Fucking speak.' he said, leaning in.

'Well, that's lovely.' she said, eyes narrowing.

'What did you mean by asking me if I'd seen my dad?'

'And your uncle.'

'What did you mean?'

'They would have come for your mother. You were there when she died. I just assumed you would have seen them.' she said.

'Please, don't do this,' he said and the desperation in his voice made her wrinkle her nose in disgust.

'You sound scared,' she said, making no effort to conceal her disgust. 'She always did protect you too much. Sometimes people need to be disabused of their notions. I learnt the truth when I was Francis's age. Not that I had much choice in the matter. That's why I never had children. Or married for that matter. Not that any man would want me after they saw...' she sighed and scratched her nose absently, leaving a bright red smear of blood on her cheek. Ben gasped. She winked, eyes glassy. He looked at her wrists, followed the trickle from her wrists to the carpet. There were two large dark patches on either side of her feet. A razor between her feet. She shifted her weight, squeezing beads of blood up around her shoes.

'Oh my God,' whispered Ben.

'No such thing,' she said and giggled.

'What...' he said and then stopped. He had no reaction to this. She lifted up a finger to his mouth and shh-ed him, blood streaming down the underside of her arm.

'I just didn't want to wait around for them. I'd never be able to relax,' she said and laughed. 'Don't tell anyone till I'm dead. I wanted to die surrounded by people but I don't want to talk to any of them, if you don't mind,' she said, slurring her words. She laughed weakly and then slumped against the wall, the banal chatter of the crowd increasing as though compensating for the loss in their number.

'This is fucked up,' said Elizabeth, grinning nervously.

'What did you tell Francis?' Ben asked.

They sat in the lounge. The evening had been crimped somewhat by his aunt. Another pointless ambulance had been called. Ben was beginning to take them for granted.

The crowd had dispersed pretty rapidly soon after, hushed, unable to think of anything to say.

'I didn't tell him anything. I just said we had to go home,' she said.

Elizabeth flumped back on the couch and sighed. 'Did she give a reason?'

Ben settled beside her and shook his head. 'She was

insane. That's all,' he said.

She was insane.

That's all.

'I want this month to be over.'

Ben nodded, stayed silent. She patted him on the shoulder and announced she was going to bed. They both went up together and they lay there quietly, eager for sleep to finish the day. Soon she was snoring and Ben was still awake. Hours passed. The dark grew darker. A small cry sounded out. Francis. He was prone to night terrors. He and Elizabeth had sworn not to indulge him, lest he become dependent on them, but Ben considered this an exception and he slipped out from under Elizabeth's arm and tip-toed out of the room and into the hall. Francis's door was closed. Francis never closed his door.

Ben stepped quietly along the hall, every sound magnified, causing his ears to move involuntarily as though eager and greedy for noise. He placed his hand on the handle and turned it. The room was black. No night-light. Surprised, he bent down and searched for the socket near the door. The small plastic night-light was still plugged in. He switched it on and it filled the room with soft orange light.

'Oh,' he said.

His father was perched on the edge of Francis's bed like a bird. Tears welled up in Ben's eyes, blurring his vision, something that used to happen when he was a child and afraid of the dark. Fear had paralysed him. He thought of his aunt in that second, the expression of disgust on her face as the last of her pissed from her wrists.

His father rocked back and forth excitedly on the bedframe, grinning. Francis lay perfectly still on the bed, eyes fixed on the ceiling.

'Francis,' whispered Ben. The effort made his nose bleed.

His father stopped rocking and slowly turned his head. 'Shhh,' he said, finger to lips. His eyes were yellow and bright with amusement.

Ben blinked the tears from his eyes and backed out of the door. His father began to growl, a horrible, animal sound, and Francis's door closed over.

Ben could feel breath on his neck. 'Hello,' whispered his uncle. 'We missed you down there.'

Ben turned to him, breath now coming in wheezing bursts.

'I missed you.' His uncle's eyes burned in the darkness and Ben could feel his bladder give way.

'God,' he moaned and his uncle began to kiss him.

'No...such...thing,' he said in between each kiss. 'Only ours. You'll meet him soon. He'll like you. And your wife. But I think...' he licked Ben's throat, Ben's bowels gave way. 'I think he'll like your son best of all.'

Ben closed his eyes as his uncle embraced him, the stink of sulphur filling his nostrils.

'It's been so long. Longer than we meant. We made a lot of friends while we were away,' he giggled. 'You won't like them,' said his uncle, squeezing him hard, something long and bony and wet pressing against his side, fingers everywhere, and suddenly Ben remembered.

A Storm of Ice

Joel A Sutherland

It was hard to focus on the road in her present state of mind, but the raging November weather demanded it.

The cracked pavement under Tara's Jetta was slick with water that was just beginning to curdle into ice. The night had grown old and the car's windshield wipers struggled to keep up with the rain that splattered the windshield. Winding through the thick and brooding forest on her way to St. Paul, Tara turned up the heat and said to the emptiness surrounding her, 'Goddamn Minnesota.'

A puddle of water exploded as the car plowed through it, sending thousands of icy beads flying through the air like daggers.

Soon the hail began to fall.

Pulling up to the three-story mansion with the four-car garage and the pillars standing guard at the front door and the manicured lawn and the barbwire gate surrounding it all, Tara quietly whistled. The pompous sight of the house never failed to impress upon her.

Leaving her overnight bag in the trunk, Tara held her purse above her head and ran from the car, having a hard time gaining traction on the ice-slicked driveway. Her right foot fell awkwardly on a large chunk of hail and the heel of her shoe snapped; her ankle twisted in a vain attempt to regain balance, and Tara fell on her knee; amidst the deafening clatter of the falling hail, a loud pop sent shivers through her brain; Tara, eyes shut tight, ground her teeth and toppled over onto her side. As tears seeped from her lids she let herself scream.

'Where the hell is she?' Inside, a woman with fiery red hair paced around a stately wooden dining table the size of a small pool. Her skin was beginning to swell around her green eyes in exhaustion. She dropped down in a chair and even though her feet were stilled, her hands kept moving, scratching her forearms, white track-marks that soon turned red trailing her long nails on her pale skin. 'Probably found some country bar along the 47 and couldn't resist.'

A handsome man, well dressed and well groomed, stepped close behind her and placed a glass of red wine on the table. 'It's shit weather; the driving will be slow. She'll get here.'

'It wouldn't be the first funeral she'd miss.'

'That's in the past. She's apologized more times than I can count. Besides, it's not until eleven tomorrow morning.'

The woman drank half of the wine in her glass in one long pull. 'Lawyer will be here at eight. She's got to be here for that.'

The man looked out the window at the falling hail, not letting up or slowing down. 'The lawyer's not going to make it, either, if this keeps up much longer', he thought.

A grandfather clock bellowed once, twice, three times, its deep chimes bouncing around the large room.

The red-haired woman spilled the rest of her wine across the table when she heard the heart-twisting screams tearing into her house from the cold, black night outside.

Jagged shards of ice had collected in the wrinkles of Tara's clothes and had begun to freeze to her auburn hair, damp with sweat. Her face was drained of color. Steam lifted from her feverish body in the late autumn air and wisped away in the wind.

The couple picked Tara up off of the ground and quickly carried her inside.

Letting sleep wrap its writhing tentacles around her, pulling her away from the night and the pain and the hail, Tara didn't say a word.

She woke early the next morning, the blankets on her bed strewn around her and soaked, her head pounding from the pain in her knee and from the incessant thundering of the hail still falling outside.

Tara lifted the sheet from her leg and peered under. Her knee was swollen and red, like a ripe grapefruit. She turned her head and moaned.

The door opened.

'Hey, Evey,' Tara said, sitting up in bed.

The red-haired woman stepped in. 'Hey, sis,' she said.

Tara waved a hand over her knee, a thin smile pulling on her lips. 'Hell of a way to kick off what's sure to be a shitty visit, isn't it?'

Evelyn sat down on the edge of the bed. Looking at the wall she said, 'Peter crushed up some painkillers in a glass of water and made you drink it last night. How you feeling?'

Tara shrugged. 'I'm fine.'

'You fall because you were drinking?'

'Fuck you,' said Tara. 'I haven't had a drink in three years. You know that.'

'Whatever,' said Evelyn as she stood up and walked to the door. 'Lawyer's here. Since you're feeling all right, I'm sure you can make it down to the living room. Crutches are at the foot of the bed.'

Tara tentatively bent her knee. She tried to keep the pain from showing in her face. 'I'll be fifteen minutes.'

'This guy ain't cheap. Make it five.' Evelyn closed the door behind her.

Tara let the pain overtake her body and exhaled loudly. She raised her middle finger at the space previously occupied by her twin sister.

The lawyer, power suit and slicked-back hair, was the kind of cheap millionaire who had attached a plow to the front of his truck so he could cut off the blue collar guy he used to pay fifty bucks to shovel his driveway.

That truck was now parked in front of Evelyn and Peter's house, the clear path behind it quickly being covered by hail once again.

'Only reason I made it here,' the lawyer said, nodding at the plow on the truck as Tara hobbled in on crutches. She sat down in a plush chair next to the couch the others were sitting on. 'Crazy weather. There were cars stranded everywhere.'

Evelyn looked at her sister. 'Good. Now we can get started.' She made the necessary introductions; the lawyer offered Tara his condolences and then stood up. 'I just have to run out to my truck. I left behind some paperwork.'

'It's coming down pretty hard out there,' Peter said.

Evelyn stood as well. 'You sure it's that important?'

'Unfortunately it is,' the lawyer said. 'I'll just be a moment.' He left the room before any more objections could be made.

Peter looked out at the grey swirling sky. 'We might have to postpone the funeral.'

Tara gently rubbed the skin around her knee and sighed.

'We can't inconvenience Tara,' Evelyn said, still standing. 'I'm sure she needs to get back to her partner in crime, Mandy.' She left the room.

Turning away so Peter wouldn't see the water pooling in the bottom of her eyes, Tara looked outside. The lawyer was rummaging around inside his truck. The hail was getting bigger and falling harder, thicker.

'How's the knee?' Peter asked, clearly feeling awkward being alone with his sister-in-law.

'Shitty.'

'When the storm dies I'll go to my office and get you some more Codeine and a brace.'

Tara nodded. Evelyn re-entered carrying a tray filled with tea and croissants. She was about to set it down on the coffee table when she looked out the window.

The tray crashed to the floor. Evelyn stood in silence, shocked. Tara and Peter followed her stunned gaze.

Outside, the truck's windshield was covered in a web of tiny cracks. One of the cracks grew too large and the front seat was showered in shattered glass as the windshield exploded. The truck bounced up and down on its suspension, jostled by the mighty barrage of hail that had instantly intensified.

The lawyer's body was sprawled next to the truck in an awkward position, legs and arms bent at irregular angles. His skull was split above his forehead, blood and brain mixing on the ground like the tea and croissants on the floor inside.

His dead eyes looked heavenward. His body twitched — a macabre dance — as it was pelted from above. Blood oozed from a multitude of protrusions; blood-soaked clothing; blood-splattered tires. Blood was everywhere.

The hail kept falling.

'Jesus, Jesus, Jesus.' Tara pulled on her hair, head bent between her knees, trying to resist the need to vomit all over her sister's fifteen-thousand-dollar rug.

Peter slammed the phone down. 'There's no dial tone.'

'We have to help him,' Evelyn said. She turned and ran for the front door.

Her husband grabbed her and sat her down. 'You can't go out there; it's too dangerous. None of us can. Besides, there's nothing you could do. He's dead.'

The finality of his words created a heavy silence that hung in the air between them like thick black smoke.

The grim hush proved too much; Tara's stomach heaved, her throat convulsed, her lips parted and a swell of frothy yellow bile splashed to the floor. She gurgled and coughed, wiped her mouth and covered her face. 'I'm sorry,' she said feebly as her body shook.

'That's just great,' her sister said.

Peter stood up. 'Never mind,' he said. 'I'll get some cleaner.'

'Forget about the fucking cleaner!' Evelyn screamed. 'What are we going to do about the dead body in our driveway?'

'Like I said before,' Peter said gravely. 'None of us are going outside. We're going to wait out the storm.' His face tightened and he sighed, his eyes fruitlessly searching for a better answer. 'That's all we can do. Wait out the storm.'

Tara, seated in the same spot as an hour before, chewed on a croissant. Her empty stomach moaned in pleasure, barely audible over the racket of the pounding hail.

'...from across the state reports are pouring in of massive destruction caused by the relentless hail. Officials are baffled by the duration of the storm, currently the longest on record...'

The reporter's voice that streamed out of the radio sounded tired, shaken, and desolate.

'...the death toll has reached sixty-six, and continues to climb...'

Evelyn lay on the couch in a state of shock, her head resting on her husband's lap. Peter gently brushed some errant strands of hair out of her eyes.

'...stay indoors...'

Tara looked outside at the hail building on the ground, now three or four feet deep, and longed for the company and security of her father more than she ever had while he was alive.

Her head throbbed with the precision and intensity of a marching band. Bam bam bam. It almost drowned out the crush of the clattering hail. Tara moaned. The Tylenol she had swallowed could no longer mask the pain. She stood in the large pantry, discouraged by the sight of so many empty shelves.

'Where is all the food?' she asked, having rejoined Evelyn and Peter in the living room. She held her right hand behind her back. The stench of vomit was thick in the air.

'Huh?' her sister said, rubbing her red eyes.

'The food. I checked the fridge and cupboards, and the

pantry, too. Unless we're going to survive on mustard and dust, we'll starve.'

Evelyn shrugged her shoulders. 'We eat out a lot, and order in.'

Peter, clearly unaccustomed with the kitchen, looked dumbfounded. 'Really? We have nothing?'

'I found this.' Tara revealed a bottle of Jack Daniel's from behind her back and tossed it on the couch beside her sister.

Evelyn picked it up and examined it closely.

'Yeah, it's still sealed,' Tara said.

Evelyn shot Tara a dirty look.

On the radio, the reporter had given up with the news, droning on in a croaked voice. '...I'm trapped, alone, trapped, doomed, hungry, hopeless, trapped...'

The first floor windows imploded by the time Tara had nervously gnawed through the nails on her right hand. Explosions of shattered glass went off one after another from all sides of the ground floor, followed by the deafening racket of ice pellets flooding in through the new openings.

All three crazed prisoners swore simultaneously as their bodies instinctively clenched up at the racket.

Once Tara realized what had happened she stood up. Leaving the crutches behind, she limped awkwardly as she left the room. Evelyn and Peter made no attempt to help her or stop her, too numb from shock and confusion. Tara returned a moment later with an empty glass.

'Fuck it,' she said. 'Whole world's gone to shit.' She picked up the bottle of Jack Daniel's, savagely twisted off the cap, and walked to one of the shattered windows. She held her glass under the torrent of ice for a second, allowing it to fill with fresh cubes. She filled the glass with golden whiskey and held it up in cheers. 'To the end of the world!' she said, and downed the drink.

Evelyn sat stock-still, her eyes bloodshot and moist, her lids heavy. 'That almost killed you before,' she said without empathy. 'It'll do it again.'

'Good,' Tara said, refilling her glass with more ice and booze. 'Got nothing left to live for here.'

'Why don't you speed up the process and jump out a window?'

Lowering the glass from her lips, Tara regarded her sister gravely. Without a word she turned and left the room.

Evelyn and Peter listened as her footsteps faded up the stairs.

'Aren't you going to tell me that was over the line?' Evelyn asked her husband with a mocking expression on her face. 'Tell me not to give up hope?'

Peter sighed, unblinking. 'No. I'm not. Tara was right. It's all ending. It's just a matter of time.' He stood up and followed Tara, leaving his wife behind.

Tara hobbled up the stairs slowly, covering her ears with the glass and the bottle of whiskey, trying to get the mind-numbing racket of the hail out of her head. The drink had numbed the pain in her knee, but could do nothing for her persistent headache.

'Tara! Wait.'

She stopped at the top of the stairs and looked back. Peter walked up towards her.

'I need a drink,' he said.

'You don't drink.'

'Good time to start.' Peter took the whiskey. Tara offered the glass but he shook it off and drank straight from the bottle, one, two, three hard gulps. He coughed and pulled the bottle from his lips, spilling a long stream of booze onto the stairs that pooled on the hardwood. 'Hard stuff,' he said. 'It burns.'

'That's enough, now.' Tara gently took the bottle back from Peter. She looked upon her brother-in-law and felt pity, something she never thought she'd feel for someone who had so much.

'You know, I feel better,' Peter said. 'The hail has got to stop eventually, right? It can't be much longer. We'll get out of this, you'll see.'

Tara smiled for the first time since she had arrived, but shook her head all the same. 'I don't know, Peter...'

'No more negativity. We'll be ok. Now, let's you and me take that bottle back downstairs and give your sister a drink. I think she needs one.'

He smiled to himself and turned around. He took one step and his foot slid through the spilt whiskey. His hand came free of the banister under the weight of his body and his neck snapped backwards. The back of his head smashed against the corner of the top stair and the thin layer of skin beneath his thick hair split apart. Blood streamed freely onto the stairs, mixing with the whiskey, splattering Tara's numb toes. Peter tumbled helplessly down the stairs in a rolling ball of cracks and snaps. His body crumpled on the ground below, twitched once, twice, then stopped. Open eyes looked out from a twisted and bent body, a sharp bone protruded from a shin, a spewing laceration covered the forehead; there was no life in those eyes.

Tara sobbed and ran down the stairs, the pain in her knee returning, the horror of what she just witnessed sobering her. She reached Peter's body but stopped herself a few feet short. The pool of blood around his shattered skull was spreading quickly. She reeled back moaning and scratched at her face, unable to look away.

Evelyn ran into the hallway and stopped. Her face blanched and she stared at the mess of her husband, eyes wide and uncomprehending. She peeled her gaze from Peter and frowned at Tara. 'What did you do?'

Tara began to cry freely. Her words were choked out of her. 'He slipped. He fell.'

Evelyn shook her head. 'I don't understand.' She looked back at her husband's body. 'Peter, get up.'

'Evey, he's dead.'

'No, that can't be.'

'He's dead.'

'No, no.'

'It was an accident...'

Evelyn clenched her jaw and exhaled. Her head jerked back up at Tara, the colour flooding back to her face, her eyes troubled. 'You did it,' she said.

Tara blinked. 'What? No...'

Evelyn took a step towards Tara. 'You pushed him.'

'Evey, for Christ's sake, I didn't! He slipped!'

Another step. 'You've always been jealous of us.'

'Evey, stay back.'

Evelyn's sock soaked up her husband's blood like a quickly spreading disease. 'You murdered by goddamn fucking husband!'

Evelyn flung herself at Tara and clawed at her throat. Thick strips of skin peeled away under her long painted nails. Tara screamed and fell backwards, her sister landing on top of her. The wind was knocked from her lungs and Evelyn clasped her hands around her neck. Tara began to thrash and kick and claw at her sister, her vision fading. Spittle flew from her cracked lips and she gasped for air desperately, but her sister wouldn't let go.

Evelyn's face dripped sweat and her eyes filled with broken blood vessels. She grunted and pushed down hard, her muscles straining. She stopped breathing, too focused on the kill. Stars danced in front of her eyes and her clasp loosened.

Tara saw her chance. She pushed her sister's arms to the left and slid out to the right from under her.

Evelyn fell on her chest to the ground and rolled herself over just in time to see her sister pounce on her stomach. The blow nearly popped her eyes from their sockets and she wheezed in suffocating pain.

Tara sucked in air in long strained gasps. He throat was nearly sealed shut with swelling and her chest heaved with every strained breath. Her neck was covered in deep gashes, all bleeding fiercely. The skin that was left was a deep purple hue. She yanked her sister up off the ground and dragged her struggling body from the hallway to the living room, adrenaline coursing through her veins, fogging her mind.

'I'll kill you,' Evelyn gasped.

Tara didn't respond. She pulled Evelyn to the broken window and clambered up the steep slope of ice. Without a pause and without remorse, she shoved Evelyn's head through the small opening between the built-up ice outside and the top of the window frame.

For a few ghastly seconds, Evelyn's body was gripped by an unearthly spasm as the sounds of her head being pulverized flooded in from outside. After a brief moment, Evelyn's body stopped shaking. Tara let go her grasp on her sister's body and jumped down from the ice pile, her face drawn and expressionless.

Evelyn's decapitated body slid down the ice and came to a rest on the floor, a thick stream of blood trailing behind her jagged open neck. The sound of ice cracking as it melted under warm liquids filled the room.

Over the thundering of the hail, a faint cry could just be heard.

'...I've made up my mind. If anyone's still listening, anyone still alive, anyone I know, I love you, and I hope you fare better than me. I've lost my mind. The pounding isn't ending. It fills my head, my soul. I need to stop it, stop it myself. Goodbye. Goodbye...'

Tara picked up the radio and unceremoniously threw it against the wall. It shattered and the only sound left in her head was the hail. The godforsaken hail. But I'll end that, too, she thought.

She walked around Peter's blood and stepped over his corpse. She made her way up the stairs, carefully avoiding all the red puddles. The pain in her knee was far from her thoughts.

Tara walked into her bedroom and opened the window. Ice rebounded off the sill and stung wherever it hit her. She looked outside. There was only ice, ice piled as high as a bus, ice in all directions. The hail kept falling.

She stepped up into the window frame. I'm coming, father, she thought to herself and smiled.

Her body was punctured relentlessly as it fell to the ground below. She died before she hit the ice, landing next to the remains of Evelyn's head.

It didn't take long for her to disappear, covered in an icy grave.

When the hail relented and finally stopped falling six hours later, Evelyn and Paul's house was completely buried, wiped out, gone, as if it had never been there.

The silence was deafening.

Falling Stars

Samuel Minier

Meteors.
That's what I thought, hoped for — solitary fire-balls arcing the night. But these soared too low, too close to home, and when one crashed through my bedroom window — shattered glass like a rattled cage, three burn-mark skips across the area rug before plonking against the baseboard and rolling back, the sinewy twine snapping and the leather casing cracking apart so that the rubber-encrusted cork core crumbled out like a rotted walnut from its shell — then I had to face what it was, a charred baseball, and I knew she was back.

I stamped out the ball, ruined my slipper, left a soot trail as I plodded downstairs. Through the screen door I could see her small form far out in the yard, almost at the tree line. I pulled on boots but no coat — bathrobe instead, to show I wasn't staying outside long.

Snow like fine sand, easily sifted on the surface but hard-packed beneath. Cold for me but far too cold for her, in her cut-offs and thin white Troy's Hardware Summer League t-shirt from 1963. She'd fired three more into the sky by the time I reached her. They never came down to fizzle out in the white field, just keep streaking smaller and smaller until they looked as distant as all the other pinpoints of light.

'Angela,' I tried to sound like the adult I was, not her best friend. 'You can't keep doing this.'

She smiled. Peachy cheeks, barely pink lips. I remembered melting crayons with her — everything but pink, she'd always hated pink — on her parent's living room radiator when we were in second grade. 'You wouldn't come out,' she said.

Three nights of this — against all logic, the fear was starting to wane. 'Well, I'm out here now.'

'Thanks.' Blur of the bat, crack like lightening, another shooting star.

'Why now?' I asked.

'You forgot my birthday.'

She was right. Forty years would do that. 'No I didn't,' I stalled as my memory chugged. 'It was January...January...'

'Twelfth,' she said.

Three days ago. The wind grabbed at my robe, prickled my stomach flesh.

She began drawing nonsense lines in the snow with the tip of the bat. 'What does fifty feel like?'

Old, when I look at you. 'Why are you here, Angie?'

'Want to show you something.'

If she wanted vengeance, there was little I could do. Whatever this was, though, it couldn't possibly help. No sense in picking at scabs. 'No,' I said.

A fireball rocketed through my car, taking out the windshield.

'You have to see!' she tantrumed. Another small explosion against my house — smoke and charred siding. 'I'll burn it all down if you make me!'

I held up both hands in surrender. She won't hurt you, she won't hurt you. 'Are we going somewhere?'

She nodded tightly, eyes drawn down, suddenly bashful. I missed her terribly at that moment, maybe more than I'd ever let myself. 'I need a coat,' I choked out. 'I'm cold — '

She grabbed my hand. Just like her, to defy stereotypes

— she was burning up. Her fingertips scorched tiny ridges into my palms.

'Better?' she asked.

She led me across the field. I kept my eyes down, watched the snow powder her ankles and then rapidly evaporate. She was a flame in the darkness, her movements flickering. I tried to hesitate when we entered the thicket, afraid the trees would erupt into fiery pillars, but her grip was unquestionable. Not strong, just inescapable.

The moon carved swaths of light through the woods. She dragged the bat in the snow with her free hand, tracing a path. A string through the labyrinth. Indeed, the trees had quintupled into a no-walled maze, but she just kept towing me through innumerable right angles of faded birch, effervescent pine.

The house that shouldn't be here, that had been two hundred miles from here on the day she'd died — that house was in the next clearing. Like a boxy shadow against the silver glow of the snow, so that any hint of trim or definition slipped away. It remained shapeless, hulking.

I forced myself not to cower. That house was far from here, back in the town of my childhood, if it still existed at all. Probably had been leveled years ago. That's all this was — a ghost, just like her. Let the memories parade and be done with it.

She handed me my old bat — handle still duct-taped for grip, sweet spot still worn to a fine grain. I balled my hands, trying to resist — please, just leave me on the bench, I'm only here to watch — but she curled my fingers back without pressure. Like peeling an onion, or opening a secret.

'You were the only boy who could hit farther than me.' This said with pre-teen flirtation. 'That's why I followed you after practice that day — because you were better than me. Different.'

I was different? She was a creature unheard of: a girl who could name all the Yankees and who never cried, even when Tommy Stamos tripped her in practice and she'd bit clean through her lip.

I'd been so nervous that day, couldn't stop chattering. She'd stoically listened as I buzzed in circular logic over and over why our team had the championship in the bag. I only managed to silence myself by chasing the words away with the bat: a toss and a swing every couple of hundred feet, imaginary grand slams guiding us across old man McNamara's back field, until that very last one.

She lofted a ball before me. I swung immediately, on instinct, as if I'd been waiting forty years to play this out again. Everything just like when we were kids — a crushing connection, the ball rocketing farther than ever before but foul, far foul...

The ball punched a pupil through one of the house's dull, vacant eyes.

'I wouldn't give you the chance to go in.' Her soft voice floated next to my ear. When I turned, though, I found only tennis shoe tracks that peeled away from me and lead to the house's front door.

'I was as tough as you,' the voice continued. 'Not scared of getting in trouble, trespassing, some boogeyman. You knew that, right?'

I knew. She'd just been faster than me, that's all. It just as easily could have been me, picking my way up the rotted stairs, peeking through the ragged refuse of the bedrooms until spotting the ball, standing amid the broken glass and calling down into the field, teasing, never hearing the closet door slowly ease open...

'You could have yelled, screamed, waved your arms.' She was in the house, her face again peering through the blasted hole of window. 'You saw him coming. Why didn't you tell me?'

Not raging, or even hurt; those would have been easier.
Just curious, eternally wondering. I didn't have an answer,
even as I watched it happen again: the bearish figure padding
behind her, seeming to swell with each step. A good five, ten
seconds, seconds like years, more than enough time to save
her, or at least try.

I didn't — throat of stone, rooted feet. He lifted a roughly
severed table leg, a savage's club, a bat of his own.

She never looked back — eyes still on mine when they
burst. Glistening constellations against the remains of the
glass pane.

As before, I fled — stumbling through the snow and
back into the thicket, soon lost amid trees and memories.
They had found Angie, congealing in the summer heat,
but nothing else. People came forward with sightings of
staring strangers — always unclean, often black. A drifter,
the police speculated. Some wandering monster. The town
grieved, spoke of cruel and meaningless loss, then moved
on. It was the Sixties; soon there was blood everywhere.

I never came forward. By the time I got home, I had
screamed myself hoarse. Over Angie, or my inaction? Mom
reasoned my croaked voice and shaking as signs of a summer
cold. I went to bed with the sun still up, and days later I gave
a fine performance for my parents, as if I was just learning
that Angie was gone.

Winter branches whipped my face — just get back home,
get back home. And just like that, the wish was granted. I
cleared the woods.

No tracks in the snow but mine. No shattered windshield,
no scorched siding, my bedroom window unbroken.

Unbroken but occupied.

His bulk filled the entire pane. Face still as undefined as
the McNamara house, but I had no trouble distinguishing

my old bat, snug in his swollen southpaw. A gentle, patient tapping against the glass.

Waiting.

'That's why I came back,' she said.

She was nowhere. When I looked to the sky, though, I could make out two globes of light brighter than the others. Like eyes, or maybe just two of her baseballs, caught in binary orbit, now forever linked.

'I just wanted to tell you to not be afraid. It doesn't hurt, when he takes you. Just like the cartoons. Stars — all you'll see is stars.'